Ramsay on
Technology Transfers
and Licensing

Second Edition

Ramsay on Technology Transfers and Licensing

Second Edition

John T. Ramsay

Butterworths
A Member of the LexisNexis Group

Ramsay on Technology Transfers and Licensing Second Edition

© Butterworths Canada Ltd. 2002
May 2002

The Butterworth Group of Companies

Canada:
75 Clegg Road, MARKHAM, ONTARIO L6G 1A1
and
1732-808 Nelson St., Box 12148, VANCOUVER, B.C. V6Z 2H2

Australia:
Butterworths Pty Ltd., SYDNEY

Ireland:
Butterworth (Ireland) Ltd., DUBLIN

Malaysia:
Malayan Law Journal Sdn Bhd, KUALA LUMPUR

New Zealand:
Butterworths of New Zealand Ltd., WELLINGTON

Singapore:
Butterworths Asia, SINGAPORE

South Africa:
Butterworth Publishers (Pty.) Ltd., DURBAN

United Kingdom:
Butterworth & Co. (Publishers) Ltd., LONDON

United States:
LEXIS Publishing, CHARLOTTESVILLE, VIRGINIA

National Library of Canada Cataloguing in Publication

Ramsay, John T.
    Ramsay on technology transfers and licensing/John T. Ramsay — 2nd ed.

Previously published under title: Technology transfers and licensing.
Includes index.
ISBN 0-433-43813-4

    1. Technology transfer — Law and legislation — Canada. 2. License agreements — Canada.
3. Software protection — Law and legislation — Canada. 4. Copyright — Computer programs —
Canada. I. Title. II. Title: Technology transfers and licensing.

KE2908.R35 2002   346.7104'8   C2002-901823-4

Printed and bound in Canada.

FOREWORD

When I joined DuPont as a young bench chemist 28 years ago, I had no idea that I would someday manage intellectual assets and technology licensing. Today, however, that is exactly what I do — although this eventuality did not develop by design. Rather, it evolved from an assignment as a venture manager. In addition to my R&D management responsibilities, during my venture management assignment, I was responsible for developing a patenting strategy and for overseeing freedom-to-operate issues, including issues related to in-licensing rights any foundational patents that would have blocked plans to make and market our intended product. Armed only with a strong technical, managerial, and (to a lesser extent) business background, I was indeed fortunate to be able to benefit from the expertise and guidance of our patent counsel and likewise able to draw from my participation in training programs offered by the Licensing Executives Society and the Intellectual Capital Management Gathering. During the past 10 years, my work has focused almost exclusively on technology licensing and licensing strategy development — and it has been a very challenging, interesting and rewarding 10 years. I know many others whose careers have moved in the same direction, and I am certain there will be still others who will follow this route in the years ahead. At the same time, I suspect that technology transfer will soon emerge as a discrete career path and will become — like the legal, scientific, and business professions — something that one can elect to prepare for and pursue from the start. Indeed, there is evidence that the professionalization of technology transfer is already underway.

It is difficult to attribute the groundswell of interest in licensing and technology transfer to any one factor. Certainly the rise of global markets, the wider competition that globalization brings, and the effects of declining product life cycles result in increased stress on the firm's ability to meet customer needs in the shortened time frames that competitive markets now demand. On the not-for-profit side, universities and the National Laboratories play an important role as innovators and technology providers. Partially fueled by recent legislation (notably, the *Bayh-Dole Act*), universities in the United States can now own the patents that result from government funding and can seek licensees and partnership relationships to commercialize innovations that arise from faculty research. These factors have worked to increase both the supply of intellectual capital and the demand for it.

Smart companies have learned that they no longer need to invent everything internally. And they have discovered that building a strong technology base through strategic partnering, collaborative research agreements, and in-licensing makes sound economic and business sense. Likewise, more companies of all sizes are actively exploring opportunities to out-license non-strategic, and in some cases even core, intellectual assets. These same companies are taking a more aggressive look at patent infringement (and likely violators) and are licensing accordingly — or are seeking settlements in the courts.

The bottom line is that enterprises, especially those that must answer to customers and shareholders, are looking for new ways to extract value from their working assets — in particular, their intellectual assets — through out-licensing, cross-licensing, or outright sale of technology. Thus, the firm's knowledge base has become an increasingly important component in any assessment of the firm's "competitive edge". Financial markets have noticed this trend and are awarding higher market multiples to firms with significant intellectual assets. At the same time, analysis of market capitalization demonstrates that an increasing portion of a firm's total market value is attributable to its intangible assets and to the heightened expectations for ROI implied by ownership of those intangible assets. Equally important is the value-creation side of the equation. Here the key to achieving maximum return on invested capital is to strategically integrate R&D with patenting and licensing and to employ business strategies that capitalize on the firm's intellectual asset portfolio.

The past decade has been marked by a substantial increase in the number of tech transfer conferences; a growing corpus of books and professional publications on the subjects of licensing, intellectual assets, and capital management; and a general proliferation of *how to* and *who's doing it* articles in the business press. Reputable societies, such as the Licensing Executives Society and the Association of University Technology Managers ("AUTM"), offer courses to their members on virtually all aspects of technology transfer. All this activity and interest attests to the widespread and growing demand for access to the tools of the trade and the lessons learned by others.

Licensing used to be almost exclusively the domain of the attorney. But while acknowledging the still critical role of counsel, it must be observed that other professionals in industry and academia (with backgrounds and formal training in areas as diverse as engineering, science, business, and finance, or combinations thereof) have entered the field of technology transfer. Technology transfer has become a synthesis of all these disciplines, and today's successful practitioner needs to have a working understanding of all these elements and how they interact to create opportunities for harvesting value. This book covers each subject area in surprising detail (considering its length) and will serve as an excellent primer for the professional entering into the technology transfer and technology-licensing arena. It will be equally useful to the seasoned professional, providing those with a technology-based focus with the insights required for understanding copyright and trademark issues, business, legal, or otherwise. Importantly, unlike any other book on technology transfer that I am aware of, the author(s) provide clear distinctions when discussing differences in U.S. and Canadian law and custom on matters governing procurement, maintenance or enforcement of contracts, and intellectual property. Once read, this book will serve as an excellent ongoing reference in the library of any licensing or technology transfer professional, including those professionals whose primary expertise is legal.

Robert R. Gruetzmacher, Ph.D.
Director, Technology Commercialization
Center for Collaborative Research and Education
DuPont
Wilmington, DE

PREFACE

No matter the state of the economy, we look to the fundamentals: Where does the value reside? How do we prudently extract that value? Increasingly, businesses recognize that enduring value resides in intellectual property, strategically protected. Some can extract that value through their own efforts; others can extract it by transferring it to others, such as by licensing.

Since the first edition, the sophistication of the techniques available to us has vastly increased. The intellectual capital movement has generated more studies that provide useful tools, even though it is still in its early stages of maturity. The valuation chapter (Chapter 2) was revised and expanded to try to capture some of these new tools.

Competitive intelligence tools, including patent citation and patent mapping, have been developed as a result of patents becoming readily available to all through the Internet from the patent offices. Patent strategies, once the domain of the larger companies, can now be created by smaller ones. This edition attempts to address those topics; as a result the patent chapter (Chapter 3) was extensively revised.

The world of copyright has exploded with the Internet allowing dissemination of music and other copyrighted content in a popularly endorsed open violation of the established rules. Once more the law of copyright is being pushed to determine issues far beyond its original scope of protection for relatively easily controlled distribution of writing, art and music. The era of the first edition dealt with the interplay between copyright and computer programs; the era of the second edition tries to deal with the likes of Napster and its millions of eager fans and the repressive judicial response that relied on copyright. I rewrote the copyright chapter (Chapter 4) so the thoughts flow better and to provide new strategies and tactics.

The intellectual property rights govern the subject matter of the grant of license; *i.e.*, what is being transferred. This edition focuses on the structure of the rights granted more than the first edition.

The last edition developed issues around how improvements should be shared; a very difficult topic to negotiate with so little published material to review. This edition adds to that topic by providing more discussion about the problems resulting from co-ownership and expands its coverage on ownership generally.

This edition provides more guidance on the effects of invalidity of the granted intellectual property rights on the ongoing obligations of payment, a very difficult area to find fair grounds let alone understand the legal ones which are different in Canada and the U.S.

Since the last edition, the Canadian government has released guidelines about the interaction between rules that are designed to encourage competition with the rules that encourage investment recovery by the protection of intellectual property — rules that are in some ways monopolistic. This edition provides a comparison of the U.S. and Canadian guidelines.

Also there has been considerable development in the law of warranties: warranties of quality, title and against infringement. How do warranties that were developed for the physical economy apply to the digital economy? The warranty chapter (Chapter 14) had to be essentially rewritten to cover the changes.

The sharing of taxation revenue in this global economy has still not yet been well resolved by the government players. This edition does not address those important discussions and leaves the issue until the rules become more refined.

This continues to be a text for the practitioner. It is not intended for the scholar or litigator; the law is developed to set the groundwork for the techniques and strategies that can be extracted. Although it is written with a Canadian bias, its comparison of U.S. and Canadian rules will be helpful in cross-border transactions and for Canadian and U.S. practitioners who are trying to understand the local rules for a solely domestic transaction.

As with first edition, I continue to learn from my clients, from those who publish papers, and those who present at conferences, such as those at meetings of the Licensing Executives Society. For this edition, I was assisted by many at my new firm, Gowlings, and in particular by Irene Bridger, Stephen Burns, Bob Fink, Pam Kent, Irene MacDonald, Randal Penman, Joann Schwager, Lisa Tessier and our 2001 summer students, Christie Adamo, Laurel Funk and Jeff Bright and Shawna Wolch, all of whom patiently provided comments, editorial revisions and updates on the law and practice.

Like the first edition, this one is dedicated to my partner in life and law, Margaret Copithorne Ramsay.

TABLE OF CONTENTS

PART IV — RESTRICTIONS ON ABILITY TO CONTRACT

PART V — CONSIDERATION

PART VIII — LEGALESE

Part I

COMMERCIALIZING METHODS AND VALUATION

Chapter 1

METHODS OF TECHNOLOGY TRANSFER

Nor do men light a lamp and put it under a bushel, but on a stand, and it gives light to all in the house.[1]

Technology can be thought of as the system of knowledge, skills, experience, and organization used to produce and utilize goods and services to satisfy human demand for sustenance and comfort. Thus, technology transfer means much more than the simple exchange of a product, process or service. It includes all of the supporting systems and development processes for a product, process or service that may result from an exchange of knowledge, skills, experience and organization. This distinction is important because there are fundamental differences in each party's rights and liabilities when negotiating either in its embodied or disembodied form as compared to buying goods.[2]

1.1 Methods

Technology and the related intellectual property rights by themselves bring no value to either society as a whole or the individual innovator. The technology must be employed in some manner. It may be released to the general public for all to use, the innovator (whether an individual or a company) may keep the technology for its own use or the technology may be made available to others for their use in exchange for valuable consideration. The innovator who keeps the technology for itself or who allows others to commercialize it will gain the maximum economic advantage only if the innovator has a method of excluding others from freely duplicating the technology. This chapter will discuss the various ways innovators may benefit from the development of technology.

1.1.1 Release to the Public

The innovator may release the technology to the world for the benefit of humankind. For example, a professor who has developed a method of purifying water in rural areas may altruistically publish his or her findings and, thus, freely permit everyone to use his or her technology. The reward would come

---

[1] Matthew 5:15, R.S.V.
[2] UNIDO, United Nations Manual on Technology Transfer Negotiation (Vienna: UNIDO, 1996). Cat. No. UNIDO-ID/SER. 0/18 UNIDO-95.2.

from the prestige and honor of publishing those findings. Less idealistically, an innovator who publishes may also receive an indirect economic reward by satisfying the scholastic "publish or perish" requirements of many colleges and universities. Some commercially oriented innovators choose to publish their innovations because they do not wish to patent them but do want to prevent others from gaining a patent on similar technology. For example, IBM produces its monthly *Technical Disclosure Bulletin*, in which it publishes its own innovations and those of others who wish to publish anonymously. Apparently this is "one of the most frequently cited prior art sources by the USPTO" (United States Patent and Trademark Office).[3] The Software Patent Institute[4] has developed a database that can be used by inventors wishing to make "defensive disclosures",[5] which also can be made anonymously.[6] An innovator may release to the public details of technology that it wants to be accepted as a standard for all to use. This practice is used by some of the developers of software usable on the Internet. Netscape used the model of releasing an entry level version of its Web browser with the hope that the user would pay to upgrade to a version with more features. Where an innovative product has not yet been proven in the marketplace, units could be given away or provided at a very reduced cost to test sites or luminary sites. For example, a medical device could be given to a hospital where it would be used and the hospital would make itself available as a reference site. Intellectual property may be gifted to universities or other institutions where it can be further developed or used for educational purposes; tax benefits may result from such a gift. More frequently, however, technology offered freely to everyone is not used in practice; most business entities are not prepared to make any investment to improve or to commercialize technology so readily available to all of its competitors. Unfortunately, considerable amounts of promising technology developed in universities or in government research laboratories remain unused because no one is prepared to make the investment to commercialize it.

1.1.2 Keep the Technology for Itself

The innovator may decide to keep the innovation for itself and exclude others from using it. This may give the business an edge that sets it apart in a highly competitive market. To keep the competitive advantage, the business entity will have to find a way to prevent its competitors from legally cloning its technology. An innovator may decide to keep the technology to itself if: (a) it can afford to complete further stages of the research and development, (b) it can commercialize the technology itself in the ordinary course of its business, (c) the technology is essentially know-how of a type that is difficult to pass on to

---

[3]   See advertisement in Technical Disclosure Bulletin, Vol. 38, No. 1, January 1995.

[4]   See <http://www.spi.org>.

[5]   See American Bar Association, Section on Intellectual Property Law, *Annual Report* 1994/95, p. 328.

[6]   Although the inventor may wish to make the disclosure, it may have good business reasons not to let others know that it is even working in the area of the disclosure.

others, or (d) the product or process resulting from the exploitation of the technology is highly volatile and the innovator could suffer from an adverse product liability claim or adverse publicity.

1.1.3 Sell All the Rights to the Technology

The innovator may decide that it will not commercialize the technology itself but rather will transfer all of its rights to someone else. This decision could result from:

(a) the market-place being controlled by a few large business entities who will make the innovator's entry into the market-place extremely expensive;

(b) the innovation being usable only in conjunction with other technology;

(c) the innovator's immediate need for cash not allowing it to wait for royalties under a licence agreement to flow in to cover its continuing expenses and research. In the early stages of some technology ventures, even though a licence with a running royalty would produce more money in the long run, an outright sale might be necessary to fund the business' short-term future;

(d) the innovation being outside the innovator's business altogether and the innovator not wanting any further involvement with it;

(e) the innovator's unwillingness or inability to fund foreseeable infringement or product liability suits;

(f) the innovator's preference to be a researcher or a research institution;

(g) the innovator not having the desire or the resources to take the product to market; or

(h) the innovator not having economic access to the raw resources required to manufacture the innovative product.

1.1.4 Transfer Only a Portion of the Rights

The innovator may be able to transfer or assign a portion of its rights to the intellectual property related to the innovation. For example, the innovator could partially transfer its copyright for a specified application (a "field of use"). The same principles that apply to a full assignment of its rights will have general application to a partial assignment (protection, value, payment and allocation of risks) in addition to principles that apply to co-ownership,[7] all of which will be discussed later in this text (see §§9.11-9.23). It is important to remember that a partial assignment may not be possible for all types of intellectual property, for example, where the partial assignment of patents as to fields of use has not been developed in practice.

---

[7]   See §4.29 of this text.

1.1.5 License or Establish an Alliance

The innovator may decide to grant only a right of use reserving to itself certain rights ("licence"). The licence could exclude everyone, including the innovator, from using the licensed technology ("exclusive licence"), could exclude all others but not the innovator ("sole licence") or could be non-exclusive.[8] Exclusivity could relate to fields of use,[9] time periods or geographic territories.[10] Instead of continuing to develop or market the technology independently, the innovator may decide to enter into some sort of an alliance (*e.g.*, strategic alliance, joint venture, industry consortium) to further develop or market the innovation jointly.[11] Each party may have technology desired by the other party. Then there could be cross-licences whereby each party licenses to the other either all or only part of its intellectual property, perhaps restricted to a particular application. A variation of a cross-licence is a pooling arrangement where holders of intellectual property "pool" their intellectual property either for their own benefit or to offer the package to third parties in a common marketing effort. The advantages of cross-licensing and pooling include integrating complementary techniques, reducing transaction costs and removing patent "blocking" positions.[12]

1.2 Common Elements

Although the methods of commercializing technology are diverse, there are many common elements that will apply to each of them. In each case, the extent of the reward to the innovator that chooses to commercialize its technology may depend on its ability to exclude others from replicating and using the technology without compensation,[13] the extent of the rights transferred and those retained,[14] the continuing contributions of each party,[15] the tax effect on those contributions[16] and the allocation of risks of liability.[17]

---

[8]   See §7.15 of this text.
[9]   See §7.5 of this text.
[10]   See §7.9 of this text.
[11]   See "Module 19, Technology Transfer by Strategic Partnering" in United Nations Manual on Technology Transfer Negotiations (Vienna: UNIDO, 1996), p. 317-331. Adverse tax and anti-trust implications of an alliance must always be reviewed.
[12]   See §3.25(c) of this text but anti-trust rules must be kept in mind; see also Chapter 10 of this text.
[13]   See Chapters 3, 4, 5 and 6 of this text.
[14]   Generally, see Chapter 7 of this text.
[15]   See §2.14 of this text.
[16]   See Chapter 12 of this text.
[17]   See Chapters 14, 15 and 16 of this text.

Chapter 2

VALUATION

There is a risk of profit and loss in everything involved in a license. No matter how the license is structured, the most intelligent price is a balance between the risks of profit and loss — a risk balance.[1]

Before you build a better mousetrap, it helps to know if there are any mice out there. Yogi Berra

2.1 Introduction

There is no one "right way" to value technology. Indeed, the method chosen may depend on the reason for performing the evaluation, which may include obtaining financing, determining of value for purpose of acquisition, establishing reasonable royalty rates with respect to a licence, establishing transfer pricing for tax purposes between related companies, purchasing specific intellectual property rights, and allocating a purchase price for accounting or tax purposes.[2] Whatever the purpose, the valuation will involve a risk assessment by the parties involved.

2.1.1 Roll your own[3]

There are many measurements of value, many of which have not been adequately tested. Each evaluator will select from a list those measurements that yield the most trustworthy results for his or her purposes. There are no "plug-and-play formulae"; no one single value measurement that serves the purpose.[4] The result from one set of measurement tools will be different from the results of another set. When making a comparison between two valuations, one must

---

[1] Tom Arnold, "100 Factors Involved in Pricing the Technology Licensing," in *Licencing Law Library, 1988 Licensing Law Handbook* (New York: Clark Boardman Co. Ltd., 1998), (hereinafter "Arnold, '100 Factors'").

[2] Line Rachette, "Valuing Intellectual Properties and Technology Companies," in *1999 Corporate Tax Conference*, pp. 10:1-3, Canadian Tax Foundation, "Rachette".

[3] See A. Stewart and A. Thomas, "The Wealth of Knowledge: Intellectual Capital and the Twenty-first Century Organization", in 2001 *Utopia Limited* (New York: Doubleday, 2001), at pp. 292-93, (hereinafter "Stewart, 2001").

[4] See Stewart, 2001, p. 293.

examine what measurements were used and the extent that the factors taken into account were subjectively established.

2.1.2 Subjective vs. objective

Although evaluators may have objective and sophisticated tools available to use such as score cards, discounted cash flow or adoptions of the Black-Scholes Option Pricing Model,[5] they will ultimately have to use subjective assessments of the importance to them of the various factors to be ranked by the objective tools.

2.2 Risks

Each party to a transaction, no matter the nature of the transaction, must examine a number of factors and come to a balance of risk and profit that endeavours to produce a fair result for all concerned. "Risk can be described as the possibility that the actual return from engaging in an economic activity will deviate from the expected return".[6] The extent of risk involved will influence the value; the actual allocation of these risks between the parties to the technology transfer will influence price.[7] "The risk is most effectively measured by placing probabilities on a supposed return on investment, thereby taking into account all deviations from the actual return that was expected".[8] The factors outlined below may assist in determining what are the risks and what is a fair "risk" balance. In the end, all of these tools may lead to a method of calculating discounted cash flow. The multiple risks that must be analyzed for each transaction include:[9]

(a) *Research Risks.* If the technology is still in the research and development stage, there is the risk that the research will be unsuccessful – that the underlying hypothesis cannot be proven in practice – or, more likely, that it cannot be made to work in an economic manner.

(b) *Manufacturability Risks.* There is the manufacturability risk — that a production environment cannot be created that will repeatedly and cost-effectively produce the product designed by the research and

---

[5]   For a discussion on discounted cash flow and Black Scholes, see Richard Razgaitis, *Early-Stage Technologies, Valuation and Pricing* (New York: John Wiley & Sons, Inc., 1999) ("Razgaitis") Chapter 7.

[6]   Terry L. Fox, *New Techniques for Valuation of Intellectual Property: Stock Option Pricing and the Black-Scholes Model*, at p. 3 posted on the Internet <http://home.earthlink.net/~terryfoxesq/ IntProp.html>.

[7]   Risks can be allocated between the parties to the technology transfer by the type of performance requirements demanded (see Chapter 7); warranties granted – product quality, title, and infringement warranties (see Chapter 14); by the payment structure that was chosen (see Chapter 11); and exposure to, or limitations on, liability (see Chapter 15).

[8]   Fox, p. 3.

[9]   Razgaitis, p. 23 sets out these five types of risks on which the following material is based.

development process. The producer may not be able to scale up the prototype that was proven in the laboratory or simulation.[10]

(c) *Marketing Risks.* There is the marketing risk – the risk that the products successfully manufactured will not be welcomed by the consumer enough to warrant their existence.

(d) *Legal Risks.* There are the legal risks – there may not be adequate intellectual property protection or existing patents may be infringed. These patents could be difficult to find if the technology is new and the search terms have not yet been adequately refined; patent applications may be hiding in the patent office that have not yet been issued or at least been laid open for review by the public.

(c) *Competitive Risks.* There are the competitive risks – how fast competitors will respond may be yet unknown – they may respond with patent infringement claims, founded or not, with actions to strike down the intellectual property protecting the subject technology, or by reverse engineering and working around that intellectual property.

Stewart writes it this way:[11]

> On its simplest level, the value of a core competence is the product of five factors: its added value (what it's worth to customers) x competitiveness (how it compares to your competitors' skill in the same area) x potential (how much demand for this ability is growing) x sustainability (how difficult it is to duplicate) x robustness (how much at risk it is). You can put numbers on all of them. The most delicate part of the job is to determine how much added value to ascribe to each knowledge asset that contributes to a product or service.

2.3 Value Versus Price

Valuation focuses on the intrinsic worth of the technology and perhaps the surrounding intellectual capital. Valuation tends to produce a range of numbers using some or all of the techniques discussed in this chapter. When establishing the price, the parties use the valuation assessments to reach an agreement. "Pricing is the internal and external communication of perceived value; … the concrete answer to valuation, the specification in monetary or equivalent terms of what is offered for sale. Pricing issues, then, relate to negotiation tactics and, in some cases, company strategy".[12]

---

[10] *Ibid.*, p. 23.
[11] Stewart, 2001, p. 304.
[12] Razgaitis, p. 7.

2.4 Checklists

Checklists are very useful to remind the valuator of the various factors to consider. In U.S. litigation, you will be expected to refer to the American judicial checklist.[13] If you are dealing with Canada Customs and Revenue Agency you should refer to its checklist.[14] If you want a checklist that allows you to weigh the values given to the various factors, you could refer to IPSCORE.[15]

2.4.1 Judicial Checklists

The 1970 U.S. decision of Georgia-Pacific has served as a template for calculating royalty rates in U.S. patent infringement matters, which contemplate a hypothetical negotiation between the holder of the patent as licensor and the infringer as licensee; and may provide helpful guidance in determining intrinsic value in a technology. It provides the following 15 factors that can be considered for their relevance to the subject transaction, some of these 15 factors apply only to the calculation of royalties, some have broader application.[16]

1. The royalties received by the patentee for the licensing of the patent in suit, proving or tending to prove an established royalty.

2. The rates paid by the licensee for the use of other patents comparable to the patent in suit.

3. The nature and scope of the license, as exclusive or non-exclusive; or as restricted or non-restricted in terms of territory or with respect to whom the manufactured product may be sold.

4. The licensor's established policy and marketing program to maintain his patent monopoly by not licensing others to use the invention or by granting licenses under special conditions designed to preserve that monopoly.

5. The commercial relationship between the licensor and licensee, such as, whether they are competitors in the same territory in the same line of business; or whether they are inventor and promoter.

6. The effect of selling the patented speciality in promoting sales of other products of the licensee; the existing value of the invention to the licensor as a generator of sales of his non-patented items; and the extent of such derivative or convoyed sales.

7. The duration of the patent and the term of the license.

---

[13] See §2.4.1.

[14] See §2.4.1.

[15] See §2.4.3.

[16] The Georgia-Pacific checklist is reprinted in Razgaitis, p. 79. A much more extensive checklist is the one prepared by Tom Arnold, "100 Factors". It does not really contain 100 separate factors; they can be lumped together in categories that are not then dissimilar to the Georgia-Pacific categories. It does have value in its detail; many of the points are illustrations of risk allocations that are the subject matter of many technology transfer agreements. Arnold's checklist has been reprinted in Razgaitis' text, pp. 87-93.

8. The established profitability of the product made under the patent; its commercial success; and its current popularity.

9. The utility and advantages of the patent property over the old modes or devices, if any, that had been used for working out similar results.

10. The nature of the patented invention; the character of the commercial embodiment of it as owned and produced by the licensor; and the benefits to those who have used the invention.

11. The extent to which the infringer has made use of the invention; and any evidence probative of the value of that use.

12. The portion of the profit or of the selling price that may be customary in the particular business or in comparable businesses to allow for the use of the invention or analogous invention.

13. The portion of the realizable profit that should be credited to the invention as distinguished from non-patented elements, the manufacturing process, business risks, or significant features or improvement added by the infringer.

14. The opinion testimony of qualified experts.

15. The royalty that a licensor (such as the patentee) and a licensee (such as the infringer) would have agreed upon if both had been reasonably and voluntarily trying to reach an agreement; that is, the amount which a prudent licensee – who desired, as a business proposition, to obtain a license to manufacture and sell a particular article embodying the patented invention – would have been willing to pay as a royalty and yet be able to make a reasonable profit and which amount would have been acceptable by a prudent patentee who was willing to grant a license.

There is no objective way of ranking the importance of the 15 factors to the subject situation. Instead there is a "multiplicity of factors bearing upon the amount of a reasonable royalty ... there is no formula by which these factors can be related precisely in the order of their relative importance".[17] This checklist can be criticised on the basis that assessing the merits of each of these factors may involve highly subjective interpretations rather than objective science. However, it is still useful if it is treated as a part of the analytical process. Many of its principles will appear in other risk assessing tools described in this chapter.

2.4.2 Canada Customs and Revenue Agency

Canada Customs and Revenue Agency (formerly Revenue Canada) has a shorter but somewhat similar list of "matters expected to have a bearing on the determination of a royalty rate or licence fees":

---

[17] See Atanu Saha and Roy Weinstein, "Beyond Georgia-Pacific; the Use of Industry Norms as a Starting Point for Calculating Reasonable Royalties," posted on the Internet at <www.micronomics.com/pubs/georgia.html> (undated) ("Beyond Georgia-Pacific"). The Georgia-Pacific checklist is reprinted in Razgaitis, p. 79.

- prevailing rates in the industry;
- terms of the licence, including geographic limitations and exclusivity rights;
- singularity of the invention and the period for which it is likely to remain unique;
- technical assistance, trademarks and know-how provided along with access to the patent;
- profits anticipated by the licensee; and
- benefits to the licensor arising from sharing information on the experience of the licensee.[18]

2.4.3 IPSCORE

IPSCORE[19] has developed a score card methodology that deserves study. It develops a matrix of varying "Assessment Factors" personalizing them by allocating an "Importance Factor" and then allows you to rank them on a scale: zero to four. A zero rating could be treated as a fatal flaw. The IPSCORE study provides a useful commentary on its matrix as well. Table A to this Chapter provides a sample: the "Basic Property and Technical Status of a Patent". An IPSCORE measurement can only be used for a company's internal purposes. It does not provide a basis for comparison to scores attained by other companies since the importance of the factors are established respectively.[20]

2.5 Strength of Intellectual Property Protection[21]

Some technologies may have little or no value even with the best intellectual property protection; however, the best technologies may have an unduly limited economic life if they are not protected by appropriate intellectual property protection. According to Razgaitis, "IP protection is a necessary but not a sufficient condition for value to exist".[22] Think of where Vis.calc (assuming it was the first developer of an electronic spreadsheet) would be if it obtained a business method patent protecting its innovation from replication by the likes of Lotus and Microsoft Excel!

---

[18] Nathalie Bouard and Marc. D. Milgrom, "Exploiting Intellectual Property Rights: A Myriad of Opportunities and Tax Issues," *1999 Corporate Tax Conference, Canadian Tax Foundation*, p. 14:1 at 14:22.

[19] See IPscore.dk for a full development of this score card methodology.

[20] Thus it is not comparable to a Profit Impact of Market Strategy where there is a database that can give information about comparable companies – described in Stewart, 2001, pp. 299 – 302. All measurement tools that Stewart, 2001 discusses are relevant to establishing the overall value of a business rather than individual components of technology which are addressed in this Chapter.

[21] The various forms of intellectual property protection will be reviewed in Chapters 3, 4, 5 and 6 of this text.

[22] Razgaitis, p. 4.

Although traditionally patents are the favoured intellectual property, patents are not always the best form of protection. Some technologies may be protected in a number of ways, including patent, copyright and trade secrecy. The successful innovator of technology will develop an intellectual property strategy appropriate for his or her circumstances (which include available resources). He or she may have to choose among the various protections that are available given the subject technology and prevailing circumstances.[23] A summary of the primary Canadian intellectual property right appears as Table B to this Chapter.[24] The following may help to place the issues in context:

(a) Patent protection requires disclosure and loss of trade secrecy.[25]

(b) Copyright and trade secrecy do not prevent independent development,[26] but the ability to maintain secrecy[27] may successfully delay a competitor from "cloning" the technology, perhaps providing an adequate competitive advantage especially with rapidly evolving technologies.

(c) The type of protection chosen will depend on the type of technology involved and its economic life. The strength of the chosen intellectual property protection strategy will affect the value of the technology.

2.5.1 Strength of a Patent

When evaluating the strength of the protection offered by a patent, consider:[28]

(a) the scientific expertise and sophistication of the patent attorney who drew the patent;

(b) has the patent been previously litigated?

(c) has the patent been subject to re-examination?

(d) have other sophisticated parties licensed the patent?

(e) how frequently the patent has been cited by other patents as "prior art"?

(f) does the patent apply to the entire product that it is intended to protect, or merely to a feature of the product, or to the product at all?

(g) the effect on the target transferee's ability to obtain substitute technology if it could not obtain a licence for the patented technology;

(h) the ability to detect infringement;

(i) the ease of working around the patented claims; and

---

[23] These intellectual property rights are discussed in more detail in Chapter 3 – Patents, Chapter 4 – Copyright, Chapter 5 – Trademarks, and Chapter 6 – Trade Secrets.

[24] Courtesy of Jane E. Clark, Partner, Gowling Lafleur Henderson LLP.

[25] See §§3.15 to 3.17 of this text.

[26] See §§4.12 and 6.3 of this text.

[27] For copyright see §4.15.1 of this text.

[28] The above points were adapted from the American Bar Association, Section on Intellectual Property Law, Chicago, Illinois, *Annual Report 1994/95*, pp. 487-88 (hereinafter "ABA *Annual Report 94/95*").

(j) has competent patent counsel provided an opinion on the validity of the patent taking into account the credibility of the claims, their application to the intended use and any potential for a claim of "patent abuse".[29]

2.6 Stage of Development

The stage of development of the innovation is very material in determining its value. A transferee will pay more if the certainty of profits is increased and the risk of loss is decreased.[30] The more certain the qualities of the product are, the better will be the profit/risk ratio. The value of technology increases in the following order of development:

(a) The undeveloped idea has the least value.[31] Although it may require the greatest level of genius, capturing its value is difficult without further development. Razgaitis writes:

A recent study published in *Research Technology Management* ...examines data looking at seven stages in the new product development process, starting with 'raw ideas' and ending with 'economically profitable'. The study concludes that the ratio from Stage 1 (raw idea) to Stage 7 (economically profitable) is 3000 to 1: that is, it takes 3000 starting raw ideas to make one profitable success."[32] How does one disclose the idea without losing all value? Rarely will a confidentiality agreement be signed by a recipient of information if the agreement covers only a mere idea and not the method of its implementation. The potential transferee will be very reluctant to even receive a disclosure of an undeveloped, unpatentable idea because the transferee's independent development may become tainted. It will not want to risk any suggestion of misappropriation of the idea and therefore may require a disclaimer of confidentiality.

(b) The development of the idea to the research stage has more value, particularly if the research data confirms the inherent hypothesis or the author of the research is highly reputable. A successful research project gives credibility to the researcher/innovator and encourages further participation.

(c) When the resulting product becomes ready for market even though still unproven, market value is added. The strategic partner does not have to perform the research to see whether or not a product can even be produced.

(d) Once the product is proven to perform and function as anticipated, more value is added.

---

[29] See §3.2 of this text.
[30] See Arnold, "100 Factors", p. 297.
[31] See §§3.5, 3.15, 4.3 and 6.4 of this text.
[32] Razgaitis, p. 25.

(e) When the product, proven as to performance, is shown to have strong market appeal, more value is added.

(f) Provision of not only a proven product, both as to performance and market appeal, but also the financial strength to allow a credible and supportable performance guarantee gives further value.[33]

2.7 Cost

Although frequently referred to, the cost of development is generally the most irrelevant factor to a transferee.[34] Costs that are likely to be irrelevant are those expended on:

(a) the inventor who is wasteful of time and resources in developing the technology in contrast to the inventor who is highly productive;

(b) eliminating unworkable variables that will not be incurred by competitors;

(c) development work that may have produced a well-researched product, but the benefit offered by that product may have little correlation to the cost expended;

(d) an invention with features the market does not need; or

(e) a very narrow market.

Richard Razgaitis in his article, "Pricing Intellectual Property",[35] points out that the cost to Picasso of oils, brushes and canvas had no correlation to the market value of his resulting paintings.

2.8 Relevant Costs

The following costs are likely to be relevant:

(a) The cost that the licensee will save by not having to independently develop the subject technology, for examples, the costs of:
   (i) completing the research and development;
   (ii) obtaining the requisite governmental approvals;
   (iii) intellectual property protection; obtaining, maintaining and protecting;
   (iv) manufacture/reproduction;
   (v) packaging;
   (vi) advertising; and
   (vii) distribution.

---

[33] See Arnold, "100 Factors", pp. 297–98.

[34] See Association of University Technology Managers, Inc., *Technology Transfer Manual 1993*, VII–Chapter 4, p. 1, at 9 (hereinafter called "AUTM *Manual*").

[35] AUTM *Manual*, VII, Chapter 4, p. 1, at 10.

(b) the cost of working around the intellectual property protecting the invention in a reasonable period of time given the lead time established by the licensor;

(c) the cost of acquiring in the market-place a competitive/displaced product — this cost may set an upper limit on the value and on the extent of the competitive advantage;

(d) the cost of reproducing clinical studies for a pharmaceutical product;

(e) the cost of obtaining governmental approvals;

(f) savings to the user resulting from the innovative technology; and

(g) the cost of policing the licence agreement:

   (i)   availability and cost of performing a meaningful audit of a "running royalty", especially in a foreign country;

   (ii) ease of access to a suitable court on a cost-effective basis to enforce payment;

   (iii) availability of an effective court order to restrain continued breach of contract or infringement.

Pitkethly has developed a useful matrix for the application of costs to patent option valuation decisions. See Table A to Chapter 3 (Patents) of this text.[36]

2.9 Comparable Rates

If they can be located, comparable royalties or royalty rates can be very helpful for royalty based compensation. What the transferor may have received from other licensees, what the licensee may have paid for a licence of substitute technology and what is the customary rate, if any, in the particular industry are all very relevant factors.[37] There are two significant challenges: first, finding any material that is useful and, second, seeing how it compares to your situation. All variables must be compared, not just the resulting royalty rate. For example, a royalty could be lower in one case than in another if the licensee contributes more in the first case, such as contributing material improvements or complementary technology.[38] There are two types of comparable rates that could be considered.

•   First, there are rates that are comparable for that or similar technology;
•   Second, there are rates that are industry-wide.

---

[36] Figure 3 of Pitkethly, p. 30. The Valuation of Patents at <www.oiprc.ox.ac.uk/EJWP0599. html>.

[37] See items 1, 2 and 11 of the list of classic valuation factors in *Georgia Pacific Corp. v. United States Plywood-Champion Papers Inc.*, 318 F. Supp. 1116 (1970), as placed in a software patent context in ABA, *Annual Report 94/95*, pp. 488-89.

[38] Ashley J. Stevens has contributed a useful chapter entitled "Finding Comparable Licensing Terms" in the AUTM *Manual*, VII– Chapter 5, p. 1.

The latter may initially be thought of as too general to provide meaningful guidance to the value of specific technology; however industry-wide rates may provide a barrier that must be overcome if the specific technology warrants a rate well above the industry-wide range. Saha and Weinsten write:

> Despite unique characteristics of patented inventions and differences in investment risks, market size and growth potentials of entities involved in royalty agreements, our experience is that royalty rates within a particular industry tend to cluster around a specific mean. In such cases, industry-wide average royalty rates, supplemented by further statistical analysis, can provide a meaningful starting point to which the Georgia-Pacific template can be applied. Note that while unique characteristics of the patented invention may ultimately cause one to reject its use, the availability of an industry norm provides experts and fact finders with an extra piece of potentially useful information.[39]

2.9.1 Sources of Comparable Rates

Ashley J. Stevens suggests that the licensor look first to its own in-house data base for comparable deals.[40] These deals will provide guidance as to techniques previously used, with both good and bad results. In a rapidly changing market, however, what worked in the past may not be appropriate in the future. Stevens' second source of material is surveys, but Stevens points out that "There aren't many good surveys on average or comparable royalty rates. This is difficult information to obtain on a wide and consistent basis".[41] Court judgments can also be used as a source of comparable rates, although they may be based on narrow and very explicit issues. Razgaitis[42] offers these additional cautions against using court-originated royalty data:

1. The patent or know-how involved has been judged as valid and infringed which tends to make the license more valuable than the customary case where the validity of patent is unknown and in some cases the patent has not yet been issued.
2. The data is very situation specific.
3. The data can be old because litigation often starts after manufacturing by an infringer has begun and can take many years. By the time it is available to the public it can be 10 years after the research and development stage.
4. The biggest limitation is simply that there are very few cases in which the royalty rates (or other financial information) become publicly known.

---

[39] Beyond Georgia-Pacific, p. 3.
[40] AUTM *Manual*, VII– Chapter 5, p. 2.
[41] *Ibid.* See also Patrick H. Sullivan, "Royalty Rates Conform to 'Industry Norm'", in *les Nouvelles, The Journal of the Licensing Executive Society,* Vol. XXIX, No. 3, September 1994, p. 140, at 145 (hereinafter "Sullivan, 'Royalty Rates', *les Nouvelles*, September 1994").
[42] Razgaitis, p. 59.

2.9.2 Further Difficulty in Making Comparisons

Goldscheider cautions us to review precedents carefully for the "many distinguishing circumstances that could effectively negate [their] relevance". As examples, he recommends watching for "differences in market conditions for any reason, variations in the competitive strengths of the parties at different points and times, or whether a particular license was part of the broader transaction, where other conditions may have been paramount".[43] Other authors point out that:

> statistically significant "industry rates" are generally not available; even if they were, they more than likely would neglect many of the economic conditions that should be factored into any specific royalty negotiation.[44]

Razgaitis points out that comparable rates may be a deceptive source for comparison since they only consider one of the many factors in a technology transfer. This is certainly the case in most licensing surveys.[45] He sets out a number of reasons why survey data has limited value:[46]

1. These data frequently cite a wide range of possible royalties within each technology category.

2. There may be limited characterization available that connects the royalty rate data to the extent and value of the IP: i.e., patents only, many patents, new patents, strong patents, patents suitable to make high margin products for a large market, for a small market, etc.

3. The royalty base in some cases may not be clear. Without understanding the base it may be impossible to determine the significance of a royalty rate (royalties based upon the entire selling price of a large assembly), say an automobile, or upon a small component.

4. The upfront and other fixed payments may not be defined or correlated to the specific royalty rates.

5. Overall there may be lacking a characterization of the many other important terms of a license such as exclusivity, term of the agreement, right to sublicense, improvement rights, etc.

6. There may be inherent vagueness in product categories: "electrical" would presumably cover an integrated circuit and a curling iron. "Mechanical" could cover everything from a complete automobile engine to a staple remover.

---

[43] Robert Goldscheider, "Litigation Backgrounder for Licensing", in *les Nouvelles, the Journal of the Licensing Executive Society*, Vol. XXIX, No.1, March 1994, p. 20, at 24 (hereinafter "Goldscheider, 'Litigation Backgrounder', *les Nouvelles*, March 1994").

[44] Daniel M. McGavock, David A. Haas and Michael P. Patin, "Factors Affecting Royalty Rates", in *les Nouvelles, the Journal of the Licensing Executive Society*, Vol. XXVII, No. 2, June 1992, p. 107, at 107 (hereinafter "McGavock et al., 'Factors', *les Nouvelles*, June 1992").

[45] Razgaitis, p. 46.

[46] Razgaitis, pp. 53-54.

7. There is usually an inadequate number of segments of data (because of the scarcity of data). For instance, there are multiple important areas within tele-communications, entertainment/media, pharmaceuticals and medical products, software, and e-commerce. Generally these are omitted entirely or subsumed within very different types of technology licensing.

8. Surveys by their nature contain dated information, which may not be relevant to the present time. Also it is not usually clear how far back in time the data reported by respondents was gathered.

9. Surveys tend to be biased by the nature of the survey segment, membership in a particular society, trans-national licensing to a specific country, and so on.

10. Many of these agreements likely had other commercially significant provisions that affected the numbers. One of the common elements of licenses between companies is a supply agreement provision; often this takes the form of the licensee agreeing to supply the product to the licensor for use or resale. The pricing of such a supply agreement can be such that it influences the valuation of the license; one extreme would be a licensor's willingness to provide a licence for no upfront money or royalty in exchange for favourable pricing under a supply agreement. Without a specification of such terms, it is impossible to interpret the meaning of a table of negotiated royalties. Another example would be the existence of cross licenses.

11. There is no characterization of the stage of development of the technology licensed. In some cases the licenses were for fully-developed products with an already proven market; in other cases, the licenses may have been for unproven inventions still at an early R&D stage.

2.9.3 Publications

A number of periodicals on licensing economics and valuation are published on a regular basis, and now such material is becoming available on the Internet. Another source of material is that which becomes publicly available through security/corporate disclosure requirements, such as those mandated by the Toronto Stock Exchange, SEDAR, or the U.S. Security and Exchange Commission (SEC)[47] and published court cases. Unfortunately, even with the SEC, when agreements are filed "the specific dollar figures as well as percentage rate data" are usually deleted.[48]

2.9.4 Networks

One study showed that although lawyers and licensing executives were "slow to reveal specific examples of running [royalty] rates from their own experience"[49]

---

[47] Stevens, AUTM *Manual*, VII– Chapter 5, p. 5. The Internet site, <www.sedar.com>, is an excellent Canadian resource. See also <www.findlaw.com> under the Tech Deals and Contracts section for U.S. materials.

[48] Sullivan, "Royalty Rates", *les Nouvelles*, September 1994, p. 140, at 144.

[49] *Ibid.*

and "although royalty rate information is held highly confidential, lawyers and executives involved in this activity have an informal network of communication that keeps them advised of the results of recent agreements".[50] Networks can be built through active memberships in industry associations such as the Licensing Executives Society and the Association of University Technology Managers and their various committees.

2.10 Profit to Licensor

The profits to the licensor are one of the most relevant valuation factors.[51] Consider the following:

(1) savings that may be expected by the licensee as a result of the use of the licensor's innovation;

(2) economic life of the technology — how soon obsolescence will occur (particularly rapid in the computer/software industries); and

(3) costs that the licensee will save by not having to independently develop the subject technology.

2.10.1 The 25% Rule

There is a widely cited tool of pricing known as the "25% Rule" made popular by Robert Goldscheider; it is appealing in its apparent simplicity. In the appropriate circumstances, it will provide a fair risk balance. The 25% Rule has been judicially applied in Canada.[52]

The AUTM Manual provides a summary of the "25% Rule".[53]

4.8.A. The 25% Rule

One of the most widely cited tools of pricing is the infamous "25% Rule". It has various manifestations, but when most managers invoke it they usually mean either of the following:

(1) The royalty in $ should be 1/4th of the *savings* in $ to the licensee by the use of the licensed subject matter, or

(2) The royalty in % of the net sales price should be 1/4th of the *profit* before taxes enjoyed by the licensee as a result of selling products made by the licensed subject matter.

---

[50] *Ibid.*, p. 145.

[51] See, for example, item 12 of the "Georgia-Pacific classic valuation factors placed in the context of software patents," ABA *Annual Report 94/95*, pp. 488–89.

[52] *Allied Signal Inc. v. Du Pont Canada Inc.* (1998), 78 C.P.R. (3d) 129 ("Allied Signal"). For a good discussion of the 25% Rule, see The Financial Aspects of Technology and Intellectual Property Licensing: The 25% "Royalty Rule" and "Investment" Approaches, Alexander J. Stock, A. Scott Davidson, and Stephen J. Cole 13 I.P.J. 109, August 1999.

[53] AUTM *Manual*, VII-Chapter 4, p. 28.

Although this looks simple, it is not. One of the key issues is the degree the licensed subject matter accomplishes the savings or produces the profit. For example, an invention incorporated into a process may produce a savings of $1 a unit. However, when one examines in detail how such savings are attained, it may be that there are several other technologies that already belong to the licensee and that will need to be exploited in order to realize the full $1. In such a case is the licensor deserving of 25 cents, or should the savings be discounted in some way before the 1/4th fraction is computed? The issue seems to hinge on whether the invention opens the door to an otherwise locked room called "I can save you $1" or whether it is a link in a multi-link chain that together combine to save $1. [When using a savings approach, the technology transfer manager should build in some inflation factor to avoid collecting 25 cents a unit over a 15-year period when inflation eats into the real value of the royalty. Remember the $1 savings is $1 in the currency of the year that the royalty is calculated (in this example). Ten years later, with inflation or increasing costs of electricity or a particular raw material, the savings could be $8 in the currency of that 10th year; the agreement should have some provision for the calculation of royalty to similarly inflate in $ so that, as in this example, it would yield $2 in the 10th year.]

In the second (profit) manifestation of the rule, things get even more complicated. Although "net sales" is generally a straightforward term to apply, profit before tax is subject to many interpretations. Normally, the royalty rate is applied to the royalty basis defined by "net sales" as follows:

> Net sales price is the gross invoice price charged less all allowances for returns, and less cash and other discounts granted, charges for packaging and shipping, and sales and excise taxes included. [This particular form of the definition is adapted from an article by Evelyn M. Sommer, "Patent and Technology License Agreements Explained", The Licensing Journal, August 1993, p. 3 ff. This article and other similar sources also deal with an important but complicated issue of transfer pricing: that is, when a licensee "sells" or transfers the product made by the practice of the technology to another division or a subsidiary of the licensee.]

2.10.2 25% of What

The rule loses its appealing simplicity as you try to apply it. How do you calculate the savings for the user? At what point on the revenue and expense statement do you calculate profit? How do you allocate overhead and amortize fixed costs? Is this profit calculated before or after research and development costs?

2.10.3 Fine Tuning the 25% Figure

Robert Goldscheider suggests that one start with a "25% split to the licensor and then either 'tune' this figure up or down, depending on the peculiar circumstances of each case, including the significance of the intellectual property portfolio and the location of the principal burden of risk".[54] Goldscheider states that with "the benefit of considerable experience", the 25% Rule has been useful. This experience perhaps allows the evaluator to move the 25% factor to a fair allocation of the risk of profit and loss. Thus the 25% rule can be characterized and thus criticised as highly subjective and not sufficiently scientific or analytical. The *Allied Signal Inc. v. Du Pont Canada Inc.* case sets out some factors that "would effect the specific percentage in each case:[55]

(i)   Transfer of technology: There would have been no need to transfer technology, so the rate should be reduced.

(ii)   Differences in the practice of the invention: The plaintiff and the defendant have two different process[es] to create their products. The defendant brings its own technology to the product development. This factor would tend to reduce the royalty rate.

(iii)   Non-exclusive licence: The defendant is not being given an exclusive license. It is not given total control over the market. This factor would reduce the royalty rate.

(iv)   Territorial limitations: The patent is limited to the manufacture of the product within Canada. This factor would reduce the royalty rate.

(v)   Term of the license: The license is only for six years of infringement, not for the entire term of the patent. This factor would reduce the royalty rate.

(vi)   Competitive technology: The availability of competing technologies, such as polyethylene and coextruded film, would reduce the royalty rate.

(vii)   Competition between licensor and licensee: The fact that the plaintiff and the defendant would be competing against each other would increase the royalty rate.

(viii) Demand for the product: Demand for nylon film was growing. This factor would increase the royalty rate.

(ix)   Risk: The risk that the product would not sell is very low. This factor would tend to increase the royalty rate.

(x)   Novelty of invention: The practice of using nylon films as a barrier to gas transmission has been commercially exploited for decades, and this invention is not the result of extensive laboratory studies. This would reduce the royalty rate.

(xi)   Compensation for research and development costs: Such costs for this product are quite low. This factor would reduce the royalty rate.

(xii)   Displacement of business: A royalty rate will tend to be higher if it results in increased revenues to the licensee. Mr. MacKillop suggests that it would not increase revenues to the defendant, but would simply "maintain existing business."

---

[54] Goldscheider, "Litigation Backgrounder," *les Nouvelles*, March 1994, p. 25.

[55] See *Allied Signal Inc.*, *supra*, note 52 at 179.

(xiii) Capacity to meet market demand: The royalty rate will be reduced if the patentee does not have the capacity to produce enough of the product to satisfy the market.

2.10.4 Razgaitis' Pros and Cons for the 25% Rule

Razgaitis writes:[56]

Some cautions in the use of the 25 Percent Rule:

1. The appropriate number is not always 25 percent.

    The figure "25" (and 33-1/3) has emerged as a common generalization and is almost always a useful initial calculation. However, one should always consider whether more or less than 25 percent of the gain is the appropriate reward for the seller.
2. The base against which the 25 percent is applied is subject to interpretation.
    The idea of the base against which 25 percent is applied is that the gain (profit) should be divided 25:75 between seller and buyer. However, determining the "gain" requires analysis. In the cost savings approach, it is important to determine the costs of operations without the benefit of the subject technology, and the costs with the technology or as compared to the next best alternative.
3. A pro forma income statement needs to be created.
    In the case of new sales, the result of the 25 Percent Rule should be expressed in terms of a royalty against sales so as to create an auditable system. Likewise, in the case of cost savings, some conversion may be necessary so that the royalty can be paid on something that is counted in an accounting sense and adjusts for inflation.
4. The 25 Percent Rule does not provide guidance on upfront payments.
    The 25 Percent Rule suggests how future savings or profits should be divided between seller and buyer. In normal circumstances there is an upfront license fee paid by the buyer. In order to determine what an appropriate upfront figure should be, some additional methodology is needed.

Some positive aspects of the 25 Percent Rule that make it popular and worth using are as follows:

*   It gives a feeling of fairness. Because it is based on apportioning anticipated gain, it creates a basis for considering the respective contributions of the seller and buyer.
*   It is based directly on resulting benefits. The 25 Percent Rule is focused on the EBIT line in the income statement, which is an appropriate measure of the direct benefit of the subject license (subject to potential adjustment in allocated costs). "This is still the subject of some controversy – should the 25% be calculated on gross profit, net profit, or the excess of the profit

---

[56] Razgaitis, pp. 117-118.

earned as a result of using the licensed technology over the profit that
would have been earned had the licensed technology not been used".

- It can be the basis of an early agreement. Parties beginning a negotiation
  can sometimes agree that their negotiations will be governed by the 25
  Percent (or some other) Rule. This can be helpful in determining mutual
  expectations at any early stage and in reaching closure.

2.11 Controlled Greed

If the price is established so that it produces a very high profit margin for the
commercialization of the technology, others will be encouraged to replicate the
technology. High profit margins may have to be limited to the time period in
which it would take others to get to market with competing technology, or, perhaps, even a shorter time to discourage others from continuing research on
clones or substitutes. High royalty rates may also encourage competitors to infringe or challenge the validity of the intellectual property protection rather than
concede to licensing. The risk of future litigation may be more attractive than
the present certainty of high licence fees.

2.12 Market Characterization

The characteristics of the market will influence the overall value of the innovation. This requires consideration of:

(a) the market for the technology — leading edge technology may not be
     needed and may be characterized as technology that "was, is, and always
     will be the technology of the future";[57]
(b) the distinctiveness of the market niche;
(c) the size of the market;
(d) the extent of competition;
(e) the size and nature of competitors;
(f) the lead time before technology is "cloned":
     (i)   ease of design around;
     (ii)   the lead time compared to the economic life;
(g) access to alternate and competing technology;
(h) effect of restraint of trade rules;
(i) availability of cross-licensing to avoid intellectual property infringement
     suits;
(j) difficulties in repatriating money from a country that has currency
     controls; and

---

[57] John T. Preston, "Success Factors in Technology Development", An Entrepreneurial Approach
      to the Commercialization of Technology, March 7 and 8, 1995, Edmonton, Alberta, Canada,
      Workshop Sponsored by PACT (Partnership/Alberta for the Commercialization of Technology)
      (unpublished) (hereinafter "Preston, 'Success Factors', in Edmonton").

(k) local market requirements:
  (i) local agent requirements;
  (ii) need to adapt technology to local market (*e.g., electrical device*);
  (iii) inflation (*e.g.,* Brazil/Russia); and
  (iv) currency devaluations.

2.13 Spin-off Potential

Some technologies are more valuable than others due to their "spin-off" potential. Technology that has many uses in different industries or applications may have more enduring value than technology that can be used only one way in one industry or application.

2.13.1 Trickle-down/ Trickle-up Spin-off

Some technology may have a "trickle-down" spin-off effect.[58] If the technology has a high performance and will be sold in low volumes at a high cost with a high margin, the entity commercializing the technology may gain the opportunity to learn about cost reduction techniques before it introduces the technology to a much larger mass market. On the other hand, technology could be introduced to a market-place that is already well served by competitive products, where the product introduced has low incremental performance and a high volume sold at low cost with low margins. In that case, the commercializing entity may decide to introduce the product into that market to learn more about the manufacturing and marketing and then to use that knowledge in areas with higher incremental performance and higher margins. For example, a company may decide to market liquid displays in digital watches (a well established, perhaps even saturated market) to learn more about producing liquid displays for laptop computers or, perhaps, even television monitors (a low-volume higher margin market).[59]

2.13.2 Convoyed Sales

Another spin-off is "convoyed" sales.[60] Although the convoyed sales must be included as part of the overall value, different royalty rates may be applicable to

---

[58] Lewis M. Branscomb, "Building Capacity to Create, Share, and Use Technology: Civil and Military Models", An Entrepreneurial Approach to the Commercialization of Technology, March 7 and 8, 1995, Edmonton, Alberta, Canada, Workshop Sponsored by PACT (Partnership/Alberta for the Commercialization of Technology) (unpublished).

[59] *Ibid.*

[60] See Goldscheider, "Litigation Backgrounder", *les Nouvelles*, March 1994, p. 20, at 24. See also McGavock et al., "Factors", *les Nouvelles*, June 1992, p. 107, at 109. See also item 6 of the Georgia-Pacific classic valuation factors.

the convoyed sales than to sales on the basic technology.[61] One study ranked the value of convoyed sales fairly low in relation to other valuation factors. The authors, expressing caution as to the validity of their study, state that "it is possible that convoyed sales relationships are very difficult to identify, especially for new technology, and therefore do not carry much weight in negotiations".[62] Some of us in practice, however, have found that convoyed sales were the main reason for the acquisition of the targeted technology.

2.13.3 Sell, Design, Build

A company may use the "sell-design-build" business model to its advantage. It may enter into a contract for the development of technology for a particular customer on a cost recovery basis, but may retain the rights to market the technology to others. The company may give the customer exclusivity for certain specified uses, reserving other uses for itself; this exclusivity may be forever or for only a limited period of time.

2.14 Contribution of the Parties

The contribution of each party to the development and commercialization of the technology will affect the amount it will have to pay to participate. Some of the factors to consider are:

  (a) who will significantly contribute to future enhancements?:[63]
      (i)   continued contributions of the inventor in research and development;
      (ii) expertise of the licensee and its presently developed improvements that can be easily integrated;
  (b) corporate reputation of either party, which will ease the opening of markets;
  (c) access to markets:
      (i)   established distribution network;
      (ii) complementary products being distributed — tag-along or derivative sales;
  (d) insight that recognizes a significant pending shift in the market;
  (e) network of connections, ability to introduce strategically placed individuals to the innovator's technology for continued research and development, and the ability to find or locate additional funding or market entry are all highly valuable contributions.

---

[61] See Goldscheider, "Litigation Backgrounder", *les Nouvelles*, March 1994, p. 20, at 24.
[62] McGavock et al., "Factors", *les Nouvelles*, June 1992, p. 107, at 110.
[63] For a discussion on improvements generally, see Chapter 9 of this text.

2.15 Unique Attributes of the Team: Preston's Four Non-technical Components for Success

It is not only the quality of the technology that produces commercial success. The attributes of the various members of the commercializing team will also contribute to the success or failure in instances where there will be an enduring relationship. Preston sets out four non-technical components for success.[64]

(1) Quality of Management:

management gets high quality ratings if it maintains a healthy balance sheet; has a clearly focused strategy; and is realistic about marketing;[65]

(2) Quality of the Investor:

there are a number of factors that influence the quality of the investors: first, the track record in building successful businesses; second, the network of connections with potential partners or customers; third, the level of personal involvement the investor is willing to devote to the business; and fourth, their access to money and long-term vision.[66]

(3) Passion for Success:

the passion of the various players is a key deterrent of success. Worded differently, any new business will encounter hundreds of barriers before it succeeds. People with no passion will use the first barrier as excuse for failure, while people with high passion will do whatever it takes to overcome the barriers. . . . Should any of these three groups be indifferent about success, the future of the company will be greatly impacted. Some companies succeed despite low marks in one or more areas, but as competitive pressures increase, it becomes more important that the start-up company have dedicated personnel. People with high passion will achieve spectacular results, and do whatever is necessary to reach their goals. As a result, it is important to evaluate and modify, if possible, the strength, determination and commitment (or 'passion') of the technologists, the managers and the investors.

There are many ways to kill passion, but greed takes first place.[67]

(4) Image:

the image factor is the way the company is perceived by potential strategic partners, investors, customers, employees . . . for example, a biotech company with a Nobel Laureate on its Board of Directors will have more credibility in presenting a joint venture plan to a large pharmaceutical company than a company with unknown scientists. Similarly, a computer company in partnership with IBM will have an easier time selling its next product than a company without such an endorsement. Also, a company deriving its technology from

---

[64] Preston, "Success Factors", in Edmonton.

[65] *Ibid.*, p. 6.

[66] *Ibid.*

[67] *Ibid.*, p. 7.

Stanford, Harvard, or MIT will have a higher image rating than technology from a lesser known university.[68]

2.16 Intellectual Capital

Preston's points are merely some of the non-technical aspects required for success. A well implemented intellectual capital management program is also important. Stewart writes: "Knowledge assets, like money or equipment, exist and are worth cultivating only in the content of strategy. You cannot define and manage intellectual capital assets unless you know what you are trying to do with them".[69] Kochikar says: "However knowledge intensive a company's work may be, it cannot survive on knowledge alone. It is the overall human capital, harnessed via organizational structures and processes, that ultimately determine its success. Knowledge is one critical component of human capital, the others being social and emotional capital".[70] Stewart further provides:

> Intelligence becomes an asset when some useful order is created out of free-floating brainpower – that is, when it is given coherent form (a mailing list, a database, an agenda for a meeting, a description of a process); when it is captured in a way that allows it to be described, shared, and exploited; and when it can be deployed to do something that could not be done if it remained scattered around like so many coins in a gutter. Intellectual capital is packaged useful knowledge.[71]

Stewart goes on to say:

> Systematic management of intellectual capital creates growth in shareholder value. This is accomplished, among other things, through the continuous recycling and creative utilization of shared knowledge and experience. This, in turn, requires the structuring and packaging of competencies with the help of technology, process descriptions, manuals, networks, and so on, to ensure that the competence will remain with the company when the employees go home. Once packaged, these become part of the company's structural capital – or more precisely, its organizational capital. This creates the conditions for rapid sharing of knowledge and sustained collective growth. . . . Lead times between learning and knowledge sharing are shortened systematically. Human capital will also become more productive through structured, easily accessible and intelligent work processes.[72]

---

[68] *Ibid.*, p. 8. Note that Preston is from MIT.

[69] Stewart, p. 70. See also §3.24 of this text for a discussion of intellectual property strategies.

[70] V. P. Kochikar, "Knowledge – The Currency of the New Millennium," posted on the Internet at <www.inf.com/corporate/thought-papers/knowledge3.html>.

[71] Stewart, p. 67.

[72] *Ibid.*, p. 110. Stewart has an excellent summary of the "Ten Principles for Managing Intellectual Capital" found at pp. 163-165.

2.16.1 Definition of Intellectual Capital

Intellectual capital can be defined as "Intellectual material that has been formalized, captured, and leveraged to produce a higher-valued asset".[73] Intellectual capital is "the sum of an organization's patents, processes, employees' skills, technologies, information about customers, and old-fashioned experience".[74] Others would say that not only is it the sum of those items, but also "the practical translation of this knowledge".[75] In financial terms, "intellectual capital is anything that can create value but you cannot drop on your foot – in other words, it is intangible; it is the difference between the total value of the company and its financial value".[76] There are three main types of intellectual capital: human capital, structural capital and customer capital. "Each is intangible – each reflects the knowledge assets of a company".[77] "Crucially, intellectual capital is not created from discrete wads of human, structural, and customer capital but from the *interplay* among them".[78]

2.16.2 Human Capital

Human capital is the unstructured resource comprised of the individuals that work for the company. Human capital, when properly enabled, is the source of "innovation and renewal".[79] For a competitive advantage, human capital needs to be harnessed into structural capital.

Roos et al. write that human capital is made up of competence, attitude and intellectual agility.[80] "We believe that intellectual capital is composed of (and generated by) a thinking part (the human capital) and a non-thinking part (structural capital). We have then suggested that structural capital has an internal and an external component (organisational and relationship capital respectively), while human capital comes from the knowledge, the attitude and the intellectual agility of employees".[81]

Competence is a combination of knowledge and skills. An indication of knowledge is the level of technical and academic education; knowledge has to be taught.[82] But knowledge must be combined with skills to have any value, as well as an attitude that applies then to the greatest advantage of the company.[83] The "attitude" characteristics will vary from company to company and must be

---

[73] Klein and Prusak as quoted by Stewart, p. 67.
[74] Stewart, p. 66.
[75] Johan Roos, Göran Roose, Nicola C. Dragonetti, and Leif Edvinnsson: *Intellectual Capital: Navigating the New Business Landscape,* (New York: New York University Press, 1998), p. 27.
[76] Roos et al., p. 27.
[77] Stewart, p. 75.
[78] *Ibid.*, p. 78.
[79] *Ibid.*, p. 76.
[80] Roos et al., p. 35.
[81] *Ibid.*, p. 34.
[82] *Ibid.*, p. 35.
[83] *Ibid.*, p. 37.

consistent with each company's strategic vision. Valued personnel will demonstrate intellectual agility – "the ability to transfer knowledge from one context to another, the ability to see common factors in two distinct pieces of information and link them together, and the ability to improve both knowledge and company output through innovation and adaptation…. Intellectual agility is tightly linked to competence, more so than attitude is. If competence is the content, intellectual agility is the ability to use the knowledge and the skills, building on it, applying it in practical contexts and increasing it through learning. Behaviour, on the other hand, relates to the ability to create a climate conducive to the development of intellectual capital in general".[84] To be intellectually agile, one must:

(a) have the "ability to build on previous knowledge and generate new knowledge".[85]

(b) have the "ability to try something totally new, imitation is the ability to look around, perceive innovation in other industries, fields of activity and companies and then apply it to one's own situation".[86]

(c) have the "ability to turn an idea into a product or service". – *i.e.* "package" the knowledge, skills and competence.[87]

2.16.3 Structural Capital

Structural capital includes the traditional intellectual property – patents, copyright, trademark, industrial design, etc., and the structures that manages and shares knowledge. "Sharing and transporting knowledge – leveraging it – requires structural intellectual assets, such as information systems, laboratories, competitive and market intelligence, knowledge of market channels, and management focus, which turn individual know-how into the property of the group. Like human capital, structural capital exists only in the context of a point of view, a strategy, a destination, a purpose".[88] Structural capital is "all intellectual capital that remains in the company when the employees go home for the night".[89] A key component of structural capital is relationships. "The most important sources of relationship capital are customers, suppliers, allies, shareholders and other stakeholders…

> It is common knowledge that gaining a sale with a new customer is much more expensive than gaining the same sale with an existing client. Claes Fornell, of the University of Michigan, suggests that customer satisfaction (that is, relationship value originating from the customer) can increase the life expectancy of the relationship, reduce price elasticity, reduce the efficiency of the competitors' effort, lower the cost of attracting new customers and enhance the reputation of the firm.

---

[84]   *Ibid.*, pp. 39-40.
[85]   *Ibid.*, p. 40.
[86]   *Ibid.*, p. 40.
[87]   *Ibid.*, p. 41.
[88]   Stewart, p. 74.
[89]   Roos et al., p. 42, using the Skandia definition.

It is quite obvious, then, that the ability of a company to retain customers is essential to its long-term profitability.[90]

Structural capital also includes organizational capital. "Organisational value includes all the physical and non-physical manifestations of intellectual capital related to the internal structure or the day-to-day operations. Databases, process manuals, invisible assets, culture and management styles are all sources of organisational value. Also, organisational value is usually the result of the effort of a company to turn human capital in proprietary information, and to share that information among all employees. Internal networks thus are part of this category of capital".[91] Organisational capital includes intellectual property rights.[92]

But again, we come back to strategy: the culture of the organization – the "'wetware' of organisational capital".[93]

2.17 Type of Licence

The more security the licensee has to attain desired profits, the more it should be expected to pay. Some of the features of a licence that will influence value are:

(a) exclusivity:[94]
   (i)   excluding all future licensees;
   (ii) excluding all licensees, including the present ones;
   (iii) excluding the licensor;
(b) field of use restrictions;
(c) territorial restrictions;
(d) value added restrictions; and
(e) duration of the licence: the shorter the term, the less may be the value.[95]

2.18 Type of Consideration to be Paid

There are many different types of considerations and the method of selection may very well influence value. The more paid up front, the more the risk to the transferee increases and the greater the discount rate for anticipated cash flow can become. The type of consideration may significantly affect value, whether such consideration be a running royalty, one or more lump sum payments, eq-

---

[90] Roos et al., p. 44. See also Stewart, p. 77.
[91] Roos et al., p. 46.
[92] Roos et al., p. 48. See the charge that puts it all into visual context at <www.matrilinks.ca/intellectualcapital.html>.
[93] Roos et al., p. 49.
[94] For a further discussion of these topics, see Chapter 7.
[95] See, for example, item 7 of the "Georgia-Pacific classic valuation factors, as placed in a software patent context," ABA *Annual Report 94/95*, pp. 488–89. These factors are set out in §2.13 of this text.

uity shares issued by the licensee, lending of continued research, fees for support, appointment to advisory boards, consulting/employment fees, certain first rights, most favoured licensee rights, grant backs and settlement of outstanding litigation.

2.19 Warranties

The extent of credible and supportable warranties against product defects and infringement will also influence value. Consider the following:

(a) product warranties,[96] their scope and limitations, the track record of the licensor in remedying defects, the service record of the transferor, such as providing support, training on methods of use and the provision of seminars to enhance general knowledge that will encourage use;
(b) infringement warranties,[97] their scope and limitation as to type of infringement, amount of damages and territory covered; and
(c) risk of bankruptcy of the transferor and its effect on the technology transfer agreement.

---

[96] For further discussion on warranties against product defects, see Chapter 14 of this text.
[97] For further discussion on infringement and its consequences, see Chapter 16 of this text.

Table A
IPSCORE

	B: Basic properties and technical status of the patent.		POINT SCORE						
	Assessment factors	Importance	4	3	2	1	0	Maximum point score	Actual point score
	I. Basic Properties								
1	Status of the patent (applied for, issued)								
2	Tenability of the patent?								
3	Stage in life cycle of the patent (new, mature, about to expire).								
4	Is it possible to extend period of protection afforded by the patent?								
5	How likely is it that the period of protection afforded by the patent will be extended?								
6	The geographical coverage of the patent, number of countries.								
	II. Technical Status								
7	To what extent is the invention developed for a superior technology?								
8	To what extent is the invention described by the use of examples of different applications?								
9	To what extent has the invention been tested?								
10	To what extent is further development necessary before commercialisation is possible.								
11	To what extent is the invention technically superior compared to substitutable technology?								
	Total								

TABLE B

OVERVIEW OF INTELLECTUAL PROPERTY IN CANADA

	PATENTS	COPYRIGHT	TRADE-MARKS	TRADE SECRETS	INDUSTRIAL DESIGN
Governing Legislation	*Patent Act*, R.S.C. 1985, c. P-4 as amended	*Copyright Act*, R.S.C. 1985, c. C-42, as amended	*Trade-marks Act*, R.S.C. 1985, c.T-13, as amended	— Common law protection only	*Industrial Design Act*, R.S.C. 1985, c. I-9, as amended
Definition	Any new, useful and non-obvious art, process, machine, manufacture or composition of matter, or any new and useful improvements in the same. Broad range of sources, including, mechanical, electrical, chemical, pharmaceutical and biotechnical industries.	Original works of authorship including artistic, choreographic, dramatic, literary (including software), musical works and compilations. Also neighbouring rights for certain types of works.	A symbol (words, design, colours, logos, a device, or any combination) that is used in relation to goods or services and distinguishes a trader's goods or services from that of another.	Secret identifiable information, which gives an advantage over competitors who do not know or use it (*e.g.* chemical formulations, compositions, recipes, source code).	Ornamentation, patterns, configuration or a shape applied to a functional article. The design must solely appeal to the eye and cannot serve a functional purpose (for example, the shape of a bottle that is not dictated by function or the pattern applied to carpets).

TABLE B

OVERVIEW OF INTELLECTUAL PROPERTY IN CANADA CONT'D

	PATENTS	COPYRIGHT	TRADE-MARKS	TRADE SECRETS	INDUSTRIAL DESIGN
Rights	Exclusive right to exclude others from importing, making, using and selling the claimed subject matter – granted in exchange for disclosing the invention to the public.	**Owner Rights:** Sole right to, among other things, copy, publish, make translations, of the work or a substantial part. **Author rights:** Moral rights: (1) to be associated with the work where reasonable, (2) to be anonymous; and (3) to the integrity of the work.	Exclusive right to *inter alia* use mark to distinguish a trader's wares or services from others. Identical marks can co-exist as long as there is no confusion.	An owner has the sole right to use, and decide when to publish, the secret. Courts have held it is not a property right.	Exclusive right to *inter alia* make, import, or sell the design.

TABLE B
OVERVIEW OF INTELLECTUAL PROPERTY IN CANADA CONT'D

	PATENTS	COPYRIGHT	TRADE-MARKS	TRADE SECRETS	INDUSTRIAL DESIGN
Scope	Protects claimed idea. Protects against independent creation. Patent awarded to first to file for patents applied for after October 1, 1989.	Protects expression, not idea, from a substantial taking. Does not protect against independent creation. Can have concurrent industrial design and trade secret protection.	Protects against confusing use.	Does not generally stop third parties who receive the secret information acting in good faith. Does not protect against independent creation. Can have overlapping copyright protection.	Protects claimed design from a substantial taking. Protects against independent creation. Can have concurrent copyright protection.
Registration	**Mandatory.** Examination procedure. Jurisdiction by jurisdiction basis, treaties facilitate.	**Voluntary.** Notice Procedure. Confers certain additional benefits (deemed notice and litigation presumptions). Protection arises automatically upon creation, in all treaty countries.	**Voluntary.** Examination procedure. Common law rights exist but registration confers many additional benefits. Jurisdiction by jurisdiction basis, treaties facilitate.	None	**Mandatory.** Examination procedure. Jurisdiction by jurisdiction basis, treaties facilitate.

TABLE B
OVERVIEW OF INTELLECTUAL PROPERTY IN CANADA CONT'D

	PATENTS	COPYRIGHT	TRADE-MARKS	TRADE SECRETS	INDUSTRIAL DESIGN
Term	20 years from date of filing if filed after October 1, 1989, subject to payment of an annual maintenance fee.	Generally, life of the author + 50 years.	Perpetual, subject to continued use, and if registered, in addition to continued use, payment of renewal fee every 15 years.	The term is perpetual, subject to keeping it secret.	10 years, subject to payment of a five year maintenance fee.

Part II

INTELLECTUAL PROPERTY PROTECTION

Chapter 3

PATENTS

The primary goal of the patent system is to encourage innovation and commercialization of technological advances. To this end, the patent system offers an incentive to inventors to publicly disclose their inventions in exchange for the exclusive right to prevent others from making, using, offering for sale or selling the inventions throughout the [country that issues the patent] or importing the inventions into the [country that issues the patent].[1]

3.1 Applicable Legislation

Patent rights, which are restricted to the country that issues the relevant patent, come only from the legislation of that country.[2] There are no common-law rights to a patent in Canada or the United States. If the legislation does not cover the subject-matter, then a patent is not available.

Strategy: What you see is what you get. If the subject-matter of your invention is not covered by the applicable Patent Act, your invention is not patentable under that Act. Consider another form of intellectual property protection.

3.1.1 Exclusionary Rights

A valid patent gives the holder the right to exclude others:

(a) if the patent covers a process:
   (i) from practising the patented process;
   (ii) from making, using, offering to sell, or selling a product made by the patented process;

---

[1] United States, *Intellectual Property in the National Information Infrastructure*, the report of the Working Group on Intellectual Property Rights, Bruce A. Lehman, Assistant Secretary of Commerce and Commissioner of Patents and Trademarks, Chair, September 1995 (hereinafter "NII"). This report is available on the Internet by pointing the Gopher Client to IITF. DOC.GOV and is located on many other sites on the Internet.

[2] In Canada, this is the *Patent Act*, R.S.C 1985, c. P-4 (hereinafter "*Patent Act* (Canada)"). In the United States, this is Title 35 of the *United States Code* (U.S.C.), 1952 (hereinafter "U.S. Patent Act").

      (iii)   from importing into the country issuing the patent a product made by the patented process;

  (b) if the patent covers a product:

      (i)   from making, using, offering to sell or selling that product;

      (ii)   from importing that product into the country issuing the patent.

Strategy: The "grant" clause must contemplate what exclusionary rights are being licensed.

3.1.2   *The Patent Application Process (Drafting, Filing, Prosecution, Issue and Maintenance)*

The process of obtaining a patent is commenced by the filing of a patent application in the appropriate patent office. A formal application consists of:

  (a) a specification, "which must have a written description of the invention telling what the invention is, how it works, and how to make and use it so as to enable others skilled in the art to do so".[3] "The written description typically includes a short introductory abstract of the invention, a description of the field of the invention, a description of the background of the invention, a brief description of the drawings and a detailed description of the invention. . . . The detailed description includes a discussion of particular embodiments or examples of the invention, often with references to the drawings". The specifications may include drawings.[4]

  (b) the specification concludes with one or more numbered sentences. These are the claims. The purpose of the claims is to provide notice of what the applicant regards as his or her specific invention. When the patent is eventually issued by the PTO, the claims define the scope of the patent owner's exclusionary rights during the life of the patent.[5] "The claims are 'word pictures' intended to define, in words, the boundaries of the invention described and illustrated in the patent. Only the claims can be infringed. Neither the written description nor the drawings of a patent can be infringed". The "claims of a patent must state distinctly and in explicit terms the things or combinations the applicant regards as new and in which he or she claimed an exclusive property or privilege".[6] In Canada the claims must be interpreted by the words and drawings of the

---

[3]   AIPLA's Guide to Model Patent Jury Instructions, p. 8 found at <www.aipla.org/patent-jury.html>, hereafter "AIPLA Jury Instructions". This is an excellent primer on the U.S. law.

[4]   *Guide to the Interpretation of Patent Claims for the Judiciary*, American Intellectual Property Association, Patent Litigation Committee, Markman Procedures Committee, draft 4/19/00 p. 3.

[5]   AIPLA Jury Instructions, p. 8.

[6]   Dino P. Clarizio, "Whirlpool and Free Trust: Claim Construction and the Test for Infringement; 18 C.I.P.R. 139 at 140 (November 2001), quoting Binnie J. in *Whirlpool v. Camco*, [2000] S.C.R. 67, ("Clarizio") — *Whirlpool Corp. v. Camco Inc.*, [2000] S.C.C. 67 – and - *Free World Trust v. Électro Santé Inc.*, [2000] S.C.C. 66.

patent specification as a whole,[7] but in the United States material disclosed in the patent prosecution history (also known as the "file wrapper") may be looked to as well.[8] Each of the claims must be considered individually, and not all claims of a patent have to be infringed for the patent to be infringed".[9]

3.1.3 The Examination Process

The AIPLA Jury Instructions set out the examination or review process (all references to PTO are to the U.S. Patent and Trademark Office, "USPTO"):

After the applicant files the application, a PTO patent examiner who reviews (or examines) the patent application to determine whether the claims are patentable and whether the specification adequately describes the invention claimed. In examining a patent application, the patent examiner considers, among other things, whether each claim defines an invention that is new, useful and not obvious in view of this prior art. The prior art is defined by statute, but generally it is technical information and knowledge that was known to the public either before the invention by the applicant or more than a year before the effective filing date of the application.

Following the prior art search and examination of the application, the patent examiner advises the applicant in writing what the examiner has found and whether he has "allowed" any claim. This writing from the PTO examiner is called an office action. More often than not, the initial office action by the patent examiner rejects some claims. The application may go back and forth between the patent examiner in the PTO and the applicant for several months or even for years until the examiner is satisfied that the specification and the claims meet the conditions for patentability.

The papers generated during this time of correspondence collectively constitute the prosecution history. This history of written correspondence is contained in a file in the PTO, and consequently some people over the course of the trial may refer to this history as the "file wrapper".

In prosecuting patent applications to protect inventions in the field of certain "market timing" sensitive technologies, circumstances are likely to arise in which it will be appropriate to have the patent issue at the earliest possible time after filing. The current rules contemplate this possibility and for an additional fee permit requests for "expedited examination" to accelerate the prosecution of

---

[7] Clarizio, p. 142.

[8] Clarizio, p. 151.

[9] AIPLA Jury Instructions Claim Construction and Infringement No.1, p. 12 – see also Timothy M. Lowman , LES Summer Meeting 2001, (hereafter "Lowman, 2001"), p. 18.

the application with a view to earlier issuance of whatever specific protection the examiner is willing to grant.

PATENTS VERSUS RESTRAINT OF TRADE

3.2 Patents Give Right to Prevent

In practice, the Canadian and U.S. Patent Acts do not give the patentee the right to exploit any technology; they give only the right to prevent others from doing certain things. The patentee may need the consent, or a "licence", from the holder of another patent or intellectual property right if the making, using or selling of the patented invention infringes that other person's intellectual property right.[10] The right to make, use or sell a patented invention may be regulated by federal, provincial, state or local law.[11]

3.2.1 Patents as Monopolies

Patents are often referred to as "monopolies"; this is a misnomer arising out of the title to the first patent legislation in England — the Statute of Monopolies.[12] Patent protection is better described as an exclusionary right, particularly in the United States where the word "monopolies" has profound antitrust ramifications.[13]

Strategy: Patents are exclusionary not monopolistic.

---

[10] It is not the holding of the patent that gives rise to the infringement; it is the making, using or selling of the invention covered by the patent. In Canada there may exist a right of a prior user to continue using the patented technology – where it is possible to have prior use without destroying novelty. See Gregor Binkley "Prior Use and the Canadian Patent Act" in (2001), 18 C.I.P.R. 207.

[11] See Art. 28 of the *Agreement on Trade-Related Aspects of Intellectual Property Rights* (hereinafter "TRIPPS") where it identifies the difference between "product" patent rights and "process" patent rights, stating:

    1. A patent shall confer on its owner the following exclusive rights:

        (a) where the subject matter of a patent is a product, to prevent third parties not having his consent from the acts of: making, using, offering for sale, selling, or importing for these purposes that product;

        (b) where the subject matter of a patent is a process, to prevent third parties not having his consent from the act of using the process, and from the acts of: using, offering for sale, selling, or importing for these purposes at least the product obtained directly by that process.

    2. Patent owners shall also have the right to assign, or transfer by succession, the patent and to conclude licensing contracts.

[12] 1623, 21 Jac. I, c. 3.

[13] R.M. Milgrim, *Milgrim On Licensing*, rev. ed. (New York: Matthew Bender, 1995), §2.28 (hereinafter "Milgrim, *On Licensing*").

3.2.2 Constitutional Protection Versus Restraint of Trade

In the United States patents and copyrights are constitutionally protected and therefore prevail over government policies such as the federal anti-restraint of trade policy — policy that otherwise opposes monopolies. Thus, the courts are forced to reconcile these competing policies: the courts and technology transfer agreements that involve an American party must "walk a thin line" between these two bodies of law. On the one hand, they must protect, as broadly as possible, the rights of the intellectual property holder and its licensees; on the other hand, they must avoid protecting these rights so broadly that they cross the line between the legitimate exercise of intellectual property rights and the violation of competition law. This gives rise "to the 'rule of necessity', which seeks to limit patentees to exercising their rights in a manner least restrictive of competition".[14]

3.3 Remedy for Restraint of Trade Violation

Although anti-restraint of trade rules and patent misuse rules could have been restricted to criminal actions, in the United States they have given rise to civil remedies, including damages, that may be sought by competitors.

3.3.1 Unique to the United States?

This protection versus competition tension does not exist in other countries. In agreements where all parties are Canadian, one must be careful not to expect anti-restraint of trade policy to have the same restrictive effect on patents and copyrights as it would on American parties. Yet,

> U.S. antitrust jurisprudence must . . . be borne in mind when drafting and reviewing Canadian technology transfer agreements that might affect in some way commerce or consumers in the United States. Where the effect of such agreement is deemed substantial enough, the courts in the United States will assert jurisdiction extraterritorially and review the agreement for conformity to the requirements of U.S. antitrust law.[15]

Strategy: In the United States, patents may not be abused to unduly restrain trade.[16]

---

[14] R.J. Roberts, "Technology Transfer Agreements and North American Competition" in M. Goudreau, G. Bisson, N. Lacasse and L. Perret, eds., *Exporting our Technology: International Protection and Transfers of Industrial Innovations* (Montreal: Wilson & Lafleur, 1995), p. 151, at 158; also printed in Intellectual Property Journal, December 1995, Vol. 9, No. 3, p. 247.

[15] *Ibid.*, p. 155.

[16] See Chapter 10 of this text.

3.3.2 Canadian Patent Abuse Rules

The Canadian patent abuse rules are very different from the U.S. rules. In Canada the following acts amount to abuse:

> If the demand for the patented article in Canada is not being met to an adequate extent and on reasonable terms;

> If, by reason of the refusal of the patentee to grant a licence or licences on reasonable terms, the trade or industry of Canada or the trade of any person or class of persons trading in Canada, or the establishment of any new trade or industry in Canada, is prejudiced, and it is in the public interest that a licence or licences should be granted;

> If any trade or industry in Canada, or any person or class of persons engaged therein, is unfairly prejudiced by the conditions attached by the patentee, whether before or after the passing of this Act, to the purchase, hire, licence or use of the patented article or to the using or working of the patented process; or

> If it is shown that the existence of the patent, being a patent for an invention relating to a process involving the use of materials not protected by the patent or for an invention relating to a substance produced by such a process, has been utilized by the patentee so as unfairly to prejudice in Canada the manufacture, use or sale of any materials.

The Canadian rules permit an application to the Commissioner of Patents who has the following powers:

> *Powers of Commissioner in cases of abuse* — On being satisfied that a case of abuse of the exclusive rights under a patent has been established, the Commissioner may exercise any of the following powers as he may deem expedient in the circumstances:
>
> (a)   he may order the grant to the applicant of a licence on such terms as the Commissioner may think expedient, including a term precluding the licensee from importing into Canada any goods the importation of which, if made by persons other than the patentee or persons claiming under him, would be an infringement of the patent, and in that case the patentee and all licensees for the time being shall be deemed to have mutually covenanted against that importation:
>
> (b)   [Repealed 1993, c. 44, s. 197(1).];
>
> (c)   if the Commissioner is satisfied that the exclusive rights have been abused in the circumstances specified in paragraph 65(2)(f), he may order the grant of licences to the applicant and to such of his customers, and containing such terms, as the Commissioner may think expedient;
>
> (d)   if the Commissioner is satisfied that the objects of this section and section 65 cannot be attained by the exercise of any of the foregoing powers, the Commissioner shall order the patent to be revoked, either forthwith or after such reasonable interval as may be specified in the order, unless in the meantime such con-

ditions as may be specified in the order with a view to attaining the objects of this section and section 65 are fulfilled, and the Commissioner may, on reasonable cause shown in any case, by subsequent order extend the interval so specified, but the Commissioner shall not make an order for revocation which is at variance with any treaty, convention, arrangement, or engagement with any other country to which Canada is a party; or

(e) if the Commissioner is of the opinion that the objects of this section and section 65 will be attained by not making an order under the provisions of this section, he may make an order refusing the application and dispose of any question as to costs thereon as he thinks just.

(2) Proceedings to prevent infringement — A licensee under paragraph (1)(a) is entitled to call on the patentee or take proceedings to prevent infringement of the patent, and if the patentee refuses or neglects to do so within two months after being so called on, the licensee may institute proceedings for infringement in his own name as though he were the patentee, making the patentee a defendant, but a patentee added as defendant is not liable for any costs unless he enters an appearance and takes part in the proceedings.

(3) Service on patentee — Service on a patentee added as a defendant may be effected by leaving the writ at his address or at the address of his representative for service as appearing in the records of the Patent Office.

(4) Considerations by which Commissioner to be guided — In settling the terms of a licence under paragraph (1)(a), the Commissioner shall be guided as far as possible by the following considerations:

(a) he shall endeavour to secure the widest possible use of the invention in Canada consistent with the patentee deriving a reasonable advantage from his patent rights;

(b) he shall endeavour to secure to the patentee the maximum advantage consistent with the invention being worked by the licensee at a reasonable profit in Canada; and

(c) he shall endeavour to secure equality of advantage among the several licensees, and for this purpose may, on due cause being shown, reduce the royalties or other payments accruing to the patentee under the licence previously granted.[17]

PATENTABLE SUBJECT-MATTER

3.4 Works Covered

The Canadian *Patent Act* provides protection to any "new and useful art, process, machine, manufacture or composition of matter, or any new and useful improvement in any art, process, machine, manufacture or composition of matter".[18] The U.S. *Patent Act* is substantially similar, speaking in terms of "proc-

---

[17] R.S.C. 1985, c. 33 (3rd Supp.), s. 24; 1993, c. 44, s. 197.
[18] *Patent Act* (Canada), s. 2.

esses, machines, manufactures or compositions of matter".[19] The latter three categories define "things" while the process category defines inventions that consist of "actions" (*i.e.*, a series of steps or acts to be performed).[20] The scope of the subject-matter of a patent may be summarized as follows:

(a) An art is abstract in that it is capable of contemplation, but concrete in that it involves applying physical forces to physical objects to change the character or condition of material objects; it is broader than a method or process.[21]

(b) Process is a method involving the application of materials to produce a result. Although the method and materials may be known, combining them to produce something new may be patentable.[22]

(c) A statutory process (*i.e.*, one within the scope of the U.S. *Patent Act*).

(d) is a series of one or more acts that manipulate physical matter or energy resulting in some form of a physical transformation. Accordingly, a claimed process is statutory if it:

  (i) manipulates some form of physical matter or energy; and

  (ii) results in a transformation or reduction of the subject matter manipulated into a different state or into a different thing to achieve a practical application.[23]

(e) A machine is any instrument used to transmit force and modify its application.[24]

(f) 'A manufacture' may mean either a completed machine or the mode of constructing it. It is a principle connected with or embodied in tangible substances to produce a practical effect, whether manually or with instruments.[25]

Strategy: An invention must be within the scope of "art, process, machine, manufacture or composition of matter" to be protected by a patent.

---

[19] 35 U.S.C. §101. See also TRIPPS, Art. 27.

[20] *Legal Analysis to Support Proposed Examination Guidelines for Computer-implemented Inventions*, October 3, 1995, Patent and Trademark Office, United States Department of Commerce, Section III.A (hereinafter "*Legal Analysis*"). In the U.S. *Patent Act* "the term 'process' means process, art or method, and includes a new use of a known process, machine, manufacture, composition of matter, or material".

[21] George Francis Takach, *Patents: A Canadian compendium of law and practice* (Edmonton: Juriliber, 1993), p. 18, Section 2.2 (hereinafter "Takach, *Patents*").

[22] *Ibid.*, Section 2.3.

[23] *Legal Analysis*, Section III.B.2.(b).

[24] Takach, *Patents*, p. 19, Section 2.4.

[25] *Ibid.*, p. 19, Section 2.5.

3.4.1 Industrial Designs

In Canada, industrial designs are protected under the *Industrial Design Act*;[26] in the United States they are protected as "design" patents under the U.S. *Patent Act*.[27] Industrial designs are aesthetic and not utilitarian. They appeal to and are judged by the eye alone[28] and are protected for their "ornamental qualities".[29] This text will not further discuss industrial design or design patents, and the word "patent" will refer to a utility patent.

3.4.2 Plants

Reproduction of plants is covered in Canada by the *Plant Breeders' Rights Act*[30] and in the United States by the *Plant Variety Protection Act*.[31] In addition, in the United States, "plant patents" are available for a "distinct and new variety of a plant which asexually reproduces".[32] This text will not further discuss "plant patents".

3.4.3 Patents for Micro-organisms

The Canadian patent system currently does not offer patent protection for some life forms, protection for animal life forms is presently especially uncertain.[33] In the United States, the law is different. The United States Supreme Court has "decided that a new, human-made single-celled organism can be patentable subject matter under Section 101".[34] In 1980, the U.S. Supreme Court, ruling that certain micro-organisms could be patented,[35] wrote "[the inventor's] discovery is not nature's handiwork, but his own. Accordingly, it is patentable subject matter under 101".[36] By 1988, U.S. Patent and Trademark Office ("USPTO") had issued its first animal patent (a transgenic mouse).[37]

---

[26] R.S.C. 1985, c. I-9, as amended.

[27] U.S. *Patent Act,* 35 U.S.C. 171.

[28] Takach, *Patents*, p. 161, citing *Industrial Design Act*, R.S.C. 1985, c. I-9, s. 2 as amended.

[29] Milgrim, *On Licensing*, §219.

[30] S.C. 1990, c. 20.

[31] 35 U.S.C. §§1562, 1611, 2321, as *per* Milgrim, *On Licensing*, §2.18.

[32] Milgrim, *On Licensing*, §2.18. See U.S. *Patent Act*, 35 U.S.C. §§161–64.

[33] *Pioneer Hi-Bred Ltd. v. Canada (Commr. of Patents)*, [1989] 1 S.C.R. 1623, 60 D.L.R. (4th) 223, 97 N.R. 185, 25 C.P.R. (3d) 257, 25 C.I.P.R. 1.

[34] Phillip B.C. Jones "Overview of United States Patent Law", Foley & Lardner home page: <http://biotechlaw.ari.net> (hereinafter "Jones, 'Overview'").

[35] *Diamond v. Chakrabarty*, 447 U.S. 303, 206 U.S.P.Q. 193 (1980) .

[36] *Ibid.*, at 197.

[37] For further discussion on this topic see Jones, "Overview".

3.4.4 Patent Protection Varies From Country to Country

Not all countries, even those with patent systems that appear to be similar to the Canadian or American systems, provide the same scope of protection from independent development. Some countries may have adopted narrower doctrines of equivalents "in order to stimulate local efforts to work around issued patents".[38]

3.5 Works Not Covered: Scientific Principles

A Canadian patent will not be granted "for any mere scientific principle or abstract theorem".[39] Although the U.S. Supreme Court has held that "anything under the sun that is made by man" is patentable,[40] that is an overstatement even for the United States. The U.S. *Patent Act* cites four categories of appropriate statutory material for patents, processes, machines, manufactures or compositions of matter.[41] These four categories do not include "mental processes as such", which are "not afforded patent protection".[42] The issue of non-patentability comes to the forefront when dealing with the patentability of computer programs, as illustrated by the following review of the principles involved:

> Subject matter not within one of the four statutory invention categories or which is not "useful" in a patent sense, accordingly, is not eligible to and cannot be patented.

> The subject matter courts have found to be outside the four statutory categories of invention is limited to abstract ideas, laws of nature and natural phenomena. While this is easily stated, determining whether an applicant is seeking to patent an abstract idea, a law of nature or a natural phenomena has proven to be challenging. These three exclusions recognize that subject matter that is not a practical application or use of an idea, a law of nature or a natural phenomena is not patentable.

> Courts have expressed a concern over "preemption" of ideas, law of natures [sic] or natural phenomena. The concern over preemption serves to bolster and justify the prohibition against the patenting of subject matter. Such concerns are only relevant to claiming a scientific truth or principle. Thus, a claim to an "abstract"

---

[38] Jerome H. Reichman, "GATT, TRIPS and NAFTA, the TRIPS component of the GATT's Uruguay Round: Competitive Prospects for Intellectual Property Owners in an Integrated World Market", Fordham Intellectual Property, Media and Entertainment Law Journal, Vol. 14, Summer 1993, No. 1, p. 1, at 17 (hereinafter "Reichman, 'GATT'"). Also printed in M. Goudreau et al., *Exporting our Technology*, p. 3.

[39] *Patent Act* (Canada), s. 27(3) (rep. & sub. S.C. 1993, c. 44, s. 192).

[40] Section III. A of *Legal Analysis*, citing *Diamond v. Chakrabarty*, 447 U.S. 303 at 308-09, 206 U.S.P.Q. 193 at 196–97 (1980).

[41] 35 U.S.C. §101.

[42] Milgrim, *On Licensing*, §2.22.

idea is non-statutory because it does not represent a practical application of the idea, not because it would preempt the idea.[43]

. . .

A process that consists solely of mathematical operations is non-statutory. Mathematical algorithms do not manipulate physical matter and cannot cause a physical effect. Courts have, however, recognized a distinction between types of mathematical algorithms, namely, some define a "law of nature" in mathematical terms and others merely describe an "abstract idea".

Certain mathematical algorithms have been held non-statutory because they represent a mathematical definition of a law of nature or a natural phenomenon. For example the formula $E=mc^2$ is a "law of nature" — it defines a "fundamental scientific truth" (i.e., the relationship between energy and mass). To comprehend how the law of nature relates to any object, one invariably has to perform certain steps (e.g., multiplying a number representing the mass of an object by the square of a number representing the speed of light). If an applicant defines a process to consist solely of those steps that one must follow to solve the mathematical representation of the law of nature, the "process" is indistinguishable from the law of nature and would "preempt the law of nature". A patent cannot be granted on such a process.

Other mathematical algorithms have been held non-statutory because they merely describe an abstract idea. An "abstract idea" may simply be any sequence of mathematical operations that are combined to solve a mathematical problem. The concern addressed by holding such subject matter non-statutory is that the mathematical operations merely describe an idea and do not define a process that represents a practical application of the idea.[44]

3.6 Computer Programs

Until the early 1990's, the exclusion of scientific principles was considered sufficient to deny patent protection for computer programs because they were made up of algorithms (*i.e.*, mathematical formulae). In 1994, the Canadian Patent Office released new rules that will broaden its previous position concerning the patentability of computer programs and will now allow patent protection for computer programs to the extent that the claims of the patent are not "unapplied mathematical formulae" that are "considered equivalent to mere scientific principles or abstract theorems which are not patentable . . .".[45]

---

[43] *Legal Analysis*, Section III.
[44] *Ibid.*, Section III-3(a).
[45] The January 1995 *Newsletter of The Patent and Trademark Institute of Canada.*

3.6.1 Patentability Neutral

The presence of a computer program in the invention will not add to or detract from patentability in the United States. In the U.S. case *In re Meyer*[46] it is stated:

(a) The presence of a mathematical algorithm or formula in a claim is merely an indication that a scientific principle, law of nature, idea or mental process may be the subject matter claimed and, thus, justify a rejection of that claim under 35 USC 101; but the presence of a mathematical algorithm or formula is only a signpost for further analysis.[47]

Legal Analysis states that as a matter of policy of the USPTO ". . . [Its] Office personnel will no longer begin examination [of a patent application for a computer program] by determining if a claim recites 'mathematical algorithm'".[48] In essence, applications for patents of computer programs, even though they include mathematical algorithms will be treated like patent applications for other inventions. All the principles of general application must be examined to see how they apply to the particular patent application. *Legal Analysis* usefully sets out the process the patent examiners will use for U.S. applications and can be expected to influence the examinations in other jurisdictions.

3.6.2 Business Method Patents

The scope of U.S. software patents was increased in the late 1990's to include "business methods" that satisfy the usual requirements of patentability.[49] It is not as clear in Canada that business methods are patentable subject matter.[50] Unfortunately in the initial stages, some business methods resulted in patents that were overreaching. In the early 2000's it is unclear how far common sense will prevail.[51]

---

[46] 688 F.2d 789, at 794–95, 215 U.S.P.Q. 193, at 197 (C.C.P.A. 1982).

[47] Quoted in *Legal Analysis*, note 32.

[48] *Legal Analysis*, Part II, "Determine what applicant has invented and is seeking to patent".

[49] For example, see *State Street & Trust v. Signature Financial Group*, 47 U.S.P.Q. 2d 1596, 149 F3d 1386 (Fed.Cir. 1998).

[50] See "Debunking Canada's Business Method Exclusion from Patentability"; Michael D. Manson and Stephen J. Ferance, presented at the Licensing Executive Society, Summer 2001 Meeting, Kananaskis, Alberta, Canada.

[51] See BarnesandNoble.com's victory over Amazon.com in an appeal of Amazon's claim that Barnes and Noble infringed on Amazon's one-click shopping patent, as reported in "The year in Internet Law", December 28, 2001, *The New York Times*.

ESSENTIALS FOR PROTECTION

3.7 New, Useful and Unobvious

To be protected by a Canadian or U.S. patent, the invention must be new, useful and unobvious.[52]

3.8 The Invention Must Be New

For an invention to be "new" for the purposes of a Canadian patent, the invention must not have been disclosed to the public in Canada or anywhere else in the world by anyone other than the inventor before the patent application is filed, subject to patent treaties.[53] Such a disclosure will include any patent application that has been laid open for inspection by the public or that has issued anywhere in the world. "The 'new' requirement is referred to as the requirement of novelty. The lack of novelty, referred to as 'anticipation' is a basis for invalidating a patent and is a complete defense in an action for infringement".[54]

3.8.1 Extra-U.S. Inventive Act: Prior Art

Prior to changes in the 1990's, an "applicant for a [U.S.] patent was not able to establish a date of invention by reference to activity in a foreign country except as provided in 35 U.S.C. 119 and 365. Thus, applicants who made their invention outside the territorial limits of the United States were able to rely only on the filing date of a foreign priority application or the filing date of an international application filed under the Patent Cooperation Treaty to establish a date of invention before the U.S. filing date of their application".[55] In other words, the United States had a first-to-file system for inventions made outside the United States and a first-to-invent system for inventions made in the United States. The U.S. Act was amended to provide that:

> [i]n proceedings in the Patent and Trademark Office, in the courts, and before any other competent authority an application for a patent, or a patentee, may not establish a date of invention by reference to knowledge or use thereof, or other ac-

---

[52] See the *Patent Act* (Canada), ss. 2 and 28.3 (re-en. S.C. 1993, c. 15, s. 33) and the U.S. *Patent Act*, 35 U.S.C. §§101–103.

[53] *Patent Act* (Canada), s. 27(1) (rep. & sub. R.S.C. 1985, c. 33 (3rd Supp.), s. 8). For disclosures made voluntarily to the public see Chapter 1, §1.1.1. Disclosure by the inventor more than one year prior to filing is also a statutory bar.

[54] "Swords and Shields, The Enforcement and Defense of Intellectual Property Rights", Timothy M. Lowman, Licensing Executives Society 2001 Summer Meeting, p. 5 (hereafter "Lowman 2001"). See also AIPL Jury Instructions Anticipation No.1, p. 22.

[55] *Effects of GATT and NAFTA on PTO Practices*, <http://www.uspto.gov/web/uruguay/URPAPER. html> (hereinafter "*Effects of GATT*").

tivity with respect thereto, in a foreign country, *other than a NAFTA country or a WTO member country*, except as provided in sections 119 and 365 of this title.[56] [Emphasis added.]

As a result, inventors in the *North American Free Trade Agreement* ("NAFTA") or in the World Trade Organization ("WTO") member countries will be entitled to rely on the first-to-invent criterion.[57] Additionally, the Patent Acts of other member countries can be expected to permit a reference to prior art disclosed in other WTO member countries.

3.8.2 Grace Period in Canada and the United States

The inventor can generally file a patent application in Canada even if the inventor (but not someone else) has disclosed details of it within the previous year, since Canada allows a one-year grace period.[58] The United States also offers a one-year grace period.[59] Relying on this grace period, however, may be dangerous because most countries, other than Canada and the United States, require "absolute novelty". No grace period is allowed, and a patent will be denied if any public disclosure has been made anywhere before the application is filed. It is to be hoped that the movement towards global harmonization of the patent system will result in other countries adopting this attractive feature of the U.S. and Canadian patent systems.[60] Thus, if a professor invents a process and publishes details of that process in a learned journal, application for a patent may be made in Canada or the United States during the "grace period". Application, however, cannot be made for a patent in many other countries, including those in the European Community, because of this disclosure: the invention is deemed to have lost its novelty due to the disclosure. The professor may also be prevented from relying on a Canadian or U.S. application to file later in those countries if absolute novelty was lost by disclosure prior to filing.

> With a grace period inventors would be able to test their products in the marketplace, and academics allowed to discuss their research with peers, at conferences and in journals, and they would still be able to file for patents in respect of those inventions. Without a grace period system, inventors and academics have got into the practice of keeping projects secret, using confidentiality agreements when dealing with others, and filing patent applications as early as possible. These prompt patent filings may have to be made before market success can be judged.

---

[56] *Effects of GATT*, p. 2.

[57] See §3.8.3 of this chapter.

[58] *Patent Act* (Canada), s. 28.3(a) (re-en. S.C. 1993, c. 15. s. 33).

[59] U.S. *Patent Act*, 35 U.S.C. §102.

[60] For a further discussion on this harmonization, see American Intellectual Property Law Association, *A Guide to Patent Law Harmonization: Towards a More Inventor-Friendly Worldwide Patent System*, 1994, 1995, p. 4 (hereinafter "AIPLA").

Grace periods therefore afford greater flexibility to inventors, but also increase uncertainty for businesses who must wonder if a competitor's technology is free to use or will later be protected by a patent. [61]

3.8.3 Inadvertent Disclosure

It is well understood that if the inventor "publishes" sufficient information (often in the form of a "White Paper" or marketing material and demonstrations at a trade show) in the public that a "person of ordinary skill in the art" could practice the invention, then absolute novelty is lost and any available grace periods start to count down. Less obvious is the fact that even if the inventor takes all appropriate care and effectively imposes binding non-disclosure obligations of confidence on the people with whom he or she deals, there is still a risk of an enabling public disclosure being made by the organizations to whom the inventor disclosed (*e.g.* in the course of seeking financing, or pursuing joint venture opportunities), which results in the same loss of novelty. In such cases the inventor's patent value is compromised and his or her remedy is against the organization that breached its secrecy obligations. Consequently, it is very important for inventors to tell no one of their discoveries without a clear need to know, and then only to persons who are truly trustworthy.

3.8.4 First-to-File Versus First-to-Invent

On October 1, 1989, Canada developed a "first-to-file" system[62] that brought its system into line with the patent systems of most of the industrialized countries other than the United States. If two people independently develop an invention, the first person to file a patent application at the Canadian Patent Office will have priority. This provides more certainty than the "first-to-invent" criterion previously used in Canada and still used in the United States. The benefits of a "first-to-file" system are certainty and encouragement to inventors to file their applications at the earliest opportunity. On the other hand, the necessity to file early under this "first-to-file" system, to avoid being displaced by another invention independently developed, may discourage a thorough examination of the demand in the market-place prior to filing the patent application. As a result, patents may be filed for inventions that have no commercial application or that may be incorrectly structured due to the lack of time to do the proper business research. The "first-to-invent" system may produce fairer treatment to the inventor; the first one to the patent office does not necessarily win, but this advantage must be balanced against an increased likelihood for litigation to determine who, in fact, was the first to invent.

---

[61] See <http://www.patent.gov.uk/about/consultations/live.html>.
[62] *Patent Act* (Canada), s. 28.2 (re-en. S.C. 1993, c. 15, s. 33).

3.8.5 Supporting Documentation

Documentation to establish an invention is important to establish the identity of the inventors and, in the United States particularly, which inventors were the first to arrive at the point of invention. Each party to a technology transfer agreement will wish to perform due diligence to satisfy itself that the claims to the invention (ownership and timing) are supportable. Proper documentation often consists of notebooks and documents generated during the inventive process. Patricia D. Granados writes:[63]

> The following guidelines are offered for purposes of ensuring that a notebook practice produces the quality of evidence needed for establishing inventorship and date of invention:
>
> (1)   Keep bound notebooks or journals for purposes of recording ideas and experiments. Loose papers get lost and are subject to challenge if they are not properly dated.
>
> (2)   Use permanent ink. Remember, you don't want someone to challenge the authenticity or dates of your recordations.
>
> (3)   Record experiments contemporaneously with the actual work.
>
> (4)   Date each experiment on the first and each subsequent day. All too often, scientists forget to date each page of their notebook. It is not uncommon to see a date followed by a subsequent date two or three weeks later. If the important work occurred in between those dates, only the later date would be relevant. If the notebook isn't bound, you have an even more serious problem.
>
> (5)   Define the objective of the experiment. This eliminates subsequent speculation as to why you were conducting the experiment.
>
> (6)   Record all relevant facts, e.g., type of equipment used, conditions, times, materials, including sources and data, etc. If standard procedures are used and not discussed in the notebook in detail, note where full descriptions of such standard procedures can be found. Use only well-known or defined abbreviations and codes. This type of information is probably what is most valuable to the scientist anyway. It explains exactly what was done and why and what the results were. Subsequent work may be based upon such facts. If possible, state a conclusion but do not make derogatory remarks about the results.
>
> (7)   Attach or copy into the notebook equipment generated data or note where such data can be found. Cross-reference the notebook and the data that is not actually in the notebook.
>
> (8)   Have a non-inventor who understands the work being recorded sign and date the relevant recordation.

---

[63]   Patricia D. Granados, "How to prove that you are an Inventor or were the first to Invent", article no longer posted on a website.

3.9 Novelty and Anticipation

Since the Canadian and U.S. rules concerning novelty have been changing over the past several years, it is recommended that the legislation that was in effect on the date of filing for a particular patent be checked. In Canada, novelty is a question of fact that is presumed and is established as of the filing date.[64] In Canada and the United States, prior art (or what is previously known about the subject-matter of the patent application) is examined to see if the invention disclosed within the application has been anticipated in the prior art to such an extent that it is not novel. If a claim set out in a patent application was "anticipated" in a single source or piece of prior art, then it will be invalid.[65] It may not matter that the possessor of the prior art did not realize that an invention had a particular application, so long as the prior art sufficiently described the subject-matter of the claim. However, the test of anticipation is quite narrow and it is not satisfied if it is necessary to gather the required elements together from a variety of prior publications and then meld them together in order to come up with the invention claimed.

3.10 The Invention Must Not Be Obvious

"The subject-matter defined by a claim in an application for a patent in Canada must be subject-matter that would not have been obvious on the claim date to a person skilled in the art or science to which it pertains".[66] "An invention satisfies the non-obviousness requirement if a 'person of ordinary skill in the art' would not have viewed the invention as having been obvious in view of the prior art at the time the invention was made".[67] Lowman writes:

> . . . Thus, there must be some aspect of ingenuity to the invention, something which would not be obvious to a person skilled in the art; the applicable art being that related to the invention. In Canada the notional person skilled in the art is the unimaginative skilled technician. The test for obviousness is:
>
> (a) Would the unimaginative skilled technician have come directly and without difficulty to the invention in light of the prior art of which the person skilled in the art would be aware of at the time the invention was made and with the skilled person's general knowledge;
>
> (b) The difference between "anticipation" (novelty) and obviousness" has been described as follows: Anticipation suggests that "your invention, though clever, was already known" while obviousness suggest that "any fool could have done that".[68]

---

[64] Takach, *Patents*, p. 29, Section 3.5.
[65] Takach, p. 29, Section 3.6.
[66] *Patent Act* (Canada), s. 28.3 (re-en. S.C. 1993, c. 15, s. 33).
[67] NII, pp. 157–58.
[68] Lowman, 2001, p. 5.

In contrast, a U.S. judge wrote:

> Invention is not always the offspring of genius; more frequently it is the product of plain hard work; not infrequently it arises from accident or carelessness; occasionally it is a happy thought of an ordinary mind; and there have been instances where it is the result of sheer stupidity. It is with the inventive concept, the thing achieved, not with the manner of its achievement or the quality of the mind which gave it birth, that the patent law concerns itself.[69]

Commercial success for the invention tends to lend support to a finding of unobviousness. If a technologically sophisticated enterprise takes a licence under the patent, this is evidence of unobviousness.[70] Similarly, if a competing enterprise working on the problem is unable to generate a successful product (without infringing the patent) that is evidence of invention.[71]

A mere scintilla or spark of invention is sufficient to support validity. Simplicity of the invention is no bar to patentability.[72] After the fact analysis of the invention or synthesis of an artificially contrived mosaic of documents is insufficient to establish obviousness.[73] The mere fact that previous work in the technology points in the general direction of the invention or suggests that it is "worth a try" does not negative inventive ingenuity, nor does the fact that several inventors reach the invention about the same time.[74] This rejects the "worth a try" jurisprudence in the U.K., *i.e.*, Canada may have a lower standard of invention than the U.K. If skilled persons working in the field have recognized the problem, but failed to make the invention, this is evidence of unobviousness.[75] If the patented device solves a long standing problem, it is evidence of unobviousness, *i.e.*, there still may be inventiveness even if there was no difficulty in putting an idea into effect once conceived, *e.g.*, paper clips or pop up headlamps. In other cases, the objective may have been known for some time (long felt want) but the preferred means of achieving the objective may not have been obvious, *e.g.*, a photocopier or an airplane.

3.10.1 When Obviousness Exists

Milgrim writes that obviousness exists where

> there has been [i] exercise of only ordinary mechanical skill; [ii] mere perfecting a quality or workmanship; [iii] mere logical extensions from the teachings of the

---

[69] *88 Specialty Co. v. H.W. Buhot*, 4 U.S.P.Q. 205, at 209 (3rd Cir. 1930), quoted in *"Resolving Inventorship"* by Sandra M. Nolan, in *Blast*, The Bulletin of Law/Science and Technology, American Bar Association Section of Science and Technology, October 1995, No. 95, p. 5, at 9.

[70] *Diversified Products v. Tye Sil* (1991), 35 C.P.R. (3d) 350 (F.C.A.).

[71] *Windsurfing v. Bic* (1985), 8 C.P.R. (3d) 241 (F.C.A.).

[72] *Diversified Products v. Tye Sil., supra*, note 70.

[73] *Consolboard v. MacMillan Bloedel (Saskatchewan) Ltd.*, [1981] 1 S.C.R. 504.

[74] *Farbwerke v. Halocarbon* (1979), 42 C.P.R. (2d) 145 (F.C.A.).

[75] *Windsurfing v. Trilantic* (1984), 8 C.P.R. (3d) 241 (F.C.A.).

prior art, [iv] substitution or alteration or modification of known elements, or dimensions, or form; or [v] application of an existing machine or process to an analogous use.[76]

3.11 The Invention Must Be Useful

In Canada "useful" means "having industrial or commercial value in a manner that benefits the public".[77] The appropriate test will be "whether the invention will be practically fit for the purpose described in the specification in the hands of a competent person".[78] To satisfy the "useful" requirement, the invention must be reduced to practice; it must be more advanced than mere research.[79]

> The purpose of this requirement [as to usefulness] is to limit patent protection to inventions that possess a certain level of "real world" (value), as opposed to subject matter that represents nothing more than an idea or concept, or is simply a starting point for future investigation or research.[80]

There is no requirement that an invention be an improvement; the practical usefulness of the invention does not matter, unless the specification promises commercial utility, nor does it matter whether the invention is of any real benefit to the public, or particularly suitable for the purposes suggested. It is sufficient utility to support a patent that the invention gives either a new article or a better article, or a cheaper article, or affords the public a useful choice.[81] A claim is not invalid merely because a non-useful embodiment is within its compass. There must be something in the claim positively pointing towards something useless.[82]

3.12 Licence Estoppel

In Canada, the law is not clear of whether or not executing a licence somehow gives rise to or an implied covenant that prevents the licensee from challenging the validity of the patents that are covered by that licence. If no such estoppel or implication covenant, then the licensee may be able to attack the validity of associated patents, but even that is not clear.[83] In the United States, the licensee cannot be directly prevented from challenging the validity of a patent.[84]

---

[76] Milgrim, *On Licensing*, §2.11.

[77] Takach, *Patents*, p. 31, Section 4.1.

[78] *Ibid.*, p. 34, Section 4.2.

[79] See Association of University Technology Managers, Inc., *Technology Transfer Manual 1993*, IV-2.1, p. 12, s. 2.1.5. (hereinafter called "AUTM *Manual*").

[80] Section III.A of *Legal Analysis*.

[81] *Consolboard v. MacMillan Bloedel*, *supra*, note 73.

[82] *Proctor & Gamble v. Bristol Meyers* (1978,) 42 C.P.R. (2d) 33 (F.C.A.).

[83] See *R. v. Curtiss – Wright Corp*, [1969] S.C.R. 527.

[84] See §11.9 of this text — Payment.

Strategy: If a Canadian license, consider including an express covenant that the licensee is not estopped from challenging the validity of a patent. Silence on the issue is not appropriate.

3.13 Patents are for INVENTIONS Not Products (Point of Invention Analysis)

Inventors and their companies normally think in terms of Products rather than Inventions. Products often contain a number of Potentially Patentable Subject Matters ("P^{2}SMs") that need to be identified and isolated before searching, analysis, and application drafting. Most new technology can be broken down into elements only some of which are "inventive" in nature, these are the P^{2}SMs that justify investigation to determine whether or not they are also novel and non-obvious such that they can support an application for patent protection. In order to determine whether or not the P^{2}SMs are novel – each P^{2}SM must be the basis for a search of both the patented and non-patented prior art. After an appropriate analysis of the search results for each P^{2}SM produces a favourable outcome, there is a sound foundation from which to apply for a patent. Also, once the P^{2}SMs are isolated it will be possible to rank or prioritize them and determine whether for a variety of reasons (*e.g.*, short life-cycle, fragility, narrow application, etc.) one or more P^{2}SMs should NOT be the subject of a patent application — even where that protection is available. Once the surviving P^{2}SMs are ranked in terms of their commercial importance, it will be possible to allocate an appropriate investment to make in the search, drafting and prosecution processes.

3.13.1 Reasons to Search

Searches are done to determine the inventor's novelty, infringement by the inventor of rights of others, and infringement by others of the inventor's rights. The novelty searches should be done before significant reliance is placed on the subject invention as a source of value. The search for infringement of others' rights should be done before the inventor undertakes an expensive research and development program or invests significantly in a business bond on the subject invention. Investors will want at least a preliminary patentability review and a serious infringement review. Once the patent is issued, the inventor will monitor the patents issued to competitors for business intelligence and will monitor its competitors' activities for infringement of its patent. Patent citation analysis is a good source of intelligence.

3.14 Provisional Patent Applications (informally known as an "incomplete" in Canada)

As a result of the *General Agreement on Tariffs and Trade* ("GATT"), the U.S. *Patent Act* allows "a new type of patent application called a provisional application . . . designed to be a simple inexpensive patent application that will not be examined except for certain formal requirements". Provisional applications have been filed in the U.S. since December 8, 1995.[85] The benefits of filing a provisional application are:

(a) a provisional application acts as an internal priority document that is followed by another application within 12 months of the filing of the provisional application;[86]

(b) a provisional application helps "an applicant to establish a filing date for inventions that may be useful in establishing senior party status in an interference proceeding (in the U.S.) or establishing a date of invention in almost every other country in the world that follows a first-to-file principle. The filing date of an application in the U.S. also establishes a prior art date effective under the provisions of 35 U.S.C.(E)";[87] and

(c) a provisional application is an "effective tool in deferring examination of an invention for a period of a year. This tool will be useful to those applicants who may want to seek financial assistance from third parties before the cost of prosecution begins, or the applicant who updates the content of an application within one year of the original filing before presenting a C-I-P application for examination".[88]

3.14.1 No Examination for Provisionals

Unlike regular patent applications in the United States, which are set up for automatic examination on filing,[89] provisional applications are not examined. Provisional applications are given a filing date that, in itself, is an "essential critical achievement for the protection of rights in the U.S. and every foreign country".[90] Filing gives the inventor one year in which to file an application that meets the standards of a regular application.

---

[85] *Effects of GATT*, <http://www.uspto.gov/web/uruguay/URPAPER.html>, p. 3.

[86] *Ibid.*, pp. 3-4.

[87] *Ibid.*, p. 4.

[88] *Ibid.*

[89] This is not the case under the revised Canadian Patent System — a separate application must be made for examination. If an application for examination is not made within seven years, the application will be deemed abandoned. For further discussion on this topic, see Canadian Intellectual Property Office, "Patent Guide" and *"Manual of Patent Office Practice"* available on the Internet at URL: <http://strategis.ic.gc.ca/sc_mrksv/cipo/patents/mopop/mopop-e.html>.

[90] AIPLA, p. 4.

3.14.2 Provisionals and First-to-File

The provisional filing option may overcome some of the perceived difficulties of a first-to-file system because it may avoid loss of priority, as further and necessary development is done before filing a formal application.[91] The provisional application, however, still requires a disclosure of the invention, and this disclosure "must be complete enough to enable a person skilled in that particular field to be able to understand how to make and use the invention without having to resort to experimentation to do so".[92]

WHERE TO FILE

3.15 Where to File: Generally

The inventor must initially decide in which jurisdiction(s) to file a patent application to obtain appropriate protection. An inventor based in Canada need not file in Canada first. Many countries belong to the Paris Convention for the Protection of Industrial Property, a treaty that allows for "convention priority". Thus, an inventor's filing date in one country will be recognized in other countries if the inventor files in those countries within one year of the original filing.[93]

3.15.1 Where to File: Patent Cooperation Treaty

Often, in the early stages of the development of technology, it is difficult to determine how successful the innovation will be. If the technology proves to be more successful than initially expected, to avoid losing out in some countries, the patent application can be made pursuant to the Patent Cooperation Treaty ("PCT"). At the time of making the first application "[i]nstead of the multiplicity of foreign applications, only one initial application has to be filed. This means that only one set of documents is required instead of several. . . ."[94] The PCT "offers [the inventor] an improved basis for taking decisions, permits time to be gained before making additional commitments, provides an improved possibility for checking the appropriateness of the international application and of the country coverage, and gives the opportunity for cost saving".[95] For example, rather than incurring the cost of translations, official fees and foreign representatives that the inventor would incur with separate applications, only the cost of

---

[91] *Ibid.*

[92] *Ibid.*

[93] Canadian Intellectual Property Office, "Patent Guide", S.B.8.2.

[94] Albert Tramposch, "Harmonization of Industrial Property Laws" in M. Goudreau et al., *Exporting our Technology,* p. 101.

[95] *Ibid.*

one application need be initially expended.[96] Making a PCT application allows more time for the inventor to choose in what countries he or she wishes to pursue patent protection.[97]

TERRITORY

3.16 Territorial Limitations

A patent prohibits infringement arising only within the country that issues the patent. Thus, a patent issued in the United States has no exclusionary effect in Canada, unless a comparable patent has been issued by the Canadian authorities. Indeed, in Canada there would be free access to the details of the U.S. invention, because these details were disclosed to the public world-wide once the U.S. patent issued.[98] Moreover, the holder of a U.S. patent may not be able to contractually prohibit its licensee from exploiting the patented technology outside the United States if that would be considered an antitrust violation.[99]

3.17 Full Disclosure

In exchange for the exclusionary rights provided by a patent, the patentee must disclose sufficient details of an invention in "full, clear, concise and exact terms" sufficient to permit a person experienced in the relevant art or science to implement the protected innovation.[100]

3.17.1 Best Mode

In the case of a process patent, in both Canada and the United States, the applicant must explain the necessary sequence of the various steps involved.[101] For a machine, the applicant must explain its principle and the best mode in which the application of that principle has been contemplated.[102] This description of the best mode is in addition to disclosure adequate to enable one skilled in the art to practice the invention.[103] The purpose of the disclosure is to "teach a person in each art [for each field of technology involved in the claimed invention] how to make and use the relevant aspect of the invention without undue experimenta-

---

[96] *Ibid.*, at 105.

[97] *Ibid.*, at 104.

[98] Patents are available for review via the USPTO's at: <http://www.uspto.gov/main/patents.html>.

[99] See Reichman, "GATT", p. 38.

[100] *Patent Act* (Canada), s. 34(1)(b); U.S. *Patent Act*, 35 U.S.C. §112.

[101] *Patent Act* (Canada), s. 34(1)(d) (am. S.C. 1992, c. l, s. 113; rep. S.C. 1993, c. 15, s. 36); U.S. *Patent Act*, 35 U.S.C. §112.

[102] *Patent Act* (Canada), s. 34(1)(c) (am. S.C. 1992, c. l, s. 113; rep. S.C. 1993, c. 15, s. 36); U.S. *Patent Act*, 35 U.S.C. §112. See also Milgrim, *On Licensing*, §53.

[103] Milgrim, *On Licensing*, §2.53.

tion".[104] The U.S. guidelines for patenting computer programs state: "Applicants should be encouraged to functionally define the steps the computer will perform rather than simply providing the source or object code".[105] The AIPLA Jury Instructions offer the following in its "Best Mode" section:

> The law requires that "the specification shall set forth the best mode contemplated by the inventor of carrying out his invention." If the inventor had specific processes, techniques, compositions, material or conditions that he or she recognized at the time of filing as the best way of carrying out the invention, then he or she must include that information in the patent disclosure.

> The purpose of this requirement is to ensure that a patent applicant "plays fair and square" with the patent system by restraining inventors "from applying for patents while at the same time concealing from the public preferred embodiments of their invention which they have in fact conceived." An inventor must disclose his or her best mode to the public in exchange for patent protection. The law does not give an inventor the right to exclude others from practicing the invention unless he or she has provided an adequate disclosure of the best way known to him or her at the time of filing of the application of carrying out the invention. To determine whether the inventor complied with the best mode requirements you [the jury] must answer two questions:
>
>   (a) At the time the patent application was filed, did the patentee have a best mode for practicing his or her invention; and
>
>   (b) If so, did the patentee adequately disclose the best mode in the patent specification?[106]

3.17.2 Disclosure of Prior Art

Prior art relating to an invention must be disclosed in an application to patent that invention. As *Legal Analysis* states: "The written description will provide the clearest explanation of the applicant's invention by exemplifying the invention, explaining how it relates to the prior art and by explaining the relative significance of various features of the invention".[107] A U.S. applicant and anyone involved in a re-examination of a U.S. patent "has a duty of candor and good faith in dealing with the [USPTO], which includes a duty to disclose to the Office all information known to that individual to be material to patentability . . .".[108] If the patent applicant is not sufficiently candid, the applicant may have committed fraud on the patent office. Milgrim writes:

---

[104] *Legal Analysis*, Section IV.A.

[105] *Ibid.*, Section IV.E.

[106] P. 42, citations deleted.

[107] *Ibid.*, Section II.B.

[108] *Manual of Patent Examining Procedure*, USPTO, Chapter 2000, Duty of Disclosure, August 2000, located at <http://www.uspto.gov/web/offices/pac/mpep/index.html>.

(a) there are numerous ways of not fulfilling one's duty of candor with the Patent Office; one obvious way is not to disclose matter known to be material, with the intent to deceive; another way of doing it is burying that which is plainly material in a welter of other citations;

(b) a district court must determine, but need not make explicit findings on, whether undisclosed art in fact anticipated or rendered the claimed invention obvious in order for the district court to assess the requirement that the omission be sufficiently material to constitute inequitable conduct;

(c) in essence, where conduct before the USPTO has resulted in an infirmity, such as failure to disclose best mode, a court must scrutinize all the evidence to determine whether the omission was merely negligence or whether there was an absence of good faith;

(d) fraud on the [USPTO] turns on the materiality of the material not disclosed and intent.[109]

3.17.3 Licensing Risks as a Result of "Best Mode" Requirement

A U.S. patent may be challenged and invalidated on the basis of failure to describe the invention using the "best mode". Problems arising out of the "best mode" requirement are:

(a) it is "difficult to understand and apply in many cases";[110]
(b) it frequently causes litigation;
(c) it leads to extensive litigation expenses; and
(d) it can result in patent invalidation by a district court judge or jury with little understanding of the "inventive or patenting process".[111]

It "is difficult or impossible for patent practitioners to avoid all best mode issues".[112]

Strategy:
(1) *Determine who will have control over the conduct of defending a challenge.*
(2) *Allocate fairly between the parties the cost of defending a challenge to the validity of a licensed patent, based on failure to disclose the best mode.*

---

[109] Milgrim, *On Licensing*, §256.
[110] ABA *Annual Report*, 94/95, p. 84.
[111] Summarized from ABA *Annual Report*, 94/95, p. 142.
[112] ABA *Annual Report*, 94/95, p. 142.

3.18 Disclosure via Publication 18 Months After Filing

In Canada, since October 1, 1989, and in the United States, since June 8, 1995, the details of a patent application will be "laid open" to public inspection at the relevant patent office 18 months after the filing date of the application or, where a request for priority has been made in respect of the application, 18 months from the earliest filing date of any previously regularly filed application on which the request is based.[113] The issuance of a Canadian patent, for infringement purposes, will have a retroactive effect to the date the application was laid open for public inspection.[114] This disclosure will occur even though it may be likely that at the expiry of that 18-month period the patent will not have issued and may not issue for some considerable time thereafter. The United States now publishes patent applications 18 months from the earliest filing date for which a benefit is sought unless the applicant makes a request upon filing, certifying that this invention disclosed in an application has not and will not be the subject of an application filed in another country that requires publication after 18 months.[115]

3.18.1 Trade Secrecy and "Laying Open" Patent Application

Everyone is entitled to review the application and to study the disclosure after the patent application is "laid open". Because Canadian and U.S. patent applications must disclose the "best mode" of applying the principles of the invention covered by the patent application, the underlying trade secrets will likely be disclosed. These secrets become part of the public domain even if, subsequently to the laying open, the patent application is rejected or withdrawn. Thus, the applicant must decide prior to the 18-month disclosure whether he or she wants to rely on trade secrecy or patents; after that date these protections are mutually exclusive as to the technology disclosed by the application.[116] The applicant may wish to expedite the examination process or to obtain opinions of patentability and defensibility from a qualified patent attorney and agent before the 18-month period expires.[117]

Strategy: In a technology transfer agreement, agree which party will decide to continue or to withdraw the application prior to it being "laid open".

---

[113] *Patent Act* (Canada), s. 10(1) (rep. & sub. R.S.C. 1985, c. 33 (3rd Supp.), s. 2; re-en. S.C. 1993, c. 15, s. 28).

[114] *Patent Act (Canada)*, s. 55(1)(b) (rep. & sub. R.S.C. 1985, c. 33 (3rd Supp.), s. 21; re-en. S.C. 1993, c. 15, s. 48).

[115] See URL: <http://www.uspto.gov/web/patents/pubs>.

[116] See E. Robert Yoches, "Strategies for Patent Protection", in *Corporate Counsel's Guide to Intellectual Property* (Chestertand, Ohio: Business Laws Inc., 1996), p. 1.205 (hereinafter "Yoches 'Strategies'").

[117] AIPLA, p. 7.

3.19 Disclosure Benefits Business in Other Countries

Reichman emphasizes the beneficial effect of the best mode disclosure to users of the disclosed technology who are located in countries where no patent application has been made:

> The lack of a grace period enables alert entrepreneurs in countries where no timely application has been filed to exploit technical disclosures published in other countries . . . . In effect, the disclosure requirements constitute a vehicle for direct acquisition of foreign technological knowledge. Potential competitors in developing countries who monitor information flowing from the international patent system will find it easier to work around or improve foreign inventions.[118]

Because of this, some innovators will increasingly choose to rely on trade secrecy as their preferred means of intellectual property protection.[119]

3.19.1 Cost of European Patent Office May Give Europeans a Free Ride

Some writers have complained that the cost of seeking patent protection in the European Patent Office ("EPO") is becoming prohibitive and, thus, inventors may not pursue patent protection in Europe. This allows exploitation of technology disclosed in a U.S. or Canadian patent application by permitting a free ride in Europe without reward to the U.S. or Canadian inventor.[120]

Strategy: When negotiating who will pay the cost of prosecuting patent applications in which countries, consider the benefit that the disclosure of the technology through the patent application will have for competitors in territories where there is no patent protection for the subject inventions.

TERM

3.20 Duration

For patent applications filed in Canada after October 1, 1989, or in the United States after June 8, 1995, the term of the patent is for 20 years from the filing date.[121] Patents filed before those dates have a term of 17 years from the date of issue.

---

[118] Reichman, "GATT", p. 18.

[119] *Ibid.*

[120] ABA *Annual Report*, 94/95, p. 166.

[121] *Patent Act* (Canada), s. 44 (rep. & sub. R.S.C. 1985, c. 33 (3rd Supp.), s. 16; re-en. S.C. 1993, c. 15, s. 42).

Strategy: When licensing rights under any patent, determine the duration of the patent protection period remaining.

3.21 Maintenance Fees

To maintain issued patents, many jurisdictions require the payment of maintenance fees periodically. In Canada, these fees must be paid annually and cannot be prepaid;[122] a reduction in fees is available for small entities.[123] No advance notice is given requiring payment.[124] The United States also imposes maintenance fees[125] and has reduced rates for small entities.[126] The Canadian and U.S. maintenance fees are modest in comparison with those charged by some other countries.[127] Failure to pay the maintenance fee will result in the termination of the patent.[128]

Strategy: In a technology transfer agreement, negotiate which party will pay the fees necessary to maintain a patent. Do not assume that the obligation is implicitly the licensor's. And, establish controls to ensure that the fees are paid.

3.21.1 Submarine Patents Under Old System

Under the system that prevailed before the adoption of the patent term of 20 years from the date of filing, rather than 17 years from the date of issue,[129] and the requirement to lay open to the public the patent application 18 months after filing[130] (which old system still applies to patents filed before the applicable date of the reform), a patent application could be processed very slowly and could issue once the technology was well established in its use by competitors, to the surprise of many unauthorized users of the patented technology. The move to protection starting 20 years from the date of filing is viewed by some as "an effective weapon against these 'submarine' patents",[131] thus limiting the "submarine" to a more reasonable duration and giving more certainty to other innovators and their marketing entities.[132] Under the former Canadian and American patent systems, the term of the patent was calculated from the date of issue. This created the risk that applications filed many years back could issue. This risk continues for applications filed prior to the revised systems becoming effective.

---

[122] Section 76.1 of the Rules under the Canadian *Patent Act*.

[123] *Ibid.*, s. 77.1 and Schedule 2.

[124] Takach, *Patents*, p. 89, Section 7.64.

[125] U.S. *Patent Act*, 35 U.S.C. §41(b).

[126] U.S. *Patent Rules*, 37 C.F.R. §1.9.

[127] Milgrim, *On Licensing*, §2.61.

[128] *Patent Act* (Canada), s. 46(2) (re-en. S.C. 1993, c. 15, s. 43), U.S. *Patent Act* 35 U.S.C. §5.41.

[129] See §3.18 of this text.

[130] See §3.18.1 of this text.

[131] ABA *Annual Report*, 94/95, p. 84. See also AIPLA.

[132] For further discussion on this topic see AIPLA.

"When these hidden or submerged applications are issued as patents, existing products or industrial processes can suddenly become infringements".[133] Under the new Canadian and U.S. system, the "submarine" period in which non-disclosure continues is only 18 months after filing.

Strategy: Determine which party bears the risk of a submarine patent issuing after execution of the licence thereby precluding continued use of the licensed technology. The licensee will not want to continue paying royalties to the transferor if it has to pay a royalty to the patent holder.

EFFECT ON INDEPENDENT DEVELOPMENT

3.22 Patents May Preclude Independent Development

A valid Canadian or U.S. patent excludes the possibility that another entity can legally practise in Canada or the United States the art covered by that patent during its term, even if the other entity independently developed the subject-matter of the patent or if its infringement was innocent. This broad protection is not available under copyright or trade secrecy. This strong exclusionary power makes patents "potent licensing tools".[134] The legally and technically stronger the patent, the more economically valuable it is likely to be.

MARKING

3.23 Requirement to Mark

In Canada and the United States there is no longer a requirement to mark a patented product to give public notice of the patented status. "Phrases such as "patent pending" and "patent applied for" have no legal effect and serve to inform only".[135]

3.23.1 Should You Mark?

Although there is no legal obligation in the United States to mark products protected by a patent, there is still good reason to mark. The amount of damages awarded in the case of infringement of a U.S. patent will increase if the product is marked with a notice concerning the patent.[136] Damages are recoverable for unmarked products only if it can be proven that the infringer had actual no-

---

[133] AIPLA, p. 5.
[134] Milgrim, *On Licensing*, §2.27.
[135] Takach, *Patents*, Section 7.63, p. 89, and U.S. *Patent Act*, 35 U.S.C. §207.
[136] U.S. *Patent Act*, 35 U.S.C. §287.

tice.[137] If marking starts part way through the infringement, damages are recoverable without proving actual notice for the period after the marking started.[138] Lack of marking does not render the patent protection unenforceable, it merely limits the damages that are recoverable; an injunction would still be available.

Strategy: The licensor should insist on patent marking by the licensee. Appropriate marking will vary according to the particular product.[139]

PATENT STRATEGIES

3.24 Patent Strategies: Practice Issues

Some of the factors to consider when one is deciding whether to patent are:[140]

    (a) the strengths of alternate protections (copyright, trade secrecy, technical protection) and the ability to commercialize the invention without patent protection;

    (b) the benefits to be obtained by the patent, which are obtained at the cost of disclosing the trade secrets. The more costly it is to enter a market (such as with a new drug), the more important it is to obtain patent protection — keeping in mind that the technology may be free for the using in any country where a patent is not obtained;[141]

    (c) the monetary cost of obtaining and maintaining patents in each of the jurisdictions where the technology will be marketed;[142]

    (d) the non-monetary cost of obtaining and maintaining patents, for example, the time consumed by the inventors that could have been used in a technically productive fashion. What would be otherwise productive time can be consumed: (i) educating the "attorney about technology and the 'state of the art' so that the attorney can properly distinguish the invention from what was done before",[143] and (ii) developing a sufficiently detailed disclosure needed for a patent application, together with a review and analysis of the prior art;

    (e) the ability to detect infringement. Total inability to detect infringement is often sufficient reason to reject patenting, but not always. The patent may be useful for defensive reasons;[144]

---

[137] *Ibid.*

[138] *Ibid.*

[139] See Carl Oppedahl, "Patent Marking of Systems", Santa Clara Computer and High Technology Law Journal (1995), Vol. 11, No. 2, p. 205 on the Internet at <http://www.patents.com/lrl.html>.

[140] See Yoches, "Strategies", p. 1.201.

[141] See §3.16 of this text.

[142] Yoches, "Strategies", p. 1.204.

[143] *Ibid.*

[144] *Ibid.*, p. 1.206.

(f) the reluctance to prosecute infringement, particularly if infringers are likely to be customers;[145] and

(g) the possibility of publishing to prevent others from obtaining a patent.[146]

3.25 Competitive Strategies

Not all patents are obtained for the same reasons. The following are some of the reasons for obtaining patents:

(a) Some are commercialized in their own right. The patentee may hold the patent with the intention of licensing it to others to produce revenue, or to keep it for use in the patentee's own business to acquire an advantage over competitors.[147]

(b) Some serve as a shield, *i.e.*, as a defence against someone else independently developing and patenting the technology. If a company is secretly developing technology and, prior to it applying for a patent or commercializing that technology, another company, who have also been developing that technology independently, applies for a patent, the first-to-file rule may take the first company out of the market-place everywhere but the United States. These defensive patents may be referred to as design freedom patents. "Some companies build up large patent portfolios to protect themselves from patent lawsuits from other patent owners. This strategy is akin to the 'mutually assured destruction' theory for avoiding nuclear war: both sides will refrain from suing for fear of countersuits".[148]

(c) Some are used as a sword. Some companies take out patents that, in an economic sense, encircle a competitor's patent like a fence and prevent or delay further enhancement of the competitor's technology. They may thus be able to force the competitor to license to them some of its patentable technology that would not otherwise be available, in exchange for licences of the constraining encircling patents. This strategy may be used to maintain or to capture market position.

(d) Some are used to gain cross-licensing opportunities. In some industries, such as the electronic industry, cross-licensing exists as a matter of course, particularly where the exclusivity offered by patents is not economic to maintain. In other industries, such as the pharmaceutical industry where the cost to enter a market is so high, cross-licensing is seldom done.

---

[145] *Ibid.*

[146] *Ibid.*

[147] Yoches, "Strategies", p. 1.202.

[148] *Ibid.* An alternative to this strategy is to publish innovations to establish prior art and, thus, prevent a patent being applied for the same subject-matter because the material is then prior art. See §§1.1.1 and 3.8 of this text.

Strategy: When licensing, be sure that the claims of each licensed patent have been carefully reviewed for their inherent strengths or lack thereof. Not all patents are created equal.

3.25.1 Patent Strategies and Corporate Evolution[149]

The evolution of the patent strategies deployed often co-relate to the overall corporate evolution of the corporation itself:

(a) an emerging company adopts the "get it out the door" business model, where the financial and business resources are focused on product development and production. Often this business model is built on one key breakthrough capable of supporting a foundation patent, but formal and effective intellectual property protection is either ignored or neglected due to a lack of resources.

(b) the Foundation Patent Model is based on a scientific breakthrough that has material potential commercial value and significant work-around costs. Some entities consider a Foundation Patent a pre-requisite to commercialization starts in a new business area.[150]

Steven P. Fox writes:

In patent protection process design, it is helpful to view industrial activity from several different vantage points. A few are discussed below:

1. There are two classes of companies operating on different paradigms. One type of company is small enough and simple enough in structure that employees can still enjoy frequent direct contact through all management levels. Projects tend to be more focused and more rapidly implemented. There are fewer products and an invention on one of them is likely to be readily identifiable and easily visible throughout the organization. A patent on such an invention is likely to be viewed as very important. The other type of company is larger, and activities are diffused over a broader range of market interest. More patents are obtained on more products. While a single invention covering a product may be just as important as for smaller companies, the inventions and the patents on them are often viewed more collectively.

2. Innovation can occur several different ways. Innovation may begin as part of a linear process, sometimes starting with a major scientific breakthrough. It then moves from idea to design, then development, then production, then finally to market. The assumption is that with a major scientific breakthrough, everything else takes care of itself. The breakthroughs are relatively easy to identify and protect with patents. More often, however, in the current competitive environment, there is no clear scientific breakthrough; and the focus of innovation

---

[149] For a good discussion of patent strategies, see Ove Granstrand, *The Economics and Management of Intellectual Property,* (Cheltenham, U.K.: Edward Elgar Publishing, Inc., 1999) ("Grandstand") p. 221, from which some of this material is derived.

[150] Granstrand, p. 221.

is more on making incremental improvements. The innovation process is less linear and considerably more interactive, where the ball passes back and forth among the various players both inside and outside of the company. Within this environment, inventions are more of a challenge to identify, yet patents on the incremental advances are important to competitiveness.[151]

(c) the start up entity soon recognizes that it is too vulnerable with only a Foundation Patent. It realizes that it needs to develop a defensive portfolio to keep all avenues open for the further development and commercialization of its product line. It may adopt a policy of continually filing improvements to its Foundation Patent.[152] It will develop its Design Freedom portfolio to preclude others from obtaining patents in its technology sector and asserting them against it. This defensive portfolio may "blanket" or "flood" the space to keep open the company's ability to advance its own technology. It is a useful strategy "in emerging technologies when uncertainty is high regarding which R&D directions are fruitful or in situations with uncertainty about the economic importance of the scope of a patent".[153] A patent strategy is to "turn the area into a jungle or minefield of patents, for example, "mining" or "bombing" every step in a manufacturing process with patents, more or less systematically".[154]

(d) the growing Company may develop a family of patents built on related science, for example a Foundation Patent and related improvement patents in that technology. Successful companies often build clusters of families of patents, not all of which patents are economically motivated. It is important to recognize that patents often referred to as "petty" or "junk" patents due to their marginal technical merit may be entirely valid legal and economic tools since such patents may be part of a larger and valid business strategy to surround a core technology or barricade a fragile component of a company's intellectual property from external attack.

(e) the evolving company may eventually adopt an offensive strategy by developing a patent portfolio that surrounds or otherwise blocks its competitors' positions. Thus an extensive portfolio could be developed around a Foundation Patent, which portfolio consists of individually less scientifically important patents that collectively block the effective commercial use of the technology covered by the surrounded patent, even after its expiration.[155] In addition to blocking competition, this allows the company to adopt two business models:

    (i)   Toll Collector Model — demand royalties or other compensation for the use of patented technology. "You are free to use our

---

[151] Steven F. Fox, "How to Get the Patents Others Want", *les Nouvelles*, March 1999, p. 3 at 3 (Fox).

[152] See Granstrand, p. 222.

[153] Granstrand, p. 221.

[154] Granstrand, p. 221.

[155] Granstrand, p. 221.

technology so long as you pay for it". Companies such as IBM make their patented technology available for set royalty rates, but the licences are "patent licences" only – essentially an agreement to use.

    (ii)   Technology Access Model – use a patent portfolio to obtain access to patents held by others; the strength of a large patent portfolio could be very intimidating to the holder of a smaller portfolio especially if it feels vulnerable to attacks on the validity of its Foundation Patents.

(f) the growing Company's strategy could evolve beyond bare patent licences to the Enabler Model where it licenses both patents and trade secrets, where the secrets add value and increase the economic return to the licensee (and thus to licensor).

(g) up to this point offensive actions have resulted in the license of technology. The growing Company may eventually adopt the Synergetic Business Model, under which it uses its intellectual property portfolio as an integral part of its business strategy to obtain benefits peripheral to the intellectual property in its portfolio. Here the profitability target is that of the overall business rather than the profitability of the IP department alone.[156]

3.26 Intellectual Asset Management

Technology Managers can develop or implement the following IP strategies:

(a) Maintain a current database of all the intellectual property of the company, including any restrictions on its exploitation such as confidentiality, exclusivity and sole-sourcing arrangements and co-ownership issues.

(b) Augment the company's overall competitive intelligence by mining public patent databases (including determining who is citing the company's patents) and developing patent maps that will be helpful in identifying trends.

(c) Gather information from the company's innovators in a timely fashion. Fox writes:

> Sometimes it is a challenge to inspire inventors working on a project to dis-close their inventions to the legal department. They may have the feeling that their contributions are obvious and, hence, not of value from a patent standpoint, or that their contributions are not good enough to rise to the level of patentability.
>
> The timely capture of inventions from researchers is very important. Tech-nologists are busier than ever keeping up with the rapid advancement of

---

[156] Laws prohibiting restraint of trade must be addressed.

technology and at the same time meeting their personal productivity requirements. Work pressures often result in low prioritization of time for
writing invention disclosures and submitting them to the legal department.
Under the law, there is usually a short window of opportunity to file a patent application after an invention is made, and thereafter, the right to a patent may be lost forever. Lack of timely action may compromise a company's position and create long-term adverse impacts. Cooperation and
motivation of the inventors is needed to ensure that the inventions are disclosed in a timely manner and that patents can be obtained on them.[157]

(d) In order to attain this timely capture, a program offering investor
    incentives may be necessary:

> Traditionally, inventors have been expected to write invention disclosures
> during the course of research, and this activity has been considered part of
> the job. Some companies still rely on this understanding to capture and
> protect inventions. However, many companies recognize that more may be
> needed to motivate the timely submission of invention disclosures, particu-
> larly if the drafting of a disclosure is going to be done on an inventor's per-
> sonal time because the pressure of project deadlines leave little time during
> the course of a normal day. A common solution is to create an inventor-
> incentive program, which rewards inventors with cash payments. Such pro-
> grams serve to increase the number of invention disclosures and assure their
> timely submission. In addition, these programs can be used to encourage
> disclosures in certain specifically identified technology areas where more
> patents are needed in the portfolio.[158]

(e) Adopt an aggressive policy of filing patent applications that relate to
    core technologies or key business opportunities, but only in conformity
    with the company's patent strategy that is integrated with its overall
    business strategy.[159]
(f) Develop a patent strategy that is separate from but conforms to the
    company's overall business strategy that assesses the economic value of
    patents to be at least as important as the scientific and legal merit of
    patents.
(g) Develop a strategy of periodically abandoning patents and patent
    applications that have no continuing economic merit. See Table A to this
    Chapter that sets out an option model for the prosecuting and
    maintenance of patents.[160]

---

[157] Fox, pp. 3-4.

[158] Fox, p. 4.

[159] See the discussion on the use of intellectual property management process terms in the article
by Willy Manfroy and Harry J. Gwinnell, "Intellectual Capital in a Spin Off", *les Nouvelles*,
December 1998, 159, at p. 160.

[160] See also the 25-point business oriented checklist for patent filing decisions in Edward L. Le-
vine's article "Considerations for Patent Disclosure", Sept 1991, *les Nouvelles*, p. 137.

Ed Hendrick writes:

An Intellectual Property Program: In its most basic form, a beginning intellectual property management program requires at least three steps – the early phases of a more robust program. These three are the identification of intangible assets, the provision for some basic level of protection, and some accountability for effective utilization of developed/acquired assets so as to ensure a return on investment. It is extremely important, and very doable, that at least a minimum program of IP management be designed that fits well into the operations of the small business.

At a minimum, "an effective ... intellectual property program should:

- "Encourage employees to bring to the attention of management inventions, designs, product names and other "good ideas."
- Provide a system to evaluate the "good ideas," so that the appropriate protection can be sought for those that may have present or future value.
- Ensure that ownership is acquired for all employee developed patents, trademarks, copyrights and trade secrets.
- Ensure that all inventions and other technological developments are properly documented and corroborated.
- Provide a system to minimize risk of infringing the intellectual property of others.
- Provide a system to evaluate patents and related technology for commercial development through licensing.
- Continuously monitor the corporation's commercial products and market position that ensure that patents are providing effective commercial protection.
- Monitor the competition to identify potential infringers.[161]

Although an ambitious list for the small business owner or entrepreneur, it is difficult to ensure the existence of a viable intellectual property management program without at least a modicum of attention to all of the above issues.

DUE DILIGENCE BY LICENSEE

3.27 Matters to Review

Prior to entering into a technology transfer agreement the prudent transferee may take the following steps to avoid becoming contractually bound to unwanted obligations, and to ensure that the underlying patents are capable of delivering the technology that is being bargained for:

(a) examine the scope of the patent to confirm that the claims are broad enough to cover the transferee's proposed activities (one or more of "making, using or selling" an apparatus or system that includes at least one patented element or using some process or method claimed in the patent);

---

[161] Edward J. Hendrick, Jr., IP Management Challenges – Meeting the Competition, September 1999, *les Nouvelles* 106, at pp. 109-110.

(b) examine any opinion of patent validity that the transferor has and is prepared to make available — a transferee may also want to obtain independent opinions respecting the validity and strength of each patent that is the subject of the transfer agreement;

(c) obtain assurances from the transferor that:

    (i) the subject patent is the only intellectual property right that the transferor holds that the transferee will need to authorize its proposed activity. This is particularly relevant if a licence results from a settlement of allegations of infringement; the transferee does not want to sign an agreement and then immediately find out that the transferor holds more patents that prohibit the transferee's proposed activity; and

    (ii) the transferor is the rightful owner of the patent and that no employees, contractors or other third parties have a (potential) interest in that patent.

(d) examine the applicable law to determine the term of the patent (for example, 17 years from date of issue versus 20 years from the date of filing);

(e) examine the patent specification in the same way a patent examiner would to check that:

    (i) the claims are credible and sufficiently capture the relevant elements and processes,

    (ii) the invention is useful,

    (iii) the invention is within one of the statutory categories and not merely scientific principle,

    (iv) the detailed description portions of the disclosures clearly and adequately explains the invention and how it differs from the prior art as well as the relative significance of the various elements of the invention,

    (v) all prior art – both patented and non-patented – has been disclosed;

    (vi) there are no "forced" definitions in the patent specification that impose meanings different from the normal usage of the defined words,[162]

    (vii) the effect of every limitation set out in the claims is comprehensible and clear,

    (viii) the claims are precise, clear, correct and unambiguous,[163]

    (ix) ensure that the Claims cover all aspects (*i.e.*, methods, systems and any apparatus) of the invention and that the disclosure contains language supporting everything in the claims; and

    (x) there is no other obvious risk that the patent is not valid and enforceable or potential for allegation of patent misuse.

---

[162] For a discussion on "forced definitions", see §18.6.3 of this text.

[163] *Legal Analysis*, note 20.

3.28   Ownership of Inventions: Employer-Employee Relationship[164]

3.28.1 In Canada

In Canada, the general principle is that an invention made by an employee belongs to the employee and not to the employer. This presumption applies even where the invention relates to an aspect of the employer's business or where the employee used the employer's time and materials in completing the invention. However, there is an important exception to this general principle. Where a person is employed for the purpose of inventing the particular invention, then the employer owns the invention. To determine if one satisfies this exception from the general rule, one must consider the nature and context of the relationship, including such things as the express purpose of employment, whether the employee prior to being hired had previously made inventions, and whether invention is the product of a problem the employee was instructed to solve. If the relationship does not fit within this exception, the employer should enter into an express contract for the assignment of the intellectual property rights developed by the employee. Prudent employers will do this as a matter of course to avoid the risk that they had misunderstood the relationship. As with any contract, valuable consideration must be given for the assignment. These agreements should be entered into when an employee is hired, on an annual review which renews the employment relationship, when a stock option is granted, or when some other valuable consideration is granted.[165] With independent contractors, it is always prudent to overcome the presumption in favour of the inventor. The basic rule is that the company retaining the independent contractor will only own the invention if there is an express or implied term of the agreement that the company owns the invention and any resulting patent.[166]

3.28.2 Ownership of Inventions in the United States

In the United States, the general rule is that inventions are owned by the inventor even if an employee. However, there is also the exception that where the inventor is hired to invent and this invention was made a part of the inventor's employment duties, the ownership of the invention belongs to the employer. Conversely, where the employee was not hired to invent or to work in areas where inventiveness is expected, the employee owns the invention. The U.S. has a rule that might not exist in Canada: if the invention was made using the employer's facilities or time, but was not made as a result of the duties of the employment, the employer receives a "shop right" to the invention (a non-exclusive, non-transferable, royalty-free licence to use the invention and any patent on the invention).

---

[164] See Paras. 9.16 and 9.17 and references cited there.
[165] See *Dableh v. Ontario Hydro* (1996), 68 C.P.R. (3d) 129 (F.C.A.), and *Techform v. Wolda* (2000), 5 C.P.R. (4th) 25 (Ont. Sup. Ct.) (2001), 56 O.R. (3d) 1 (C.A.).
[166] See *Techform v. Wolda, ibid.* (Ont. Sup. Ct).

Table A Patent Option Valuation Decisions

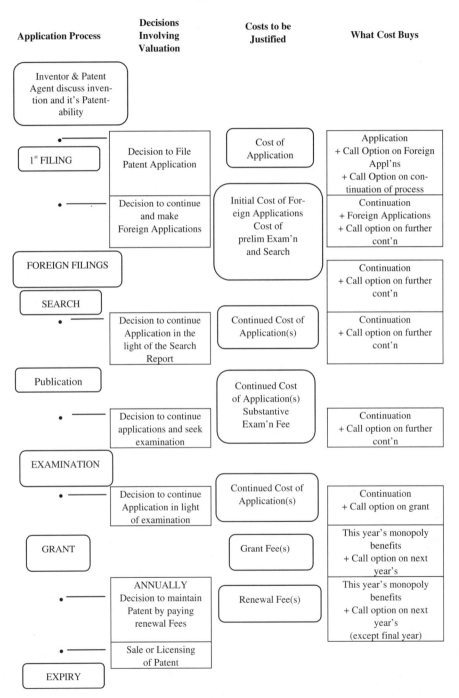

Application Process	Decisions Involving Valuation	Costs to be Justified	What Cost Buys
Inventor & Patent Agent discuss invention and it's Patentability			
1st FILING	Decision to File Patent Application	Cost of Application	Application + Call Option on Foreign Appl'ns + Call Option on continuation of process
	Decision to continue and make Foreign Applications	Initial Cost of Foreign Applications Cost of prelim Exam'n and Search	Continuation + Foreign Applications + Call option on further cont'n
FOREIGN FILINGS			Continuation + Call option on further cont'n
SEARCH			
	Decision to continue Application in the light of the Search Report	Continued Cost of Application(s)	Continuation + Call option on further cont'n
Publication		Continued Cost of Application(s) Substantive Exam'n Fee	
	Decision to continue applications and seek examination		Continuation + Call option on further cont'n
EXAMINATION			
	Decision to continue Application in light of examination	Continued Cost of Application(s)	Continuation + Call option on grant
GRANT		Grant Fee(s)	This year's monopoly benefits + Call option on next year's
	ANNUALLY Decision to maintain Patent by paying renewal Fees	Renewal Fee(s)	This year's monopoly benefits + Call option on next year's (except final year)
	Sale or Licensing of Patent		
EXPIRY			

Chapter 4

COPYRIGHT

The primary objective of copyright is not to reward the labor of authors, but [t]o promote the Progress of Science and useful Arts. To this end, copyright assures authors the right in their original expression, but encourages others to build freely upon the ideas and information conveyed by a work. [1]

Copyright is a queer thing. It arises effortlessly. It is easily traded and difficult to protect. It applies to almost every original artistic, musical or literary creation from a computer database to a photograph of the Mona Lisa. It is exceedingly difficult to define. There are encyclopedia-length treatises on copyright law that chronicle attempts by British and American courts to delineate copyright. Underlying copyright is the fundamental tension between the need to protect and encourage authors and society's interest in having access to their works. [2]

INTRODUCTION

4.1 Where Copyright Exists

Copyright exists by virtue of legislation but is afforded protection only in that country offering the copyright protection, unless there is some arrangement that extends the rights to another territory, such as the *Berne Convention*,[3] the *Universal Copyright Convention* ("UCC")[4] and agreements between World Trade Organization ("WTO") members.[5]

---

[1] United States, Intellectual Property in the National Information Infrastructure, the report of the Working Group on Intellectual Property Rights, Bruce A. Lehman, Assistant Secretary of Commerce and Commissioner of Patents and Trademarks, Chair, September 1995, p. 20 (hereinafter "NII"), quoting from *Feist Publications, Inc. v. Rural Telephone Service Co.*, 113 L.Ed. 2d 35A at 349-50, 113 S. Ct. 1282 at 1290 (U.S. 1991). All page references are to the page numbers as printed using Adobe Acrobat Reader.

[2] E. Susan Vogt, Copyright 101, <www.gowlings.com/resources/publication>.

[3] Convention for the Protection of Literary and Artistic Works concluded at Berne on September 9, 1886 and includes revisions such as the *Paris Act* of 1971.

[4] Adopted on September 6, 1952 in Geneva, Switzerland and revised in Paris on July 24, 1971.

[5] See the *General Agreement on Tariffs and Trade* ("GATT"), specifically, the *Agreement on Trade Related Aspects of Intellectual Property Rights* ("TRIPS").

4.1.1 Berne Convention

Most of the industrialized countries of the world are long-time parties to the *Berne Convention*. This Convention establishes the minimum protection that must be given to creators of works that are within the scope of copyright. Canada and the United States are members of this Convention. The United States became a party effective only on March 1, 1989. American works created before that date may therefore have different treatment. This extra-territorial protection for copyright through the *Berne Convention* is unlike protection for patents, which is restricted to the country where the patents issue. Even though a country is party to the *Berne Convention*, this does not necessarily mean that there are appropriate courts and remedies available in that country, or that all countries provide the same protection.

Strategy: A review of any licensing situation in a foreign country must include (a) an examination of the ability to enforce contractual and intellectual property rights, and (b) the scope of copyright protection to make sure your particular work is covered to the extent you expect.

4.1.2 Universal Copyright Convention

The UCC operates separately from the *Berne Convention*; however, countries may be parties to both conventions. The underlying protection offered through the UCC is that certain minimum levels of copyright protection will be offered to individuals of the other signatory countries, through the portion of the *General Agreement on Tariffs and Trade* ("GATT") known as the *Agreement on Trade Related Aspects of Intellectual Property Rights* ("TRIPS").

4.1.3 World Trade Organization Members and Others

Canada has extended copyright protection to all member countries of the World Trade Organization. In addition, Canada has entered into reciprocal agreements with a number of other countries expanding copyright protection beyond the *Berne Convention*, UCC and WTO.

4.1.4 Copyright in the Digital Age

On June 22, 2001, the Government of Canada launched a major initiative for reforming Canadian copyright legislation for the digital age by releasing for comment a number of discussion papers. This was the first step in what could be a lengthy process of reform.[6]

---

[6] On June 22, 2001, Industry Canada and the Department of Canadian Heritage released three papers: (1) '*A Framework for Copyright Reform*'; (2) '*Consultation Paper on Digital Copyright Issues*'; and (3) '*Consultation Paper on the Application of the Copyright Act's Compulsory*

ESSENTIALS OF COPYRIGHT: WORKS COVERED

4.2 Categories

Canada offers copyright protection to an extensive list or "bundle" of exclusive rights:

> Copyright applies to all original literary, dramatic, musical and artistic works. Each of these general categories covers a wide range of creations. Here are just a few examples:
> - literary works: books, pamphlets, poems and other works consisting of text and computer programs;
> - dramatic works: films, videos, plays, screenplays and scripts;
> - musical works: compositions that consist of both words and music or music only (note that lyrics without music fall in the literary works category);
> - artistic works: paintings, drawings, maps, photographs, sculptures and architectural works.
>
> Copyright also applies to three other kinds of subject-matter in addition to the works listed above:
> - performer's performances: performers such as actors, musicians, dancers and singers have copyrights in their performances;
> - communication signals: broadcasters have copyrights in the communications' signals that are broadcast;
> - sound recordings: makers of recordings, such as records, cassettes, and compact discs, which are called "sound recordings "in the *Copyright Act*, are also protected by copyright.[7]

The U.S. *Copyright Act* lists essentially the same categories in eight parts:

(1) literary works;
(2) musical works, including any accompanying words;
(3) dramatic works, including any accompanying music;
(4) pantomimes and choreographic works;
(5) pictorial, graphic and sculptural works;
(6) motion pictures and other audiovisual works;
(7) sound recordings; and
(8) architectural works.[8]

Retransmission Licence to the Internet'. Copies of these papers can be found at Industry Canada's website at <www.strategis.ic.gc.ca> under Copyrights; Copyright Reform Process.

[7] *"A Guide to Copyrights"* published by the Canadian Intellectual Property Office, January, 2002.

[8] 17 U.S.C. §102(a) (1988 and Supp. V 1993).

4.2.1 Expanding Coverage

In either case, the list of covered works is intended to expand with changing technology. For example, the Canadian definition of "every original literary, dramatic, musical and artistic work" is defined to *include* specific types of works, *i.e.*, it is not intended to be restricted to those works. These works are "every original production in the literary, scientific or artistic domain, whatever may be the mode or form of its expression, such as compilations, books, pamphlets and other writings, lectures, dramatic or dramatic-musical works, musical works, translations, illustrations, sketches and plastic works relative to geography, topography, architecture or science".[9] In Canada and the United States the "literary work" classification covers computer programs.

4.2.2 Effects of Separate Classifications

For technology licensing, the separate classifications for "literary, dramatic, musical and artistic works" become very important. Each classification gives rise to a different ownership and use rights that may be held by different people.[10]

REQUIREMENTS FOR COPYRIGHT PROTECTION

4.3 Eligibility

There are "three basic requirements for copyright protection: originality, creativity and fixation.[11] Substantial effort alone is not sufficient to qualify a work for copyright protection; it must be coupled with an original form of expression. The extent of the effort, often referred to as "sweat of the brow" or "industrious collection," is not, by itself, relevant.[12] The method of recording the work is irrelevant. The work must merely be "fixed in some fashion for more than a 'transitory duration'";[13] *i.e.*, its fixation must have some "permanent endur-

---

[9]   Section 2 of *Copyright Act*, R.S.C. 1985, c. C-42 (Canada), definition of "every original literary, dramatic, musical and artistic work" (rep. & sub. S.C. 1993, c. 44, s. 53 (2)).

[10] For further discussion, see §4.13 in "Multimedia: The Information Highway" later in this Chapter.

[11] NII at 24. See R.T. Hughes, S.J. Peacock, N. Armstrong, and D. Smith, *Hughes on Copyright and Industrial Design*, rev. ed. (Markham, Ont.: Butterworths, 1984) at §7, p. 341 (hereinafter "Hughes On Copyright"). See also s. 16C respecting fixation and performers, producers of Phonograms and Broadcasting and s. 25A for the 50-year term applying from the date of fixation.

[12] See, for example, the leading U.S. Supreme Court case on this point, *Feist Publications, Inc. v. Rural Telephone Service Co.*, 113 L. Ed. 2d 35A, 113 S. Ct. 1282 at 1290 (U.S. 1991). For a Canadian case see *Tele-Direct (Publications) Inc. v. American Business Information Inc.*, (1997), 76 C.P.R. (3d) 296 (F.C.A.).

[13] See 17 U.S.C. §101 (1988) (definition of "fixed").

ance".[14] "The form of fixation and the manner, method or medium used are virtually unlimited".[15]

4.3.1 What is Not Protected

In both Canada and the United States "an author has no copyright in ideas or information, but only in his expression of them".[16] As the U.S. Supreme Court has ruled: "the most fundamental axiom of copyright law is that no author may copyright his ideas or the facts he narrates".[17] "Spontaneous speech and signing are obviously not protected". But email?[18] *Vaver* writes "The Internet may have spawned a new hybrid; a communication literary in form, but oral in substance. Unlike most other laws, copyright usually celebrates form over substance. Whether this will continue with communication flows on the Internet remains to be seen".[19]

4.3.2 Idea Originator Versus Work Author

The creator of an idea who does not record the idea, or otherwise affix the idea in any way, may find that he or she is not the owner of the copyright to the work when someone else takes the idea and records it in some fashion. *Vaver* writes:

> A person may have a brilliant idea for a story, or for a picture, or for a play, and one which appears to him to be original; but if he communicates that idea to an author or an artist or a playwright, the production which is the result of the communication of the idea to the author or the artist or the playwright is the copyright of the person who has clothed the idea in form, whether by means of a picture, a play, or a book, and the owner of the idea has no rights [i.e. copyright] in that product.[20]

4.3.3 Quality Versus Originality

It is not the quality of the work that is important; the key factors are that it is the original work of the author and involves some intellectual effort.[21] "Quality and

---

[14] See Hughes et al., *Hughes On Copyright*, §8, p. 353, and cases cited in the footnotes.

[15] NII, p. 26.

[16] Hughes et al., *On Copyright*, §16, pp. 383-84 quoting *Delrina Corp. v. Triolet Systems Inc.* (1993), 9 B.L.R. (2d) 140, 47 C.P.R. (3d) 1 (Ont. Gen. Div.). Also see NII, pp. 20 and 33.

[17] *Feist Publications, supra*, note 1, pp. 344-45 (L.Ed.). The U.S. Supreme Court has stated the principle: "copyright assures authors the right to the original expression, but encourages others to build freely upon the ideas and information conveyed by a work". See also, Art. 9, Section 2.

[18] Vaver, p. 27.

[19] *Supra*, note 17, at 350.

[20] Vaver, p. 52. However, there may still be an issue of misappropriation of trade secrets.

[21] Vaver, p. 41.

legality" are irrelevant; "trash and the sublime ... all have been found equal under the copyright law".[22]

MORAL RIGHTS

4.4 Economic Rights Versus Moral Rights

In many countries, the copyright legislation distinguishes between an author's economic rights (the right to prevent copying, publishing, performance, public display, etc.) and moral rights (the right of "paternity" and the right of "integrity"). "Moral rights" is somewhat of a misnomer; these rights do not have anything to do with morality or ethics. Waiving "moral" rights does not mean that the author has thrown off all propriety and will now engage in immoral or licentious behavior. Canada has adopted a broad variety of moral rights; the United States has adopted a narrow variety in its *Visual Artist Rights Act of 1991*.[23]

4.4.1 Paternity Rights

In Canada, the moral rights of paternity are the "right...to be associated with the work as its author by name or under a pseudonym and the right to remain anonymous".[24] The rights of integrity are infringed "only if the work is, to the prejudice of the honor or reputation of the author, (a) distorted, mutilated or otherwise modified, or (b) used in association with a product, service, cause or institution".[25] In the case of a painting, sculpture or engraving, the prejudice is "deemed to have occurred as a result of any distortion, mutilation or other modification of the work".[26]

4.4.2 Multimedia and Moral Rights

With the ability to manipulate artistic works, copies of which have been scanned in a digital format, moral rights become a realistic problem, particularly in the multimedia area. In Canada, unless moral rights have been waived, the author of any textual material can require that his or her name be used in connection with the reproduction of work, even if copyright has been assigned. Conversely, the author(s) of a book can require that his or her name not be used in connection with that book (joining that great group of authors known as "Anon."). As a result of the Canadian rules, even though a creator of a formation of flying geese on display in a Toronto shopping center had assigned copyright, he re-

---

[22] Vaver, pp. 21-22.

[23] 17 U.S.C. §106A.

[24] *Copyright Act* (Canada), s. 14.1 (en. R.S.C. 1985, c. 10 (4th Supp.), s. 4).

[25] *Ibid*, s. 28.2(1) (en. R.S.C. 1985, c. 10 (4th Supp.), s. 6).

[26] *Ibid.*, s. 28.2(2) (en. R.S.C. 1985, c. 10 (4th Supp.), s. 6).

quired the removal of red ribbons that had been placed around the necks of the geese by an over-exuberant Christmas decorator. (Rudolph may have a red nose, but geese may not have red ribbons.)[27]

4.4.3 U.S. Variety of Moral Rights

The United States has adopted a modest variation of "moral rights" by the *Visual Artist Rights Act*, "which created certain rights of integrity and attribution to works of visual art".[28] The right of integrity is the right "to prevent any intentional distortion, mutilation, or other modification of [a work of visual art] which would be prejudicial to his or her honor or reputation"[29] if a work of visual art is:

a painting, drawing, print or sculpture existing in a single copy, in a limited edition of 200 copies or fewer that are signed or consecutively numbered by the author, or, in the case of a sculpture, in a multiple cast, carved, or fabricated sculptures of 200 or fewer that are consecutively numbered by the author and bear the signature or other identifying mark of the author; or (2) a still photographic image produced for exhibition purposes only, existing in a single copy that is signed by the author, or in a limited edition of 200 copies or fewer that are signed and consecutively numbered by the author.[30]

4.4.4 Waiver of Moral Rights

Traditional moral rights cannot be assigned. In some countries, such as Canada, they can be waived. In Canada, moral rights apply to all types of works without limitation.[31] This computer program may involve moral rights.

Strategies:
(1)   Assess the impact of moral rights on source code of software and other digitized works.
(2)   Require all employees/consultants to waive their moral rights in addition to assigning their copyrights.

---

[27]   *Snow v. Eaton Centre Ltd.* (1982), 70 C.P.R. (2d) 105 (Ont. H.C.J.).
[28]   D. Bender and D.A. Jarvis, "Multimedia Licensing" (address to the U.S. and Canada Licensing Executive Society's Annual Meeting, Advanced Software Licensing Issues Seminar, Thursday, October 20, 1994 (unpublished) (hereinafter "Bender and Jarvis, 'Multimedia Licensing'")).
[29]   17 U.S.C. §106A.
[30]   *Ibid.*, §101.
[31]   *Copyright Act* (Canada), s. 14.1(1) (en. R.S.C. 1985, c. 10 (4th Supp.), s. 4).

ORIGINAL EXPRESSION

4.5 Copyright Protects Original Expression in Software

Copyright in Canada and the United States protects any "original" work, *i.e.*, a work independently created and not copied from other works.[32] The work does not have to show inventiveness as a patented innovation would. The work expressed may merely be a "unique form of expression of widely understood computer functions".[33] *Delrina Corp. v. Triolet Systems Inc.* sets out the basic rules:

> The most basic principle of copyright law is that copyright cannot subsist in an idea but only in the way the author of a work expresses that idea. Perhaps the next most fundamental principle is that to give rise to copyright, the work must be original, that is to say, it must not have been copied by the author from another work, whether that other work was protected by copyright or was in the public domain and free for the taking.[34]

4.5.1 No Copyright Protection for Ideas

In *Delrina*, the judge helpfully enumerates some general principles applicable to the law of copyright.

1. An author has no copyright in ideas or information, but only in his or her expression of them.
2. Copyright subsists in original literary works. There is no copyright where the author has copied from something already in the public domain or from a work in which another holds the copyright.
3. Even if the expression originated with the author, the expression of the idea is not copyrightable if the expression does no more than embody elements of the idea that are functional in the utilitarian sense: see *Lotus v. Paperback*, 740 F . Supp. 37 (D. Mass. 1990) at 57-58.
4. If an idea can be expressed in only one or in a very limited number of ways, then copyright of that expression will be refused for it would give the originator of the idea a virtual monopoly on the idea. In such a case it is said that the expression merges with the idea and thus is not copyrightable.
5. Copyright does not subsist "in any arrangement, system, scheme, method for doing a particular thing, procedure, process, concept, principle, or discovery,

---

[32] See *University of London Press Ltd. v. University of Tutorial Press Ltd.*, [1916] 2 Ch. 601 at 608, 86 L.J. Ch. 107; and *NEC Corp. v. Intel Corp.*, W.L. 67434, at 5 (N.D. Cal. 1989), quoting M. Nimmer, *Nimmer on Copyright*, s. 2.01[A] at 2-8, s. 2.01[B] at 2-15.

[33] August and Smith "Software Expression", at 680.

[34] *Supra*, note 16, 47 C.P.R. (3d) 1 at 32.

but only in an author's original expression of them. Consistent with accepted thinking in copyright law, therefore, a particular expression of a mathematical algorithm or other procedure for solving a problem or accomplishing some end in the form of sets of instructions or statements may be protected by copyright, but the mathematical algorithm or other procedure as such cannot be protected by copyright": Sookman Computer Law, pp. 3-96.[35]

Courts are forced to deal with the grey issues. Would one person's method of expression, if protected, preclude others from developing a competitive program if there is only one way of expressing the underlying idea? These issues significantly involve public policy. The garden-variety infringer[36] clearly should be restrained, but copyright should not give patent-like protection.

4.6 Ideas Versus Expression

The courts have tried to develop methods of separating from software the expression that is not protectable because it is not the one and only embodiment of the idea.[37] *Delrina* summarizes the issue as follows:

[I]t seems clear that before a computer program or some part of it can be held to be copyrightable, some method must be found to weed out or remove from copyright protection those portions which, for the various reasons already mentioned, cannot be protected by copyright. After the portions that are not copyrightable have been filtered out, there may or may not be any kernels or golden nuggets left to which copyright can attach.[38]

4.6.1 Analytical Method of Filtering Out Ideas from Expression

Delrina follows the analytical method offered by the court in *Computer Associates Inc. v. Altai Inc.*,[39] *i.e.*, the abstraction, filtration and comparison method. In the first step of the analysis, *i.e.*, abstraction, the program is broken down into its constituent structural parts. The second step, filtration, requires the court to examine "each of these parts for such things as incorporated ideas, expression that is necessarily incidental to those ideas, and elements that are taken from the public domain".[40] The court is thus "able to sift out all non-protectable material".[41] This leaves "a kernel, or possibly kernels, of creative expression"[42] that is

---

[35] *Supra*, note 16, at 41 (C.P.R.).

[36] McCabe, "Reverse Engineering" p. 10, quoting from Atari.

[37] *Ibid*, at 37.

[38] *Delrina Corp. v. Triolet Systems Inc.* (1993), 9 B.L.R. (2d) 140, 47 C.P.R. (3d) 1 at 37 (Ont. Gen. Div.).

[39] 982 F.2d 693 (2nd Cir. 1992).

[40] *Delrina, supra*, note 38, at 33 (C.P.R), quoting Walker, p. 4741, in *Computer Associates Inc. v. Altai Inc., supra*, note 39.

[41] *Ibid*.

[42] *Ibid*.

the protectable portion of the work. Then, in a suit for infringement, the court will compare the protectable material "with the structure of [the] allegedly infringing program. The result of this comparison will determine whether the protectable elements of the programs at issue are substantially similar so as to warrant a finding of infringement".[43]

4.7 When Has Copyright Infringement Occurred?

In cases where the idea versus expression dichotomy is not an issue, there are many ways to determine whether there has been a copyright infringement of the subject software:

(a) Access to the subject program may indicate the likelihood of copying, but it is not conclusive. In *Prism Hospital Software Inc. v. Hospital Medical Records Institute*, the defendants had access to the source code and behaved towards the plaintiff with "open arrogance bordering on contempt".[44] In *Delrina*, although the defendant had a copy of the source code, he did not use it. And in *Atari Games Corp. v. Nintendo of America Inc.*, Atari improperly obtained a copy of the source code.[45]

(b) A competitive program developed in an unusually short period of time may indicate copying, but if the creator of the computer program also wrote the subject program that is allegedly infringed, he or she could cut the time down significantly by eliminating the time wasted by design and conceptual errors that was originally encountered.[46]

(c) Programs that are functionally similar indicate copying.[47] The similarities, however, could result from:

(i) the intention to make [the computer program] capable of performing every function [the subject program] can perform,

(ii) peculiarities required by another program with which the subject program is intended to interface or support,

(iii) habits or styles developed by a programmer who developed both programs,

(iv) common ways of approaching problems,

(v) the problems encountered in programming not lending themselves to multiple solutions, and

---

[43] *Computer Associates*, *supra*, note 40, at 735.

[44] (1994), 97 B.C.L.R. (2d) 201, [1994] 10 W.W.R. 305, 18 B.L.R. (2d) 1, 57 C.P.R. (3d) 129 (B.C.), quoted from 179 (C.P.R.).

[45] 975 F. 2d 832 (Cir. 1992). There is a significant problem to developers when "a programmer has kept a copy of a copyrighted program obtained during previous employment. The use of this program, unknown to the present employer, in writing competing software is likely to lead to a finding of copyright infringement". See *Computer Associates*, *supra*, note 40, quoted by McCabe "Reverse Engineering", p. 9.

[46] See *Delrina*, *supra*, note 38, at 12 (C.P.R.).

[47] *Ibid.*, at 13 (C.P.R.).

(vi) the programmer who developed both programs using the same tools that he or she remembered using in the first program;[48]

Unusual phrasing, unnecessary instructions or mistakes common to both programs suggests copying.[49] It must be established, however, that the common item is indeed a defect and not something intrinsically necessary;[50]

(d) Both the programs working on seldom used terminals[51] may be an indication of copying, although the full offering may result only from a desire to be fully competitive;[52]

(e) A common hidden command may indicate copying so long as the same command does not result from the use of the same programming convention;[53] and

(f) An overwhelming similarity of codes may be evidence of copying.[54]

COPYRIGHT FOR GOVERNMENT-CREATED WORK

4.8 U.S. Versus Canadian Government-created Works

There is a material difference between Canada and the United States in the treatment of government-created works. Canada reserves copyright to the government for most works. The United States denies protection for most (but not necessarily all) government-created works. This denial of protection, however, may apply only within the United States; copyright may exist extra-territorially.

4.8.1 Canadian Rule

Under the Canadian rule, if "any work is, or has been, prepared or published by or under the direction or control of Her Majesty or any government department, the copyright in the work shall, subject to any agreement with the author, belong to Her Majesty ...".[55] Her Majesty includes the federal and provincial governments and any of their agencies. In an ostensibly democratic country, this has startling implications: some works, such as statutes, regulations, court decisions, parliamentary proceedings and the like should be readily available. On the other hand, the Canadian governments, both federal and provincial, have engaged in creating works that often would be produced for commercialization and, thus,

---

48 *Ibid.*
49 *Ibid.*, at 14 (C.P.R.) and *Atari*, as quoted by McCabe "Reverse Engineering", p. 10.
50 *Ibid.* at 45 (C.P.R.).
51 *Ibid.*, at 16 (C.P.R.).
52 *Ibid.*
53 *Ibid.*, at 17 (C.P.R.).
54 *Ibid.*, and *Prism, supra*, note 44.
55 *Copyright Act* (Canada), s. 12 (rep. & sub. S.C. 1993, c. 44. s. 60(1)).

are recognized as deserving protection.[56] As s. 12 of the Canadian *Copyright Act* indicates, upon entering into a relationship with a Canadian government or one of its agencies for the preparation or publication of a work by, or under control of, that government or agency an author will lose copyright to the government, unless there is an agreement to the contrary. In September 1991, the federal government, through its Treasury Board, adopted a new policy for intellectual property arising in federal government contracts. Unfortunately, it appears that this policy is not uniformly applied.[57] Intellectual property resulting from the performance of the contract is now presumed to vest in the contractor, unless the contract determines that the Crown ownership of resulting intellectual property is justified. Note that this policy applies only to the federal government and not to the provinces. In any event, the policy of any Canadian government can be changed without public consultation.[58]

4.8.2 U.S. Rule

In the United States the general rule is that copyright protection is "not extended ... to works of the U.S. Government",[59] subject to limited exceptions. "Therefore, nearly all works of the U.S. government ... may be reproduced, distributed, adapted, publicly performed and publicly displayed [in the U.S.] without infringement ... under its copyright laws".[60] Engaging in these activities in a country outside the United States may not be lawful. It is noted that "while the *Copyright Act* leaves most works created by the U.S. Government unprotected under U.S. copyright laws, Congress did not intend for the section to have any effect on the protection of U.S. government works abroad".[61]

Strategies:
   (1)   When dealing with the Canadian federal government, the government of its provinces or territories or any of their agencies, in the contract clarify the ownership of copyright.
   (2)   When licensing a work that was produced or published by, or under, the control of the Canadian federal government, the government of the provinces or territories, or any of their agencies, check the relevant contract; silence on the issue is not a good thing.
   (3)   Watch out for the copyright of Her Majesty and of Uncle Sam!

---

[56] Canada: Information Highway Advisory Council, *Subcommittee Report on Copyright and the Information Highway* (March 1995), Chapter 6.
[57] *Ibid.*
[58] *Ibid.*
[59] NII, pp. 34-35, citing 17 U.S.C. §105 (1988).
[60] *Ibid.*, p. 35.
[61] *Ibid.*

COMPUTER PROGRAMS

4.9 Computer Programs are Literary Works

In both Canada and the United States, computer programs are a subset of "literary works" that are protected by their Copyright Acts.[62]

4.9.1 Debate over Type of Protection for Computer Programs

Prior to each country deciding to expressly protect computer programs by copyright, there was considerable debate over the proper form of intellectual property protection that is appropriate for software, and this debate now continues into the courts. Computer programs do not fit easily into any of the traditional categories of copyright or patent. Copyright, traditionally, covers artistic works (paintings, sculptures), dramatic works (plays) and music and literary works (books). Patents, traditionally, protect utilitarian items, such as machinery or other kinds of hardware. Software usually achieves a utilitarian result, but operates as a result of a written work, *i.e.*, source code. Types of software range from software on chips that directs hardware, such as a vehicle's fuel system, to software that directs other software, such as operating systems, to software that interacts with people (word processing packages) or entertains them (video games). The debates on whether copyright should be applied to software may be summarized as follows:

(1) Copyright was not intended to protect essentially utilitarian tools.
(2) Software is derived from written work (source code) and, therefore, should be protected by copyright.
(3) The term of protection for copyrighted works (life of the author plus 50 years) was too long for software; even the term of protection for patents was too long (formerly 17 years after issuance, now 20 years after filing). Software should have its own shorter term of protection.
(4) Software should be protected only if it shows novelty or inventiveness as required for patent protection; copyright law requires only that the work be the original work of the author.
(5) The grant of patent protection requires disclosure of the invention; copyright protection does not require disclosure. Software, being essentially utilitarian, should be protected only if disclosure is made. It is wrong to provide a term of protection almost three times as long as the term of patent protection when there is no disclosure required to obtain copyright protection.

Copyright won the day, but we still see the debate continuing as the courts endeavor to determine the appropriate scope of protection offered by copyright.

---

[62] See also, Art. 10, Section 1 and Circular 1 "Copyright Protection for Computer Programs" published by the Canadian Intellectual Property Office, October 1, 1997.

4.10 Canadian Definition of "Computer Programs"

The following is the definition of a "computer program" that was adopted in the *Copyright Act* (Canada):

> "computer program" means a set of instructions or statements, expressed, fixed, embodied or stored in any manner, that is to be used directly or indirectly in a computer in order to bring about a specific result.[63]

4.10.1 Comparable American Provision

The Canadian and U.S. statutory definitions of computer programs are very similar.[64] This similarity will be very helpful for creators that license their software both in Canada and the United States and will be helpful to courts in Canada (the less litigious country) as they will be able to look to American decisions for guidance.[65]

4.10.2 Program on a Disk Versus Program on a Chip

It should not matter whether the program is stored on a disk or a chip or any other kind of media that may be developed in the future, so long as it is "expressed, fixed, embodied or stored in any manner".[66] The definition appears to be broad enough to include the screen display that has been described as an exact reflection "and is a visual reproduction of the instructions that a creator of the program embodied on the tape or disk".[67] Thus "[i]f someone else copies the screen display. ...for use in another program, he infringes any copyright the owner of the work held in it"[68] unless he or she has the consent of the copyright owner. However, this issue remains in doubt pending further clarification by the courts.

---

[63] Section 2 (en. R.S.C. 1985, c. 10 (4th Supp.), s. 1(3)).

[64] The U.S. equivalent is 17 U.S.C. §102 which states "A 'computer program' is a set of statements or instructions to be used directly or indirectly in a computer in order to bring about a certain result".

[65] For example, *Delrina Corp. v. Triolet Systems Inc.* (1993), 9 B.L.R. (2d) 140, 47 C.P.R. (3d) 1 (Ont. Gen. Div.), drew heavily on U.S. decisions.

[66] *Copyright Act* (Canada), s. 2 (en. R.S.C. 1985, c. 10 (4th Supp.), s. I (3)), definition of "computer program".

[67] *Delrina Corp. v. Triolet, supra*, note 65, at 28 (C.P.R.).

[68] *Ibid.* However, the owner of the work copied still has to prove he or she has copyright in the work under the abstraction, filtration and comparison analysis, discussed further in *Delrina* and in this material.

4.10.3 Produce or Reproduce

The copyright holder has the exclusive right to produce or reproduce a work or any such substantial part thereof in any manner whatsoever.[69] In software terms, this means to: copy onto a hard drive; copy onto a floppy disk or other storage media to be put away for archival purposes; copy onto storage tapes to be kept at a remote site for disaster recovery; copy onto a floppy disk to give to friends; copy onto a floppy disk for use on a home computer; copy onto a bulletin board for distribution to other subscribers;[70] copy (download) from a bulletin board for personal use;[71] scan a printed work (*e.g.*, a text or photograph) into a digital file (which file is the "copy");[72] and browse on the Internet.[73]

4.10.4 Perform

The copyright holder has the exclusive rights to perform the work. This is a broad definition and could, for example, include the display of a computer game in a public place.

4.10.5 The Work or Any Substantial Part Thereof

Substantiality may go to the quantity of material copied, particularly with software. "Part" is more than a mere particle.[74] "A copyright owner cannot therefore control every particle of her work, any little piece the taking of which cannot affect the value of her work as a whole. Transferring 60 of 14,000 lines of computer program source code into another program was found not to take a substantial part of the former work, especially since writing this routine material from scratch would have taken a competent programmer twenty minutes."[75] In the case of multimedia, a small portion of a musical work may be substantial.

4.10.6 Translation

The Canadian copyright holder has an exclusive right to translate a work. The word is defined broadly. Translation is not restricted to translation into another

---

[69]   *Copyright Act* (Canada), s. 3.

[70]   See NII, pp. 66 and 81.

[71]   See *Sega Enterprises and Sega of America v. Maphia et al.*, summarized in the Software Law Bulletin July/August 1994, pp. 1-2. See also NII, pp. 66 and 81.

[72]   NII, p. 65.

[73]   See Canada: Information Highway Advisory Council, *Subcommittee Report on Copyright and the Information Highway* (March 1995), Chapter 3 in the Section: "Should 'browsing' be permitted as a use of works in the Information Highway" (hereinafter "Browsing NII").

[74]   Vaver, p. 81.

[75]   Vaver, p. 81. See also 4.25 of this Chapter.

spoken language (such as English to French), but may include translations from one platform to another (for example, DOS to Windows or Macintosh).[76]

4.10.7 Rent

The Canadian copyright holder has the exclusive right to rent a computer program. This section was required as a result of the *North American Free Trade Agreement* ("NAFTA") and was designed to overcome the invitation to copy that was promoted by the rental of software. The Canadian prohibition on rentals applies to any "computer program that can be reproduced in the ordinary course of its use, other than by a reproduction during its execution in conjunction with a machine, device or computer".[77] The prohibition also covers commercial rental like transactions.[78] There are industry-sponsored associations that take steps to enforce the copyrights of their members (illegal copying and illegal renting), and a visit from them can be a very discomforting experience.

4.10.8 Import

The Canadian copyright holder has the exclusive rights to import a copy of a work into Canada. By court application, an order can be obtained to require the Canadian customs officials to prohibit the importation of illegal copies into Canada. This is a very strong and cost-effective weapon.

DATA PROTECTION

4.11 Data Protection

At present, databases are not protected in Canada[79] or the United States by its own form of protection (*i.e.*, a *sui generis* form of protection). The issue of a *sui generis* form of protection for databases was the subject of a study of the World Intellectual Property Office, resulting in the release in August 1996 of a "Draft Treaty on Intellectual Property in Respect of Databases".[80] The draft treaty pro-

---

[76] This would seem to be the implication of the Supreme Court's affirmation of the decisions at trial and on appeal in *Apple Computer Inc. v. Mackintosh Computers Ltd.*, [1987] 1 F.C. 173, 3 F.T.R. 118, 28 D.L.R. (4th) 178, 8 C.I.L.R. 153, 10 C.P.R. (3d) 1; additional reasons 12 F.T.R. 287, 43 D.L.R. (4th) 184, 14 C.I.P.R. 315; vard. [1988] 1 F.C. 673, 44 D.L.R. (4th) 74, 81 N.R. 3, 16 C.I.P.R. 15, 18 C.P.R. (3d) 129 (C.A.); affd. [1990] 2 S.C.R. 209, 36 F.T.R. 159*n*, 71 D.L.R. (4th) 95, 110 N.R. 66, 30 C.P.R. (3d) 257. Specifically, see the appeal decision at p. 29 (16 C.I.P.R.).

[77] *Copyright Act* (Canada), s. 3(1)(h) (en. S.C. 1993, c. 44, s. 55 (2)).

[78] *Ibid.*, s. 3(2) (rep. & sub. S.C. 1993, c. 44, s. 55) and (3) (en. S.C. 1993, c. 44, s. 55).

[79] The Government of Canada has released a discussion paper '*A Framework for Copyright Reform*' issued by the Intellectual Property Policy Directorate, Industry Canada, June 22, 2001, which raises the issue as to the appropriate protection to be given to databases in Canada.

[80] See <www.wipo.org/eng/diplconf/6dc_a02.htm#Article%202>.

vides a useful definition of a database; "Database means a collection of independent works, data or other materials arranged in a systematic or methodical way and capable of being individually accessed by electronic or other means". [81]

The primary Canadian vehicle for protection of databases is copyright, being a "compilation", one of the bundle of items protected by copyright. [82] The subject matter of the database may be within the public domain such as "facts, figures, single words, numbers" [83] and therefore not a work protected by copyright. Only the selection and the arrangement of the data is protectable in such case. [84] Protection becomes more elusive if there is only one way of selecting and arranging the data. [85] "In other words, only an original method or format of selection and arrangement will be protected by copyright". [86] Mere time, effort, industry or "sweat of the brow" is not sufficient in Canada and the United States to meet the copyright requirements of "originality". [87] The "abstraction – filtration – comparison" process used in software copyright issues may apply to data [88] to separate out what is the proper subject matter of copyright and what is not. The reaffirmation in *Feist* of a need for a small measure of "creativity" is illustrated in the cases reviewed where "copyrightability" was not present:

(i) In facts or with respect to activities (even if industrious activities) that are "mechanical", "typical", "garden variety" . . . (all involving, essentially, "names and addresses") . . . [or] (list of facts); or

(ii) In matters that are dictated by external factors . . . (format of a chart determined by the custom or convention of the industry) or for which there is only one way (or, perhaps, limited ways) of expressing the concept or idea . . . . This analysis is almost identical with the "abstraction-filtration-comparison" approach to "non-literal" infringement of computer programs. [89]

Once beyond these minimal levels, copyrightability will be present. [90] "Copyright protects *selection* and *arrangement* which may exist in the compilation *as a whole*, even if constituent elements are not copyrightable themselves . . . ." [91] The same principle applies with trade secrecy: although components of the information may be in the public domain, the selection, coordination and ar-

---

[81] *Ibid.*, section 2.03.

[82] Howell, Data Base Protection And Canadian Laws (State of Law as of June 15, 1998). Available at <www.pch.gc.ca/culture/cult_ind/pubs/fulveren.pdf>.

[83] Howell, p. 3.

[84] Howell, p. 3.

[85] See, for example, *Feist Publications, Inc. v. Rural Telephone Service Company, Inc.*, 449 U.S. 340, 113 L.Ed. 2d 358 (1991) and *Tele-Direct (Publications) Inc. v. American Business Information Inc.* (1997), 76 C.P.R. (3d) 296, 310 (F.C.A.).

[86] Howell, p. 4.

[87] See Howell, p. 4.

[88] See Howell, p. 61.

[89] Howell, p. 14.

[90] Howell, p. 14.

[91] Howell, p. 14.

rangement may not be in the public domain and therefore capable of being protected as a trade secret.

If copyright does not subsist, consider whether the data is protected by trade
secrecy (assuming it was not made available to the public) or consider whether
the misappropriation of the data could be considered to be "unfair competition"[92] or in violation of fair trade practices statutes.[93] Also note that the fair
dealing/fair usage right to use copyright work does not apply to trade secrecy.
The entire relationship between the parties must be examined but keep in mind
the issue whether copyright pre-empts trade secrecy protection in the United
States. Howell states, "...any initiative to provide non-copyright protection of
databases, say through an unfair competition theory or trade secret analysis,
especially if proceeding in provincial jurisdiction, must be appropriately differ-
entiated from the copyright protection of selection and arrangement of databases
or compilations, in order to avoid the demarcation and pre-emption difficulties
that have had to be faced in the United States".[94]

DERIVATIVE WORKS

4.12 Derivative Works

A derivative work is one "based upon one or more pre-existing works".[95] A derivative work is specifically covered by the U.S. *Copyright Act*, but there is no
equivalent provision in the Canadian Act. In Canada, derivative works are controlled, if at all, by the basic prohibition against copying of "any substantial
part" of a work. Developers of computer programs often wish to control modifications to their software, sometimes referred to as updates or improvements.
The modified software would be a derivative work in the U.S. context or would
involve a copy of all or a substantial portion of the work for the Canadian context.[96]

Strategy:

1.   *In Canada, do not use the phrase "derivative work" assuming it has
      statutory meaning; define it, perhaps using the U.S. statutory defini-
      tion.*

2.   *In a contract involving a Canadian, consider specifically controlling
      the creation of a derivative work because that is not expressly covered
      by the Canadian Copyright Act.*

---

[92] See Howell, p. 13.

[93] Howell, p. 48.

[94] Howell, p. 34, Whether unfair competition applies is discussed in *Howell;* further discussion is
      beyond the scope of this work.

[95] NII, p. 40, quoting in part from 17 U.S.C. §101 (1988) (definition of "derivative work").

[96] See Chapter 9, "Improvements and Joint Ownership".

MULTIMEDIA: THE INFORMATION HIGHWAY

4.13 Copyright Law and Multimedia

"Multimedia" brings together copyright law and entertainment law, which previously operated separately, each with "their own legal customs and traditional licence terms".[97]

The multimedia industry currently consists of an inchoate mass of computer software and hardware companies, cable television companies, telecommunications companies, publishing companies and traditional entertainment companies. All those industries have their own cultures with their own customs, practices and traditions ingrained through years of experience. Each industry seeks to impose its own vision of "order" upon the multimedia industry. This clash of cultures leaves all these cross-industry alliances uneasy and insecure. That culture clash also means that expectations of parties in different industries differ markedly in every transaction. Indeed, even approaches to negotiations differ among industries, and finding common ground can sometimes be the most important element of a successful negotiation.[98]

4.13.1 No Separate Copyright Category for Multimedia

Multimedia works are not categorized separately under the U.S. or Canadian Copyright Act.[99] The term multimedia is a misnomer;

> it is the types of categories of works that are "multiple"... not the types of media. The very premise of a so-called "multi-media" work is that it combines several different elements or types of works (e.g., texts, literary works), sound (sound recordings), still images (pictorial works), and moving images (audiovisual works) into a single medium (e.g., a CD-ROM) - not multiple media.[100]

---

[97] Mark Radcliffe, "Key Issues for User of Multimedia" in *les Nouvelles*, the Journal of the Licensing Executive Society, Vol. XXX, No. 2, June 1995, p. 93, at 95 (hereinafter "Radcliffe, 'Key Issues', *les Nouvelles*, June 1995"). See also Michael D. Scott and James L. Talbott, "Multimedia: What is it? Why is it Important and What do I Need to Know About It?" in *The Computer Law Association Bulletin* (1993), Vol. 8, No. 3, p. 14, at 15.

[98] "Multimedia Licensing Issues" written by a committee consisting of William S. Coats and David M. Barkan, presented in "Evolving Strategies in Evolving Industries", 1994 Licencing Executives Society Winter Meeting, February 16, 1994, p. 2 (hereinafter "Coats and Barkan, 'Licensing Issues'"), 129 NII, p. 42.

[99] NII, p. 42.

[100] *Ibid.*, pp. 41-42.

4.13.2 Bundle of Separate Rights

Copyright gives the holder a number of separate and independent exclusive rights.[101] For technology licensing, the separate classifications for "literary, dramatic, musical and artistic works" become very important for multimedia use. Each classification gives rise to different ownership and use rights that may be held by different people.

4.13.3 "[T]o produce or reproduce the work or any substantial part thereof in any material form whatever"[102]

Frequently, the content provider wants to include in his or her multimedia works a very minuscule portion of another copyrighted work. The content provider may think that taking such a very tiny portion will be permissible, but it must be remembered that it is the quality of the material taken, not the quantity that determines the substantiality of the copying. A tiny portion may be the "very essence" of the work and, thus, may be protected by copyright.[103] Digital technology allows the user to manipulate material that has been digitized to conceal its origin and, therefore, a content owner might never find out or even suspect, let alone establish, that an image appearing on the screen is something that originally came from his or her work.[104] Drawing the line between what is a "substantial part thereof" and what is not is very difficult to do in practice, and may be done at the taker's jeopardy.

4.13.4 "Transmit"

The Canadian *Copyright Act* gives the copyright holder of a literary, dramatic, musical or artistic work the exclusive right to communicate that work to the public by telecommunication.[105]

Strategy: Until the United States adopts transmission rights as exclusive right of the copyright holder, transmission rights should be controlled by contract. The right of transmission is a critical component of the information highway including the Internet.

---

[101] Radcliffe, "Key Issues", *les Nouvelles*, June 1995, p. 98 and NII, p. 215.

[102] *Copyright Act* (Canada), s. 3(1).

[103] Bender and Jarvis, "Multimedia Licensing", p. 12.

[104] Coats and Barkan, "Licensing Issues", p. 8.

[105] *Copyright Act* (Canada), s. 3(1)(f) (am. R.S.C. 1985, c. 10 (4th Supp.), s. 2; re-en. 1988, c. 65, s. 62(1); am. 1993, c. 44, s. 55(2)).

4.13.5 Independent Rights

Each of the rights given to a copyright holder is independent, even if relating to the same work. In addition to independent existence, each right is capable of being licensed or assigned for specific and separate applications. Thus, the multimedia content provider is faced with the almost overwhelming tasks of:

(a) identifying the holders of the various copyright interests. A clip from a musical movie may require consent of the holder of copyright for the screen play (perhaps even the novel on which it is based), the score, the lyrics and the singer and, sometimes, even the entertainment unions and the writers' guilds. Copyright notices are not required for copyright works, making the process of identification even more difficult.[106] An owner of copyright should consider placing copyright footprints in the work to overcome the problems of identification and location;

(b) determining each holder's rights. One holder may have the right to present the work as a live drama; another as a film to be shown only in a theatre, another as a video for home consumption, another as a television miniseries, and yet another as a continuing television program;[107]

(c) determining when any of the rights are jointly held. An individual who works as an independent contractor, alone or jointly with others, holds copyright to the work created either solely or jointly with others, as the case may be, unless there is an effective assignment of copyright that has not reverted to the assignor;

(d) evaluating the portion of the work to be included in the multimedia work.

(e) [E]ach licensor fears that its particular contribution will become immensely popular in this new market, which the licensor cannot then fully exploit because it has signed away at least some of its multimedia rights to the CD-ROM licensee.[108] Formula and rate structures in use for photographs and movies have not been set with multimedia use in mind, and usually run too high for a multimedia title. Many licensors charge 5 per cent of the final price, often acceptable enough for a traditional work but overwhelming where the multimedia work may use 200 or more sources.[109]

(f) negotiating which existing multimedia platforms will be the subject of the licence. The licensor will be anxious about limiting its product to a platform that may be a loser in the market-place. (Do you choose SEGA

---

[106] *Ibid.*, p. 52.

[107] See the litigation surrounding *Lonesome Dove*, referred to in Radcliffe, "Key Issues", *les Nouvelles*, June 1995, p. 95, middle column.

[108] Bender and Jarvis, "Multimedia Licensing", p. 5. See also Coats and Barkan, "Licensing Issues", p. 7.

[109] *Ibid.*, p. 9.

or Nintendo?) Will the licensor reserve the right to produce the work on other platforms?[110]

(g) negotiating the application of the licence to future platforms. "In the present environment, it will be difficult for the licensor to know what the shape of things will be in just a few years, which is within the term of the typical license. In such situations, both licensors and licensees seek to protect their interests. The licensor is worried lest it authorize applications that it does not contemplate, and as a result, grant licences to its birthright for a pittance. This uncertainty causes problems for both the business people, and their lawyers. How do you protect your rights in the end product when you're not sure what that product will be? And even if you do know what it would be, you may not be able to perceive the universe of future applications for it. Contracting parties should be careful regarding the language they use in the grant and royalty clauses. For example, from the licensee's perspective, where a broad grant is desired, the clause might recite that the license is for performance, distribution, etc., "by any means now known or later conceived". And it may speak of exploitation "in any way, medium, mode, form or language". Where a narrow grant is desired, the clause might recite that no rights are granted other than those expressly granted, and that all rights not expressly granted are reserved to the licensor".[111]

(h) granting concessions to the copyright holder for the use of the content provider's interface. The licensor may want to ensure that all its works can be enjoyed using the same interface and that interface may be controlled by the multimedia content provider.[112]

(i) avoiding infringement of an author's moral rights in the process of morphing an author's work. Assignment of copyright does not infer that moral rights have been waived.[113]

4.13.6 Clearing Houses for Multimedia Content?

It is hoped that in the near future copyright clearing houses will be operating successfully to reduce some of these difficulties.[114] Napster has accelerated the public demand for a resolution. This long-standing need for these clearing houses has been made even more urgent by the demand for music available on-

---

[110] Radcliffe, "Key Issues", *les Nouvelles*, June 1995, p. 94. See also Bender and Jarvis, "Multimedia Licensing", pp. 14ff. And see also Coats and Barkan, "Licensing Issues", p. 10, where they discuss the difficulties of deciding on an appropriate platform that will win the day with the consumers.

[111] Bender and Jarvis "Multimedia Licensing", pp. 15 and 16.

[112] Radcliffe, "Key Issues", *les Nouvelles*, June 1995, p. 94.

[113] For further discussion of moral rights, see §4.4.

[114] See Bender and Jarvis, "Multimedia Licensing", pp. 21ff.

line illustrated by the success of Napster – the complicated web of music licences[115] must be resolved to avoid consumers finding their own solutions.
As Coats and Barkan have stated:

> Unfortunately, using existing content has the disadvantage of having to deal with
> the people who own it. The producer has to negotiate with people who may not
> know whether they have the rights to license, because when the work was created
> (whether it is art, film or television programming) there was no such thing as mul-
> timedia rights or digital rights.[116]

What the content provider considers to be a clip of minor importance may be
proven subsequently in the market-place to be the sole reason for the success of
the provider's multimedia product. How can it be anticipated in advance which
portions of the multimedia work will appeal to customers? As well as being a
copyright concern, this makes it extremely difficult for the parties to agree on an
appropriate value for the individual components of a multimedia work.

DURATION

4.14 Duration

In Canada and the United States, for most works the term for which copyrights
exist is the life of the author plus 50 years (or in the case of joint ownership, the
death of the last author to die plus 50 years).[117] Under the European Directive,[118]
the duration is the life of the author plus 50 years. In Canada, where the identity
of the author is unknown, copyrighted works subsist for 50 years from the date
of publication in the case of a published work, and for 75 years of the making of
the work in the case of an unpublished work.[119]

*Strategy: If the duration of the licence is the term of the copyright, clarify the
applicable term. It may vary with the date of the creation of the work (as a result*

---

[115] Ronna Abramson and Elizabeth Wasserman, "Record Labels and Songwriter's Duet turns into a
One-on One", Law.com, May 18, 2001.

[116] Coats and Barkan, "Licensing Issues", p. 6.

[117] *Copyright Act* (Canada), s. 6 (rep. & sub. S.C. 1993, c. 44, s. 58); U.S. *Copyright Act*, 17
U.S.C. §302.

[118] European Communities Council Directive on the Legal Protection of Computer Programs, 14
May 1991, No. L 122l42. (Hereinafter "European Software Directive").

[119] *Copyright Act* (Canada), s. 6.1 (S.C. 1993, c. 44, s. 58). See also Art. 12, where it states:
> Whenever the term of protection of a work, other than a photographic work or a work of
> applied art is calculated on a basis other than the life of a natural person, such term
> shall be no less than 50 years from the end of the calendar year of authorized publica-
> tion, or, failing such authorized publication within 50 years from the making of the
> work, 50 years from the end of the calendar year of making.

of changes to the relevant Copyright Act), with the country where it was created and with the country where the restricted activity is undertaken.

4.14.1 Reversion of Assigned Rights

If an author assigns copyright, both Canada and the United States have rules relating to the reversion (*i.e.*, assignment back) of the copyright to the author. In Canada, the copyright will revert to the author's estate 25 years after the author's death.[120] In the United States, the reversion occurs 35 years after the transfer, at the option of the author.[121] Therefore, reversion is not automatic in the United States. "This right to terminate, intended to protect authors, cannot be waived by contract or other agreement. However, termination is not automatic; an author must assert his or her termination rights and comply with certain statutory requirements to regain copyright ownership".[122]

Strategy: Be cautious when dealing with the owner of a copyrighted work who has derived his or her rights as a result of an assignment because that owner, by assignment, could lose those rights as a result of a reversion.

REGISTRATION AND DISCLOSURE

4.15 Registration Not Necessary

In Canada, registration has never been required to obtain copyright protection. Registration of the work in Canada can be made by registering the title to the work. The work itself is not delivered for registration. The advantage of registering in Canada is that in the event of a legal dispute, there is a presumption of ownership of the work that must be rebutted by the other party.[123] In the United States, registration was required prior to March 1, 1989, and the registration notice had to comply with the format required by the then prevailing U.S. *Copyright Act*. Failure to register or to place the proper copyright notice resulted in a forfeiture of copyright protection. After March 1, 1989, registration is no longer required in the United States for copyright to exist, but it may be necessary to register before an action is brought to enforce copyright in court.[124] With a work that has been evolving for many years and has material parts that were copied from works publicly distributed before March 1, 1989 in the United States, out of prudence, keep registering the work and affixing the proper copyright notice to avoid loss of copyright for those works.

---

[120] *Copyright Act*, s. 14(1). This reversion does not occur with collective works.

[121] U.S. *Copyright Act*, 17 U.S.C. §203(a) (1988).

[122] NII, pp. 48-49.

[123] See "*A Guide to Copyrights*", published by the Canadian Intellectual Property Office, January 2000, for information on how to register a work in Canada.

[124] *Ibid.*, at 61, referring to 17 U.S.C. §41(a).

Strategy: Do not risk forfeiting copyright to works that were publicly distributed in the United States prior to March 1, 1989 by failing to place the requisite copyright notice.

4.15.1 Trade Secrecy Versus Registration of Copyright

Milgrim discusses the issue "whether use of a copyright notice might evidence publication denying trade secret confidentiality, and uncertainty whether widespread commercial exploitation of copyrighted software might be deemed 'publication' despite confidentiality restrictions imposed by licensing terms".[125] Since he concludes that this issue is "arguably still unsettled", he recommends "use of a form of notice which preserves both trade secret confidentiality and copyright".[126]

4.15.2 Place a Copyright Notice Anyway

It may be prudent practice to place a copyright notice on works even though there is no statutory requirement. In Canada, this registration gives the benefit of the presumption of ownership and notice to others that there is a copyright. In the United States, timely registration may entitle the copyright holder to gain statutory damages and legal fees; if a copyright notice is used, generally it must consist of three elements:

- © or the word "Copyright" or the abbreviation "Copr." (in the case of sound recordings embodied in phonorecords, ℗);
- the year of first publication of the work; and
- the name of the owner of copyright in the work.[127]

Strategy: The giving of notice may be very relevant depending on where you may seek protection. Consider: © [Date] [Name of Copyright Owner], All Rights Reserved" to obtain maximum international protection; but a prudent licensor will verify the local and current requirements.

EFFECT ON INDEPENDENT DEVELOPMENT

4.16 Copyright Does Not Give Coverage Offered by a Patent

Generally copyright does not prevent independent development of a copyrighted work.

---

[125] R.M. Milgrim, *Milgrim On Licensing*, rev. ed. (New York: Matthew Bender, 1995), §5.51, pp. 5-175 (hereinafter "*Milgrim, On Licensing*").

[126] *Ibid.*

[127] 17 U.S.C. §401(b) and 402(b) (1988).

[B]asic copyright norms recognized by all developed legal systems protect only an author's original expression, not his ideas, and independent creation constitutes a perfect defence to any charge of copying. These limitations promote competition by a built-in process of "reverse engineering" that permits third parties to freely use the facts and ideas underlying clusters of related expression.[128]

Anyone who legitimately discovers the underlying ideas of one computer program can create another that implements those ideas in a different manner. Thus, copyright protection generally is much weaker than patent protection.

Strategy: For works that can be formatted for electronic transmission, consider placing a copyright notice and specifying what uses (e.g., copying and modification) are permitted. Perhaps place a notice that discloses the address where copyright consent may be obtained.

FAIR DEALING/USE

4.17 Introduction

Both the Canadian and U.S. Copyright Acts list activities that do not constitute an infringement of copyright; in Canada, these are referred to as "fair dealings" and in the United States as "fair uses". The most significant and, perhaps, murky of the limitations on a copyright owner's exclusive rights is the doctrine of fair use. Fair use [dealing] is an affirmative defence to an action for copyright infringement. It is potentially available with respect to all manners of unauthorized use of all types of works in all media. When it exists, the user is not required to seek permission from the copyright owner or to pay a licence fee for the use.[129]

4.17.1 Canadian Fair Dealing

The Canadian rules specify limited acts that fit within the "fair dealing" exception.[130] This list appears to be finite and is not given as examples of fair dealing. To fit within the Canadian exception from copyright infringement, the dealing must be both fair and fit within the specifically stated activities. The *Copyright Act* provides that fair dealing for the purpose of:

---

[128] Jerome H. Reichman, "Intellectual Property In International Trade and the GATT", in M. Goudreau, G. Bisson, N. Lacasse and L. Perret., eds., *Exporting our Technology: International Protection and Transfers of Industrial Innovations* (Montreal: Wilson & Lafleur, 1995), p. 3, at 49.

[129] NII, p. 73.

[130] *Copyright Act* (Canada), s. 29, s. 29.1 and s. 29.2 (am. R.S.C. 1985, c. I (3rd Supp.), s. 13; R.S.C. 1985, c. 10 (4th Supp.), s. 5; S.C. 1993, c. 44, s. 64 (1) and (2)).

(a) research and private study;
(b) criticism or review; or
(c) news reporting;

does not infringe copyright. In respect of the latter two categories appropriate credit must be given to the author and the source.[131]

4.17.2 American Fair Use

The American rules are different; the items listed for "fair use" are only examples of acts that are thought to be appropriate for consideration. The main difference between the two lists is the American exemption for "teaching (including multiple copies for classroom use), scholarship or research",[132] whereas the main Canadian exemptions cover only "private study or research".[133]

The Napster case indicates that "sampling" is not fair use.[134] Also, the Napster usage was not merely time or space – shifting of copyrighted material that could be considered as fair use. "Fair use, when properly applied, is limited to copying by others which does not materially impair the marketability of the work which is copied".[135] The U.S. legislation, *Digital Millennium Copyright Act* ("DMCA") may increase the tension between copyright protection and fair use. "Fair use balances the exclusive rights of copyright laws with the public interest in the documentation of copyrighted information".[136]

This DMCA Act is designed to provide, "adequate legal protection and effective legal remedies" against the circumvention of technological measures designed to protect copyrighted works from infringement. In the *Reimerde*s and *Napster* cases, the courts were trying to deal with significant technological changes, some of which enable legitimate, some of which enable nonlegitimate uses of copyrighted material. The cases become even more complex with introduction of "imperfect technology" that cannot discriminate between legitimate and non-legitimate uses of copyrighted material".[137]

---

[131] *A Guide to Copyrights*, a Canadian Intellectual Property Office Publication, January, 2000.

[132] U.S. *Copyright Act*, 17 U.S.C. §107.

[133] *Copyright Act* (Canada), s. 29, 29.1 and 29.2 (am. R.S.C. 1985, c. I (3rd Supp.), s. 13; R.S.C. 1985, c. 10 (4th Supp.), s. 5; S.C. 1993, c. 44, s. 64(1) and (2)).

[134] *Napster,* ¶18

[135] *Napster,* ¶15, 16.

[136] *Harvard Law Review*, vol. 114, 1390 at 1394 (HLR Recent cases).

[137] See *Harvard Law Review*, Recent cases at 1397.

4.18 What is Fair

The U.S. *Copyright Act* gives some guidance that may be helpful in determining what is fair. The Canadian Act has no equivalent provisions,[138] but the U.S. rules may be of persuasive value. Section 107 provides:

> In determining whether the use made of a work in any particular case is a fair use, the factors to be considered shall include
>
> (1) the purpose and character of the use, including whether such use is of a commercial nature or is for non profit educational purposes;
>
> (2) the nature of the copyrighted work;
>
> (3) the amount and substantiality of the portion used in relation to the copyright work as a whole; and
>
> (4) the effect of the use upon the potential market for or value of the copyrighted work.[139]

Strategy: Before copying a work without permission of the author, review the fair dealing/use exceptions to the enforcement of copyright protection to determine if the copying is permissible.

The Napster case developed what is a commercial use: making a direct economical benefit was not necessary for "commercial use".[140] Here the Napster activities denied others of an economic benefit. The Napster system enabled others (through "repeated and exploitative copying of unauthorized uses of copyrighted works")[141] to "save the expense of purchasing authorized copies" of the downloaded music.[142] Also access to the infringed material acted as a draw to the Napster site and therefore Napster did engage in the commercial use.[143] *Napster* also suggests that, "under certain circumstances, a court will conclude that a use is fair even when the protected work is copied in its entirety.[144]

---

[138] Sheldon Burshtein in "Surfing the Internet: Canadian Intellectual Property Issues", presented at the 1996 McGill University Meredith Lectures, May 1996, writes at §3.2.9:

> Whether activity in respect of a work is 'fair' is left to judicial interpretation upon the facts of each case. The courts have determined that the factors which are relevant in determining the fairness of the dealings include (1) the length of the excerpts which have been appropriated from the works; (2) the relative importance of the excerpts in relation to the critic's or journalist's own comments; (3) the use made of the work; and (4) the nature of the use, be it criticism, review or summary ...even though the criteria as to what constitutes fairness set out in the United States legislation are appealing, it is only with great caution that they may be considered to determine whether an activity constitutes fair dealing in Canada.

[139] NII, pp. 74-75.
[140] *Napster*, ¶11.
[141] *Napster*, ¶11.
[142] *Napster*, ¶11.
[143] *Napster*, ¶27.
[144] *Napster*, ¶13, 14.

Strategy: In a technology licence of a copyrighted work, consider contractual prohibitions on activities that otherwise would be permitted as fair dealing/use after determining whether these prohibitions would violate public policy or be unlawful restraints of trade.[145]

SPECIAL FAIR DEALING/USE RULES FOR COMPUTER PROGRAMS

4.19 Fair Dealing/Use for Software

Because computer programs were not placed in a separate category for copyright purposes, the traditional exception of an infringement for "fair dealing" or "fair use" applies (*i.e.*, any fair dealings with, or fair use of, any work is a defence to infringement).[146] In addition, the revised *Copyright Act* (Canada) provides that the following do not constitute an infringement of copyright of a computer program (note that the word "person" refers to individuals, businesses, universities, governments and other entities):[147]

    (a) A person who owns a copy of a program may make a "single reproduction for backup purposes... if the person proves that the reproduction... is destroyed immediately when the person ceases to be the owner of the computer program" [emphasis added].[148]

---

[145] See NII, p. 49, which says

    Limitations on the exclusive rights, such as the first sale doctrine, fair use, or library exemptions, may be overridden by contract. However, such contract terms can be enforced only under state law. ...Licenses and other contracts cannot transform noninfringing uses (such as fair uses) into infringement; they can, however, make such uses violations of the terms and conditions of the agreements.

[146] For a further discussion of what is fair and what dealing/uses are listed, see §4.6 and following in this Chapter.

[147] *Interpretation Act*, R.S.C. 1985, c. 1-21, s. 35.

[148] *Copyright Act* (Canada), s. 27(2)(m) (en. R.S.C. 1985, c. 10 (4th Supp.), s. 5). In comparison, the U.S. *Copyright Act*, §117, provides:

    Notwithstanding the provisions of section 106, it is not an infringement for the owner of a copy of a computer program to make or authorize the making of another copy or adaptation of that computer program provided:

        (1) that such a new copy or adaptation is created as an essential step in the utilization of the computer program in conjunction with a machine and that it is used in no other manner, or

        (2) that such new copy or adaptation is for archival purposes only and that all archival copies are destroyed in the event that continued possession of the computer program should cease to be rightful.

Note that this section refers to "archival copies" whereas the Canadian counterpart of this section refers to a "single reproduction for backup purposes". Licensees of software should be aware of the significant difference between the Canadian and American rules.

(b) A person who owns a copy of a computer program, which copy is authorized by the owner of the copyright, may make a single reproduction of the copy, by adapting, modifying or converting the computer program, or translating it into another computer language if the person proves all of the following three things: "(i) the reproduction is essential for the compatibility of the computer program with a particular computer,[149] (ii) the reproduction is solely for the person's own use, and (iii) the reproduction is destroyed immediately when the person ceases to be the owner of the copy of the computer program" [Emphasis added]. [150]

4.19.1 Fair Dealing or Express Permission

Any copying that is not within these fair dealing (use defences) or is not authorized by the licence granted at the time of acquisition of the copy of the program will result in an infringement of copyright. At present, it is not clear whether in the United States or Canada a licence can take away any fair dealing/use. [151]

4.19.2 What Legitimate Needs for Copying and Modifying Were Not Included

There are many legitimate reasons for copying programs that should be ex-cepted from the general rules against copying: not all of these reasons were cov-ered by the fair dealing software-related amendments to the Canadian Act. A software user normally would like to be able to:

(a) make more than one back-up copy of the program for internal use to overcome the risk of inadvertent damage or destruction;
(b) alter the program to tie into the user's own program and use the derivative work for the user's own internal purposes;
(c) make other copies or modifications to the program (such as may be necessary for normal support), so long as they are solely for the user's internal use.

4.19.3 Only Owners Receive the Benefit of the Right to Copy Computer Programs

It should be noted that under the Canadian and U.S. rules only an owner is given the benefit of the fair dealing defences.[152] Thus, anyone who is not an owner (for

---

[149] Note: there is no equivalent provision for compatibility with a particular program.

[150] *Copyright Act* (Canada), s. 30.6 (en. R.S.C. 1985, c. 10 (4th Supp.), s. 5).

[151] For example, see *ProCD Inc. v. Zeidenberg*, 908 F.Supp. 640 (D. Wis. 1996), summarized in The Computer Law Association Bulletin (1996), Vol. 11, No. 2, p. 28.

[152] In contrast, the European Software Directive gives similar rights to a "lawful acquirer".

example, a person who has borrowed a copy or who is a true licensee of a copy) may not have the benefit of these fair dealing defences that specifically relate to software. The first draft of the Canadian Bill provided that the person had only to be in "lawful and actual possession" of the copy: that would have covered a "licensee". The requirement that the person be an owner may restrict the ability of many legitimately licensed-users to satisfy essential copying needs.

Strategies:

(1)   *Keep in mind that these statutory rights may be extended by a valid licence or another agreement between the owner of the copyright and the user. The licence may give more rights than the Copyright Act (Canada) would otherwise give, and users should strive to get permission for a number of archival copies reasonably appropriate for their specific purposes.*

(2)   *Anyone who has the opportunity to negotiate the terms of the software licence should request that the licence permit the number of copies and the type of modifications required. It is hoped that Canadian consumers of mass-marketed programs will demand that the tear-me-open licences provide additional rights to make back-up copies.*

4.19.4 Restricting Back-up Copying

A licensor may want to be cautious about restricting the fair dealing/use right to make a back-up copy, particularly with licences within the European community. Article 5.2 of the European Software Directive provides "the making of a back-up copy by a person having a right to use the computer may not be prevented by contract insofar as it is necessary for that use".

4.19.5 Reverse Engineering for Interoperability

Because, under the Canadian and U.S. rules, an owner may modify a computer program to make it interoperable with his or her computer, it would seem to be a necessary conclusion that he or she is authorized to reverse engineer the machine code into human readable code if that is necessary to determine how to make the modification. The reverse engineering for computer compatibility may be defensible as fair dealing/use only if there is no other way of making the necessary modification (*i.e.*, the reproduction is "essential" for this purpose).

4.19.6 Reverse Engineering Methods

"Reverse engineering" can be done in several ways. It can involve looking at the software while it is operating to determine its functional and performance specifications. Some technology can be taken apart to see its components. Reverse engineering can involve decompiling or disassembling software to determine how the software functions. Decompiling involves regenerating the form of code used just before it was converted into electronic form. Disassembling involves the translation of this low-level code into a high-level human readable form. With complex programs, however, the revelation of the source code in this fashion may be of little value without the author's annotations explaining what he or she did.

4.19.7 Reverse Engineering As Fair Dealing

Whether reverse engineering is permissible for the development of competing programs has been a subject of several U.S. cases, including *Atari Games Corp. v. Nintendo of America Inc.*,[153] and *Sega Enterprises Ltd. v. Accolade Inc.*,[154] both of which are the subject-matter of an excellent and succinct article by Philip J. McCabe.[155] In each of these cases intermediate copying of the subject program occurred. In *Sega* it was ruled, as was expected, that this intermediate copying would be an infringement. But, to the surprise of many, it was also ruled that this intermediate copying (obtained through some form of reverse engineering) was a "fair use" and therefore is permissible so long as the intermediate copying:

(a) is only for the purpose of discovering the underlying ideas and the development of the program's functional specifications, and

(b) these functional specifications are relayed to a "clean room" of developers who independently find methods of expressing (*i.e.*, developing) a new program that meets these functional specifications.

4.19.8 Reverse Engineering is Rarely Legitimately Needed

In a very useful article by Casey P. August and Derek K. W. Smith,[156] the authors suggest that reverse engineering is rarely needed to discover the functional specifications of a computer program. It is their position that:

> [f]unctional ideas expressed in a successful computer program are usually revealed through the information published by its developer or through the normal use of the program in a computer....The source code version produced by reverse compilation is useful primarily for pirates and other so-called "competitors" who do little original software authoring and who do not wish to compete on an equal development cost footing with the originator.[157]

---

[153] 975 F .2d 832 (Cir. 1992).

[154] 977 F.2d 1510 (Cir. 1992).

[155] "Reverse Engineering of Computer Software: A Trap For The Unwary?", in the Computer Law Association Bulletin (1994), Vol. 9, No. 2, p. 4 (hereinafter called "McCabe, 'Reverse Engineering'").

[156] "Software Expression (SSO), Interfaces, and Reverse Assembly", in Canadian Intellectual Property Review, (1994) Vol. 10, No. 3, p. 679 (hereinafter called "August and Smith 'Software Expression'").

[157] *Ibid.*, at 690. The August and Smith article attempts to "explain in simple terms some of the relevant concepts of a computer program, their ideas and expression, their sequence, structure

Strategy: Because, under the appropriate circumstances, fair dealings/use might be restricted by contract, consider placing a prohibition against a licensee taking any steps intended to reveal the source code of software, e.g., reverse engineering.

4.19.9 Reverse Engineering for Interoperability in Europe

Reverse engineering to make modifications for interoperability with another computer program is not explicitly covered by the Canadian and U.S. *Copyright Acts*. The European Software Directive encourages some forms of reverse engineering, where reproduction of a program's code and translation of its form are indispensable to obtain the information necessary to achieve the interoperability of an independently created computer program with other programs[158] provided that certain conditions are met and that the information retrieved is not also used for other purposes.

Strategies:
(a)   *Licences of software granted to European customers must take into account the fair dealing/use rules of the European Software Directive.*
(b)   *Consider making available some means for other developers in Europe to design their software to interoperate with yours to overcome reverse engineering authorized by the European Software Directive.*

4.19.10 Error Correction in Europe

In addition to encouraging interoperability, the European Software Directive permits the correction of errors in a copy of a program that has been lawfully acquired; this includes reproduction, adaptation and other alterations necessary to correct errors.[159] Perhaps the *Atari* and *Sega* cases indicate a movement of the U.S. judiciary to adopt the policy evidenced in the European Software Directive.[160]

Strategy: Since the European Software Directive does not give the right to the "lawful acquirer" to make improvements beyond error correction and measures necessary to achieve interoperability, a licence of software within the European Community should prohibit any use of the information disclosed in

---

and organization (SSO) software 'interfaces', and reverse assembly or reverse compilation (sometimes misnamed as 'reverse engineering')". It is a useful addition to our computer law literature.

[158] European Software Directive, Art. 6.

[159] Article 5.1 and the Recitals to the Directive.

[160] For a helpful article on this point see Timothy S. Teter, "Merger and the Machines: An Analysis of the Pro-compatibility Trend in Computer Software Copyright", in Stan. L. Rev. (1993), Vol. 45, p. 1061.

the process of correcting errors or achieving interoperability for any other purpose.[161]

EMPLOYEE-CREATED OWNERSHIP AND JOINT WORKS OWNERSHIP

4.20 Examine Local Work-for-Hire Rules

The Canadian and U.S. "work-for-hire" rules are not entirely the same; the scope of "employee" under the U.S. rules may be broader than the Canadian rules. The Canadian rules may be more representative of the international position. Parties contracting for creation of works that will be protected by copyright will be well advised to examine the applicable local laws.

4.20.1 Canadian Rules

The Canadian rule is contained in the *Copyright Act* (Canada), and components of the rule can be broken down as follows:

(a) where the author of a work
(b) was employed by some other person
(c) under a contract of service or apprenticeship
(d) and the work was made in the course of his or her employment
(e) the employer shall be the first owner of the copyright
(f) in the absence of an agreement to the contrary.[162]

4.20.2 U.S. Rules

In contrast to Canada, in the United States the scope of the relationship between the person paying for the work and the actual developer is broadly defined as more than just an "employee". The U.S. rule states that the author is "the employer or other person for whom the work was prepared".[163]

---

[161] Even if the current available technology does not now concern a licensor about the possibility of trade secrets being revealed by permitted reverse engineering, the licensor should anticipate such technology becoming available.

[162] *Copyright Act* (Canada) s. 13(3).

[163] 17 U .S.C. §201. See §4.21.2 of this text and following for a further discussion of work done in the course of employment.

4.21 Employee Versus Contractor

A person under a "contract of service" is an employee under Canadian labour law rules.[164] A useful standard in Canada for determining employment is whether deductions were made at source for income tax purposes. The economic trend of the last decade is to avoid the cost of employee benefits and to avoid making deductions at source for tax purposes, which can be achieved by hiring individuals as independent contractors ("contracts for service"). This practice may have the unexpected result of depriving copyright from the party paying for the development of a work and leaving it with the individual who created the work. It will be difficult for the commissioning party to argue that, for copyright purposes, the individual was an employee if the employer had not deducted income tax at source and had treated the creator as an independent contractor.

4.21.1 Created in Course of Employment

The issue of whether a work was created in the course of employment can be distilled to "was the work created as an integral part of the working of the enterprise, or did the author create it on his own account?"[165] One factor to consider is the control the employer had over the author, but control is not the determining factor. The more skilled the individual, the less control necessary.[166]

4.21.2 Work Done in Course of Employment — Canada

Barry Sookman, in his text, lists some other factors to consider when determining for Canadian purposes whether a computer program was created in the "course of employment" and, thus, whether the copyright is owned by the employer or employee/contractor:

(a) whether the program source code was retained by the programmer;
(b) whether the customer ever asked for or demanded it;
(c) the nature of the fees charged to the customer;
(d) the relationship of the fees to the program's development cost; and
(e) whether full documentation relating to the program was provided to the person commissioning the program.[167]

---

[164] *C.P. Koch Ltd. v. Continental Steel Ltd.* (1984), 82 C.P.R. (2d) 156 at 163-64 (B.C.S.C.).

[165] *Beloff v. Pressdam Ltd.*, [1973] 1 All E.R. 241, at 250, [1973] R.P.C. 765 (Ch. D.).

[166] *Amusements Wiltron Inc. v. Mainville*, [1991] R.J.Q. 1930 (*sub nom. Amusements Wiltron Inc. v. Mainville*), unofficially translated in 40 C.P.R. (3d) 521 (C.S.).

[167] Barry B. Sookman, *Computer Law: Acquiring and protecting information technology* (Toronto: Carswell, 1989), pp. 3-34 (hereinafter "Sookman, *Computer Law*").

4.21.3 Work Done in Course of Employment — United States

The U.S. Supreme Court in *Community for Creative Non-Violence v. Reid*,[168] identified certain factors (not a conclusive nor a complete list) to consider whether an employment relationship exists. The second circuit court in *Aymes v. Bonelli*[169] emphasized these factors:

(1) the hiring party's right to control the manner and means of creation;
(2) the skill required;
(3) the provision of employee benefits;
(4) the tax treatment of the hiring party; and
(5) whether the hiring party has the right to assign additional projects to the hired party.[170]

Subsequently, the U.S. Supreme Court has said it will apply a uniform test for determining whether an individual is an "employee" regardless of the purpose for making the determination (*e.g.*, copyright, employee benefits, Social Security tax withholding). Accordingly, in the United States additional precedents may be drawn from federal case law outside the copyright area to determine ownership under the "work-for-hire" doctrine.[171] Meadows writes:

> Facts which would support the commissioning party's claim that the consultant was its "employee" based upon payments by the commissioning party to the consultant, would include:
>
> (a) the payment of a regular periodic (e.g., hourly, daily) "salary" to the consultants;
>
> (b) a structured payment schedule (e.g., bi-weekly, monthly);
>
> (c) the provision of the employee benefits which are available to the commissioning party's regular employees, to the consultant or in the case of a consulting company, to the consultant's employees;
>
> (d) the payment by the commissioning party of applicable payroll and social security taxes (or a legal obligation for the payment thereof) on behalf of the consultant or the consultant's employees; and
>
> (e) the provision of workers' compensation coverage and contributions to unemployment insurance or workers' compensation funds on behalf of the consultant and the consultant's employees.

---

[168] 490 U.S. 730, 109 S. Ct. 2166 (1989).

[169] 980 F .2d 857, at 862 (2nd Cir. 1992).

[170] American Bar Association, Section on Intellectual Property Law, Chicago, Illinois, Annual Report, 94195, p. 291.

[171] James E. Meadows, "Ownership Issues Presented in Independent Consultant Engagements: Applying the 'Work for Hire' Doctrine to Computer Programmers", in The Computer Law Association Bulletin (1992), Vol. 7, No. 2, p. 24, at 26 (hereinafter "Meadows 'Ownership Issues").

Payment by the project or based upon milestones, and without any form of with-holding or payment of employment taxes and related charges (or legal obligation therefore), would weigh against the commissioning party's "'payment' argument."[172] [*i.e.*, since it paid, it should own.]

The U.S. courts may be applying the "integral part of the business" test used in the Canadian/English cases.

4.22 Retention of Copyright by Employee

Although the author is an employee, she or he still may own copyright to a work created on her or his own time, without orders from the employer, if the work is entirely unrelated to employment duties.[173] If an employee creates a software program entirely on the employee's own time, but the work created is function-ally similar to the employer's program, even if the employee can establish own-ership of the copyright under s. 13(3), the employee may be holding that copy-right under a constructive trust for the employer as a result of a breach of fiduci-ary duty to the employer.[174] This illustrates the need to look at all areas of the law[175] rather than narrowly focusing on one area, such as the *Copyright Act*.

4.23 Retention of Copyright by Independent Contractor

If the author of the work is an independent contractor, the author will own copy-right and may assign copyright only by written agreement.[176] The commission-ing party will not be able to prosecute infringers of "its" software unless it has a written assignment.[177]

---

[172] *Ibid.*, p. 28.

[173] *École de conduite tecnic Aubé Inc. v. 1509 8858 Québec Inc.* (1986), 12 C.I.P.R. 284, at 295 (Que. S.C.).

[174] Sookman, *Computer Law*, pp. 3-31 referring to *Missing Link Software v. Magee*, [1989] I F.S.R. 36 (Ch. D.). Sookman also refers to a U.S. case on this point, *In re Simplified Systems*, Copyright L.R. (CCH) 26, 255 (Bankr. W .D. Pa 1988). See U.S. case *Avtec Systems, Inc. v. Peiffer*, 21 F.3d 568 (4th Cir. 1994), where the employee who was hired to write computer pro-grams developed a program entirely on his own time and on his own initiative. Although the plaintiff had argued constructive trust as well as copyright ownership, the plaintiff was unsuc-cessful on both accounts. The commentary does not make it clear why the breach of fiduciary duty argument was not successful nor does the commentary make it clear whether the program was functionally similar to a program marketed by the plaintiff. However, an earlier reference in the Software Law Bulletin in April, 1994, Vol. 7, No. 4, pointed out that the employee had started the development of the program before he started his employment and no trade secrets were in violation. This commentary notes that the plaintiff had not demanded the source codes until after it had fired the defendant.

[175] Such as breach of trade secret, breach of contract or unfair trade practices.

[176] *Copyright Act* (Canada), s. 13(4). U.S. Copyright Act, U.S.C. §201(b).

[177] *Frank Brunckhorst Co. v. Gainers Inc.* (1993), 47 C.P.R. (3d) 222 (Fed. T.D.).

4.23.1 Rights Not Covered

The work-for-hire rule does not cover "moral rights" nor the reservation to the author of an article, a contribution to a newspaper, a magazine or a similar periodical, of the right to restrain publication of the work otherwise than as part of a newspaper, a magazine or a similar periodical.[178]

4.23.2 Need for Written Agreement

No written agreement is necessary for employees' work to belong to the employer;[179] ownership of copyright to works created by an employee in the course of business automatically belongs to the employer. For an independent contractor, a written agreement or acknowledgment is necessary.[180]

4.23.3 Equitable Rights in Future Works

For a work that is yet to be developed at the time the assignment agreement is executed, there is a concern that the assignment needs to be perfected from an equitable interest to a legal interest. Section 13(4) of the Canadian *Copyright Act* refers to the owner of a work assigning rights and, thus, the question is raised whether these rights can be effectively assigned before the work, and therefore the right, is created. There is very little case law on this point but the case, *Canadian Performing Rights Society v. Famous Players Canadian Corp. Ltd.*,[181] indicates that an assignment executed prior to the creation of the work creates an equitable interest that will be recognized by the courts. Section 36 of the Canadian *Copyright Act* provides that "any person...deriving any right, title or interest by assignment or grant in writing...may...in his own name...enforce such rights as he may hold ...". In *Performing Rights Society*, the court recognizes the rights of the equitable assignee to enforce the copyright in its own name, ruling that the words "assignment" and "assignee" should be given the "fuller meaning", to include both legal and equitable assignees.[182]

4.23.4 Loss of Equitable Rights

Even though the equitable assignee's rights may be recognized if the *Performing Rights Society* case properly states the law, the equitable assignee can lose those rights under s. 57(3) of the *Copyright Act*, which provides:

---

[178] See the discussion in §4.13 and following, relating to Moral Rights.
[179] *Copyright Act* (Canada) s. 13(3). U.S. *Copyright Act*, 17 U.S.C. §204(a).
[180] *Copyright Act* (Canada), s. 13(4) and Normand Tamaro, *The Annotated Copyright Act* (Scarborough, Ont.: Carswell, 1995) (hereinafter "Tamaro, *Annotated Copyright Act*"), p. 238, citing *Canavest House Ltd. v. Lett* (1984), 2 C.P.R. (3d) 386, 4 C.I.P.R. 103 (Ont. H.C.J.).
[181] [1929] A.C. 456, 98 L.J.P.C. 70.
[182] *Ibid.*, at 550 (A.C.).

Any grant of an interest in a copyright, either by assignment or licence, shall be adjudged void against any subsequent assignee or licensee for valuable consideration without actual notice, unless the prior assignment or licence is registered in the manner prescribed by this Act before the registering of the instrument under which the subsequent assignee or licensee claims.

In the United States, when dealing with priority disputes between transfers, the transfer first executed is granted priority, only if it is registered one month from execution or at least before the subsequent transfer.[183] Any equitable interest not perfected by registration can thus be defeated by the registration of a *bona fide* assignment. In the United States, however, a non-exclusive licence will not be defeated by a subsequent transfer where the non-exclusive licensee did not know of the transfer and the licence is in writing, signed by the copyright owner.[184]

4.23.5 Constructive Trust

Even if the copyright is owned by the individual, as a result of a fiduciary duty (if one can be established), the individual may be characterized as holding the copyright subject to a constructive trust in favour of the employer. An agreement for the creation of a copyrighted work could require the contractor to hold copyright, once created, in trust for the employer until the assignment is perfected, to make sure that the principles of the *Performing Rights Society* case are implemented.

4.24 Exit Interviews

As a practical matter, on completion of a program (or each module of a program), the contractor should be required to formally (*i.e.*, in writing) confirm the assignment of the copyright. Additionally, as part of an "exit" interview with the contractor (*i.e.*, on termination of the contract), all copyright should be assigned for any work in which the contractor participated.

4.25 Corporate Contractor

If the contractor is a company, then each individual whose services are being supplied as subcontractors of the corporate contractor should assign, and agree to assign, copyright.

---

[183] U.S. *Copyright Act*, 17 U.S.C. §205(e).
[184] *Ibid.*, 17 U.S.C. §205(c).

4.26 Implied Right to Use

Even if the harsh result is that the contractor does own the copyright, the person paying for the work may still have an implied right to use and to modify the work,[185] although this is not likely to prohibit the contractor from directly or indirectly competing with the person who paid for the work.

Strategies:

  (1)   *Although no written agreement is necessary for the employee's works to belong to the employer, a written agreement is necessary for independent contractors.*

  (2)   *For a work that is yet to be developed at the time the assignment agreement is executed, there is a concern that the assignment needs to be perfected from an equitable interest to a legal interest. Section 13(4) and §201 refer to the "owner", of a work assigning rights, thus, the question is raised whether these rights can be effectively assigned before the work (and therefore the right) is created.*

  (3)   *As a practical matter, on completion of a program (or each module of a program), the contractor should be required to formally (i.e., in writing) confirm the assignment of the copyright. Additionally, as part of an "exit" interview with the contractor (i.e., on termination of the contract), all copyright should be assigned for any work in which the contractor participated.*

  (4)   *If the contractor is a company then each individual whose services are being supplied should assign, and agree to assign, copyright.*

  (5)   *An agreement for the creation of a copyrighted work could require the contractor to hold copyright, once created, in trust for the employer until the assignment is perfected by a written registered assignment.*

  (6)   *The contractor should be required to acknowledge:*

   1.   *the copyright thereto shall belong to the employer when the contractor participates alone or with one or more other individuals in the creation of any computer program, data, documentation or any other written work, whether recorded in human or computer readable form; and*

   2.   *the contractor shall execute written assignments of copyright to the works on the request of the employer and do all other acts to enforce copyright as the employer may reasonably request, in each case undertaken or prepared at the expense of the employer.*

  (7)   *Due Diligence: Review the business practices of the transferor of technology to verify that it owns all of the intellectual property rights to that technology. Consider the following:*

---

[185] H. Ward Classen, Marc R. Paul and Gary D. Sprague, "Increasing Corporate Competitiveness By Utilizing Independent Contractors", in The Computer Law Association Bulletin (1996), Vol. 11, No. 1, p. 3, at 6, quoting *Aymes v. Bonnelli*, 47 F. 3d 23 (2nd Cir. 1995).

1. Are employees/consultants required to sign secrecy, non-solicitation and assignment of innovation agreements?
   (a) Is there consideration for these promises?
   (b) Are employees required to disclose innovations in a timely
       fashion?
2. How is disclosure to be made?
3. Do employees turn over to the employer regular details of research and development performed so these are not lost on termination of employment or death;
4. Is sensitive material placed in safekeeping such as an escrow
   house, to avoid employee espionage?
5. Are proper procedures set up to protect third party secrets as
   well as company secrets?
6. Is there a policy to control publications to avoid loss of an opportunity to patent by a premature publication?
7. Are the employees aware of the need to register patents, copyrights or trade-marks?[186]

JOINT COPYRIGHTED WORKS

4.27 Joint Ownership

If an independent contractor retains copyright pursuant to the Canadian or U.S.
Copyright Acts[187] there will be a risk of joint ownership if the work can be considered to be a joint work. The U.S. Act defines a joint work as a work "prepared by two or more authors with the intention that their contributions be
merged into inseparable or interdependent parts of a unitary whole".[188] The Canadian equivalent is the definition of "work of joint authorship", defined by s. 2
to mean a "work produced by the collaboration of two or more authors in which
the contribution of one author is not distinct from the contribution of the other
author or authors".

4.28 Equality Not Necessary

The contribution of the parties need not be equal either in quality or quantity,[189]
but there must be "joint labour in carrying out a common design".[190]

---

[186] Some of these items are adapted from an article "Clear Policy Can Forestall Data Piracy", in
   The Globe & Mail, January 17, 1995.
[187] *Copyright Act* (Canada), s. 13 (3); U.S. *Copyright Act*, 17 U.S.C. §101.
[188] Meadows, "Ownership Issues", p. 29, citing 17 U.S.C. §101.
[189] Tamaro, *Annotated Copyright Act*, p. 117.
[190] *Ibid.*, p. 115.

RESULT OF JOINT OWNERSHIP: CANADA VERSUS THE UNITED STATES

4.29 Forget Versus Specialty Tools

The result of joint ownership is very different in Canada from the result in the United States. The Canadian position is set out in *Forget v. Specialty Tools of Canada*.[191] Although the case relates to patent law, it also applies to copyright law since it is judge-made law rather than law required by statute and the relevant principles of the *Patent Act* and the *Copyright Act* are the same. In Canada, the points of the *Forget* case may be summarized as follows:

(1) a co-owner may assign the whole of his or her interest without the concurrence of any other co-owner;[192]
(2) a co-owner may not assign a partial interest without the concurrence of all other co-owners;[193]
(3) a co-owner may not license the work protected without the concurrence of all other co-owners.[194]

The *Forget* case acknowledges that the Canadian rule differs from the U.S. position. In the United States "joint authors own an individual interest in the whole of the work, and may independently use or license the work, subject to a duty to account for profits to the co-owner".[195]

4.29.1 Rule Is Not Always Appropriate

Neither the U.S. nor the Canadian rule of joint ownership is generally appropriate; each in its own way can produce a result totally unexpected by the parties before they seek legal advice (which, unfortunately, all too often is sought after the work has been created and the parties are adverse).

4.29.2 Contributory Infringement

The Court of Appeal in Napster reviews contributory infringement principles. First, the Court of Appeal sets out the general principles of contributory infringement: "Traditionally, one who, with the knowledge of the infringing activity, induces, causes, or materially contributes to the infringing conduct of

---

[191] (1993), 48 C.P.R. (3d) 323, 10 B.L.R. (2d) 62 (B.C.S.C.); affd. (1995), 62 C.P.R. (3d) 537 (B.C.C.A.).
[192] *Ibid.*, at 330 (48 C.P.R.).
[193] *Ibid.*
[194] *Ibid.*
[195] Meadows, "Ownership Issues", p. 29, citing *Oddo v. Ries*, 743 F.2d 630, at 633 (9th Cir. 1984).

another, may be held liable as a 'contributory' copyright infringer".[196] The Appeal Court held that "Napster had both actual and constructive knowledge that its users exchanged copyrighted music".[197] Therefore, it was liable for contributory infringement. The principles may have broader implications. The Court of Appeal states: "We agree that if a computer system operator learns of specific infringing material available on his system and fails to purge such material from the system, the operator knows of and contributes to direct infringement. … Conversely, absent any specific information which identifies infringing activity, a computer system operator cannot be liable for contributory infringement merely because the structure of the system allows for the exchange of copyrighted material".[198]

4.29.3 Allocate Risk of Infringement

Because it is so difficult to ascertain the ownership of all the aspects of copyright to a work, the allocation of risk for an infringement should be addressed in each licensing agreement.

Strategies:
   (1)   *In most licences, the licensor should be required to warrant that it "does in fact have a valid copyright and [that] the licensee is not simply buying an infringement lawsuit".[199]*
   (2)   *It may be appropriate to set "up some form of shared risk, in which liability costs are apportioned between licensor and licensee", or to involve an insurance company.*

"In the early years of [multimedia] licensing, insurance policies are likely to be too expensive, but over time a sufficient risk pool may develop and a sufficient track record of litigation may exist to justify the involvement of the insurance industry".[200]

---

[196] *A&M Records et al. v. Napster, Inc.* 239 F.3d 1004 (United States Court of Appeals, 9th Cir. 2001) ("Napster"; herein references will be to the paragraph numbers), ¶20.

[197] *Napster,* ¶21, 22.

[198] *Napster,* ¶24. The issue of the scope of liability off an internet service provider for contributory infringement was not resolved by this case and particularly the extent of relief offered by the *Digital Millennium Copyright Act* (4.5).

[199] Coats and Barkan, p. 19.

[200] *Ibid.*

Chapter 5

TRADEMARKS

The differing local trademark and unfair competition laws that conflict with federal laws, and that change from region to region, give rise to uncertainties that are unwelcome to businesses in increasingly global communities.[1]

CONSTITUTIONAL ISSUES

5.1 Introduction

"Trademarks" include words, logos, packaging and other methods of distinguishing one's goods and services from those of others. Both in Canada and the United States, appropriate trademarks are entitled to legal protection whether they are registered or not.

5.2 Origins of Trademark Law

The protection offered in Canada and the United States to trademarks, registered and unregistered, arises out of the common law prohibiting unfair competition.[2]

5.2.1 Dual Jurisdiction

Unlike patents, constitutional jurisdiction over trademarks was not reserved exclusively for the federal government in either Canada or the United States.[3] Thus,

---

[1] J.H. Reichman, "GATT, TRIPS and NAFTA, the TRIPS component of the GATT's Uruguay Round: Competitive Prospects for Intellectual Property Owners in an Integrated World Market", in M. Goudreau, G. Bisson, N. Lacasse and L. Perret, eds., *Exporting Our Technology: International Protection and Transfers of Industrial Innovations* (Montreal: Wilson & Lafleur, 1995), p. 40.

[2] For a fuller discussion on this topic, see Arthur H. Seidel, Steven J. Meyers and Nancy Rubner-Frandsen, *What the General Practitioner Should Know about Trademarks and Copyrights*, 6th ed. (Philadelphia: American Law Institute-American Bar Association Committee on Continuing Professional Education) (hereinafter "ALI/ABA *Trademarks*"); Also see Roger T. Hughes, S.J. Peacock, N. Armstrong and D. Smith, *Hughes on Trade Marks*, rev. ed. (Markham, Ont.: Butterworths, 1984), looseleaf (hereinafter (Hughes et al., *Hughes On Trade Marks*)) and John Drysdale and Michael Silverleaf, *Passing off Law and Practice*, 2nd ed. (London: Butterworths, 1995) (hereinafter "Drysdale and Silverleaf, *Passing Off*").

[3] See Hughes et al., *Hughes On Trade Marks*, §1, p. 311 and ALI/ABA *Trademarks*, p. 1.

there exists (1) a mixture of common-law rules relating to unfair competition generally, (2) provincial or state legislation relating to unfair competition with significant effect on trademarks, and (3) the federal legislation on trademarks which, on occasion, attempts to control unfair competition. This gives rise to constitutional conflicts about how much control the different levels of government (federal versus provincial/state) can exert over the areas of trademark and unfair competition.[4] Since the U.S. federal government cannot exert controls over intrastate commerce (*i.e.*, commerce that occurs only within one state), the U.S. trademark legislation passed by the U.S. federal government (including the U.S. *Trademark Act* — known as the *Lanham Act*) covers only interstate commerce, commerce with foreign nations, and commerce with Native Americans.[5] Likewise the Canadian federal government's attempt to control unfair competition has been subject to constitutional challenges. Section 7(e) of the Canadian *Trade-marks Act* attempts to prohibit a person from doing any act or adopting any "business practice contrary to honest industrial or commercial usage in Canada"; the constitutionality of this subsection is in doubt since it may be an intrusion by the federal government into exclusively provincial jurisdiction.[6]

Strategy: A review of current law applicable to the specific geographic areas involved will be required whenever trade names and trademarks are involved in a technology transfer agreement.

UNFAIR TRADE PRACTICES

5.3 Examples of Unfair Trade Practices

Some practices that might be suspect as unfair in Canada or the United States, either as a result of common law, provincial or state legislation, or federal legislation are:

  (a) an offending company *passing off* its products as if they were products of another company, either by misrepresenting the source or sponsorship of those products;[7]
  (b) an offending company claiming that another company's products either originated from the offending company or are under "sponsorship" of the offending company ("reverse passing off");[8]

---

[4] This conflict becomes most apparent in the franchising area. See the discussion of franchising later in this chapter at §§5.20–5.23.

[5] ALI/ABA *Trademarks*, p. 2.

[6] Hughes et al., *Hughes On Trade Marks*, §74, p. 658.

[7] ALI/ABA *Trademarks*, p. 12; Hughes et al., *Hughes On Trade Marks*, §§75–80, starting at p. 660. See also Canadian *Trade-marks Act*, R.S.C. 1985, c. T-13, s. 7(c) (hereinafter "*Trade-marks Act* (Canada)").

[8] See Drysdale and Silverleaf, *Passing Off*, ¶¶4.13 and 4.14, p. 83.

(c) an offending company engaging in false or misleading advertising about its own products;[9]

(d) disparagement of a competitor, its goods or services,[10] where such disparagement is not permitted by any constitutional or other right protecting freedom of speech;[11]

(e) an offending company making false statements as to its own intellectual property protection;[12]

(f) an offending company making false statements as to the intellectual property possessed by another (for example, slander of the other's title);[13]

(g) an offending company *diluting* the effectiveness of a trademark by using that trademark on an unrelated item with resulting loss of distinctiveness (this may be legally offensive in some jurisdictions only if there is "anti-dilution" legislation in effect in that jurisdiction);[14]

(h) misappropriating the reputation of a famous individual (for example, golfer, Tiger Woods) for another's commercial benefit;[15] and

---

[9] ALI/ABA *Trademarks*, p. 12. See Drysdale and Silverleaf, *Passing Off*, ¶4.19, p. 86; and see the *Lanham Act*, 15 U.S.C. §43(a).

[10] ALI/ABA *Trademarks*, p. 12, *Trade-marks Act* (Canada), s. 7(a) and U.S. *Trademark Act*, 15 U.S.C. §1125(a)(1)(B) (1994).

[11] For further discussion see American Bar Association, Section on Patent, Trademark and Copyright Law, *Annual Report* 94/95, p. 152 (hereinafter "ABA *Annual Report*, 94/95").

[12] ALI/ABA *Trademarks*, p. 12; Hughes et al., *Hughes On Trade Marks*, §70, pp. 653–52.

[13] ALI/ABA *Trademarks*, p. 12.

[14] The *Trade-marks Act* (Canada), s. 22(1) provides "No person shall use a trade-mark registered by another person in a manner that is likely to have the effect of depreciating the value of the goodwill attached thereto". For a further discussion on this topic, see ABA *Annual Report*, 93/94, Report of Subcommittee A, Subject 1, "A Federal Anti-Dilution Statute?" in the Report of Committee No. 205 "Unfair Competition — Trade Identity" (hereinafter "ABA *Annual Report*, 93/94"). See also English case *Taittinger v. Allbev, Ltd.*, [1993] F.S.R. 641 (referred to in the ABA *Annual Report*, 93/94, p. 139). Also §1125(1)(A) and (B) to the U.S. *Federal Trademark Dilution Act of 1995* provides:

> (1) Any person who, on or in connection with any goods or services, or any container for goods, uses in commerce any word, term, name, symbol, or device, or any combination thereof, or any false designation of origin, false or misleading description of fact, or false or misleading representation of fact, which,
>
> (A) is likely to cause confusion, or to cause mistake, or to deceive as to the affiliation, connection, or association of such person with another person, or as to the origin, sponsorship, or approval of his or her goods, services, or commercial activities by another person, or
>
> (B) in commercial advertising or promotion, misrepresents the nature, characteristics, qualities, or geographic origin of his or her or another person's goods, services, or commercial activities, shall be liable in a civil action by any person who believes that he or she is or is likely to be damaged by such act.

[15] See s. 2(a) of the Model Right of Privacy and Publicity Statute, which provides in part:
Right to Use of Identity
(a) No person shall have the right, except as the individual concerned may have consented thereto,

(i)   imitating the "get up", "guise", or "trade dress" of a competitor's product or service[16] (for example, imitating the shape of the "Coke" bottle or certain wine or perfume bottles). ("Trade dress" traditionally has referred to the appearance of a product or a product's packaging and may include features such as size, shape, colour, texture, graphics and the like, in varying arrangement and combinations.)[17]

In each case the plaintiff may have to prove there was confusion to the public and detriment to the "injured" party, particularly if the case is based on the common law. In any event, the law of unfair competition is a flexible, changing legal concept that does, and should, adapt itself to social and business changes.[18]

Strategies:
   (1)   A technology transfer agreement involving a trademark should prohibit specific acts that are characteristic of unfair competition, concerning both the products of the parties to the agreement and products of third parties.
   (2)   Because claims for unfair competition are becoming more popular, the parties to a technology transfer agreement involving a trademark should consider the appropriateness of insurance that provides indemnification for offences.[19]

5.3.1 Passing Off

Passing off is one type of unfair competition. As the phrase suggests, someone is trying to "pass off" its goods or services for those of another. To establish a passing off claim in a lawsuit, one must establish:

(a)   goodwill[20] attached to the plaintiff's goods or services in the relevant geographical area;
(b)   a misrepresentation

    (i)   to use an individual's identity publicly in such manner as to state or imply, for purposes of commercial advantage, the individual's endorsement of a product, service, or business, or the individual's affiliation with the source of such product, service, or business;

See ABA *Annual Report* 94/95, p. 212, for a further discussion of this Model Act. For Canada, see Hughes et al., *Hughes On Trademarks*, §81, p. 697 and the *Privacy Acts* of British Columbia, Saskatchewan, Manitoba and Newfoundland and the Quebec Civil Code referred to in *Hughes.*

[16]   See Hughes et al., *Hughes On Trade Marks*, §78, pp. 683–84 and the American Bar Association, Section on Patent, Trademark and Copyright Law, *Annual Report*, 91/92, p. 189 (hereinafter "ABA *Annual Report*, 91/92").

[17]   ABA *Annual Report*, 91/92, p. 189.

[18]   ALI/ABA *Trademarks*, p. 13. See also Hughes et al., *Hughes On Trade Marks*, §75, p. 660, and see Drysdale and Silverleaf, *Passing Off*, ¶1.04, p. 3.

[19]   See ABA *Annual Report*, 94/95, p. 219.

[20]   For goodwill to exist, the trademark must be in use. To see how the legislation handles applications for registration prior to usage, see §5.11 of this text.

(i)   made by a trader in the course of trade, or

(ii)   to prospective customers somewhere in the appropriate distribution chain;

that leads or is likely to *lead the public in that geographical area to believe* that the goods or services are those of, or are authorized by, the aggrieved plaintiff; and

(c) that causes, or is likely to cause, *actual damage* to the aggrieved plaintiff's business or goodwill.[21]

5.4 Area of Coverage

The public who may be confused by a "passing off" effort may be located in a local area; this public does not have to be in all of Canada or the United States or even an entire province or state. Goodwill that exists only in one local area therefore will be protected by the common law only within that local area. If the product or service is *known* over a broad area, even though *available* only in a local area, protection may still be available:[22] what is required for protection in an area may only be the "necessary reputation"[23] in that area. One of the advantages of the federal registration of a trademark is protection throughout the entire country rather than only a small area in which there is the necessary reputation.

5.4.1 Residual Reputation

Even if a business has been wound up, there may be residual goodwill that merits protection in a passing off action.[24]

5.5 Continuing Distinctiveness

Because a trademark is used by a business to distinguish its goods and wares from those of other businesses, either by indicating the source or quality,[25] the trademark must be sufficiently distinct to be recognized by the consumer. The

---

[21] Adapted from Drysdale and Silverleaf, *Passing Off*, ¶2.33, p. 19; Hughes et al., *Hughes On Trade Marks*, §76, p. 671; and "Tentative Draft No. 1 of the Restatement of the Law (3rd) of Unfair Competition" discussed in ABA *Annual Report*, 91/92, p. 209, at 214–15.

[22] See Drysdale and Silverleaf, *Passing Off*, ¶3.10, p. 31. Consider the difficulty of isolating the "local area" if the product or service is promoted on the Internet. See Sheldon Burshtein, "Surfing the Internet: Canadian Intellectual Property Issues", presented at the 1996 McGill University Meredith Lectures, May, 1996 (hereinafter "Burshtein, 'Surfing'"), ¶ 2.2.2.

[23] *Ibid.*, ¶3.12, p. 34.

[24] *Ibid.*, ¶3.15, p. 36.

[25] See Hughes et al., *Hughes On Trade Marks*, §12, p. 363, and §32, p. 457. See also *Trade-marks Act* (Canada), s. 2 (definition of "distinctive") and ALI/ABA *Trademarks*, ¶103, p. 4.

trademark must not be merely descriptive of the goods or wares.[26] The owner of a trademark must take the appropriate measures to maintain its distinctiveness; this can be lost if the trademark is allowed to become descriptive of the generic product. Thus, one sees considerable effort being expended to prevent trademarks like "Kleenex", "Teflon", "Rollerblades" and "Xerox" from becoming generic in the way "escalator", once a trademark, became the generic word for a moving staircase.[27] To avoid distinctiveness being lost by authorized users, controls are necessary. Distinctiveness may also be lost if the trademark is used by someone other than the owner without an appropriate licensing arrangement and such use remains unchallenged by the trademark owner.

Strategies:
    (1)   Allocate the responsibility of preventing unauthorized use of a licensed trademark, as well as related costs.
    (2)   Ensure that the licence contains the required controls to maintain distinctiveness.

TYPES OF MARKS

5.6 Different Types of Marks

The types of marks recognized by the Canadian *Trade-marks Act* are traditional trademarks (including distinguishing guises) and certification marks. The U.S. *Trademark Act* recognizes traditional trademarks, service marks, certification marks and collective marks.[28]

5.6.1 Traditional Trademarks

The statutory definitions of a traditional trademark reflect what the law of unfair competition will protect (*i.e.*, the goodwill of a business that is derived from a well-known indication of source of sponsorship or of quality used by that business). The Canadian *Trade-marks Act* in its definition of "trademark" refers to a mark that is *used* by a person to *distinguish* its goods or services from those of others.[29] The U.S. *Trademark Act* separates "service marks" (marks that identify "services") from trademarks (marks restricted to "goods"). Under the *General Agreement on Tariff and Trade* ("GATT"), the *Trade-Related Aspects of Intellectual Property Rights* ("TRIPS") does not distinguish between wares and

---

[26]   22 U.S.C. §2(e)(i) and *Trade-marks Act* (Canada), s. 12(1)(b).

[27]   For a Canadian example, see *Unitel Communications Inc. v. Bell Canada* (1995), 61 C.P.R. (3d) 12, at 59–69 (F.C.T.D.).

[28]   See also the General Agreement on Tariffs and Trade ("GATT") Agreement on Trade-Related Aspects of Intellectual Property Rights ("TRIPS"), Art. 15, §1.

[29]   *Trade-marks Act* (Canada), s. 2.

services in its definition of a trademark:[30] "A trademark shall consist of any sign, or any combination of signs, capable of distinguishing the *goods or services* of one undertaking from those of another, including personal names, letters, numerals, figurative elements, and combinations of colours".[31] Article 16(2) and (3) of TRIPS requires that "well known trademarks for wares and services shall be protected".[32] The definition in the U.S. *Trademark Act* states what a mark is, requires the feature that the mark identifies and distinguishes the goods or services from those of the competitors (mark includes a "word, name, symbol, or device, or any combination of those").[33] This definition basically applies in Canada. The U.S. "device" is reflected in s. 2 of the Canadian Act's "distinguishing guise", which includes a "shaping of wares or their containers" and a "mode of wrapping or packaging wares".

5.6.2 Certification and Collective Marks

A certification mark is used to distinguish wares of a defined standard. It may relate to the character or quality of the goods or services, the working conditions under which they are produced, the class of persons producing the goods or services or the geographic area in which they have been produced.[34] The certification mark is not used by its owner;[35] it is used by the provider of the goods or services, which obligates itself to deliver those goods or services within the defined standards on being permitted to use the certification mark. Collective marks are not specifically mentioned in the Canadian *Trade-marks Act*.[36] Like certification marks, collective marks identify qualities or groups of goods or service providers.

5.6.3 Marks Versus Names

Trademarks are not the same as trade names. A trade name is the name under which any business is carried on, whether or not it is the name of a corporation,

---

[30]   See the Uruguay Round negotiations of GATT, TRIPS Art. 15(1).

[31]   ABA *Annual Report,* 94/95, p. 177.

[32]   *Ibid.*

[33]   See ALI/ABA *Trademarks*, p. 4. Also see U.S. *Trademark Act*, 15 U.S.C. §1127.

[34]   *Trade-marks Act* (Canada), s. 2 (definition of "certification mark"). See also ALI/ABA *Trademarks*, p. 5.

[35]   Unless the same mark is also registered as a traditional trademark by that owner: see Hughes et al., *Hughes On Trade Marks*, §15, p. 367-2.

[36]   The ABA *Annual Report*, 92/93, p. 167, states:

The Canadian Act has for many decades recognized service marks and certification marks, but has given no specific statutory recognition to collective marks. However, the practice of the Canadian Trade-Marks Office for many years has been to permit U.S. collective marks to be registered in Canada as ordinary trade-marks or as certification marks, even though there has been no statutory or case law basis for doing so. Extending formal statutory recognition to collective marks would make sense of an inane practice.

a partnership or an individual. A company name is not registerable as a trademark except when the company name is also used as a trademark. A trade name, however, may be registerable (indeed may be required to be registered) under federal or provincial/state law in Canada and the United States.[37]

5.7 Prohibited Marks

Certain marks are specifically prohibited by the Canadian and U.S. *Trademark Acts*. These include anything "scandalous, obscene or immoral"[38] or marks "that disparage or falsely suggest a connection with persons, institutions, beliefs, or national symbols, or that would bring them into contempt or disrepute".[39]

STRENGTH OF TRADEMARK

5.8 Elements of Distinctiveness

The essence of a trademark lies in its *distinctiveness*.[40] The purpose of a mark is to identify and distinguish the relevant goods or services. A mark that is merely descriptive of the goods or services therefore has difficulty in attaining the requisite distinctiveness warranted for protection. Trademarks may be ranked by their strength as follows:

(a) "fanciful" or "a meaningless word specifically coined to serve as a trademark with no descriptive or even suggestive connotation in any language".[41] An example of a fanciful trademark is "KODAK".[42]

(b) "arbitrary" or "a word in normal usage that is used in an unrelated sense". The "BRICK" is a well-known Canadian furniture retailer using an arbitrary mark. The trademark "BRICK" could not be used as a trademark for a style of bricks, but when arbitrarily used for a furniture retailer, it may give significant strength.[43]

(c) protectable "descriptive" marks have something extra that serves to provide identity and distinctiveness because of usage, notwithstanding their descriptiveness. Such descriptive marks are often referred to as having "secondary meaning"[44] or having acquired distinctiveness.

---

[37] See Hughes et al., *Hughes On Trade Marks*, §13, p. 365 and ALI/ABA *Trademarks*, p. 8.

[38] Using the words contained in *Trade-marks Act* (Canada), s. 9(1)(j). See also ALI/ABA *Trademarks*, p. 7.

[39] ALI/ABA *Trademarks*, p. 7.

[40] Some trademarks get their distinctiveness from the style of print used. This distinctiveness may be lost in "domain names" used on the Internet.

[41] ALI/ABA *Trademarks*, pp. 5–6.

[42] *Ibid.*, p. 5.

[43] *Ibid.*, p. 6.

[44] See Hughes et al., *Hughes On Trade Marks*, §30, pp. 453-9 and ff. and ALI/ABA *Trademarks*, p. 6. Article 15(1) of TRIPS provides: "where a trademark is not inherently capable of distin-

5.8.1 Guidelines to Trademarks That Warrant Protection

The *Revised Model State Trademark Bill*,[45] adopted by nearly half of all U.S. states as the basis of their trademarks legislation, in determining the standards required for granting protection to famous marks, provides as follows:

In determining whether a mark is distinctive and famous, a court may consider factors, such as, but not limited to:
(1) the degree of inherent [46] or acquired distinctiveness of the mark ...;

(2) the duration and extent of use of the mark in connection with the goods and services with which the mark is used;

(3) the duration and extent of advertising and publicity of the mark ...;

(4) the geographical extent of the trading area in which the mark is used;

(5) the channels of trade for the goods or services with which the mark is used;

(6) the degree of recognition of the mark in the trading areas and channels of trade ... used by the mark's owner and the person against whom the injunction is sought;

(7) the nature and extent of the use of the same or similar mark by third parties.[47]

5.8.2 Federal Trademark Dilution Act of 1995

On January 16, 1996, the United States enacted an amendment to the *Trademark Act,* which was designed to effectively grant remedies to the owner of a famous mark to prevent activities that will lead to dilution (*i.e.*, "conduct which weakens the distinctiveness or the goodwill associated with a mark").

Dilution can occur through blurring or tarnishment. Blurring is the unauthorized use of a mark on dissimilar products or for dissimilar services that may cause the mark to cease functioning as a unique identifier of the mark owner's goods. Tarnishment occurs where a mark becomes consciously or unconsciously linked with poor quality, unsavory, or unwholesome goods or services.

For various reasons, state statutes are ineffective. First, not all states have dilution statutes, currently only about half the states have such statutes. Second, there is no uniform definition of dilution. Thus, some courts will only enjoin non-

---

guishing the relevant goods or services a Member may make registrability depend on distinctiveness through use", *per* ABA *Annual Report*, 94/95, p. 177. Note that there will be a difference between suggestive marks which are somewhat descriptive but registrable, and marks which are clearly descriptive and therefore not registrable.

45 International Trademark Association ("INTA"), Revised Model State Trademark Bill, revised November 1996.

46 Such as a "fanciful" or "arbitrary" trademark.

47 The ABA *Annual Report*, 90/91, p. 125. The *Trade-marks Act* (Canada), s. 6(5), produces substantially the same result.

competitive, non-confusing uses, while others protect uses on both similar as well as dissimilar products. Third, courts are reluctant to issue nationwide injunctions. Consequently, the recently enacted Federal Trademark Dilution Act of 1995 is expected to provide uniform and nationwide protection for famous marks.[48]

The amendment provides remedies for dilution of famous marks.

(2) In an action brought under this subsection, the owner of the famous mark shall be entitled only to injunctive relief unless the person against whom the injunction is sought willfully intended to trade on the owner's reputation or to cause dilution of the famous mark. If such willful intent is proven, the owner of the famous mark shall also be entitled to the remedies set forth in sections 35(a) and 36, subject to the discretion of the court and the principles of equity.[49]

REGISTRATION

5.9 Requirement to Register

Although sometimes beneficial, registration is not necessary under the Canadian or U.S. Trademark Acts; however, registration may be necessary under other legislation and, particularly, provincial/state legislation. Trademarks with the appropriate qualities are registrable at the separate trademarks offices for Canada and the United States. Unless specifically stated when registered, the registration offers protection for usage in the entire country (but, in the United States, not for commerce that occurs only within one state).

5.9.1 Benefits of Registering Federally

Article 16(1) of TRIPS sets out a reasonable summary of the effect of registration in Canada and the United States:

The owner of a registered trademark shall have the exclusive right to prevent the use in the course of trade of the identical or similar trademark for goods or services that are identical or similar to those goods or services in respect of which the owner's trademark is registered where such use would result in a likelihood of

---

[48] Jonathan Agmon, Stacey Helpern and David Parker, *The Federal Trademark Dilution Act of 1995*, <http://www.ll.georgetown.edu>.

[49] U.S. *Trademark Act*, 15 U.S.C. §1125(c)(2). It is questionable whether the U.S. Act or Canadian jurisprudence has yielded the protection expected: See Horowitz, E. and E. Di Lello, "Blurring Under the Federal Trademark Dilution Act", Managing Intellectual Property, June, 1999, and *United Artists Pictures Inc. v. Pink Panther Beauty Corp.* (1998), 80 C.P.R. (3d) 247 (Fed. C.A.).

confusion. Such confusion shall be presumed where there is use of the identical mark with the identical wares or services.[50]

Other benefits of registering federally include the rights to

(a) use the trademark throughout the country[51] and to preclude others from using a confusing mark anywhere in the country;[52]

(b) place the trademark on a database that is readily accessible nationally (for example, the NUANS database in Canada or the T-SEARCH database in the United States);[53]

(c) a presumption that a registered trademark is valid, placing the onus on the challenger to establish invalidity;[54]

(d) sue in the U.S. federal courts, as well as in a state court, for an infringement of a U.S. registered trademark;

(e) sue in the Federal Court of Canada, as well as in a provincial court, such as Alberta's Court of Queen's Bench, for an infringement of a Canadian registered trademark;

(f) register in other countries under international treaties;[55]

(g) prevent importation of goods bearing infringing marks;[56]

(h) a broader scope of protection than is offered under common law or provincial/state legislation;[57] and

(i) the availability of a court order compelling seizure of material bearing infringing trademarks.[58]

TERM

5.10 Term of Federally Registered Trademarks

In Canada, the term of a trademark is 15 years, indefinitely renewable for 15-year periods.[59] In the United States, the term is 10 years; however, after six years

---

[50] See ABA *Annual Report,* 94/95, p. 177. See also *Trade-marks Act* (Canada), s. 19.

[51] For Canada, see Hughes et al., *Hughes On Trade Marks,* §17, p. 371; for U.S., see *Trademark Act,* 15 U.S.C. §1051. But consider the problem raised by two businesses owning the same trademark, one in use, for example, in Canada, and one in Germany. Burshtein, "Surfing", at ¶2.3.8.6, queries: "Does the European company's advertising of its mark as a domain name worldwide on the Internet infringe the Canadian company's trade-mark in Canada?". See also Drysdale and Silverleaf, *Passing Off,* ¶3.10, p. 31.

[52] For Canada, see *Trade-marks Act* (Canada), s. 19 . For the United States, see *Trademarks Act,* 15 U.S.C. §§1051 and 1063.

[53] See ALI/ABA *Trademarks,* p. 31.

[54] For Canada, see Hughes et al., *Hughes On Trade Marks,* §17, p. 371.

[55] The "Paris Union" was established by convention in 1883 and includes Canada, the United States and most industrialized countries.

[56] See *Trade-marks Act* (Canada), s. 53(1) and (4); U.S. *Trademarks Act,* 15 U.S.C. §1124.

[57] Items (a) through (h) are adapted from ALI/ABA, *Trademarks,* p. 17.

[58] *Trade-marks Act* (Canada), s. 53(1); U.S. *Trademarks Act,* 15 U.S.C. §1116(d).

[59] See *Trade-marks Act* (Canada), s. 46(1).

the registrant must notify the registrar that the trademark is still in use.[60] Thereafter, additional terms of 10 years are available.[61] Article 18 of TRIPS provides that the initial term for protection of a trademark in the subscribing countries must be at least seven years, renewable indefinitely for terms of not less than seven years.[62]

5.10.1 Loss for Non-use

Reflecting the basics of the law of unfair competition — that protection is offered for marks that are in use and, by that usage, generate goodwill — a Canadian trademark may be expunged from the Trademark Register for non-use.[63] Article 19(1) of TRIPS allows for cancellation of a trademark "after an uninterrupted period of at least three years of non-use".

REGISTRATION PRIOR TO USE

5.11 Registration Federally Prior to Use

The basic principles of the rules against unfair competition require usage of the trademark and, thus, generation of goodwill to warrant protection (*i.e.*, existing goodwill must be injured to give rise to the claim). In practice under a registry system, however, businesses will often want to "reserve" trademarks[64] they intend to use. This will give them the requisite lead time to develop the marketing for the identified product or service. The *Trade-marks Act* of Canada currently allows an application to be filed on the basis that the applicant intends to use the proposed trademark, but final registration of the trademark will not occur until the applicant files a Declaration of Use confirming that the trademark is being used in commerce. Article 15(3) of TRIPS provides that usage, although a condition to *registration*, cannot be a condition to *filing*, and refusal of the application cannot be made "on the ground that use has not been commenced within 3 years from filing". The Canadian government passed s. 45(1) that contemplates evidence of use three years after filing. The United States implemented TRIPS, effective January 1, 1996.[65]

---

[60] U.S. *Trademarks Act*, 15 U.S.C. §1058.
[61] *Ibid.*, §1059.
[62] See quote in ABA *Annual Report*, 94/95, p. 177.
[63] *Trade-marks Act* (Canada), s. 45.
[64] See Burshtein, "Surfing", ¶ 2.2.4.3.
[65] ABA *Annual Report*, 94/95, p. 179.

MARKING

5.12 Marking Not Required

Using a mark to designate a trademark is not required under the Canadian *Trademarks Act*. It has been suggested that using ® or the letters TM as a superscript "would convey the same impression to the public, namely that the trademark was registered".[66] However, this is a valuable way to give notice to the public that the trademark is not a generic term. In the United States, the registrant has the option to display the words "Registered in U.S. Patent and Trademark Office" or "Reg. U.S. Pat. & Tm. Off." or "®". If these words are not displayed, the registrant has to show that the other person using the trademark had actual knowledge that the mark was registered or the registrant will not be entitled to any of the statutory profit and damage remedies offered by the U.S. *Trademarks Act*.[67]

REGISTRATION IN A PROVINCE/STATE

5.13 Inconsistent Rules

One of the greatest barriers to global, and sometimes even national, commerce is the lack of conformity from jurisdiction to jurisdiction for registration requirements (including necessity for registration and extent of disclosure required to the government and the prospective licensee).[68] In the United States, a *Model Trademarks Act* and its revisions were developed to provide uniformity, but it has not been adopted in all states and has not been applied consistently in the states that have adopted it.

Strategy:
   (1)   Be aware of relevant provincial/state registration/disclosure requirements.
   (2)   Make necessary revisions to standard form licence agreements to reflect regional differences.

5.14 Benefit of Registration in a Province/State

These benefits include:

---

[66]   See Hughes et al., *Hughes On Trade Marks*, §39, p. 509.
[67]   15 U.S.C. §1111.
[68]   See also American Bar Association, Section on Patent, Trademark and Copyright Law, *Annual Report*, 90/91, p. 126 (hereinafter "ABA *Annual Report*, 90/91").

(a) permission to register a trade name which might not otherwise satisfy the standards of the *Trademark Acts*;

(b) satisfaction of registration requirements that impose penalties for non-registration;[69] and

(c) protection for use of a trademark only within one state (and, thus, not covered by the U.S. *Trademark Act*).

REGISTERING INTERNATIONALLY

5.15 International Treaties

TRIPS, one of the results of the recent GATT negotiations, was included in the Final Document signed in April 1994 by Canada, the United States and over 120 other countries[70] and provides certain minimum requirements for registration. Canada and the United States are in the process of enacting the legislation necessary to bring their *Trademark Acts* into line with the requirements of TRIPS. Preceding TRIPS, Canada, the United States and Mexico established minimum standards for trademark protection when they entered into the *North American Free Trade Agreement* ("NAFTA").[71]

LICENSEES

5.16 Registration of Licensees

As a result of NAFTA and TRIPS, the Canadian *Trade-marks Act* no longer requires a licensee of a trademark to be recorded as a "registered user". Now s. 50 requires "direct or indirect control" over the "character or quality of the wares or services".[72] This brought the Canadian Act more into line with the U.S. *Trademark Act*.

5.17 Requisite Controls Over Licensees

In both Canada and the United States, the distinctiveness of trademarks can be lost due to insufficient management and policing of trademarks which gives rise to extensive uncontrolled use and may lead to the loss of distinctive trademarks.[73] The following sets out some good advice to licensors of trademarks:

---

[69] See ALI/ABA *Trademarks*, p. 16 and the Alberta *Partnership Act*, R.S.A. 1980, c. P-2, s. 110.

[70] ABA *Annual Report*, 94/95, p. 176.

[71] See Art. 1708 of NAFTA.

[72] Repealed & sub. S.C. 1993, c. 15, s. 69.

[73] See *Unitel Communications Inc. v. Bell Canada* (1995), 61 C.P.R. (3d) 12 (F.C.T.D.) and ABA *Annual Report*, 94/95, p. 246. See U.S. *Trademark Act*, 15 U.S.C. §1064.

Trade-mark owners in Canada, including franchisors, should ensure that all trade-mark licenses are in writing, and that the written agreements contained adequate control provisions over the licensee's or franchisee's goods or services. In a franchise system, the trade-mark license and control provisions will typically be found in and as part of the franchise agreement. The agreement should clearly identify every use that the franchisee is entitled to make of the marks and should give the franchisor a contractual right to exercise control over the character or quality of the franchisee's wares or services. The agreement should also specify the manner in which control may be exercised (for example, by periodic inspection). Franchisors also should include, or consider adding to the agreement, a right to terminate the agreement in the event that the franchisee fails to comply with the franchisor's quality standards.

It is not sufficient for a trade-mark owner to have an appropriate trade-mark license agreement in place if the owner does not exercise control in fact. However, . . . [the *Trade-marks Act* (Canada)] specifically allows a trade-mark owner to exercise control over a licensee's wares or services, either directly or indirectly. Direct control may be exercised by supplying proper use guidelines, approving samples of the product at various stages of its manufacture, visiting the licensee's premises, acting on consumer complaints and, in some cases, supplying the product. Indirect control, on the other hand, may be exercised by appointing an independent agent or representative to exercise direct control over the licensee. This method will frequently be used in master franchise transactions where the trade-mark owner (the franchisor) will appoint a representative (the master franchisee) to exercise quality control supervision over the use of the trade-marks by sublicensees (the franchisees).[74]

Strategy: A licensor of a trademark must impose controls over the use of the trademark to avoid loss of distinctiveness.

5.18 Protecting Licensee Against Infringers

Section 50(3) of the *Trade-marks Act* (Canada) has a provision that requires a licensor of a trademark to protect the licensee against harm caused by a third party infringer, unless the licence agreement has a contrary provision.[75]

Strategy: A technology transfer agreement that includes the licence of a Canadian trademark should address who has the obligation, if any, to take action against third-party infringers. Remember, the default provision is that the licensor has the obligation to protect the licensee.

---

[74] ABA *Annual Report*, 93/94, p. 237.
[75] Repealed & sub. S.C. 1993, c. 15, s. 69.

CO-OWNERSHIP OF TRADEMARKS

5.19 Co-ownership of Trademarks

If two or more companies have the right to use the same trademark as result of some form of co-ownership, s. 48(2) of the *Trade-marks Act* (Canada) implies that distinctiveness can be lost if the co-owners exercise their rights in a manner that confuses the public.

Strategy: Co-owners of a trademark should agree to take appropriate steps to preserve the distinctiveness of that trademark.

FRANCHISES

5.20 Franchise Legislation

There is no commonly accepted definition of a "franchise". An element common to most franchises, however, is a licence of a trademark.[76] The definition of "franchise" may vary with the particular legislation.[77]

> The types of businesses that have been found to constitute franchises for purposes of various franchise laws have included a broad array of distribution and licensing relationships in numerous industries. Whether a relationship is referred to as a distributorship, dealership, partnership, license, or by some other name, it may be subject to a variety of laws that regulate franchising if it is found to possess the legal attributes of a franchise.[78]

5.21 Disclosure Legislation

Some franchise legislation requires registration of the franchisor with a governmental authority and compulsory disclosure of facts to the franchisee and, in some cases, to the government. This legislation is intended to:[79]

---

[76] ABA *Annual Report,* 94/95, p. 246.

[77] Currently, Alberta and Ontario are the only Canadian jurisdictions to enact franchises legislation: in Alberta, the *Franchises Act,* R.S.A. 2000, c. F-23, and in Ontario, The Arthur Wishart Act (Franchise Disclosure), 2000. The definition of franchise in s.1(1), of the Alberta Act defines franchise as "a right to engage in a business . . . (ii) that is substantially associated with a trademark, service mark, trade name, logotype or advertising of the franchisor or its associate or designating the franchisor or its associate . . .".

[78] ABA *Annual Report,* 91/92, p. 182.

[79] The Alberta *Franchises Act* states a similar purpose in s. 2.

(a) prohibit misrepresentation and other potentially fraudulent activities in the sale of franchises;[80]
(b) force "disclosure of information to prospective purchasers [*i.e.*, franchisees] to aid them in making an informed decision";[81] and
(c) require "registration and approval by the [governmental] administrators prior to offering or selling franchises".[82]

Disclosure required by the Uniform Franchises Offering Circular includes descriptions of:

> all trademarks and related commercial symbols to be licensed, including information as to federal or state registration; any litigation, past or pending, in any court or administrative tribunal, state or federal; any agreements significantly limiting the rights to use the trademark; whether the franchise agreements will obligate the franchisor to protect the trademarks and the franchisee against claims of infringement or unfair competition; and whether the franchisor knows of any infringing uses which could materially affect the franchisee's use of the trademarks.[83]

5.21.1 Franchise Disclosure

The franchise disclosure rules of many states are the same as those imposed by the U.S. Federal Trade Commission ("FTC"). To be a franchise[84] within the scope of the FTC Rules generally these elements must exist:

    (i) an agreement between the franchisor and the franchisee that permits the franchisee to use the franchisor's trade name, trademark or service mark;

    (ii) significant assistance to the franchisee or significant control over the franchisee's method of business operation, or the franchisor's provision of a marketing plan to the franchisee; and

    (iii) a required payment of consideration deemed to be a "franchise fee" to the franchisor or its affiliate by the franchisee.[85]

5.21.2 Control

The FTC has indicated that any one of the following forms of control or assistance is sufficient to cause a franchise to fit within the scope of its franchise disclosure legislation:[86]

---

[80] ABA *Annual Report*, 90/91, p. 150.
[81] *Ibid.*
[82] *Ibid.*
[83] *Ibid.*, quoting "Business Franchise Guide (CCH)", para. 5813.
[84] Also see Alberta *Franchises Act*, s. 1(1)(d).
[85] ABA *Annual Report*, 90/91, p. 151.
[86] Alberta has a similar provision in the definition, in s. 1(1), of "marketing or business plan" which outlines many of the material aspects of conducting business specified by the franchisor.

(i)   restrictions on business location or sales area;

(ii)   furnishing management, marketing or personnel advice;

(iii)   restrictions on customers;

(iv)   location or sales area restrictions;

(v)   formal sales, repair or business training programs;

(vi)   furnishing a detailed operations manual;

(vii)   promotional campaigns requiring franchisee participation or financial con-
        tribution;

(viii) mandatory personnel policies and practices;

(ix)   control over production techniques;

(x)   establishing accounting systems or requiring accounting practices;

(xi)   location and site approval;

(xii)   location design or appearance requirements;

(xiii) control over hours of operation.[87]

5.21.3 Payment to Fall Within the Definition of a Franchise

For FTC purposes there must be a payment.[88] "The 'required payment' is interpreted broadly in order to capture all sources of revenue that the licensee must
pay to the licensor for the right to market goods or services under the licensor's
mark, whether those payments are required by contract or practical necessity".[89]

5.22 Business Opportunity Legislation

In addition to franchise legislation, some provinces/states have business opportunity legislation that is intended to protect against ventures that "historically
have been marketed to unsophisticated purchasers at a low level of investment
and have been subject to frequent fraudulent practices and abuses".[90] The scope
of the business opportunity legislation could pick up some franchises unexpect-
edly.[91] The provision of certain types of representations by the franchisor could
trigger the application of some business opportunity legislation, for examples,

---

[87] ABA *Annual Report*, 93/94, p. 223, quoting FTC Interpretive Guides to Franchising and Busi-
      ness Opportunity Ventures Trade Regulation Rule, 44 Fed. Reg. 49, 966, 49, 967 (1979).

[88] In Alberta, a payment is only one of the elements included in the definition of "franchise",
      however a "continuing financial obligation" is also part of the definition in the alternative to
      the payment of a franchise fee (s. 1(1)).

[89] ABA *Annual Report*, 93/94, p. 223.

[90] ABA *Annual Report*, 90/91, p. 151.

[91] *Ibid.*

(1) "the seller will refund the buyer's initial payment or buy back the materials that the buyer purchased from the seller if the buyer is dissatisfied with the business opportunity", and (2) "the seller will provide some sort of marketing plan to the buyer".[92]

Strategies:

(1) Become familiar with any applicable "business opportunity" legislation.

(2) Examine the applicable business opportunity legislation for any appropriate exemptions.[93]

(3) If possible, avoid representations and other licence provisions that trigger the application of business opportunity legislation; consider disclaiming offensive representations.[94]

(4) Restrict franchises to entities that are not covered by the legislation (i.e., purchasers having the required business experience, financial strength and sales performance history).[95]

(5) Consider marketing the products/services directly rather than through franchisees in jurisdictions where compliance will be difficult.[96]

5.22.1 Effects of Business Opportunity Legislation

In addition to registration and disclosure, if a "franchise" is within the scope of business opportunity legislation, it may be:

(a) required to repurchase inventory on termination,

(b) restricted to termination only for cause,

(c) required to permit renewal unless there is a cause for termination.[97]

5.23 Controls under Franchise Acts

As previously mentioned, the Canadian and U.S. *Trademark Acts* require a licensor of a trademark to maintain control over the use of the trademark, failing which the trademark may be lost because it loses its "distinctiveness". While the strength of a trademark may be described as the "cornerstone" of a franchise,[98] a key to the success of a franchise may be "uniformity of product and control of . . . [the] quality and distribution [of the product that] causes the public to turn to

---

[92] ABA *Annual Report*, 94/95, p. 250.

[93] *Ibid.*, p. 251.

[94] *Ibid.*, p. 252; see also ABA *Annual Report*, 91/92, pp. 185–86.

[95] ABA *Annual Report*, 94/95, p. 252.

[96] *Ibid.*, p. 253.

[97] ABA *Annual Report*, 91/92, p. 182.

[98] ABA *Annual Report*, 94/95, p. 246, quoting *Susser v. Carval Corp.*, 206 F.Supp. 636 at 640 (S.D.N.Y. 1962); affd 332 F.2d 505.

the franchise stores for the product".[99] The Trademarks Acts of Canada and the United States therefore impose the need for controls over the franchisee. The extent of control necessary may bring the franchise relationship into one governed by a provincial/state Franchise Act[100] and may, indeed, contravene the provisions of a provincial/state Act. In contrast with this federal requirement, some provincial/state franchise legislation attempts to restrict the extent of the controls a purchaser can impose on its franchisees.[101] Because these vary so much from state to state, this topic will not be discussed in this text.

Strategy: There is a "tight rope" between imposition of controls required by the Trademark Acts and imposition of controls that will bring the relationship within the scope of registration/disclosure franchise legislation or business opportunity legislation, or that will offend legislation that precludes excess controls.[102] Walk it carefully.

---

[99] ABA *Annual Report*, 94/95.

[100] See ABA *Annual Report*, 90/91, p. 207.

[101] See ABA *Annual Report*, 94/95, pp. 245 ff.

[102] See ABA *Annual Report*, 93/94, p. 228.

Chapter 6

TRADE SECRETS

Trade secrecy is such a powerful form of protection that innovators are offered a long-term monopoly via a patent in exchange for disclosure of the best mode of implementing that technology.

Although often used interchangeably, "Confidential Information" and "Trade Secrets" are not necessarily the same. In Canada, a trade secret is a subset of confidential information. Therefore, when drafting agreements one has to be careful to examine any reference to a trade secret to see if it should be a reference to the larger more encompassing phrase "confidential information".[1]

APPLICABLE LEGISLATION

6.1 North American Free Trade Agreement (NAFTA) and Trade Secrets

On becoming a party to NAFTA, Canada, the United States and Mexico agreed to ensure a minimum standard of protection to trade secrets within the three countries.[2]

1. Each Party shall provide the legal means for any person to prevent trade secrets from being disclosed to, acquired by, or used by others without the consent of the person lawfully in control of the information in a manner contrary to honest commercial practices, in so far as:
   (a) the information is secret in the sense that it is not, as a body or in the precise configuration and assembly of its components, generally known among or readily accessible to persons that normally deal with the kind of information in question;
   (b) the information has actual or potential commercial value because it is secret; and
   (c) the person lawfully in control of the information has taken reasonable steps under the circumstances to keep it secret.

---

[1] For the purpose of our discussion, however, we will refer to "trade secrecy".

[2] North American Free Trade Agreement, Art. 17.11.1 (hereinafter "NAFTA"). For corresponding provisions under the Trade Related Intellectual Property Protection Agreement (hereinafter "TRIPS"), see Art. 39, discussion relating to "undisclosed information".

2. A Party may require that to qualify for protection a trade secret must be evidenced in documents, electronic or magnetic means, optical discs, microfilms, films or other similar instruments.
3. No Party may limit the duration of protection for trade secrets, so long as the conditions in paragraph 1 exist.
4. No Party may discourage or impede the voluntary licensing of trade secrets by imposing excessive or discriminatory conditions on such licenses or conditions that dilute the value of the trade secrets.[3]

6.1.1 Canadian Rules

Trade secrecy in Canada is protected through the common law. To date, neither the federal government nor the nine common-law provinces have passed any legislation covering the protection offered to trade secrets, let alone defining what a trade secret is. Likewise, the Province of Quebec, governed by civil law, has not enacted any codes specifically related to trade secrets.

6.1.2 U.S. Rules

Many of the U.S. states have adopted variations of the *Uniform Trade Secrets Act*, though not all enactments are, in fact, uniform.[4] Courts in the United States refer to the 1939 *Restatement of Torts*, §757,[5] even though the section was not continued into the *Restatement (Second)*[6] or into the more recently adopted *Restatement (Third) of Unfair Competition.*[7]

PROTECTION OFFERED

6.2 Works Covered

There seems to be no limit to the scope of protection offered by trade secrecy.[8] Indeed the definition of the *Restatement (Third) of Unfair Competition* refers to "*any* information that can be used in the operation of a business or other enterprise" (emphasis added). The distinction between "trade secrets" and "confidential information" may depend on the nature of the secret. If in a particular U.S. State a "trade secret" is defined by the local version of the *Uniform Trade Se-*

---

[3] Items 5, 6(a) – (d), and 7 of Art. 1711 describe protections against disclosure when applying for approval of the marketing of pharmaceutical or agricultural chemical products that utilize new chemical entities.

[4] Gale R. Peterson, "Trade Secrets in an Information Age" in (1995), Houston Law Review, Vol. 32, No. 2, p. 385, at 389.

[5] *Ibid.*, p. 389.

[6] *Ibid.*

[7] *Ibid.*, p. 391.

[8] See Institute of Law Research and Reform, *Trade Secrets*, Report No. 46, p. 157.

crets Act, "confidential information" may be a better phrase to use because it may be free of limitations to the phrase "trade secret" imposed by that Act. Similarly, there does not seem to be a finite legal distinction between a trade secret and confidential information. Thus, these words should not be used interchangeably in an agreement as each has a distinct and separate meaning.

Know-how can be a trade secret, but is not necessarily so. Some expertise may be readily available; some may be peculiar to a particular company and may be subject to measures to keep it secret.[9]

Strategy: Use your own definition of trade secrets, avoid inadvertent application of statutory definitions.

6.3 Independent Development and Reverse Engineering

Like copyright, but unlike patent, trade secrecy does not prevent independent development or replication of the subject technology through reverse engineering.

NECESSARY QUALITIES FOR PROTECTION

6.4 Secrecy

To be protected, the information must be secret. Art. 17.11.1 of NAFTA specifies that the protected information "is secret in the sense that it is not, as a body or in the precise configuration and assembly of its components, generally known among or readily accessible to persons that normally deal with the kind of information in question". This seems to be a reasonable summary of the Canadian case law and of the U.S. law[10] — absolute secrecy is not necessary.[11] In the context of a business, some factors to be closely examined in determining whether there is sufficient secrecy to warrant protection include:

---

[9] See Michael D. McCoy, John P. Higgin and Lance A. Larson, "Trade Secrets and Related Licenses", presented at Technology Transfer 2001, Licensing Executives Society, May 21-24, 2001, at pp. 2-3.

[10] See generally Peterson, "Trade Secrets in an Information Age". See also TRIPS, Art. 29, ¶2, where it states:

2. Natural and legal persons shall have the possibility of preventing information lawfully within their control from being disclosed to, acquired by, or used by others without their consent in a manner contrary to honest commercial practices so long as such information:

is secret in the sense that it is not, as a body or in the precise configuration and assembly of its components, generally known among or readily accessible to persons within the circles that normally deal with the kind of information in question;

has commercial value because it is secret; and

has been subject to reasonable steps under the circumstances, by the person lawfully in control of the information, to keep it secret.

[11] Adapted from Peterson, "Trade Secrets in an Information Age", p. 429.

(a) the extent to which the information is known outside the business;
(b) the extent to which it is known by employees and others involved in the business;
(c) the extent of measures taken to guard the secrecy of information;
(d) the value of the information to the holder of the secret and to his or her competitors;
(e) the amount of effort or money expended in developing the information;
(f) the ease or difficulty with which the information can be properly acquired or duplicated by others;
(g) whether the holder of the secret and the taker treat the information as secret; and
(h) the custom in the industry concerning this specific type of information.[12]

Strategy: Agree to keep confidential only what is secret. Define what is to be kept secret carefully.

6.5 Economic Value

To warrant protection in the business context, the information must have present or future commercial value.[13]

Strategy: Agree to keep secret only information that has value.

6.6 Novelty

The degree of novelty required for patents is not necessary for a trade secret because trade secrecy does not prevent independent development.[14] Only a minimum level of novelty is required; information will not be protected if it is of a trivial nature.[15]

6.7 Imposition of Duties of Confidence

Confidentiality obligations may arise from express contract, implied contract or from a duty that arises by operation of law. In Canada, the law of confidence is *sui generis*, existing outside of the traditional property, tort or trust law. As the

---

[12] Items (a) to (h) listed in David Vavor, "What is a Trade Secret," in Roger T. Hughes, ed., *Trade Secrets* (Toronto: Law Society of Upper Canada, 1990), p. A-18 (papers presented at a conference held at Osgoode Hall, November 24, 1989). A substantially similar list appears in Peterson, "Trade Secrets in an Information Age", p. 421, quoting from the *Bando* case, 9 F.3d 823, at 848 (10th Cir. 1993).

[13] See NAFTA, Art. 17.11(1.b), and Peterson, "Trade Secrets in an Information Age", p. 417.

[14] Peterson, "Trade Secrets in an Information Age", p. 416.

[15] Peterson, "Trade Secrets in an Information Age", p. 417.

law of confidential information does not yet have a significantly reviewed body of case law summaries, consideration should be given to utilizing the law of contract to regulate the affairs of the parties. Parties may contract expressly concerning the obligations of secrecy. A contract may imply those obligations particularly in employment contracts.[16] The courts have had much more difficulty in finding non-contractual ways of protecting secrets and often seem to stretch the law of property and trust (*i.e.*, fiduciary duty).

Strategy: Be careful in your use of words; legal words, such as "trust" and "fiduciary," give rise to special remedies that may not be available under contract law.

6.7.1 Explicit Imposition of the Duties of Secrecy is Sometimes Unnecessary, but Still Recommended

At common law, a duty of confidence can arise without the parties agreeing in writing to maintain confidentiality or even discussing the need for secrecy. If a duty is so obviously an implied part of the communication, a court will impose that duty.[17] Essentially, if one party receiving the confidential information knew or ought to have known that it was a secret, only a court will impose a duty of confidence upon such party.

Strategy: Rather than having secrecy obligations imposed by the common law, the negotiations for a technology transfer shall early on establish what secrecy duties will be assumed and what duties will be disclaimed.

SECRECY AGREEMENTS

6.8 Imposing Obligations of Confidentiality by Contract

When drafting a confidentiality agreement, the drafter should not assume that there is a clear legal definition of "trade secret" or a precise distinction between the words "confidential information," or "trade secret". The word "proprietary" adds little clarity. The disclosing party may want to have expansive coverage and endeavour to cover information that "otherwise might not be entitled to protection".[18] The definition should be drafted each time for the specific circumstances.

---

[16] Peterson, "Trade Secrets in an Information Age", p. 404.

[17] *Ibid.*

[18] Roger Milgrim, *Milgrim on Trade Secrets*, § 4.02[I][d][ii].

6.8.1 Compare to Restrictions on Competition

An imposition of obligations of confidentiality may be similar to restrictions on competition and, thus, if unduly restrictive, are challengeable for being in contravention of public policy against restrictions on competition. The secrecy obligations should therefore be sufficiently precise and appropriately written for the particular circumstances.

6.9 Information that is the Subject of the Contractual Secrecy Obligations

The disclosing party will want the definition of "confidential information" to be drafted in the broadest terms available, particularly if it cannot be readily anticipated what will be disclosed in an on-going relationship. Conversely, the recipient of the information will want to restrict the definition as much as possible to narrow down its restriction on use and to limit the quantity of information that must be stored in a secured manner.

Strategy: Draft the scope of the definition of "confidentiality" to produce a fair balance between the needs of the disclosing party and the duties of the recipient.

6.9.1 Who Describes the Secret?

The drafter, taking the easy way out, may leave it to others to draft a definition of trade secrecy and write " 'Confidential Information' means the information described on Schedule 'A'". The drafter's confidence that a person with the appropriate technical skills will insert the proper words may be misplaced. That person may forget to attach Schedule "A" altogether and leave the agreement uncertain at best and entirely unenforceable at worst. The drafter may find that the scheduled definition contains puffery that could be considered to be specific statements of quality that a court might decide constitute an express warranty that overrides the effect of a general statement disclaiming all express warranties. The drafter might be upset to find that Schedule "A" is so well prepared and in such detail that the schedule itself reveals the trade secrets. Rarely is the agreement imposing confidentiality kept secret, and the instrument designed to preserve secrecy may very well be the instrument that reveals the secrets.[19]

Strategy: Too much can be as bad as too little.

---

[19] John H. Woodley, "Taking Care of Trade Secrets: Controlling and Exploiting Trade Secrets in Law and Practice" in Roger T. Hughes, ed., *Trade Secrets* (Toronto: Law Society of Upper Canada, 1990), p. C-1, at C-4 (papers presented at a conference held at Osgoode Hall, November 24, 1989).

6.9.2 Mark as Confidential

Some agreements state that the disclosing party must mark as "Confidential" all information that is to be the subject of confidentiality and restricted use. This may be appropriate when all the information will be disclosed in writing at one time; it is not as practical if the information will be disclosed orally or over a period of time.

6.9.3 Oral Disclosures

In contemplation of oral disclosure, some agreements provide that the obligation of confidentiality must be imposed by written notice delivered within a certain period of time following a verbal disclosure; otherwise there would be no obligation of confidentiality imposed. This helps to control the scope of information that is to be kept secret, but in practice is overlooked more often than not, especially during lively technical discussions. If the technical staff have been properly warned about oral disclosures, this requirement to put the disclosed information into writing may interfere with a normal robust exchange of information. With the normal pressures of negotiating and implementing a technology transfer, individuals may forget to do the requisite written confirmation (assuming they were even aware that this extra step was necessary).

Strategy: Be reasonable about oral disclosures: remember what is reasonable to the negotiators is not necessarily reasonable to the implementers.

6.9.4 Posting on the Internet

Posting on the Internet will likely result in loss of secrecy even if deleted in a short period of time.[20]

6.10 Exceptions to Information that is to be Kept Secret

The recipient will want to except out certain information from the subject-matter of the duties of confidentiality and restrictions on use, including the following standard exceptions:

(a) information that is within the public domain at the time of the disclosure;
(b) information subsequently entering the public domain without fault on the part of the recipient;
(c) information that the recipient already knows.

---

[20] See McCoy at p. 19.

Perhaps the recipient could be required to immediately disclaim confidentiality on receipt of information it already knows, though this may not be practical in a larger organization where individual employees will not know what other information is in the possession of the recipient. Often these "normal" exceptions include disclosure to professional advisors or to a court. Those provisions are misplaced – they permit disclosures which may not result in the information ceasing to be confidential for all purposes.[21]

6.10.1 Onus of Proof

The drafter could specify who has the onus to prove whether specific information is within one of the exceptions. Will the disclosing party have to establish that the information is not generally known in its trade or business? Will the recipient have to prove that it possessed the information at the time of disclosure? Will the recipient have to claim the benefit of the exception within a specified period after disclosure?

Strategy: Specify who has the onus to establish existence of an exception.

6.10.2 Public Domain

The phrase "public domain", though frequently used in Canada, may not be familiar to many licensing executives. It may have different meanings in different countries. Rather than being faced with having to determine the number of people that comprise the "public" and whether that "public" can be restricted to a narrow area of business, the drafter of the confidentiality clause could use a phrase more generally used in trade secrecy legislation, such as "not generally known in the disclosing party's trade" or "not generally known by the disclosing party's competitors".

Strategy: Avoid phrases such as "public domain" that may have conflicting legal meanings and little or no commercial meaning.

6.10.3 Public Domain and Continued Royalties

Even though information enters the public domain, a licensee may be required to pay continuing royalties unless the contract specifies otherwise. This is in contrast to the U.S. rule that permits termination of an obligation to pay continued royalties when a patent expires or is declared invalid.[22]

---

[21] See §6.16 and §6.17 of this text.
[22] See §11.9 of this text.

6.11 Mixture of Public and Private

Mixed public and secret information may be protected if the combination has been brought into "being by the application of the skill and ingenuity of the human brain",[23] but applies only to the secret portion of the material. Some collections of data may contain both information that is obtained from the public domain and information that is private, or they may present public domain information in a novel manner. To overcome a contrary inference from a disclaimer of confidentiality for information within the public domain, the confidentiality clause could specifically protect a blend of public and private information if the private information enhances the public information.[24]

COMMUNICATING TRADE SECRETS

6.12 Methods of Communication

The many different ways of communicating disclosure of trade secrets must be considered. They can be disclosed in written materials (including manuals), at training sessions, or transferred in digital format, either physically, in the form of floppy disks or compact discs, or electronically by telecommunication, including the Internet.

6.12.1 Full and Useful Disclosure

The recipient will expect a full accurate and useful disclosure. Conversely, the disclosing party will want to restrict the quantity of information that must be collected and physically transferred.

6.12.2 Training Communicates Trade Secrets

One of the most significant methods of transferring the know-how portion of technology is the training provided by the disclosing party. By this process, data is converted into useable information. The recipient will want to obtain "an appreciation of the benefits of doing things a certain way, an understanding of research objectives to achieve a certain result, knowledge of which avenues of research may be productive and insight into what mistakes to avoid".[25]

---

[23] See Peterson, "Trade Secrets in an Information Age", p. 418.
[24] See *International Corona Resources Ltd. v. LAC Minerals Ltd.*, [1989] 2 S.C.R. 574, 61 D.L.R. (4th) 14 at 78 (D.L.R.).
[25] Rule No. 3 in Alan H. Melincoe, "Locked out licensees", counsel at the San Jose law firm of Hoge, Fenton, Jones & Appel, "Intellectual Property" at <http://www.portal.com/~recorder/melon.html>.

6.12.3 Selection of the Site for Training

The selection of the training site is particularly relevant if the parties' places of business are remote from each other (for example, one party is in Cairo and the other in Calgary). An Internet "chat" line could be used to benefit multiple users if the information so disclosed is not confidential.

6.13 Factors to Consider When Offering Training

(a) Will the teacher travel to the students, or vice versa?

(b) Who pays the cost of travel and accommodation?

(c) How many students will be trained at one time (both a minimum and a maximum)?

(d) Whose equipment will be made available to the students?

(e) What is the requisite training or expertise of the teachers/students?

(f) What accreditation will be given after successful completion of the training and will the students then train other students?

(g) How long will the training sessions be (both minimum and maximum)? Consider hours per day as well as days per week, and consider religious and statutory holidays that are not shared by both the teachers and the students;

(h) How often will training sessions be given (both minimum and maximum)?

(i) What language will be used?

(j) Will interpreters with the requisite scientific and language skills be provided?

(k) Which party will pay any medical expenses incurred by the students or teachers while in a foreign country?

(l) What provisions will be made for the safe departure of the teacher and students in the event of civil unrest or political revolution, or illness?

(m) What are the minimum safety conditions required at the transferee's plant site? and

(n) Will the teacher have full and free access to the licensee's plant, phone and fax?

MEASURES TO BE ADOPTED TO MAINTAIN SECRECY

6.14 Requisite Standards

The propensity for highly skilled "hackers" to gain illegal access to computers thought to be secured will be a concern for all parties. The recent publicity that hackers have produced draws attention to an already serious problem. The most likely intruders into a computer system are competitors, followed by employees and ex-employees. Other likely intruders are customers, public interest groups, suppliers, foreign governments and junior high school students.[26] As a result, the requisite standards adopted to maintain secrecy must be specified. Some agreements provide that the "recipient shall take measures to *ensure* that secrecy is maintained". Because a strict definition of the word "ensure" is to "guarantee" or "insure,"[27] use of "ensure" may, inadvertently perhaps, impose a higher standard of care than the standard of care adopted by the disclosing party for the same information. "Ensure" does not mean to "strive" or to give a good try, though it is often used in that context. When commonplace usage and the dictionary definition seem to be contradictory, a more precise word should be used.

6.14.1 *"Use Own Precautions"*

Many agreements provide that a recipient "shall take the same precautions to hold information in confidence as it takes for its own trade secrets". This may be an acceptable standard for a company that is known to have adopted very stringent standards, but it could cause disappointment to the disclosing party if its secrets are disclosed along with those of a recipient that has allowed its standards to become dangerously lax.

6.14.2 *"All Reasonable Measures"*

Often, agreements provide that the "recipient shall take all reasonable measures available to it". What is "reasonable," however, will depend on the individual circumstances.[28] It may require a "balance of cost and benefits that will vary from case to case".[29] It is unlikely that an owner of a trade secret will be required, in order to qualify for the legal benefits offered to trade secrets, to "take extravagant, productivity-impairing measures to maintain their secrecy".[30] As encryption becomes more accessible, will it become a "reasonable mesure"?

6.15 Proprietary Rights Protection Policy

When prudent companies receive or develop confidential information, they should adopt a proprietary rights policy. This policy should be written in clear language and distributed to all employees and contractors.[31] One essential item for this policy will be confidentiality agreements with employees and statements

---

[26] Economic Security, press clippings published by Canadian Security Intelligence Service, p. 5, compiled February 1995, quoting National Security Institute's Advisory, January 1995.
[27] See *The Oxford English Dictionary*, J.B. Sykes, ed. (England: Oxford University Press, 1982).
[28] See Peterson, "Trade Secrets in an Information Age", p. 442.
[29] *Ibid.*, p. 446, citing *Rockwell*, 925 F.2d, at 178.
[30] *Ibid.*, p. 447, again citing *Rockwell*.
[31] Canadian Security Intelligence Service, "Clear Policy Can Forestall Data Piracy", January 17, 1995.

setting out company policies for the treatment of confidential information. These agreements and policies will consider

(a) the consideration granted to the employee that is sufficient to justify the promises obtained;[32]

(b) the duty of an employee/contractor to disclose innovations made by that individual while employed or retained by the company. Is the duty of disclosure restricted to innovations made in the course of employment or to any innovations made in that time period? Consider the difference between "during employment" and "in the course of employment".

(c) the ownership of innovations made in the course of employment;

(d) the ownership of innovations that were made outside the course of employment but using company time and equipment;

(e) the ownership of innovations that were made entirely on the employee's own time and off the premises of the company but that are still within the type of business conducted by the company;

(f) the duty of the company to keep confidential the innovations disclosed by the employee that are not owned by the company (most agreements with employees fail to make the confidentiality bilateral);

(g) the duty of the employee to assign or to waive any intellectual property rights vested in the employee by operation of law, keeping in mind, particularly, copyright to works that have not yet been created;[33]

(h) the company's policy towards unsolicited disclosures and any standard policy of refusing such disclosures or accepting them only with a disclaimer of confidentiality;

(i) security measures taken to prevent loss of trade secrets merely as a result of key employees taking jobs elsewhere and not creating and leaving documentation necessary to re-create the research and development done to date of termination; consider the appropriateness of continually depositing research records with a neutral third party;

(j) provisions that will prevent the employee from competing with the company or soliciting its customers and employees;[34]

(k) all the other issues related to confidentiality agreements generally.

It is essential to implement a thorough proprietary rights protection policy. This will ensure that no door is left unsecured.[35]

---

[32] For example, see *Watson v. Moore Corp. Ltd.* (1996), 134 D.L.R. (4th) 252 (B.C.C.A.).

[33] See §§4.4.4, 4.21 to 4.26 of this text.

[34] See Chapter 10, Restraint of Trade.

[35] Canadian Security Intelligence Service, "Clear Policy Can Forestall Data Piracy," January 17, 1995.

6.15.1 Other Measures to be Adopted to Maintain Secrecy

The confidentiality provisions could specify what measures must be adopted to maintain secrecy, particularly in the case of highly sensitive material or where it is not clear that the recipient has adopted strict standards for maintaining secrecy. Some of these measures are:

(a) having enforceable non-disclosure and confidentiality agreements with those individuals who are permitted access to confidential information;[36]
(b) taking sensible precautions against industrial espionage;
(c) labelling plans and documents "confidential";
(d) employing confidentiality legends, warnings and agreements;
(e) limiting visitors and employing similar types of security;
(f) locking up, or otherwise securing, sensitive information;
(g) taking technical precautions (for example, dividing the system into steps to be handled by separate individuals or departments);
(h) using copy protection and embedded codes to trace copies and carrying out regular employee exit interviews.[37]
(i) specifying physical security of areas where access may be gained to the confidential information;
(j) specifying security measures for electronic storage and transmission of data including, or derived from, any confidential information;
(k) specifying controls on access to any computer facility and tape or disk library where any confidential information may be stored; and
(l) specifying document and computer network control systems that limit access to the confidential information to employees and agents who have a need to know, which control system provides for a secured method of protection of sensitive data.

Strategy: Specify the required secrecy controls.

6.15.2 Employee Confidentiality Agreements

Like any restrictive covenant, an employee confidentiality agreement must be reasonable in scope. The rules are more relaxed for confidentiality agreements than they are for non-competition agreements. A confidentiality agreement need not be restricted by time or territory as is likely the case for a non-competition, unless the local law requires otherwise.[38] However the scope of the information will be subject to close scrutiny by the courts; this scope must be reasonable and not include professional expertise if inclusion would prevent the employee from finding alternate employment.

---

[36] Peterson, "Trade Secrets in an Information Age", pp. 441– 42.
[37] Items (b)–(h) are adapted from Peterson, "Trade Secrets in an Information Age," pp. 448 – 49.
[38] See *Milgrim on Trade Secrets*, §4.02[1][d][vi][C].

The distinction between general professional expertise and specific expertise built on company trade secrets is not clear and debate may become emotional. The drafter must be careful about changing the scope of the confidentiality agreement too narrowly or too broadly. If the drafter is too specific, he may overlook secrets that were not, or perhaps even could not, be thought of at the time the agreement was created.[39] The courts will not revise an express agreement to overcome the drafter's errors.[40] The agreement may be less restricted than what the rules of law would imply.[41] Whether it can be more restrictive would be subject to the test of reasonableness. A prudent drafter might create a separate non-disclosure agreement independent of the employment agreement.[42]

6.15.3 Exit Interviews

Exit interviews are an indication of reasonable measures adopted to maintain secrecy. The departing employee should be reminded of his or her obligation of confidence, being as particular as possible.[43] Exit interviews should be conducted even if there is no confidentiality agreement in place since the legal relationship between the parties may imply duties of confidence.

RESTRICTIONS ON USE/DISCLOSURE

6.16 Permitted Use

In the case of copyright and patents, the right to *use* is controlled by the statutory restrictions. In the case of trade secrets, however, restrictions on use will be imposed by contract in the absence of a contract or by the common law. The confidentiality clause might specify: (a) the confidential information shall be used only for the recipient's internal use or, perhaps, only for a specific project; (b) the right to reproduce material, since reproduction not only is controlled by trade secrecy but also is prohibited by copyright law; and (c) the rights of affiliates to use the disclosed material, as well as the rights of the recipient, and the responsibility of the recipient for the conduct of its affiliates.

---

[39] See *Milgrim on Trade Secrets*, §§4.02[2][b] and 4.02[2][b][I].

[40] See *Milgrim on Trade Secrets*, §4.02[2][b].

[41] See *Milgrim on Trade Secrets*, §4.02[2][c].

[42] See *Milgrim on Trade Secrets*, §4.03.

[43] See McCoy at p. 9 where he cites *Mirafi, Inc. v. Murphy* 14 U.S.P.Q 2d 1337, 1341 (W.D.N.C. 1989) where the employer had obtained a "Confidential Information and Secrecy Agreement" but failed to do an exit interview, and failed to follow up with employees to make sure they were not contrary to their obligations in respect of secrets.

6.17 Permitted Disclosure

Even though information may not have become generally available to the relevant trade or business, the recipient may require the right to use or to disclose information without breaching its duties and, perhaps, without triggering a royalty for the following reasons:

(a) if the information has been released to a third party without obligations of confidence, even though it is not generally available. This permitted use should arise only after the disclosure and should not have any prior effect. The disclosing party will want to except out disclosures that result from misappropriation by a third party.

(b) disclosure as a result of a government order or a court order, though the disclosing party could demand that it be given advance notice to permit it to oppose the disclosure;[44]

(c) disclosure to a professional advisor;

(d) disclosure to employees or consultants who have a need to know, whether subject to express confidentiality agreement in a form provided by the agreement or in the recipient's standard form; and

(e) disclosure to bankers and other lenders, to permit them to assess the merits of financing the project involving the exploitation of the confidential information.

Strategy: Specify both the permitted uses and the permitted disclosures.

6.18 Duration

The parties could agree on the duration of the obligations of restricted use and non-disclosure. There is no industry standard that can be applied in all cases since the nature of the information will vary. A reasonable anticipation of the economic life of the information may be an appropriate standard. From the recipient's point of view, the duration of its duties must not be taken lightly due to the cost of maintaining secrecy. Personnel will soon forget the confidentiality obligation as they move on to new projects or new jobs.

Strategy: Negotiate a term for the duties of confidence that reasonably matches the information's economic life.

6.18.1 Termination

On termination of the duties of confidentiality, the agreement could require that the recipient return all copies of the information that it has in material form and render unusable all materials stored on a computer. Some agreements require an

---

[44] The parties should consider the effect of any freedom of information legislation.

officer or an appropriate employee with authority to certify that the recipient has no further copies in its possession. The recipient may be reluctant to return or to destroy all copies of the confidential information if it is concerned that the disclosing party will subsequently claim misappropriation or misuse of the secrets. Having lost possession of all copies, the recipient may not be able to properly defend itself. On termination, such a recipient may require at least one copy of all of the material to be deposited securely with access limited for the purposes of such a defence. All continued rights of use should specifically be prohibited, subject to appropriate exceptions for individual circumstances. Some agreements provide for termination of the agreement rather than termination of obligations; in such cases, survival of the obligations of secrecy is required. One should not expect any implication of continued duties when explicit secrecy obligations have been agreed on. This concern will apply to employee non-disclosure agreements as well.[45]

Strategies:
    (1)   *Specify what action is to be taken on termination of the agreement.*
    (2)   *Allow confidentiality obligations to survive termination of a technology transfer agreement, where appropriate.*

---

[45]   See *Milgrim on Trade Secrets*, §4.02[b][i].

Part III

THE TRANSFER

Chapter 7

TRANSFER OF RIGHTS

7.1 Introduction

Each party will strive to clearly define what technology is being transferred as well as the extent of the transferred interest. They will precisely establish the express terms and delete the application of inappropriate compiled terms. The right to favourable terms and exclusivity will be subject to specified conditions.

7.2 Subject-Matter

The subject-matter of the transfer can be a process or product protected by patent or trade secret, a name or logo protected by trademark, or a work (literary, artistic, musical, dramatic, etc.) protected by copyright. If the process or product is protected by patent, the grant clause could specifically refer to the subject patent. The ABA Draft Model Software Agreement[1] uses a broad-brush approach. A "Licensable Activity", *i.e.*, one permitted by the license, is "an activity encompassed by one or more Intellectual Property Rights, *i.e.*, an activity which, absent a license, would give rise to liability for infringement (or inducement of infringement or contributory infringement) of the Intellectual Property Right(s)".[2] This definition may not fully cover trade secrets unless "infringement" is expanded to cover "misappropriation" or "misuse". The ABA Draft Model Software Agreement uses the words "grants to LICENSEE . . . a license under any and all Intellectual Property Rights owned or otherwise assertible by a Transferor to engage in the following Licensable Activities".[3]

---

[1] American Bar Association, Section on Patent, Trademark and Copyright Law, Committee on Computer Programs, *Model Software License Provisions*, Committee Chair: D.C. Toedt III available at <www.lawnotes.com/software> (hereinafter "ABA Draft Model Software Agreement").

[2] *Ibid.*, Section 1001.57.

[3] *Ibid.*, Section 102.2. The author would prefer to use the words "Permitted Activities". This precedent uses BLOCK CAPITALS only for Licensor and Licensee and not for other defined phrases. Perhaps this can be used as a reminder to replace each word with a word or acronym appropriate for the purpose. The use of the words "Licensor" and "Licensee," besides being unfriendly, almost guarantees that somewhere in the document one word ("Licensor") will be in-

7.2.1 Characterization of Technology Transfer

To make sure a licence agreement is characterized as a licence (with a retention of some rights) rather than as a sale or an assignment (with a disposition of all rights), the grant clause should state that the licence is subject to every term of the agreement being fulfilled.[4] Brunsvold and O'Reilley[5] characterize technology transfer agreements into assignments (a complete transfer of an interest even if that interest may be a partial interest), licences (mere permissions to do something) and exclusive licences (more than a 'mere licence' and less than an assignment). The characterization of the technology transfer may produce significantly different results for tax purposes, and these differences will vary from country to country and may differ depending on the various types of intellectual property.[6] As well, there could be a significant difference in the application of bankruptcy law. Although, for business purposes, an exclusive licence for the full term of the patent with a running royalty based on net sales may seem identical to an assignment where the consideration is a percentage of net sales, "it is possible that in the creditors' rights context, the two transactions might be treated differently".[7] In addition, in the U.S., there may be a difference between an assignment and a license in the right of the transferee to sue.[8]

7.2.2 Use of Word "Rights"

If the drafter of a licence agreement refers to a grant of "rights", it might be appropriate to specifically state that only a licence is being granted since the phrase "grant of rights" could be considered to be an assignment of intellectual property *rights* rather than the grant of a "permission" to do something.

7.2.3 Get All the Rights Needed

The licensee will want to ensure that it has received a transfer granting all of the rights the transferor has relating to the subject-matter of the transfer and that the

---

advertently switched with the other ("Licensee"), perhaps with wholly unintended and, perhaps, irreparable consequences.

4 Ronald B. Coolley, "*Drafting a Granting Clause*", in *les Nouvelles*, the Journal of the Licensing Executive Society, Vol. XXVII, No. 4, December 1992, p. 212 (hereinafter "Coolley, 'Drafting', *les Nouvelles*, December 1992"). See also Robert Goldscheider, *Companion to Licensing Negotiations, Licensing Law Handbook* (New York: Clark Boardman Callaghan, 1993-94), where he uses the phrase "subject to the terms and conditions of this Agreement", at p. 153 (hereinafter "Goldscheider, *Licensing Law Handbook*"). The ABA Draft Model Agreement uses similar words in its Section 102.2.

5 Brian G. Brunsvold and Dennis P. O'Reilley, *Drafting Patent License Agreements*, 4th ed. (Washington: BNA Books, 1998), p. 5 (hereinafter "Brunsvold and O'Reilley, *License Agreements*").

6 See Chapter 12 of this text.

7 R.M. Milgrim, *Milgrim On Licensing*, rev. ed. (New York: Matthew Bender, 1995), §15.00, p. 15-3 (hereinafter "Milgrim, *On Licensing*").

8 Brunsvold and O'Reilley, *License Agreements*, p. 6.

transferor does not possess separate rights that may overlap with the rights specifically granted to the licensee.[9]

7.2.4 Do Not Exceed Rights

The grant of licence should not exceed the rights possessed by the transferor. A holder of a U.S. patent that is not issued in any other country cannot grant the right to use that patented technology in any other country. Conversely, a U.S. transferor may run into antitrust violations if it tries to restrict the licensee from using the patented technology outside of the United States.[10] This territorial restriction in a grant of licence may be more acceptable if the subject-matter of the licence is a trade secret rather than a patent, the benefit of trade secret protection not being limited to any particular jurisdiction.

7.3 Scope of Grant

Some licensees grant rights that are restricted to specific intellectual property rights, such as an issued patent. Thus, the grant would provide that the licensee could engage in certain activities that otherwise would be prohibited as a result of the transferor's intellectual property. For example, the grant could permit the licensee to make products covered by the claims in patent 123456. "Licenses of this type are often given and taken by competitors with one another. They are sometimes referred to as 'accommodation licenses', and are concluded on fairly modest terms".[11] The patents that are licensed should be specifically listed in a Schedule attached to the agreement. The country, number, and expiration date should be indented. If pending applications are intended to be included, they should also be listed with their respective policy dates.[12] If there are patent applications, controls over their continued prosecution should be addressed, as well as the effect of patents not issuing as a result of the applications within a stated period of time.[13] With some other licensees (particularly with software), the licensee wants to be able to use specific technology and thus the grant refers to the right to use the technology in specified activities. For example, the grant would permit the licensee to use the leased software for its own internal purposes. These licensees often tend to omit any reference to the exclusionary rights that permit the license, with the assumption (hopefully correct) that they get a license of all the rights the transferor has. Prudent drafters would reference the exclusionary rights that permit the license. Fordis and Griffin gave this guidance, using a biotech example:

---

[9] This is important patented technology (see Chapter 3 of this text) for patents as well as for copyrighted works, particularly multimedia content (see Chapter 4 of this text).

[10] Coolley "Drafting", *les Nouvelles*, December 1992, p. 213.

[11] Goldscheider, *Licensing Law Handbook*, 2000-2001 ed., §7.2, p.76.

[12] *Op cit*, §7.14, p. 72.

[13] See Chapter 11, "Payment", §11.9.

Defining What is Conveyed

In most license agreements, the parties know exactly what is conveyed because the license is directed to an issued patent. In those licenses, the rights conveyed are often defined as follows:

"Any product the manufacture, use or sale of which would, but for the licenses granted herein, infringe a claim of U.S. Patent No. _____ ".

This language will not apply to all biotech products, however, because (1) many products are not the subject of issued or pending patents and (2) there are a number of ways to define biotech products. Thus, the practitioner must exercise great care to appropriately and accurately define exactly the product to be conveyed. An accurate definition should include both what product is conveyed and what forms that product may take.

Consider, for example, a license directed to a recombinant DNA invention relating to a gene sequence that codes for a specific protein. The rights to that invention might be expressed as:

The gene itself.

The vector being the gene.

The cell and cell line to which the gene encoding the protein was introduced.

The actual protein expressed by the cell.

In addition, rights to any of these aspects of the invention may be based on the structure of the product or the function of the product. Consider, for example, the protein. Rights to the protein defined in terms of structure could be defined narrowly as rights to a specific gene with a specific sequence. Alternatively, functional-type rights might be defined as the genetic sequence that encodes a particular protein, or even more broadly, rights to the genetic sequence that encode proteins that perform a specific function.

Similarly, rights in hybridoma technology can be conveyed in various forms. Most importantly, however, the practitioner should realize that a conveyance of a hybridoma will grant far greater rights than the conveyance of the monoclonal antibodies. As discussed above, the immortal hybridoma cell line will continue to produce monoclonal antibodies infinitely. The monoclonal antibodies, in contrast, have a limited lifetime.

As a final point, the practitioner should note that cell lines, including transformed cells that contain a specific gene or plasmid and hybridoma cell lines, may be deposited. In such a case, rights to the biological materials may be expressed by reference to the deposit, as follows:

Cell line shall mean the CHO cell line 1-15$_{500}$ deposited with the American Type Culture Collection and accorded accession number CRL 9696. (U.S. Patent No. 4,766,075).

Plasmids shall mean those plasmids deposited in the American Type Culture Collection, Rockville, Md., and given, respectively, A.T.C.C. Accession Nos. 39745, 39746, 39747, 39748 and 39749. (U.S. Patent No. 4,736,866).

Hybridomas shall mean hybridomas designated XMMEM-OE5 and XMMEN-LY1 as deposited with the American Type Culture Collection (A.T.C.C.), 12301

Parklawn Dr., Rockville Md., U.S.A. on Apr. 24, 1986 and given A.T.C.C. Accession Nos. HB9081 and HB9082, respectively, (U.S. Patent No. 4,918,163).[14]

7.3.1 Hybrid Licences

Grant claims can become complex when one tries to build in the entire bundle of rights needed (think of the many rights under copyright), or improperly only use the patent rights – make, use, sell, and import and overlook the other rights controlled by other intellectual property. Trade secrets produce different problems. Trade secrecy does not give rise to an exclusionary right – it is based on the rights to receive disclosure in exchange for restrictions on uses and obligations to maintain secrecy. Trade secrets are misappropriated or misused, not infringed. To reduce this complexity, Goldscheider writes: "Taking into account the differences in the various intellectual property rights, it is usually advisable to grant licenses to each one in a separate paragraph".[15]

PERMITTED/RESTRICTED USES

7.4 Uses Covered by the Grant

In addition to the subject-matter, the licence agreement should specify what uses are permitted in the case of patents, trademark and copyright and what uses are restricted in the case of trade secrets. The permitted rights for patents are variations of "make, use and sell".[16] The transferor could give Alice the right to make, but not to sell and use, and could require her to comply with quality control standards. Bob could get the right to sell only, *i.e.*, he would be allowed to act as a distributor of some kind, with a requirement for him to comply with the transferor's marketing program.[17] Charlie could get the right to use the patented technology, perhaps only at a specified plant site, and may be required to use the technology only in a specified manner, complying with all safety and environmental rules. There is a long list of permitted uses of a copyrighted work including the following: the right to produce or reproduce it; to perform it; to publish it; to translate it and to produce, reproduce or perform the translation;[18] to make a record or other way of mechanically performing a work; to import a copy of the work; and, in the case of a computer program, to rent it.[19] Each of these

---

[14] Jean Burke Foris and Susan Haberman Griffen, *"Avoiding Traps in Licensing Biotechnology"*, *les Nouvelles*, June 1991, 45 at p. 46.

[15] Goldscheider, *Licensing Law Handbook* 2000-2001, §7.20, p. 76.

[16] See §3.2 of this text.

[17] Since this may be a franchise, the rules relating to franchises, disclosures by the transferor and restrictions on permitted controls may be relevant — see Chapter 5 of this text starting at §5.20.

[18] See §4.10.3 to 4.10.6 of this text.

[19] See §4.10.7 and 4.10.8 of this text.

rights possessed by the copyright holder are independent of each other, and each may be licensed as to different, specific and separate applications.[20] The copyright holder of a painting can thus grant to Alice the right to publish the painting in a book; to Bob, the right to sell separate reproductions; and, to Charlie, the right to digitize it and place it in a clip art catalogue. The holder of a trade secret has the right to maintain secrecy. Once the secret information is released to another, the holder of the secret must impose restrictions on use; usage is not prohibited by statute, as is the case with patent or copyright. Instead of permitted uses, as are contained in a patent or copyright licence, a licence of a trade secret thus *restricts* uses as well as imposes obligations on the licensee to maintain secrecy. Often, a trade secret licence will permit one or more specific uses and restrict all other uses.

7.4.1 Non-physical Delivery

For any work that is stored in digital or electronic form, the right to transmit the work by telecommunication should be considered, as well as other methods of non-physical delivery that may be developed in the future. Developers of computer games are hard pressed to decide what computer platforms and what methods of delivery are appropriate uses for each licence (physical delivery at retail stores versus non-physical delivery over the Internet).[21]

7.4.2 "Have Made"

If a patent licence grants a right to make, the licence should clarify whether the licensee may permit a subcontractor to make the product for it, even though that may be implied by law. Likewise, rather than relying on terms implied by the local law, the agreement could specify whether a licensee that only has the right to "use" also has the right to "sell" the protected product to another user, or, if that is excluded, the right to dispose of it for scrap.

7.4.3 Grant of All Rights — What's Left?

If the grant in a patent licence is to "make, use, sell," it is possible that no rights have been reserved from the licensee since these words are co-extensive with the protection offered by the U.S. and Canadian Patent Acts. Mayers and Brunsvold thus question whether anything is added by including additional words such as "to . . . have made, . . . lease, or otherwise dispose of . . . ",[22] though these words are often added for comfort.[23] It might be appropriate to say that the rights "make, use and sell" include, without limitation, specific rights such as "have made,"

---

[20]   See §4.28 of this text.

[21]   See, for example, *Atari Games Corp. v. Nintendo of America Inc*, 975 F.2d 832 (Fed. Cir. 1992).

[22]   Mayers and Brunsvold, *License Agreements*, p. 71.

[23]   *Ibid.*, pp. 71-72.

"lease," or "dispose of". So long as the words "without limiting the generality of the foregoing" or some other phrase of similar effect is used, the business principles are often better developed by using the more explanatory language. The agreement could also clarify whether "have made" means to be made only by someone under the control of the licensee who is subject to confidentiality and restrictions on the use of any trade secrets involved.

7.5 Field of Use

The granted rights may be restricted to specific uses or purposes, often referred to as "fields of use". For example, an expert learning software system could be licensed to Alice, for use with devices that assist spine-injured individuals to walk, and to Bob, for use in the financial derivatives market.[24] If, however, the separation of fields of use are too finely divided and could "divide a naturally competitive market", in the United States there could be antitrust issues; thus, the field of use clause must be "handled with care".[25]

7.5.1 Difficulty in Separating Fields of Use

In a business sense, it is often very difficult to separate the various uses to provide exclusivity to different entities for the separate fields of use. This difficulty increases if the extent of the usefulness of the technology is not yet proven. The business deal often reflects the parties' differing predictions of the merit of the foreseeable applications. The negotiators of the technology transfer agreement will be challenged to produce language that is precise and that resolves the complications resulting from the "ever-increasing commercial and industrial complexity and overlap".[26] A licensee could be restricted to use the licensed technology, whether it be protected by patent, copyright or trade secrecy, only:

(a) in specified combinations — if the licensee has some product or process that will be combined by utilizing the transferor's technology, the licence could restrict the licensee to use the transferor's technology only with that product or process;
(b) with specified styles or sizes of product; or
(c) with product to be sold or used by specified customers, or marketed through specified trade channels.

---

[24] These varied, divergent uses are not at all the result of my imagination running rampant, but were suggested to me as appropriate uses for the product produced by one of my software clients.

[25] Cooley, "Drafting," *les Nouvelles*, December 1992, p. 213. See also Milgrim, *On Licensing*, §15.12, pp. 15–28, and Chapter 10 of this text.

[26] Milgrim, "*On Licensing*," §15.13, p. 15–29.

IMPLIED LICENCES

7.6 Implied Licences

The negotiators to a technology transfer agreement should consider not only the rights expressly granted or transferred but also those that may be implied. Brunsvold and O'Reilley point out that equitable principles "prohibit a party to a contract from taking legal actions that would interfere with the expected consideration and rights of the other party to the contract".[27] Brunsvold and O'Reilley list some grants that a court could choose to imply on equitable grounds (*e.g.*, plain indications that a grant of licence should be inferred).[28]

(a) A license to "make and sell" may imply a right to use "for if not, why would anyone purchase from the licensee".

(b) "[A] license to make and use does *not* imply a licence to sell".[29]

(c) "[A] license to sell does not logically imply the right to make if it can be presumed that the licensed product can be obtained by purchase".[30]

(d) Once a product that embodies technology covered by a patent is sold, patent rights cannot be used to control the manner of its use or the right to resell that product.[31]

(e) U.S. cases have established that the purchaser of a patented product has the right, in the absence of an express restriction imposed at or prior to sale, to also resell and repair the patented product free of patent infringement suits by the seller.[32] Any restriction imposed must not violate U.S. antitrust rules.[33]

Although the grant of licence implies the agreement of the transferor not to assert its intellectual property rights against the licensee,[34] the implied agreement may cover only the precise subject-matter of the express grant.[35] Brunsvold and O'Reilley suggest that, if there is bad faith on the part of the transferor, a court may imply a licence to exploit the undisclosed but necessary patentable technology.[36] "However, bad faith by the patent owner is not necessary to create an implied license.... Inadvertence or sloppy practise

---

[27] Brian G. Brunsvold and Dennis P. O'Reilley, "Implied Licenses", October 1993, Annual Meeting of the Licensing Executives Society (U.S.A. and Canada) (unpublished), p. 4 (hereinafter "Brunsvold and O'Reilley, '*Implied Licenses*'").

[28] Brunsvold and O'Reilley, *Drafting Patents License Agreements*, p. 246-7.

[29] *Ibid.*

[30] *Ibid.*

[31] *Ibid.*, p. 252, referring to the doctrine of exhaustion enunciated by the U.S. Supreme Court in *Adams v. Burke*, 84 U.S. (17 Wall) 453 (1873).

[32] *Ibid.*, p. 253.

[33] *Ibid.*

[34] See Brunsvold and O'Reilley, *License Agreements*, pp. 246-7.

[35] *Ibid.*, p. 16.

[36] See Brunsvold and O'Reilley "*Drafting Patents License Agreements*", at p. 248.

will also suffice if the party asserting the implied license could reasonably infer from the patent owner's actions that the patent owner consented to the use of the patented invention".[37] Brunsvold and O'Reilley suggest that if it is intended to restrict a licence grant to a specific patent, even though there are related patents, these related patents and patent applications should be disclosed by number and title, and a licence or other transfer of these other rights should be disclaimed.[38] The licensee may want an express agreement that the transferor will not assert its rights under any of its intellectual property rights against the licensee so long as the licensee is engaged only in the functions intended to be covered by the licence.[39] In the multimedia area, the licensee may need more than the traditional intellectual property rights. It may need a waiver of moral rights if the work was created outside of the United States.[40]

Strategies:
   (1)   *In a patent licence, specify whether the grant is intended to cover every activity covered by the patent. Precise wording is necessary to avoid unnecessary and undesirable questions as to what limitations, if any, were intended.*[41]
   (2)   *Expressly negate any implied licence that is not intended, or provide an express licence for the intended scope, with an exclusion of all other uses.*[42]

7.7 Quantity Limitations

In performance clauses, there is often a requirement that the licensee will manufacture or sell a minimum number of units.[43] In the "grant" clause there may be requirements that the licensee sell in minimum blocks of a stated number of products. Conversely, it could be specified that the licensee cannot sell more than a specified number of units in a year, or in total. In recognition of different distribution channels that need to be maintained, some distributors could be licensed to sell in blocks of at least 100,000 units per sale; others could sell in smaller blocks. Instead of using a fixed

---

[37] *Ibid.*, p. 2, referring to *DeForest Radio Telephone & Telegraph v. United States*, 273 U.S. 236, at 241 (1927).

[38] *Ibid.*, p. 248.

[39] Coolley, *"Drafting," les Nouvelles*, December 1992, p. 213.

[40] See §4.16 of this text and Kenneth M. Kaufman, "Legal and Business Issues for On-Line Publishers and Content Providers", in *The Internet and Business: A Lawyer's Guide to the Emerging Legal Issues*, Joseph F. Ruh, Jr., ed. (The Computer Law Association, Current Issues Publications series, 1996), p. 107, at 108.

[41] See Goldscheider, *Licensing Law Handbook* p. 316. See also Goldscheider, *Licensing Negotiations,* where he provides examples of activities described by a reference to a patent as well as activities that are functionally described.

[42] See Brunsvold and O'Reilley, *"Drafting Patent License Agreements"*, p. 247.

[43] For further discussion see §12.3 ff. of this text.

number of units, the licence could restrict the licensee from selling more than 10 per cent of the product's total sales, perhaps to prevent it from obtaining a dominant position as a buyer.

7.8 Price Limitations

Some transferors would like to restrict the licensee from selling below a specified price. Such a restriction will contravene anti-restraint of trade rules against price maintenance and should be avoided.[44] An alternative might be to let the licensee charge the price it chooses, but to provide for a minimum level of royalty. Increasingly, royalties are being based on suggested retail price to allow the licensee the maximum flexibility and to provide the transferor with an assured level of royalties without having to resort to price fixing. The licensee then can engage in price wars but, without the consent of the transferor, the transferor's revenue will not drop below a pre-agreed level.[45]

TERRITORY

7.9 Territory

The licence may permit the licensee to engage in the licensed activities only in a particular territory. In the United States and Canada, there seem to be few legal restrictions on the size of the territory (for examples, the portion of the City of Calgary lying north of the Bow River, all of the Province of Alberta, or all of Canada). The licence may give exclusive rights to some territories and non-exclusive rights to others, and it may give the right to manufacture and sell in one territory, but only the right to use in another. These territorial restrictions, frequently seen in trademark licences or franchises, are useful in distribution agreements and manufacturing licences. These restrictions must be carefully reviewed for any licence to a licensee within the European Community where the market is intended to be seamless.[46]

7.9.1 Doctrine of Exhaustion

Once an item has been manufactured and sold, it may be impossible to restrict the purchaser from reselling the item, causing a relocation of the item from a permitted territory into a restricted territory. There is a rule of law referred to as

---

[44] See Chapter 12 of this text.

[45] In any event, local advice on restraint of trade rules is essential.

[46] See Goldscheider, *Licensing Law Handbook* 2000-2001 at pp. 74-75 for examples.

the "doctrine of exhaustion" of rights that must be reviewed to determine the ability to control such movement of goods.[47]

7.9.2 Site Licences: Relocation and Replacement

If a licence of technology is specific to a certain site or plant, the possible relocation or replacement of the plant must be addressed. The intent of the restriction is to limit the number of sites at which the licensee can engage in a licensed activity, and the restriction should not prevent an appropriate relocation or replacement.

7.10 Transferring Knowledge

Unless the licensee is merely an agreement not to sell for infringements, such as a bare patent licence, the licensee will likely require assistance to employ the licensed technology. The transfer agreement should contemplate that knowledge will be transferred and technical assistance provided. This could be done by:

(a) Training sessions;
(b) Well organized manuals that will be easily understood by the licensee;
(c) The transferor's manual being available to provide support on an as-needed basis; and
(d) Plant visits and periodic personnel exchanges.

MOST FAVOURABLE TERMS

7.11 Most Favourable Terms and Conditions

A licensee who is in a strong bargaining position will want to have a deal that is at least as good as those its competitors have.

> There is no general rule of law which requires the patent owner to extend identical licensing terms to all licensees, or to refrain from granting to a subsequent licensee terms which are more generous in some respect than those contractually assured to a prior licensee. It is therefore quite natural for the prospective acceptor of a license to request that the agreement contain provisions assuring him [of most favoured licensee terms].[48]

---

[47] For additional discussion, see Ronald B. Coolley, "*Recent Developments in Emerging Issues in Licensing*" in The Licensing Journal, Vol. 14, No. 86, p. 7, and Michael Burnside, "*Intellectual Property as a Non-Tariff Barrier*", presented to the Canadian Bar Association, September 26, 1990, at its annual meeting in London, England.

[48] Brunsvold and O'Reilley, *License Agreements*, p. 117.

Thus, the licensee may request that if the transferor grants to anyone else a licence of the same patent on more favourable terms, the transferee will give notice of this subsequent licence and offer the licensee the benefit of the lower royalty rate. O'Reilley and Morin write:

> The fundamental purpose of the MFL clause is to protect prior licensees from a competitive disadvantage should subsequent licenses be granted on more favourable terms, conditions or royalties. Different terms, however, are not always a concern, for not all subsequent licenses could impose a competitive disadvantage, regardless of the terms, conditions or royalties. For instance, the licensees may be in different fields or territories, making it totally irrelevant, from a competitive standpoint that one licensee pays a 10% royalty while the other pays 5%. The licensor must carefully draft the MFL clause to ensure his flexibility to license, on any basis, to subsequent parties not in competition with his prior licensees. Competitive disadvantage, even though difficult to ascertain, should be the touchstone of an MFL clause.
>
> In general, the MFL clause provides a first licensee with an option to obtain more favourable terms granted to a second licensee. Thus, the MFL clause is triggered by the subsequent granting of a license. But what is a license as contemplated by this provision? Obviously, an express agreement covering future use of a property right (whether it be exclusive rights or otherwise) would qualify as such a license. Express agreements covering past use of the property right and the doctrine of implied license, however, have created problems, especially for the licensor. The general form of the MFL clause is ill equipped to combat these problems. To prevent an unintended application of the MFL clause, the licensor must clearly understand the possible ramifications of subsequent settlements and other conduct relative to infringers. A well informed licensee will be able to take advantage of the licensor's mistakes.
>
> Perhaps the most troublesome problem in administering a typical MFL clause is correctly evaluating whether a second licensee is more, or less, favourable than the first. If the MFL clause does not define the phrase "more favourable terms" or "a more favourable royalty", it is extremely difficult to compare the costs to different licensees of the respective licenses, particular when the rights licensed and the terms and conditions are not precisely the same in both licenses. What value is accorded to the rights licensed, the variety of considerations, the methods of payment, and the restrictions placed on the licensee and licensor in each license? Who should determine whether the subsequent license is more or less favourable?[49]

7.11.1 Cherry-picking Selected Terms

The transferor will wish to avoid allowing the licensee to "cherry-pick" the terms it likes best. For example, consider a more favourable royalty rate due to a greater access to the licensee's improvements. Some transactions may be so

---

[49]   D. Patrick O'Reilley and Michael H. Morin, "Troubles for Most Favoured Licensees", *les Nouvelles*, March 1998, 26 at 27.

unique, due to the nature of the players, that no concession should be made to other licensees who do not have the same market presence. For example, inclusion in the IBM product line may warrant terms that others should not have. The licensee should be required to match all the terms, not just one such as the royalty rate, so that they accept the more unfavorable terms as well.[50]
O'Reilly and Morin write:

> What renders one license more or less favourable than the next? Howe does one go about determining the relative value of licenses? Because a license is a contract, the terms of the contracts should control this inquiry. The typical MFL clause, however, offers no guidance for determining this important issue.
>
> This lack of specificity suggests that license agreements are easily comparable or that the governing standards are clear in the case law. In reality, neither of these assumptions is correct.
>
> Because licenses are frequently negotiated and tailored to the needs of a specific licensee (and licensor), the valuation and comparison of terms of license agreements are exceptionally difficult. Often the amount and/or type of technology licensed varies, grantbacks of technology are sometimes included, and obligations of the licensor or licensee, and restrictions on the licensee, differ. Each such variation in the agreements could conceivably, and in reality, often does affect the license's value.[51]

They recommend establishing benchmarks for comparing agreements as where one is more favourable:

> Another method of resolving uncertainties is for the licensor and licensee to establish meaningful and predictable parameters for determining whether a second license is "more favourable" by agreeing on an exclusive list of controlling parameters and to incorporate them into the MFL clause. Naturally, these standards should be limited to the important aspects of the license agreement. As an example, such a list of parameters might include: (a) the scope of technology transferred (e.g. know-how, technical assistance); (b) technology grant-backs (e.g. cross-licenses, know-how); (c) major restrictions placed on the license (e.g. territory, field-of-use, export); (d) major obligations assumed by the licensee (e.g. best efforts to develop markets), and (e) the terms of the agreement (e.g. termination or extension provisions). This exclusive list clearly will reflect the expectations of the licensor and licensee concerning the scope of the "more favourable" determination. When such parameters are provided, an express statement should be included to reflect that only those terms and conditions common to both licenses should be considered.[52]

---

[50] See O'Reilley and Morin, p. 31.
[51] *Ibid.*, p. 30.
[52] *Ibid.*, pp. 30-31.

They recommend caution when dealing with settlements and MFL clauses, and in particular they emphasize the difference between amounts paid to settle a claim and amounts paid for continuing rights:

> If the licensor insists on a "settlement-for-past-infringement" exception, the licensee must ensure that "past infringement" is expressly defined. Specifically, the exception should be limited to those aspects of the settlement dealing with past infringement as opposed to future use of the rights. In addition, the licensee should restrict the exception to those property rights licensed by the licensor, thus avoiding the situation where his licensed rights are a part of the consideration paid in a settlement of the infringement of some other rights.[53]

7.11.2 Alerting the Licensee to more favourable Terms

O'Reilley and Morin write:

> Another problem is the procedure by which a licensee is to discover a subsequent, more favourable license agreement. The licensor may be obligated to inform the licensee about all subsequent related licenses, obviating the licensee's problem but often creating an administrative or competitive problem for the licensor. The licensor could be required to disclose to the licensee only those license agreements that have more favourable terms. Where the licensor decides whether one license is more favourable than the other, he may have a bias in favour of his own interests. Even where a licensor evaluates subsequent licenses in good faith, an error in such evaluation may expose the licensor to liability.[54]

7.11.3 Most Favoured Clauses and Settlement of Infringement Suits

The transferor will try to avoid the most favoured clause applying to a license granted to settle an infringement suit. The transferor should not be placed in the situation of having to choose between prosecuting infringers where a court may award a lower royalty rate triggering off the most favoured clause.

Strategy: The most favoured licensee clause could require the licensee to elect to take all terms in the licence that appear more favourable, rather than cherry-picking selected terms.[55]

---

[53]   See O'Reilly and Morin, p. 30.
[54]   *Ibid.*
[55]   See Goldscheider, *Licensing Law Handbook*, p. 327.

7.11.4 Checklist of items to be reviewed for a most-favoured licensee claim

Strategy:
The most favoured licence clause will address the following:
(a)   *how and when the transferor will notify the licensee of the details of another licence. Obligations of confidentiality owed to a subsequent licensee must be protected and the most favoured provision should be restricted to stated patents;*[56]
(b)   *a territory or field of use in which the favourable terms apply;*
(c)   *the duration of the more favourable terms;*[57]
(d)   *the method of valuing non-cash consideration (for examples, cross-licences or equity);*
(e)   *the method of dealing with lump sum payments;*[58]
(f)   *whether the adjustment will be retroactive;*
(g)   *how to deal with prior licences;*
(h)   *how to deal with licenses to infringers;*
(i)   *how the licensee will elect to accept the most favoured licensee clause, if the adjustment is not made automatically.*

OTHER LICENCES

7.12 Right to Receive Other Licences

A licensee, which has received rights for a restricted territory or field of use, may wish to be considered as a candidate when the transferor is ready to licence other territories or fields of use. The right to be considered may range from a first right to negotiate, to a soft first refusal (where the transferor has not yet located the potential licensee and established the terms), to a hard first refusal (the name of the licensee and pertinent terms are both established), or to an option to acquire rights to additional territories on pre-determined terms.

7.13 Use of Other Party's Name in Promotions

A licence may restrict the right of either party to use the other party's name in promotions; some licences even prevent the licensee from even announcing that it has a licence.[59]

---

[56]   See Michael R. McGurk, *Problems of Careless Drafting, les Nouvelles*, September 1997, 148 and 149.
[57]   *Ibid.*
[58]   O'Reilley and Morin, p. 31.
[59]   See, for example, Goldscheider, *Licensing Negotiations,* Model Clause M24-3, p. 273.

EFFECT OF INVALIDITY

7.14 Effect of Invalidity of the Licenced Intellectual Property Right

The licensee may want to be protected against paying royalties if one of the intellectual property rights that it considers material subsequently is established to be invalid or of no beneficial effect. See Chapter 11 of this text.

7.14.1 Estoppel

In Canada, the licensee is estopped from disputing the validity of its transferor's intellectual property right; entering into the licence is considered to concede that point.[60] In the United States, there is no such estoppel; in contrast the anti-restraint of trade rules encourage the licensee to dispute such validity.[61] A Canadian licence might disclaim an admission of validity when appropriate.

EXCLUSIVITY

7.15 Exclusive Licence

If the licence is exclusive, it will exclude the transferor as well as all third parties.[62] If the transferor wishes to reserve some rights to itself, these rights must be expressly reserved and, thus, make the licence exclusive subject to these specified reservations. A transferor may be using the licensed technology in its own business or may have outstanding licences, "limiting [its] ability to grant total exclusivity".[63]

7.15.1 Sole Licence

A "sole" licence does not exclude the transferor; it agrees only that the transferor will not grant any other licences to third parties.[64]

---

[60] *Rymland v. Regal Bedding Co.* (1966), 59 D.L.R. (2d) 316, 58 W.W.R. 182, 51 C.P.R. 137, 34 Fox Pat. C. 145 (Man. C.A.).

[61] Milgrim, *On Licensing*, §18.50.

[62] See D.G. Henderson, "*Patent Licensing: Problems from the Impression of the English Language*" in (1970), 4 Ottawa L. Rev. 62, p. 66 (hereinafter "*Henderson 'Patent Licensing'*") and Mayers and Brunsvold, *License Agreements*, p. 39.

[63] Milgrim, *On Licensing*, §15.09.

[64] See Henderson, "*Patent Licensing*," p. 66 and Milgrim, *On Licensing*, §15.33.

7.15.2 "Sole and Exclusive"

The use of these words together is a contradiction of terms.[65] This specialized legal meaning, however, is not clearly apparent and, perhaps, it would be more appropriate to specify in the technology transfer agreement:

(a) what rights granted exclude all others, including the transferor;
(b) what rights are reserved by the transferor for its use alone;
(c) what rights are reserved by the transferor for its use and for the use of others currently licensed, but to the exclusion of all others except the licensee; and
(d) what rights are reserved by the transferor for its use and for the use of others now or hereafter licensed.

Strategy: Assist the negotiators: set out the business issues, alternatives and consequences in the early draft agreements, perhaps using annotations.

7.16 Limited Exclusivity

Exclusivity can be restricted to:

(a) specified fields of use;
(b) specified distribution methods;
(c) specified territories;
(d) specified time periods;
(e) specified levels of sales, production, purchases or other appropriate milestones.

7.17 Conditional Exclusivity

It could be a condition of maintaining continued exclusivity that the licensee:

(a) attain certain levels of sales, purchases, production or other appropriate milestones;
(b) produce specified royalties;
(c) pay specified amounts if required royalty levels are not attained;
(d) engage in certain research, development, production or sales activities appropriate to the circumstances.

---

[65] Henderson, *"Patent Licensing"*, p. 66.

PERFORMANCE REQUIREMENTS

7.18 Best Efforts

The phrase "best efforts" is often used in technology transfer agreements, and not always as a result of drafting laziness. It may be used because:

(a) the parties have developed a level of trust between them and do not want to disrupt the relationship by pressing for more precision;

(b) the parties are unable to predict market acceptance of the product; and

(c) the negotiators think the phrase has a well recognized meaning.

Unfortunately, when the trust relationship collapses or the transferor feels that its technology is not being adequately exploited, the parties will find that although the term "best efforts" has been the subject of frequent litigation, particularly in the United States, its meaning is uncertain and ambiguous. In Canada, there is case law that would indicate that the phrase means "leave no stone unturned". The words "do not mean second-best endeavours . . . . They do not mean that the limits of reason must be overstepped with regard to the cost of the service; but short of these qualifications the words mean that the [licensee] must, broadly speaking, leave no stone unturned . . . ."[66]

In the United States as well, there does not seem to be a clear meaning of the phrase "best efforts". Its use gives little or no guidance — indeed there is no "direct reference . . . to the scope or direction in which the efforts should be made".[67]

Strategy: The best advice is do not use the phrase "best efforts".[68]

7.19 Minimum Levels

The parties might be better served if they addressed what "minimum performance" will be acceptable. This performance may be in terms of:

---

[66] *C.A.E. Industries Ltd. v. R.*, [1983] 2 F.C. 616, at 638, 639 (T.D.); additional reasons at (1983), 79 C.P.R. (2d) 88 (Fed. T.D.); leave to appeal refused (1985), 20 D.L.R. (4th) 347*n*, [1986] 2 W.W.R. *xxin* (S.C.C.), referring to *Sheffield Dist. Ry. Co. v. Great Central Ry. Co.* (1911), 27 T.L.R. 451. There seems to be no distinction between "best efforts" and "best endeavours" for this purpose. This case law seems to be totally out of line with commercial expectations in technology transfer agreements.

[67] Brunsvold and O'Reilley, *License Agreements*, p. 25, quoting *Western Geophysical Co. of America v. Bolt Associates*, 285 F. Supp. 815, 157 U.S.P.Q. 129 (D. Conn. 1968).

[68] See Charles W. Shiftley, and Bradley J. Hulbert, "'Best Efforts' May Not Be The Best Advice" in *les Nouvelles*, the Journal of the Licensing Executive Society, Vol. XXVII, No. 1, March 9, 1992, p. 37, at 39. This article has an interesting analysis of "best efforts" clauses providing a summary of legal decisions, practical examples of difficulties caused by the phrase and suggested improvements.

(a) media advertising to be undertaken;
(b) displays at trade shows;
(c) direct mail promotions;
(d) minimum number of licences to be obtained in a year; and
(e) minimum revenue to be earned in a year.

The request for "minimum performance" requirements cuts through the "puffery" of the licensee; suddenly, the transferor sees the licensee realistically assessing the product and the market-place.

7.20 Effect of Not Satisfying Performance Requirements

If the licensee does not satisfy the conditions for maintaining exclusivity, some of the consequences may be

(a) loss of exclusivity — the licence could convert from an exclusive licence to an non-exclusive licence.[69] This allows the transferor either to exploit the technology itself or to license others for that purpose. It may, however, not always be possible to find other licensees who are prepared to compete with the formerly exclusive licensee, and the benefit of the conversion from exclusivity to non-exclusivity may be illusory;
(b) maintenance of exclusivity by payment of a specified amount;
(c) termination of agreement;
(d) loss of rights only after a "cure" period has expired, giving the licensee a second chance to attain the specified milestones; and
(e) forbearance of loss of rights if the failure to attain the milestones is due to factors beyond the licensee's control. A good and prompt dispute resolution mechanism will be necessary for the transferor to avoid any dispute over whether the failure was caused by the transferor or by the licensee or by external causes.[70]

---

[69] Mayers and Brunsvold, *License Agreements*, p. 41.
[70] See Milgrim, *On Licensing*, §15.14.

Chapter 8

CUSTOMIZATION AND ACCEPTANCE TESTS: WHO, WHY, WHEN, WHERE AND HOW

8.1 Introduction

Frequently, the transferor's existing technology must be adapted or further developed for the licensee's particular needs. This adaptation may give rise to an issue over ownership of improvements[1] and over joint ownership.[2] In any event, acceptance criteria for the adaptation must be addressed; this is the subject-matter of this Chapter.

8.2 Specifications/Acceptance Tests Yet to be Developed

When technology is being adapted or improved, the licensee will want to subject the resulting product or process to appropriate acceptance tests. Often, when a technology transfer agreement is being prepared, the parties have not yet developed mutually acceptable function or performance specifications, thus it is unlikely that acceptance tests will be established. A mechanism is necessary for establishing acceptance tests as the project proceeds. The negotiators must contemplate how the parties will interact in the further development of the technology. The agreement might set out, perhaps in chronological order, flexible provisions covering the remedial action to be undertaken if the acceptance tests are not passed. Although legally trained individuals like certainty in their agreements establishing such a working relationship, "an on-going dynamic process" may be more desirable than the "locked-in" relationship that is produced in most agreements.[3]

---

[1] See Chapter 9.

[2] See §4.27 of this text.

[3] American Bar Association, Section on Patent, Trademark and Copyright Law, Committee on Computer Programs, *Model Software License Provisions*, Committee Chair: D.C. Toedt III (hereinafter "ABA Draft Model Software Agreement").

8.2.1 Conceptual Description of Specifications

The development agreement could provide a conceptual description of what the parties intend to achieve in the development project, perhaps discussing the general business or scientific problems intended to be solved. Although only concepts can be described at this point of the research and development, the expectations of the parties should be stated as precisely as possible to avoid uncertainty and unrealistic expectations. If the licensee is inexperienced, it may be wise for the transferor to insist that a consultant be retained to clarify the licensee's expectations. In any event, each party "should have experienced technical advisers to help establish the specifications".[4]

8.2.2 Types of Specifications

Lawrence Chesler's useful article on system specification and acceptance testing guidance may be summarized as follows:[5]

(a) there are two types of specifications that may be defined for a system: functional specifications and performance specifications;[6]

(b) functional specifications define the capabilities of the system at a functional level, *i.e.*, what features and functions the system will have;

(c) performance specifications define *how efficiently* the system will per-form its functions;

(d) although accurately defined functional capabilities of a system can be complex, it is usually the performance specifications that are most difficult to define with sufficient clarity to avoid contractual disputes; and

(e) to the extent practicable, define all acceptance tests criteria, and especial-ly performance specifications, by reference to well-drafted bench-mark tests in which all relevant variables are carefully and systematically controlled.

8.2.3 Development Team

Appropriately trained and experienced personnel should be appointed to a team that will co-ordinate the development of the customized technology;[7] the team

---

[4] Pegi A. Groundwater, "General Considerations in Drafting Software Licenses", a paper presented at the Licensing Executives Society Annual Meeting, October 26, 1992 (unpublished), p. 3-64. See also William P. Andrews, Jr., "Limiting Risks in International Transactions: Current Legal Issues in the United States Domestic Transactions for Computer Goods and the Unsigned Services", a paper presented to the World Computer Law Congress, 1991, p. 12 (hereinafter "Andrews, 'Limiting Risks'").

[5] Lawrence Chesler, "Specifications, Acceptance Testing, Acceptance Procedures and Risk Allocations in Agreements for Complex Systems: The Vendor's Perspective" in The Computer Law Association Bulletin, 1991, Vol. 6, No. 1, p. 8 (hereinafter "Chesler 'Specifications'").

[6] *Ibid.*, p. 9.

[7] ABA Draft Model Software Agreement, Section 211.1.

could be the same group that established the specifications. This development team could be given the exclusive right to approve the initial specifications and any deviations from them.

8.3 Needs – Study Plan

The first task of the development team might be to design the method for performing a detailed study of the parties' goals or a "Needs – Study Plan".[8] The agreement could address what would happen if the development team cannot reach agreement on a Needs – Study Plan within the desired time period, as well as the method and timing of any payment to each of the parties for its contribution to the Needs – Study Plan.

8.3.1 Development Plan

Once the parties have achieved agreement on a Needs – Study Plan, they can move on to prepare a detailed Development Plan and a related Progress Schedule. The Development Plan could consist of critical path charts setting out the generally anticipated project tasks and task phases with reasonable estimates of the time anticipated and charges for each project task. "The contract must provide a clear, well-defined mechanism for finalizing the specifications and acceptance test procedures well in advance of system installation, in order to avoid disputes when the time comes for acceptance testing."[9] As Chesler writes:

> The best mechanism for accomplishing this goal is to build into the contract a series of milestones, to set forth in the contract the interim tasks that must be completed in order to insure that such milestones are met, and to assign responsibility for those tasks to the appropriate party. There should be a clear understanding that the vendor's ability to meet milestones by the dates projected is contingent upon timely performance by the user of all tasks for which the user is responsible.[10]

8.3.2 Contributions of Each Party

The responsibility of each party must be specified, including: (a) payment, (b) provision of previously developed intellectual property, personnel and equipment, (c) the right to use previously developed intellectual property contributed to the project by one party, and (d) consideration of the ownership of any derivative work.

---

[8] *Ibid.*, Section 213.1.
[9] Chesler, "Specifications", p. 10.
[10] *Ibid.*

8.3.3 Binding Effect of Development Plan and Progress Schedule

The agreement must consider what, if any, binding effect the Development Plan and Progress Schedule will have — whether it will be established for guidance only, or will a unilateral deviation result in damages or, perhaps, termination. The parties might agree to periodically review the Development Plan and Progress Schedule with the intention of revising both the specifications and the timetables to take into account the result achieved to date. The agreement must address the effect of parties being unable to agree on the initial Development Plan and Progress Schedule or on deviations that are "essential" in the eyes of one party.

8.4 Performance of Acceptance Tests

The Development Plan and Progress Schedule should also include methods of testing the resulting technology; some payments may depend on acceptance tests being passed. The agreement could consider:

(a) the time period within which the acceptance tests must be conducted, and the effect of a test not being performed within that period;

(b) the location of the test;

(c) the rights and obligations of the developer to attend at the test and to conduct or participate in the test;

(d) the right of the non-testing party to receive full details of the test results;

(e) control over quality of material to be processed in the test, and which party has the right or obligation to provide that material (if the user is performing the test, the developer may want to pre-test the material to make sure it is appropriate to be used in the test);

(f) detailed standards that will establish acceptance or rejection, perhaps as to quality, quantity and speed of input/output;[11]

(g) partial acceptance if the test is "almost passed";

(h) the consequence of a failure, including an extension to allow the developer to attempt to remedy the problems (with or without a penalty), and the ability of either party to abandon if the remedial action is not done in a timely fashion or cannot be done economically;

(i) allowances for failures or delays not attributable to the parties;

(j) the right to re-test after modifications have been made, and how many times tests must be performed; and

---

[11] *Ibid.*, p. 9. Andrews, "Limiting Risks" writes that the "single best avenue for avoidance of litigation in computer contracts is to establish in excruciating detail the expectations for the performance of the system" (p. 12). The author of this text has experienced too much excruciating detail in contracts, and, as a plain language drafter, would prefer "precisely accurate detail".

(k) the effect on any warranty if the tests are passed — are the tests in lieu of a warranty?

8.4.1 Delays and Deficiencies

Chesler writes:

> In some instances it may be reasonable for the vendor's performance dates to slip by one day for each day the user is late in performing its obligations; in other instances, it may be reasonable for the vendor's performance dates to slip by a longer period of time than a one for one slippage, where, for example the vendor is forced to divert resources to other projects while waiting for the user to complete its obligations. The contract should also specify that if the user's approval of specifications and acceptance tests procedures is delayed beyond a specified milestone date, all subsequent vendor milestone dates for implementation and delivery will be delayed . . . If the vendor submits specifications or acceptance test procedures to a user for review and approval, the user should be required to approve or disapprove such materials in writing in a reasonably short period of time (*e.g.*, fifteen business days). Because of the possibility that a user may never approve specifications or acceptance criteria, or the process may drag on for extended period, the contract should specify that the user's failure to provide written notice of disapproval within the specified period of time constitutes approval; . . . The contract also should provide a mechanism for terminating the contract if such specifications or test procedures are not approved by a certain date.[12]

8.4.2 Rejections

One potential consequence of technology failing to pass acceptance tests is the right to reject the technology and, perhaps, to cancel any remaining obligations under the technology transfer agreement.[13] In allowing for rejection, the following might be considered:

(a) the extent of failure of the acceptance tests that permit rejection or other reasons giving rise to such a drastic remedy;

(b) the time within which rejection must be made;

(c) the consequences of not rejecting within that time period;

(d) the method of giving notice of rejection;

(e) any period in which the transferor has the opportunity to cure the defect giving rise to the rejection;

(f) which party has the responsibility to remove the rejected technology from the licensee's premises (this is particularly important if the technology is embodied in a plant or major system) and the incidental costs of restoring the condition of the licensee's premises;

---

[12] *Ibid.*, p. 11.
[13] See also §13.5 of this text.

(g) whether rejection is the sole remedy available to the licensee; and

(h) whether the contractual right to reject is instead of any implied right of rejection granted by any applicable Sale of Goods legislation.[14]

8.4.3 Abandonment

Each party may want the opportunity to abandon the project if it feels that the project is not viable or that it is not getting what it anticipated out of the project. Either party may come to the conclusion that a project is not economically viable and, thus, may wish to abandon the entire project or only the tasks that are causing the uneconomic result (assuming that viable tasks can be separated from non-viable tasks). The agreement could allow for abandonment on a specified, but reasonable notice and provide for a pre-agreed payment for the abandonment. The agreement could also go on to resolve the rights of ownership and the continued use of the abandoned technology.

8.5 Documentation to be Delivered

If documentation will be required, its details and format must be established by the parties. In many cases, particularly with software, the completeness of documentation may determine the actual usefulness of the technology. The details of the documentation could vary depending on the stage of development.

8.6 Records and Reports

In order to establish independent development, the parties might require that their researchers maintain records of all third-party sources of research, scientific principles and data used in the development. These records might be necessary to defend against a claim of misappropriation of copyrighted material (including source code for software) or trade secrets. They could include the names of all individuals who worked on the project and a cross-reference to their files which contain the appropriate secrecy and assignment of innovations agreements.[15]

---

[14] For example, ss. 36 and 37 of Alberta's *Sale of Goods Act*, R.S.A. 2000, c. S-2, or the *Uniform Commercial Code,* Art. 2.

[15] See, for example, the ABA Draft Model Software Agreement, Section 215.3.

Chapter 9

IMPROVEMENTS AND JOINT OWNERSHIP

9.1 Introduction

In many technology transfer relationships, either party may make improvements to the technology that was initially transferred. The negotiators must determine how these improvements will be shared and which party will own them. The law does not imply that improvements must be shared; that is the subject of contract.[1]

9.2 Business Reasons for the Transferor to Share Improvements

The transferor may want to share improvements with its licensees for a number of reasons including:

(a) to keep its product competitive, maintain customer loyalty and, thus, maintain the income flow from running royalties;

(b) to maintain a position for the technology as the one that sets the standard for the industry;

(c) to increase its royalty income by exploiting the improvement throughout its distribution chain;

(d) to extend the economic life of the product/process and, thus, extend the life of the income stream;

(e) to decrease the licensee's exposure to product liability by keeping the product/process in a state-of-the-art condition.

---

[1] See Gordon F. Henderson, Q.C., 'Problems from the Imprecision of the English Language', 63 C.P.R. 99 (1969), at 107.

9.3 Business Reasons for the Licensee to Want Access to Improvements

The licensee may want to gain access to improvements for the following reasons:

(a) to maintain or improve sales;
(b) to improve its productivity if it is a user of the licensed technology;
(c) to maintain its revenue stream from sublicensees; and
(d) to share improvements made by other licensees, as well as those made by its transferor.

9.4 Business Reasons for the Transferor to Want Access to Licensee's Improvements

The transferor will want access to improvements that the licensee makes to the transferor's technology:

(a) to be able to provide support. If the licensee has changed the technology without disclosure to the transferor, the transferor's attempts to provide support may be frustrated. If all users are not implementing the same technology, support will become increasingly complex. Most software suppliers will cease to support obsolete products after a period of time, and will want their licensees to have only the improved versions. Many updates to software are made to overcome problems that caused a high demand for support; implementation of these updates will reduce the cost of providing support. If standardization is the goal, lack of implementation of all the improvements will detract from standardization;
(b) to share the improvements with its other licensees and thus develop an "improvement club", or a patent pool;[2]
(c) to maintain the base product as the standard in the industry;
(d) to gain the benefit of improvements that would not have been made but for the disclosure of the transferor's trade secrets.

---

[2] A significant difficulty in designing a patent pool is the belief of each party that its contribution will exceed the value of contribution by the other licensees. In any event, licensees will be concerned about what other licensees will be gaining access to its technology that is granted back, and very concerned if they are competitors. Unfortunately either in practice or as a result of restraint of trade they may not be able to select who are these other licensees that are entitled to gain access to its improvements.

9.5 Additional Compensation for Providing Improvements

The transferor may not want to automatically extend the licence to include improvements without obtaining further compensation:

(a) if the improvement can be marketed independently;
(b) if the improvement will not be fully commercialized by the licensee but, rather, could be "locked-up" by a disinterested exclusive licensee.

The licensee may not want to share its improvements with its transferor without compensation

(a) if the improvement can be used independently of the licensed technology;
(b) if the improvement could be more valuable than the licensee technology;
(c) if it is toward the end of a licence term; and
(d) if the obligation to disclose can be considered too broad or onerous.

9.6 Patent Versus Copyright Improvements

Improvements for patented technology are fundamentally different in a legal sense from improvements to copyrighted works.[3] A patent holder does not have the exclusive right to improve its technology, whereas the copyright holder has the exclusive right to make "translations", "adaptations" to its work and, in the United States, "derivative works".[4] In Canada, the exclusive right (if any) to make "adaptations" and "derivative works" must be inferred from the exclusive right to copy since it is not expressly covered by the Canadian *Copyright Act*.[5] That it may be inferred is suggested by the express provision in the Canadian *Copyright Act* that provides a fair dealing defence for modifications of computer programs for use on a different computer.[6]

9.7 Types of Improvements to Patented Technology

Some agreements may leave the scope of the word "improvement" to be determined by the courts, but the business decision makers should be alerted to the fact that the word "improvement" by itself may not have a precise legal meaning even with patents. "Improvement" does not have a well established meaning;

---

[3] R.M. Milgrim, *Milgrim On Licensing*, rev. ed. (New York: Matthew Bender, 1995), §17.00 (hereinafter "Milgrim, *On Licensing*").
[4] Note according to *Canadian Guide to Uniform Legal Citation* (Carswell), it is not necessary to put "U.S." before the citation. The current format (at p. 40) is: (title)(division code) (abbreviated code name)(section)(year) *Copyright Act*, 17 U.S.C. §106 (1976).
[5] R.S.C. 1985, c. C-42.
[6] *Ibid.*, s. 27(2) (am. R.S.C. 1985, c. 1 (3rd Supp.), s. 13; R.S.C. 1985, c. 10 (4th Supp.), s. 5; 1993, c. 44, s. 64(1) and (2)). See also §4.4 of this text.

neither does "modification" or "enhancement". One Canadian court has said that the word "improvement" should not be interpreted in a technical sense but "in its ordinary meaning within the context of the contract and the intentions of the parties".[7]

Indeed, this is an area where words are mangled by the practitioners giving the drafter instructions that are never uncertain but often wrong. Justice Edenfeld made this well-known comment in relation to terminology used in the computer industry:[8]

> After hearing the evidence in this case the first finding the Court is constrained to make is that, in the computer age, lawyers and courts need no longer feel ashamed or even sensitive about the charge, often made, that they confuse the issue by resorting to legal "jargon", law Latin or Normal French. By comparison, the misnomers and industrial shorthand of the computer world make the most esoteric legal writing seem as clear and lucid as the Ten Commandments or the Gettysburg address: and to add to this Babel, the experts in the computer field, while using exactly the same words uniformly disagree as to precisely what they mean.

The situation is inherently difficult since the parties are endeavouring to address the legal characteristics of what they will develop in the future. Improvements will only "occur" at some uncertain time in the future and will have currently undefined characteristics. In addition, the future status of patents, copyrights and/or third party rights cannot now be known". [*Milgrim on Licensing §17.01*]

9.8 Share Some, Keep Others

Some improvements could be subject to sharing and other improvements could be retained to the exclusion of the other party. The distinction must be carefully made, considering the appropriate circumstances, and one definition may not be sufficient throughout the agreement.

There could be a different definition for those improvements the licensor is obliged to deliver to the licensee (the grant-forward) and the licensee is obliged to deliver to the transferor (the grant-back).

---

[7] *Dyform Engineering v. Ittup Hollowcore Ltd.* 71 C.P.R. (2d) 72 (B.C.S.C.), at p. 86-87. See "*Fundamentals*", Dawn H. Giebelhaus – Mains, [Insights Vancouver] hereafter "*Giesbelhaus-Mains*". See also Daniel R. Bereseken and Meredith Brill, '*Patent Licensees – Improvements, Enhancements and Modifications*', Negotiating and Drafting Intellectual Property Session Agreements (November 25, 1999).

[8] *Honeywell Inc. v. Lithonia Lighting Inc.* 317 Supp 406 at 408 (N.D. Ga 1970), as quoted by Giebelhaus-Mains at p. 6.

9.9 List of Types of Improvements

A list of types of improvements[9] to patented technology may assist in negotiating what improvements are to be shared. Some types are:

(a) improvements that cannot be used without infringing the transferor's patent;

(b) improvements that are disclosed in a patent that cites the licensed patent as prior art;

(c) improvements that are patentable, whether or not patented, and that are within the scope of at least one of the claims of the licensee patent;[10]

(d) improvements, whether or not patentable, that satisfy certain criteria;[11]

(e) improvements that will be considered to result from disclosure by the transferor of trade secrets related to the patented technology, unless the licensee can establish it made the improvement independently or as a result of prior knowledge;

(f) improvements that relate to function,

    (i) those that reduce the cost of the manufacture of the product by at least a specified per cent;

    (ii) those that increase the sales of the product by at least a specified per cent;

    (iii) those that reduce the cost of the application by at least a specified per cent;

    (iv) those that increase the output of the application of the process by at least a specified per cent;[12]

(g) improvements that relate to similarity, for example, any product/process that has substantially similar features to the transferor's products/process;[13] and

(h) improvements that relate to competitiveness, for example, an improvement is any product/process that could competitively displace demand for the transferor's product/process.

The definition of "improvement" could operate by the elimination of what it does not include as well as by what it does include.[14] In any event, "because of uncertainty as to what individual courts may, in their wisdom, do with this term

---

9   Including modifications, enhancements and additions.

10 Timothy J. English, "Improvements in Patent Licensing, Journal of the Patent and Trademark Office Society", November 1996, 730 at 742. What is patentable and what is not can ultimately only be decided by a court; this criteria may not give as much comfort as might be expected.

11 The concern here would be a requirement to disclose inconsequential improvements.

12 John Crispen and Terry Marsh, "Preparing for the Future — Implement a Grant-Back", presentation at the 1994 Annual Meeting of Licensing Executives Society (Canada). See also *Milgrim On Licensing*, §17.02.

13 This criteria might be very vague and thus of limited use.

14 See B.G. Brunsvold and D.P. O'Reilley, *Drafting Patent License Agreements*, 4th ed. (Washington, D.C.: BNA Books, 1998), p. 85.

if it is undefined, it is highly desirable that the parties eliminate potential argument by providing a stipulative definition of their choosing".[15] The definition chosen may be different for improvements that are included by the transferor in its grant than for improvements that are the subject of a grant-back by the licensee.

9.9.1 Infringement is Not a Good Standard for Copyright

The case law has established that copying of the literal code of a computer program is prohibited, but it does not establish what non-literal copying is prohibited.[16] An original method of expressing an idea is protected under copyright rules unless it has merged with the idea being expressed (the idea not being protected by copyright). Recently, Canadian and American courts have been struggling to "weed out or remove from copyright protection those portions [of a computer program] which, . . . cannot be protected . . . ".[17] Cases relying on *Computer Associates v. Altai, Inc.*[18] use the abstraction/filtration method and reject the structure, sequence and organization analysis propounded by *Whelan Assoc. v. Jaslow Dental Lab Inc.*[19] Whether either analytical method is practically sound, let alone legally correct, remains unsettled and the scope of protection offered by copyright to computer programs presently is far from clear.[20] Relying on copyright infringement as a standard for a software improvement thus provides little certainty to the business decision makers.

9.9.2 Functionality May be a Better Standard for Software Improvements

The following are examples of different kinds of improvements that could be made to licensed software.

> *Type A.* An improvement[21] to the source code (the human readable portion of a computer program) that is made to remedy or "work around" an error that prevents the program from working as intended.

---

[15] *Ibid.*, p. 86.

[16] See Chapter 4 of this text.

[17] *Delrina Corp. v. Triolet Systems Inc.* (1993), 47 C.P.R. (3d) 1 at 37, 9 B.L.R. (2d) 140 (Ont. Ct. (Gen. Div.)).

[18] (alternative cite shown) 982 F.693, at 705 (2nd Cir. 1992). *Computer Associates International Inc. v. Altai Inc.* 23 U.S.P.Q. (2d) 1241 (2nd Cir. 1992).

[19] 797 F.2d 1222, 230 USPQ 481 (3d Cir. 1986), cert. denied, 479 U.S. 1031 (1987).

[20] See P.J. Mcabe, "Reverse Engineering of Computer Software: A Trap for the Unwary?" (1994) 9 No. 2 The Computer Law Association Bulletin 4 at 10-11. Philip J. McCabe, "Reverse Engineering of Computer Software: A Trap for the Unwary?" in The Computer Law Association Bulletin (1994), Vol. 9, No. 2, p. 4, at 10–11.

[21] Often referred to as a "modification". There seems to be no difference between "improvement" and "modification" or "enhancement".

Type B. An improvement to the source code that is made to provide features that were described in the functional specifications, but were not achieved in the current version.

Type C. An improvement[22] to the source code that provides features that were not contemplated by the current version.

Type D. An improvement that provides new features but does not modify the source code of the transferor's program, though it interfaces with it and can call upon the transferor's program to perform functions; this type of improvement is sometimes called a "stand-alone module".

The transferor needs disclosure of Type A and B improvements made by the licensee. Even with Type C improvements, errors in normal operation may relate to a change of the source code that inadvertently disrupted other operations, making support difficult or impossible. The transferor needs disclosure of, and the rights to use, Type A and B improvements in order to maintain standards. The transferor may need the right to use Type A, B and C improvements to keep its product vibrant and in the current state of the art. The transferor would like to have Type D to expand the life of its technology and related income stream.

9.9.3 Improvements to Biotechnology

Fordis and Griffen write:

> *Defining and Allocating Rights to Derivatives.* Biological materials are living growing, and reproducing entities which, as living entities, will undergo the same type of random mutations that occur in nature. An insignificant mutation may have no effect on the rights conveyed in a license, but any type of significant change may drastically affect the licensed rights.
>
> For example, if Company A licenses in a hybridoma that introduces monoclonal antibodies for use in its program to treat a particular disease, a mutation in hybridoma that inhibits the production of monoclonal antibody X will make the license worthless. Alternatively, if Company B licenses in a cell line that produces a protein Z, and the cell line mutates to produce an even more valuable protein W, Company B might be able to use that protein without paying royalties.
>
> Thus, it is critical to carefully consider and define what derivatives of biological products, if any, are conveyed. There are no definitive answers to this issue, but the Biotechnology Committee of the Licensing Executives Society (USA & Canada) has suggested some definitions:
>
> 1. Derivative means any progeny or subclones of parent; or
>
> 2. Derivative means progeny, clones, subclones or products of parent wherein such progeny and subclones include nonidentical progeny and subclones of

---

[22] Often referred to as an "enhancement".

parent; and such progeny includes progeny which would not have been made but for parent.

More specific definitions are:

3.　Derivative means any progeny and any genetically engineered modification wherein:

Such progeny and genetically engineered modification is based on and incorporates all of the essential features of parent; or

The genetic material is substantially unchanged; or

The genetic material is substantially based on and incorporates an essential element of parent and is verifiably distinct from parent; or

The structural and/or functional characteristics are identical to or are predictable, expected result of genetically engineered modifications of parent; or

The genetic material is substantially similar to the material from which it is derived and having a substantial portion of the characteristics of parent genetic material; or

Any genetically engineered modification that is substantially based on and incorporates an essential element of parent without a substantial change in phenotypic expression.

Once the derivatives are defined, the parties must determine who should maintain rights on those derivatives. This will be a subject for negotiation between the parties, but a rather common solution is to specify that derivatives belong to the licensor and that the licensee will grant back rights to those derivatives to the licensor.[23]

9.10 Grant-backs

The rights granted back by the party making the improvement (the "improver") in favour of the party that produced the basic technology that was modified (the "basic innovator") can be either a transfer of all rights, a transfer of ownership with a reservation of rights of continued use, or a licence back to the basic innovator.

(a)　*Transfer of Rights.* Generally, a transfer back of all rights will be resisted by all improvers. Indeed, anything more than a non-exclusive grant-back may be a violation of rules against restraint of trade in the United States.[24] There is a barrier, sometimes only an emotional barrier, to

---

[23]　Jean Burke Fordis and Susan Haberman Griffen, '*Avoiding Traps in Licensing Biotechnology*', *les Nouvelles*, June 1991, 45 at 46-47.

[24]　Anti-Trust Guidelines for the Licensing of Intellectual Property. These guidelines are reproduced in "Expanded European Communities Interfacing with North American, Technology, Marketing and Commercial Implications", Symposium 4, Licensing Executives Society (U.S.A. and Canada) September 11–13, 1994 (hereinafter "LES Symposium 4"). (Guidelines hereinafter referred to as "U.S. Anti-Trust I.P. Guidelines"). Also, see Chapter 10 of this text.

giving up ownership to an improvement. Historically, such a transfer has been demanded when there has been an imbalance of bargaining power, for example, a large multinational corporation dealing with a national in a developing country. In many such countries, a grant-back that involves a transfer of ownership is prohibited.[25]

(b) *Transfer of Ownership With a Reservation For Continued Use.* There may be good reason for a transfer of ownership. If one party is charged with prosecuting third-party infringes or with obtaining patents for all improvements, it may find it more expedient to own the improvements. Where the transfer of the improver's improvement is made to the basic innovator, the rights reserved to the improver should address whether the improver has the right to sublicense the rights of use to its affiliates or to any other third party and, if so authorized, whether there is a duty to report such licences and account for royalties. The term of continued use of the improvement by the improver who transferred its rights to the basic innovator should not necessarily cease with expiration of the term of the basic improvement, or the improver may find itself unable to use its own innovation on expiry of the basic licence.

(c) *Grant of a Non-exclusive Licence-back.* A grant of a non-exclusive licence-back of an improvement is more generally acceptable to improvers, particularly when there is a real or a perceived imbalance of bargaining power, and may be the only way to share improvements when a grant-back assignment is prohibited or potentially illegal, whether on account of rules against restraint of trade or otherwise.[26] The licence must state the respective rights of the basic innovator and the improver to produce, improve and sell the improvement and the duties to account between themselves for its use, essentially covering most of the points contained in any licence of technology of a similar nature.

9.10.1 Disclosure of Improvements

Because the disclosure of the improvements will be similar to any disclosure of confidential information, the basic principles that apply to trade secrets will apply to these improvements.[27] The time when a disclosure of an improvement must be made should be specifically set out in the agreement. It could be at one of the following stages of development:

(a) reduction to practice for a patentable improvement;[28]
(b) commercially marketable stage;
(c) third party site beta testing stage;

---

[25] See Chapter 10 of this text.
[26] A non-exclusive grant-back does not necessarily pass the U.S. rules against restraint of trade but it has a better chance of passing them than an exclusive grant-back does. See the U.S. Anti-Trust I.P. Guidelines, Section 5.6.
[27] See Chapter 6 of this text.
[28] See *Milgrim On Licensing*, §17.13, pp. 17-21.

(d) alpha testing stage; or

(e) first conception stage.

The choice of the timing will be important, especially toward the end of the relationship when each party will want to retain everything from the other. The parties may wish to choose a cut-off date that is earlier than the termination date.[29] Milgrim suggests that a licensee could negotiate for disclosure to occur as the improvement develops module by module to avoid losing all disclosure if completion of the improvement will not occur until after the cut-off date.[30] Additionally, the agreement will have to specify how often disclosure will be made, for example, at least quarterly. The agreement could provide what details of the improvement must be disclosed. These details could be:

(i) enough information to permit the user to commercially use the technology;

(ii) only the material disclosed in a relevant patent; or

(iii) only that an innovation has been made and a brief description of its functional specifications.

9.10.2 Declining Improvements

A licensee may want to retain the right to decline a patented improvement if, to accept them, would extend the term of the licence where the term of original licensee patents have expired. Therefore it might be required to pay a royalty for higher than the improvement would warrant on its own.

9.10.3 Conditions to Continued Grant-Forward

The transferor may wish to make its continued obligation to disclose and provide improvements conditional on certain events:

(a) The licensee has not challenged the validity of its patents. The U.S. law permits a licence to challenge validity, but does not seem to prevent a grant-forward being conditional on no challenge;

(b) The licensee then being in compliance with all the terms of the licence agreement.[31]

In any event the obligation should terminate on termination of the licence.[32]

---

[29] *Ibid.*, pp. 17-20.

[30] *Ibid.*, pp. 17-22.

[31] See *Milgrim on Licensing*, §17.17

[32] The licensee may be concerned if it has transferred to the transferor ownership of an improvement the licensee made. On termination of the licence, the licensee may no longer be able to use its own improvement.

JOINT OWNERSHIP

9.11 Introduction

Joint Development Agreements or Collaboration Agreements provide difficult challenges to the participants: what rights should each have to the jointly developed intellectual property, which is often improvements to existing technology separately owned by the participants.

9.12 Reasons for Collaboration

Often the individual participants do not have the independent financial or technical resources to develop the proposed technology, or do want to develop technology that sets a standard for the group of participants, and thus decide to collaborate. If the business plan is not well thought out and the complex and confusing legal principles are not dealt with, the goals of the business leaders might be defeated.

9.13 Collaboration Business Plan

The business plan will define clearly the business and competitive objectives expected to be achieved. It will address

(a) "Where the common advantages and benefits of the joint project exist, *i.e.*, what each party can do that the other party cannot do itself";[33]
(b) What capital each party can contribute (human intellectual capital, structural intellectual capital – equipment and intellectual property – and financial capital);
(c) The strengths and weaknesses of each party's human and structural intellectual capital;
(d) The scope of the work to be undertaken and the milestones to be established for GO/NO GO decisions and benchmarks used to measure performance;
(e) The markets in which each participant operates, both now and in the future, and desires to have exclusive use of the project technology; and
(f) The markets in which each participant is best positioned
    (i)   To license the project technology; and
    (ii)   To prosecute and enforce the related patent rights against third party infringers.[34]

---

[33] T. Gene Dillahunty, '*How To (And How Not To) Deal With Inventorship in Joint Development Agreements*', *les Nouvelles*, Vol. XXXVII No. 1 at 1, 3 ("Dillahunty"), at p. 3.
[34] Dillahunty, at p. 4.

This business plan will allow the parties to develop a market driven, application focused, exclusive territory approach rather than an inventorship/ownership approach which, as will be discussed below, is both frustrating in its lack of clear answers and disappointing in its results.

9.14 Legal Principles

In order to focus on the effects of joint ownership, first one needs to review how ownership is derived and how it relates to inventorship; then one needs to review the rules that relate to the exploitation of joint intellectual property rights held by the co-owners.

9.15 Joint Inventorship Rules in Canada

Woodley writes:

> Where two or more persons by their joint efforts make an invention, then the joint inventors become joint applicants. It is the person who conceived the idea, not the one who commercializes it who is the inventor, having regard to the invention as claimed. A person seeking to displace the presumption of joint inventorship made by the fact that more than one inventor signed the petition, bears a heavy onus of proof to displace such presumption. On discovering that one or more further applicants should have been joined in applying for a patent, such further applicant or applicants may be joined by a request accompanied by a new petition naming all of the original inventors together with the added inventors. Similarly, where it appears that one or more of the joint inventors had no part in the invention, the application may be revised.[35]

In Canada, an inventor must be the person who first conceives of a new idea or discovers a new thing that is the invention and the person that sets the conception or discovery in a practical shape.[36] Presenting a problem to another for a solution is not an act of invention. Where a person is directed to engage in a purely mechanical act for the purpose of testing whether an invention will work, in circumstances where the whole train of ideas put into motion were those of others, the person is not be treated as an inventor. If a person merely verifies another's previous predictions, the person is not an inventor. Each inventor must generally contribute to the formation of a definite and permanent idea of the complete and operative invention. Joint inventors do not have to work together at the same time, make the same type or amount of contribution, or contribute to the subject matter of every claim in the patent.

---

[35] John H. Woodley, '*Allocations of Ownership of Inventions in Joint Development Agreements*', *les Nouvelles*, December 2000, 183 at 183, references deleted ("Woodley on Joint Ownership").

[36] See *Apotex Inc. v. Wellcome Foundation Ltd.*, [2000] F.C.J. No. 1770, [2001] 1 F.C. 495 (Fed. C.A.).

To be considered a co-inventor one must be able to say that without his contribution to the final conception, it would have been less efficient, less simple, less economical or less beneficial. Joint authorship on a scientific paper does not necessarily equate to joint inventorship — joint authorship may be granted as a matter of courtesy for involvement in a small segment of the work performed rather than significant and active participation in originating or reducing the idea/concept to practice.

This professional courtesy offered for papers should not be extended to patents; each named inventor must really have made such a material contribution.

9.16 Employee Inventions and Ownership – Canada

Woodley writes:

> The Patent Act does not provide guidance as to the ownership of patents and patent applications and thus it is the common law that governs the issue of ownership.

> Unlike the case in the United States, or the more recent trend in England, the general rule in Canada is that an employee producing and invention, even on the employer's time and using the employer's equipment, can patent it in the absence of a contrary agreement, unless the employer can establish at least a partial beneficial interest. The exception is when a person is hired to develop and invention or is duty bound to do so, in which case equitable principles may be invoked to enforce trust obligations to the employer. When a person is hired for the express purpose of developing an invention, whatever new material, method or process the inventor discovers belongs to the inventor's employer. It is an implied term in a contract of employment that an employee is trustee for the employer in an invention made in the course of research as an employee, unless such implied term is displaced by a contrary agreement having legal effect. However, the invention belongs to the employee, in the absence of agreement, if the invention does not directly arise out of the work assigned to the employee; each case must be examined on its own facts. The court should consider the nature and context of the employer relationship. Exceptions to the presumption which favour the inventive employee include:

> (1) an express contract to the contrary, or

> (2) where the person was employed for the purpose of inventing or innovating which requires considering nature and context of the employer/employee relationship which include:
>   (a) the express purpose of employment;
>   (b) whether the employee at the time he was hired had previously made inventions;
>   (c) whether the employer had incentive plans encouraging product development;
>   (d) whether conduct of the employer once the invention had been created suggested ownership was held by the employer;

(e) whether the invention is the product of a problem the employee was instructed to solve (*i.e.*, whether it was his duty to make inventions);

(f) whether the employee's inventions arose following his consultation through normal company channels (*i.e.*, was help sought);

(g) whether the employee was dealing with highly confidential information or confidential work;

(h) whether it was a term of the servant's employment that he could not use the idea which he developed to his own advantage.

9.17 Employee Inventions and Ownership – U.S.

O'Reilley writes:

> In the United States, inventions are owned by the inventors unless they are under some express or implied obligation to another. If several inventors jointly make and invention, the invention is owned jointly be each of them.

> Where the inventors are hired to invent and inventions are made as party of their employment, those inventions are the property of the employer. If an invention is jointly made by employees of different employers, the invention is jointly owned by the employers.

> In the United States an employer is entitled to own any invention made by an employee who was hired to invent. Without a contract with the employee, the employer will not have complete title until either the employee executes an assignment or a court orders transfer of title. If such an employee has left the company after making the invention or otherwise refuses to cooperate in transferring title to the employer, confirming title to an invention and related patents can be very difficult, expensive and time-consuming.

> If an invention is made by an employee who was not hired to invent or to work in areas where invention is expected, normally the employee would own the invention. The employer would only receive a nonexclusive, non-transferable, royalty-free license to use the invention and any patent on the invention (a "shop right"), but only if the employee used the employer's time or facilities to make the invention. Since a shop right is not transferable, a party to the joint development agreement who acquired only a shop right could not give rights to the other party.

> To avoid such problems, most employers require employed inventors, and sometimes all employees, to sign an employment contract that automatically assigns the employee's inventions and patent rights to their employer. In terms of employment contracts, it is important to note the difference between a promise to assign an invention in the future and a present assignment of a future invention. Under U.S. law, an employment contract can provide for the present assignment by an employee of all future inventions. Such a provision results in immediate and automatic assignment to the employer of any invention. This avoids any dispute over who owns legal title to the invention.

Under U.S. law, inventions and patents on the inventions are different rights. An employer's ownership of an invention made by an employee does not automatically result in the employer's ownership of any patent on the invention. Thus, in addition to a contract provision that automatically transfers legal title to an invention, the contract provision also should provide for the present assignment of all future patents on such inventions.

Since employees normally are not parties to a joint development agreement between their employers, the joint development agreement cannot impose obligations on the employees. It is good practice therefore, to require each party to the joint development agreement to place each employee who is likely to work on the R&D project under a contract to presently assign to his employer all future inventions and patents thereon.[37]

9.18 Patent Prosecution and Joint Ownership

In the U.S. there is a potential for serious difficulties if each party has the independent right to process patent applications for jointly developed technology. O'Reilley writes:

> Where inventions are made by different inventors who are obligated to assign to different employers, a patent application on one invention may be used as prior art against a patent application on the other invention. This can be a real problem where the two employers are involved in joint R&D since it is likely that all inventions made in the course of such effort will be related and therefore likely to be available as prior art.[38]

9.19 Independent Exploitation of Co-owned Intellectual Property

The rules in Canada and the United Sates are very different as to the rights of each co-owner to independently exploit its interest in the jointly owned intellectual property; neither rule has much economic sense.
In Canada:

(a) Each co-owner can use the jointly owned intellectual property for its own internal benefit without the consent of the other co-owner or a duty to account to it;

---

[37] D. Patrick O'Reilley, '*Allocations of Ownership of Inventions in Joint Development Agreements – The United States Perspective*', *les Nouvelles*, December 2000, p. 168 at 168, ("O'Reilley on Joint Ownership"). Note that the U.S. "shop right" concept has not been well received in Canada, *per* Woodley on Joint Ownership, p. 184.

[38] O'Reilley on Joint Ownership, p. 169.

(b) Each co-owner can assign its entire interest in the jointly owned intellectual property without the consent of the other co-owner or a duty to account to it;

(c) It is unclear if each co-owner can exclusively license its rights in the jointly owned intellectual property without the consent of the other and without a duty to account to it, but that may be a logical extension of the principle set out in (b); and

(d) Neither co-owner can partially assign its interest or grant a non-exclusive license of its rights without the consent of the other party. A patent right is considered to be an exclusionary right – partial assignments and non-exclusive licenses are considered to violate this exclusionary principle.[39]

In the United States, each co-owner can assign in whole or in part its interest in the jointly owned intellectual property and can separately grant non-exclusive licenses without the consent of the other party. O'Reilley writes:

> In the United States, inventions and patents may be assigned in whole or in part and may be licensed exclusively, non-exclusively and in fields of use. Ownership of and rights to inventions made under the joint development agreement and patents on such inventions may be allocated in any way the parties agree.[40]

This can produce surprising results. One co-owner may be suing a third party for infringement only to find that the other co-owner, perhaps out of competitive mischief, licenses the third party and negates the infringement suit.

9.20 Ownership of Joint Project Inventions

All too frequently, the parties agree that each will own the inventions it separately develops and that they will co-own the inventions they jointly developed. The approach of : "What's ours is ours, what's yours is yours, and what's joint is both of ours" is a prescription for disaster.[41] This approach may seem appealing on the expectation that its allocation is simple and clear cut, but the appeal is lost when in rushes the legal uncertainties.

> Determination of inventorship for a particular invention is not exact; inventorship is subject to differing opinions on underlying facts, is subject to legal interpretation and may legally change (due to claim amendments) during the prosecution of a patent application.[42]

---

[39] See Woodley on Joint Ownership, pp. 184-5. See also *Forget v. Specialty Tools of Canada Inc.* (1993), 48 C.P.R. (3d) 323 (B.C.S.C.); affd (1995), 62 C.P.R. (3d) 537 (B.C.C.A.) and *Marchand v. Peloquin et al.* (1978), 45 C.P.R. (2d) 48.

[40] O'Reilley on Joint Ownership, p. 168.

[41] Dillahunty, at p. 2.

[42] Dillahunty, at p. 2.

Dillahunty writes:

> [The] determination of inventorship under U.S. Patent law, has been the subject of much litigation and many different interpretations by the courts of the legal requirements for inventorship and co-inventorship on U.S. patents. In setting forth these legal requirements, the courts have enumerated various criteria for trying to determine whether an individual has sufficiently contributed to an invention to qualify as the inventor or as a co-inventor under the law. ... In general the courts try to determine whether an individual qualifies as the inventor or a co-inventor under the patent law by having intellectually contributed to the inventive concept at the conception of invention and/or to the reduction to practice of the invention. One of the few consistent requirements in the various court decisions is that the determination of inventorship under the law must be based on the invention defined in the specific patent claims in question. However, since patent claims are usually amended and changed during prosecution of the application, it is not unusual that inventorship on a particular application must be changed because of a change in the claims in the patent application before the patent is granted.

> What becomes clear from the above is that, from a practical standpoint, it is impossible to divide up and determine with any degree of certainty allocation of future property rights on new technology based on inventorship. The business people and the technical people of one party to the joint project will look to their own patent attorney to determine what technology and what patents that party will own exclusively, what technology and patents they must give up ownership of to the other party and which they must share ownership with the other party. This puts the patent attorney in the position of judge, jury and executioner with respect to establishing property rights based on legal evaluations of inventorship. Of course, whatever the patent attorney concludes for that party's rights is unlikely to agree with the conclusions reached by the patent attorney for the other party. Moreover, the legal conclusions on inventorship and patent ownership reached by a patent attorney for one party are frequently unpopular with (if not unacceptable to) that party, i.e., the attorney's own client.[43]

A problem of allocating ownership by the "what's ours is ours, what's yours is yours and what is joint is both of ours approach" is stated by Woodley:

> One problem with allocating ownership in this fashion is that the parties may not end up owning rights which are critical to their commercial objectives as it may be the other party's employees who are solely responsible for the particular invention of interest and from which technology they are now excluded.[44]

---

[43] Dillahunty, at p. 2.
[44] Woodley on Joint Ownership, p. 185.

This may lead to the following attitudes adopted by each party:

(a) We must independently develop as much as possible so we can be the sole owner of what is important to us; and

(b) We must participate in as much as possible the development of the remaining technology with the other party so we can be co-owners.

This attitude could lead to the destruction of the intent of the business leaders – a free exchange of ideas to produce collaboratively technology that could not be produced separately with the same benefits.[45]

9.21 Allocation of Ownership by a Market Driven, Application Focused, Exclusive Territory Approach

Rather than relating ownership to contribution or inventorship, it may be preferable to relate ownership to the subject matter or application (field of use). If the business plan reveals that each party has a different market focus, then ownership of inventions could be allocated by this focus. For example if one party is a manufacturer of motor vehicles (LCC) and the other a manufacturer of paint (BAC).[46]

> ...all inventions and patents solely related to paint formulation will be owned by LCC and all inventions and patents solely related to paint systems and methods will be owned by BAC. The agreement would require BAC to assign to LCC all paint formulation inventions made solely or jointly by BAC employees and would require LCC to assign to BAC all other inventions made solely or jointly by employees of LCC. To the extent this approach avoids joint ownership of patents, many complications are avoided.[47]

Dillahunty writes:

> Under this market-define, exclusive field of use approach, each party will have sole ownership of all new technology inventions and related patents which primarily relate to its own present market, including control of the prosecution, issuance, maintenance and enforcement of those patents in its market. These inventions and related patents will be exclusively licensed to the other party for the other party's present, future and license markets. The best way to determine which party should have ownership of a particular patent is to determine which party will most likely need to use that patent to sue infringers to stop competition and protect its competitive position in its present market. That party will own the patent for

---

[45] See Dillahunty, at p. 3.

[46] These are the examples used by O'Reilley on Joint Ownership at pp. 168-172 and Woodley on Joint Ownership at pp. 183-188.

[47] O'Reilley on Joint Ownership, p. 169.

use in its present market, and, consequently for its future and license markets. Having the patent issue in that party's name also provides the deterrent effect with respect to that party's competitors in that party's markets. The other party is exclusively licensed under that patent for the other party's present, future and license markets, i.e., that patent cannot be licensed by the owner to any third party in the other party's markets.

Since a particular patent may be important to both parties in their respective present or immediate future markets for protection of a competitive position, the parties will have to decide on a case-by-case basis which party will own and maintain that patent. In each case, there will need to be a provision that the other party may participate in the filing and prosecution of the patent, and may require assignment to the other party to maintain the patent in the event the owner party elects not to prosecute or maintain the patent. More importantly, there will need to be a provision to require assignment of any necessary patent from the owner party to the other party for purposes of enabling the other party to sue an infringe in the other party's market area, then assignment of the patent back to the original owner party when the litigation is completed or settled. This enables each party who needs to take legal action to protect a competitive position in its market to have sole ownership and sole control of the patent for litigation, without joining the other party in the lawsuit.

For the unknown remainder markets, the parties will be required to agree with respect to commercial exploitation of the new technology inventions and related patents in the unknown markets on a case-by case basis as the opportunities rise. This assures that the parties will share the benefits of future unknown markets, if any, and that neither party can operate or license in those markets without permission of an accounting to the other party.[48]

Note that in Canada, according to Woodley:

It is not necessary to name both parties in a suit for infringement to maintain the action. Nonetheless, there may be advantages to having both parties before the Court, or at least participating in a cooperative manner in support of the action. A joint development agreement, therefore, should include a provision that requires each joint owner to cooperate with the other joint owner in any infringement suit. The joint development agreement may place limitations on the cooperation which a joint owner must provide. Moreover, the agreement should also allocate costs of the litigation and the process therefrom amongst the joint owners. Additionally, other issues may arise in connection with the litigation which may impact on the parties' rights in the patents. For example, should there by any constraints on the parameters of trial strategy pertaining to admissions affecting patent validity or claim construction. An attempt to address these issues or a mechanism for responding to them should be provided for in the joint development agreement.

---

[48]   Dillahunty, at p. 4-5.

Since a joint owner's consent will be required to any license of the patent, there is little concern for the issues raised by recent U.S. decisions. However, the ability to grant a license may be required as part of a settlement of an infringement suit and the joint development agreement may, subject to appropriate terms, require the parties' cooperation in this regard.[49]

9.22 Cross-licensing

Even with the allocation of ownership by the market driven, exclusive field of use approach suggested by Dillahunty, there is still a risk that one party will exclusively own intellectual property required by the other party to fulfill its needs in its field of use. Thus, the allocation of ownership process could be coupled with a cross-licence for the other parties field of use, with or without compensation.[50]

9.23 Background Technology

Each party to a joint development agreement will need to address its rights to use the technology contributed by the other party or parties, often referred to as "Background Technology". There is a concern that if the agreement does not discuss the right to use contributed background technology, then the courts will imply a right of use.[51] This background technology could be defined as

> any technical information and related intellectual property rights owned by one party which may be desirable for use by the other party in the commercial use of the new technology in the other party's present, future or license market.[52]

In contrast the new technology could be defined as

> any invention in the technology area conceived by other parties separately or by the parties jointly between the date of the project and a definite ending date of the project. Thus the new technology governed by the agreement is clearly defined and is trackable by inventor conception records.[53]

The parties will watch for any implications of separate but independent projects being conducted in the same time period.

---

[49] Woodley on Joint Ownership, p. 188.
[50] All cross-licences must be examined for restraint of trade issues.
[51] See O'Reilley on Joint Ownership, p. 170.
[52] Dillahunty, at p. 4.
[53] Dillahunty, at p. 4.

9.24 IP Holding Company

In order to isolate the co-owned intellectual property, to allow for an orderly handling of the patent prosecution, enforcement and licensing matters, and to mitigate against perceived concerns in Canada about the possibility that the bankruptcy of a licensor could result in a trustee in bankruptcy terminating an exclusive licence, the collaborators may wish to transfer to a holding company all intellectual property rights to new technology created by the joint development project. This holding company would not conduct any active business other than holding and managing these intellectual property rights, and could be governed by the parties as they agree through a shareholders agreement.[54] This may cause a disadvantage to small companies that gain value by owning intellectual property more than those that are beneficiaries of a Canadian research program where ownership may be a prerequisite to the benefits of the program.

---

[54] This may cause a disadvantage to small companies that gain value by directly owning intellectual property, or that are beneficiaries of a Canadian research program where ownership may be a prerequisite to the benefits of the program.

Part IV

RESTRICTIONS ON ABILITY
TO CONTRACT

Chapter 10

RESTRAINT OF TRADE

Monopolies in times past were ever without the law [i.e., illegal], but never without friends.[1]

10.1 Introduction

There are three main types of restraints of trade that apply in technology transfers: monopolies or cartels, employee non-competition agreements and non-competition covenants granted concurrently with a sale of a business. Restraint of trade resulting in monopolies is essentially covered by legislation: in Canada, the *Competition Act*,[2] and in the United States, the *Clayton Act*[3] and the *Sherman Act*.[4] The other types of non-competition agreements may be the subject of the common law and specific local legislation.

10.2 Exclusionary Intellectual Property Rights Versus Free Competition

There is an innate tension between the monopolistic rights given by intellectual property and society's desire for free and vibrant competition. Each of Canada and the United States have issued guidelines to assist practitioners to find the appropriate balance.[5] The U.S. Guidelines provides this statement as to the need of balance of interests:

> The intellectual property laws and the antitrust laws share the common purpose of promoting innovation and enhancing consumer welfare. The intellectual property

---

[1] Coke, 3 *Institutes of the Laws of England*, 4th ed. (1670), p. 182, quoted by Michael J. Trebilcock, *The Common Law of Restraint of Trade, A Legal and Economic Analysis* (Toronto: Carswell, 1986), p. 13 (hereinafter "Trebilcock, *The Common Law*").

[2] R.S.C. 1985, c. C-34.

[3] 15 U.S.C. §12(b).

[4] 15 U.S.C. §§1-7.

[5] Intellectual Property Enforcement Guidelines, issued by Competition Bureau, Government of Canada September 21, 2000 found at <http://Strategis.ic.gc.ca/SSG/ct01992e.html> ("Canadian Guidelines") and Anti-Trust Guidelines for the Licensing of Intellectual Property, issued by the U.S. Department of Justice and the Federal Trade Commission, April 6, 1995 ("U.S. Guidelines").

laws provide incentives for innovation and its dissemination and commercialization by establishing enforceable property rights for the creators of new and useful products, more efficient processes, and original works of expression. In the absence of intellectual property rights, imitators could more rapidly exploit the efforts of innovators and investors without compensation. Rapid imitation would reduce the commercial value of innovation and erode incentives to invest, ultimately to the detriment of consumers. The antitrust laws promote innovation and consumer welfare by prohibiting certain actions that may harm competition with respect to either existing or new ways of serving consumers.[6]

10.3 Standard Rules for Intellectual Property

Although many consider intellectual property ("IP")to be materially different from other types of property, neither the Canadian nor the U.S. Guidelines apply fundamentally different principles to intellectual property than it does for other forms of property. The differences in intellectual property from other types of property include "the frequency of disputes over the boundaries of each person's property and the degree to which multiple complements may be necessary to produce a product".[7] Instead of there being different rules for intellectual property, the standard rules can be applied with the different characteristics "taken into account by standard antitrust analysis".[8] As stated by the U.S. Guidelines:

> Intellectual property law bestows on the owners of intellectual property certain rights to exclude others. These rights help the owners to profit from the use of their property. An intellectual property owner's rights to exclude are similar to the rights enjoyed by owners of other forms of private property. As with other forms of private property, certain types of conduct with respect to intellectual property may have anticompetitive effects against which the antitrust laws can and do protect. Intellectual property is thus neither particularly free from scrutiny under the antitrust laws, nor particularly suspect under them.[9]

---

[6] U.S. Guidelines, pp. 1 and 2. The Canadian IP Guidelines have a similar statement on p. 2 (pagination in each case may vary depending on printer).

[7] Richard J. Gilbert and Willard K. Tom "Is Innovation King at the Antitrust Agencies? The Intellectual Property Guidelines Five Years Later", working paper No.CPC01-20, Competition Policy Centre, University of California, Berkeley, available at <http://www.haaf.berkeley.edu/group/cp/c/pws/Publications.html> ("Gilbert").

[8] U.S. Guidelines, para. 2.1, see Canadian Guidelines, p. 2.

[9] U.S. Guidelines, para 2.1.

10.4   Intellectual Property and Marketing Power

The essence of anti-competitive action is an improper exercise of market power. The Canadian Guidelines state a position essentially shared by the U.S. Antitrust IP Guidelines:[10]

> The principle underlying competition law is that the public interest is best served by competitive markets, which are socially desirable because they lead to an efficient allocation of resources. Competition law seeks to prevent companies from inappropriately creating enhancing or maintaining market power that undermines competition without offering offsetting economic benefits. Market power refers to the ability of firms to profitably cause one or more facets of competition, such as price, output, quality, variety, service, advertising or innovation, to significantly deviate from competitive levels for a sustainable period of time. However, a firm would not contravene the *Competition Act* if it attains its market power solely by possessing a superior product or process, introducing an innovative business practice or other reasons for exceptional performance.[11]

The U.S. Guidelines pick up the same theme:

> Market power is the ability profitably to maintain prices above, or output below, competitive levels for a significant period of time. The Agencies will not presume that a patent, copyright, or trade secret necessarily confers market power upon its owner. Although the intellectual property right confers the power to exclude with respect to the *specific* product, process, or work in question, there will often be sufficient actual or potential close substitutes for such product, process or work to prevent the exercise of market power. If a patent or other form of intellectual property does confer market power, that market power does not by itself offend the antitrust laws. As with any other tangible or intangible asset that enables its owner to obtain significant supracompetitive profits, market power (or even a monopoly) that is solely "a consequence of a superior product, business acumen, or historic accident" does not violate the antitrust laws. Nor does such market power impose on the intellectual property owner an obligation to license the use of that property to others. As in other antitrust contexts, however, market power could be illegally acquired or maintained, or, even if lawfully acquired and maintained, would be relevant to the ability of an intellectual property owner to harm competition through unreasonable conduct in connection with such property.[12]

---

[10]   U.S. Guidelines, para. 2.2.
[11]   Section 2.2 of the Canadian Guidelines.
[12]   U.S. Guidelines, para. 2.2.

10.5 Analytical Process

The Canadian Guidelines provide a five-step analytical process to determine if there is an anticompetition issue:

> In general, the Bureau's analysis for determining whether competitive harm would result from a particular transaction or type of business conduct comprises five steps:
>
> - identifying the transaction or conduct;
>
> - defining the relevant market(s);
>
> - determining if the firm(s) under scrutiny possess market power by examining the level of concentration and entry conditions in the relevant market(s), as well as other factors;
>
> - determining of the transaction or conduct would unduly or substantially lessen or prevent competition in the relevant market(s); and
>
> - consider, when appropriate, any relevant efficiency rationales.

This analysis applies to all industries and all types of business transactions and conduct, and is sufficiently flexible to accommodate differences among the many forms of IP protection, as well as between IP and other types of property. For example, the Bureau takes differences among the various forms of IP protection into account when defining the relevant market and determining whether a firm has market power. In addition, although IP rights to a particular product or process are often created and protected by statute and are thus different from other forms of property rights, the right to exclude others from using the product or process does not necessarily grant the owner market power. It is only after it has defined the relevant market and examined factors such as concentration, entry barriers and technological change that the Bureau can conclude whether an owner of a valid IP right possesses market power. The existence of a variety of effective substitutes for the IP and/or a high probability of entry by other players into the market (by "innovating around" or "leap-frogging over" any apparently entrenched position) would likely cause the Bureau to conclude that the IP has not conferred market power on its owner.

The Bureau's analysis may reveal that an IP owner does indeed have market power. In general, to violate the Competition Act a firm must engage in anti-competitive conduct that creates, enhances or maintains market power. Again, consistent with its approach with respect to all forms of property, the Bureau does not consider an owner of IP to have contravened the Competition Act if it attained market power solely by possessing a superior quality product or process, introducing an innovative business practice or other reasons for exceptional performance.

Licensing is the usual method by which the owner of IP authorizes others to use it. In the vast majority of cases, licensing is pro-competitive because it facilitates the broader use of a valuable IP right by additional parties. In assessing whether a particular licensing arrangement raises a competition issue, the Bureau examines whether the terms of the license serve to create, enhance or maintain the market power of either the licensor or the licensee. The Bureau will not consider licensing agreements involving IP to be anti-competitive unless they reduce competition substantially or unduly relative to that which would have likely existed in the absence of the license.[13]

10.6 Types Of Technology Transfer and Competition Rules

Illustrations of the various types of technology transfer and how they can be viewed as anticompetitive measures may be helpful to develop the principles. However the reader should look for principles only in this text and then seek qualified counsel for advice. The U.S. and Canadian Guidelines are only guidelines, and open to varying interpretations according to the political view of the day, and further are open to re-interpretation by the courts who might adopt entirely different rules. In addition this discussion of a very complex topic can be treated only as conceptual.

10.6.1 Ownership

Ownership of IP rights by itself is not reviewable.[14] This will come as no surprise since it is only the exercise of intellectual property rights that causes competition issues. The U.S. Guidelines state:

> Intellectual property typically is one component among many in a production process and derives value from its combination with complementary factors. Complementary factors of production include manufacturing and distribution facilities, workforces, and other items of intellectual property. The owner of intellectual property has to arrange for its combination with other necessary factors to realize its commercial value. Often, the owner finds it most efficient to contract with others for these factors, to sell rights to the intellectual property, or to enter into a joint venture arrangement for its development, rather than supplying these complementary factors itself.[15]

This ownership does not in fact result in the market power, but is coupled with some other activity other than the exercise of the basic rights inherent in the intellectual property (that is the right to exclude others from making, using or selling a product), then the situation may become reviewable.[16] Acquiring the intellectual property rights of others could become reviewable if the purpose of the acquisition is to acquire excessive market power. The Canadian Guidelines state at paragraph 4.2.1:

---

[13] Canadian Guidelines, Section 4.1, pp. 5, 6.
[14] See Canadian Guidelines, para. 4.2 and U.S. Guidelines, para. 2.2.
[15] U.S. Guidelines, p. 4, para. 2.3.
[16] Canadian Guidelines, para. 4.1 and U.S. Guidelines, para. 5.7.

Sometimes upon examination, what appears to be just a refusal to license or to grant others access to a firm's IP rights turns out to have included conduct which goes beyond such a refusal. The conduct which goes beyond the unilateral refusal to grant access to the IP could warrant enforcement action under the general provisions of the *Competition Act*. for instance, if a firm acquires market power by systematically purchasing a controlling collection of IP rights and then refuses to license the rights to others, thereby substantially lessening or preventing competition in markets associated with the IP rights, the Bureau could view the acquisition of such rights as anti-competitive and review the matter under either section 79 (abuse of dominance) or section 92 (mergers) of the *Competition Act*. Without the acquisition, the owner's mere refusal to license the IP rights would have been unlikely to cause concern.

10.6.2 Licensing

Licensing is often considered to be pro-competitive. The U.S. Guidelines state:

> Licensing, cross-licensing, or otherwise transferring intellectual property (hereinafter "licensing") can facilitate integration of the licensed property with complementary factors of production. This integration can lead to more efficient exploitation of the intellectual property, benefiting consumers through the reduction of costs and the introduction of new products. Such arrangements increase the value of intellectual property to consumers and to the developers of the technology. By potentially increasing the expected returns from intellectual property, licensing also can increase the incentive thus promote greater investment in research and development.
>
> Sometimes the use of one item of intellectual property requires access to another. An item of intellectual property "blocks" another when the second cannot be practiced without using the first. For example, an improvement on a patented machine can be blocked by the patent on the machine. Licensing may promote the coordinated development of technologies that are in a blocking relationship.
>
> Field-of-use, territorial, and other limitations on intellectual property licenses may serve pro-competitive ends by allowing the licensor to exploit its property as efficiently and effectively as possible. These various forms of exclusivity can be used to give a licensee an incentive to invest in the commercialization and distribution of products embodying the licensed intellectual property and to develop additional applications for the licensed property. The restrictions may do so, for example, by protecting the licensee against free- riding on the licensee's investments by other licensees or by the licensor. They may also increase the licensor's incentive to license, for example, by protecting the licensor from competition in the licensor's own technology in a market niche that it prefers to keep to itself. These benefits of licensing restrictions apply to patent, copyright, and trade secret licenses, and to know-how agreements.[17]

---

[17] Para. 2.3, pp. 4, 5.

10.6.3 No Requirement to License

Normally there is no requirement that an owner of intellectual property must license it to others.[18] The competitive harm must stem from something more than the mere refusal to license.[19] Robert Pitofsky, Chairman of the U.S. Federal Trade Commission writes:

> Let me be clear that I have no quarrel with the fundamental rule that a patent holder has no obligation to license or sell in the first instance. A patent holder is not under any general obligation to create competition against itself within the scope of its patent.[20]

But any licence to actual or potential competitors must be reviewed to see if it "creates, enhances or maintains market power".[21] The issue gets muddier however when the patent holder couples the access to making, using or selling its patented products with some other condition that is anti-competitive, such as a requirement that the purchaser not buy from a potential competitor, or that the licensee not engage in price cutting activities.[22] The essence of the issue is how much protection does the intellectual property right give to activities that without the exclusionary rights granted by the intellectual property would be actionable as anti-competitive. The Canadian Guidelines express it this way:

> When joint conduct of two or more firms lessens or prevents competition, the competitive harm clearly flows from something more than the mere exercise of the IP right to refuse. To the extent that conduct such as conspiracy, bid-rigging, joint abuse of dominance, market allocation agreements and mergers restricts competition among firms actually or potentially producing substitute products or services, the presence of IP should not be a mitigating factor. Such conduct would be subject to review under the appropriate general provision of the *Competition Act*.
> A transfer of IP rights that lessens or prevents competition is a further example of a situation in which competitive harm results from something more than the mere exercise of the IP right to refuse. Two examples of this are when a licensor ties a non-proprietary product to a product covered by its IP right, and when a firm effectively extends its market power beyond the term of its patent through an exclusive contract. In either case, if the conduct leads to the creation, enhancement or maintenance of market power so as to substantially lessen or prevent competition, the Bureau may intervene.[23]

---

[18] Canadian Guidelines, 4.2.1 and U.S. Guidelines, para. 2.2.

[19] Canadian Guidelines, 4.2.1, p. 7.

[20] Robert Pitofsky, Chairman of Federal Trade Commission, "Challenges of the New Economy: Issues at the Intersection of Antitrust and Intellectual Property", American Antitrust Institute, Conference: Agenda for Antitrust in the 21st Century, June 15, 2000, at p. 6.

[21] Canadian Guidelines, section 4.2.1, p. 7.

[22] See Pitofsky, p. 7, items 1 and 2.

[23] Canadian Guidelines, p. 7.

10.6.4 Cross-licensing

Cross-licensing that is designed to eliminate or restrict competition is normally unlawful. However, there are cases where it is legitimate. Pitofsky states

> When competitors control patents that include legitimate conflicting claims, so that each patent holder is blocked from bringing a superior, non-infringing product to the market, the courts consistently have allowed cross-licenses, even when the cross licenses incorporate agreements on price or where the combination of blocking patents had dominant or even monopoly power.[24]

The U.S. IP Guidelines provide:

> Cross-licensing and pooling arrangements are agreements of two or more owners of different items of intellectual property to license to one another or third parties. These arrangements may provide pro-competitive benefits by integrating complementary technologies, reducing transaction costs, clearing blocking positions, and avoiding costly infringement litigation. By promoting the dissemination of technology, cross-licensing and pooling arrangements are often pro-competitive.[25]

Shapiro expands on that point:

> Cross-licenses commonly are negotiated when each of two companies has patents that may read on the other's products or processes. Rather than blocking each other and going to court or ceasing production, the two enter into a cross-license. Especially with a royalty-free cross-license, each firm is then free to compete, both in designing its products without fear of infringement and in pricing its products without the burden of a per-unit royalty due to the other. Thus, cross-licenses can solve the complements problem, at least among two firms, and thus be highly pro-competitive.
>
> A cross-license is simply an agreement between two companies that grants each the right to practice the other's patents. Cross-licenses may or may not involve fixed fees or running royalties; running royalties can in principle run in one direction or both. Cross-licenses may involve various field-of-use restrictions or geographic restrictions. Cross-licenses may involve some but not all relevant patents held by either party; "carve-outs" are not uncommon. And cross-licenses, like regular licenses, may be confined to patents issued (or pending) as of the date of the license, or they may include patents to be granted through a certain time in the future.[26]

---

[24] At p. 4.
[25] At para. 5.5.
[26] At p. 9.

Cross licensing of blocking patents are seen as having the benefit of establishing a "litigation free zone".[27] But cross-licensing, even IP for IP licenses must be examined to see whether it is a "beneficial way to cut through the patent thicket" or is a "strong-armed tactic by a dominant firm that enjoys powerful patent rights and seeks access to other's intellectual property in exchange".[28]

The comments in the Canadian Guidelines can be summarized as follows:[29]

(a) If a firm is blocked from using its technology because it infringes on another firm's patent, and if it is not possible to "the blocking patent, then these firms cannot be considered to be horizontal competitors" and thus the matter will not likely be reviewed;

(b) The blocking must go both ways; each party must have patents that block the other party; and

(c) A patent pool must be necessary to permit new technology to enter the market place to avoid being initially considered as anti-competitive.

10.6.5 Standards

Patent pools are often used to establish standards. In the case of a patent pool to establish standards, it should include only those patents that are essential to the standard; it may be wise to "employ an independent patent expert to determine whether a patent in the pool is essential", and thus weed out "patents that are competitive alternatives to each other".[30]

10.6.6 Collaboration of Agreement

Any collaboration of Agreement amongst competitors must be reviewed for any competitive possibilities.[31]

10.6.7 Patent Litigation Settlement and Antitrust Issues

Settlements of patent infringement suits have to take into account anti-competitive outcomes of the settlement. Gilbert writes:

> Courts recognize the rights of parties in litigation to settle their differences privately, and parties may have legitimate interests in a patent settlement that does not involve anti competitive objectives. Parties have an incentive to negotiate a settlement if the total economic value that the parties could achieve in a settlement exceeds the total economic value they could achieve by proceeding with litigation.

---

[27] Shapiro, p. 16.
[28] Shapiro, p. 16.
[29] Canadian Guidelines, p. 17.
[30] Shapiro, pp.17, 18.
[31] See the Antitrust Guidelines for Collaborations Amongst Competitors issued by the Federal Trade Commission and the U.S. Department of Justice, April, 2000.

The settlement value can be higher because settling may avoid litigation costs or provide an opportunity for the parties to structure arrangements that add social value to the products at issue (such as coordinating the pricing and supply of complementary' products). These are potentially pro-competitive benefits from settling a patent dispute. Unfortunately, settlement of a patent dispute also involves the welfare of third parties (that is, consumers of patented drugs) who have an interest in the outcome of the litigation. Consequently, settlements can be privately profitable, but socially undesirable because consumers who may be affected by the settlement are not present at the bargaining table.

The limits placed on the ability of a patentee to settle validity suits affects the protection afforded by the patent grant and should be considered in the context of patent policy more generally. Permitting a patentee to settle a dispute over the validity of the patent effectively extends the breadth of the patent grant. If the patent is indeed invalid, settlement allows the patentee to reap a reward even though it has failed to achieve a patentable innovation. On the other hand, prohibiting a settlement incurs the risk that a court may erroneously conclude that a patent is invalid.

Clearly there are instances where settlements of patent disputes are socially harmful. If the patent is likely invalid, a settlement can be justified only if the social costs of proving invalidity are very large.

FTC Commissioners Anthony and Leary both note that settlements involving patent disputes may be pro-competitive and caution against blanket prohibitions of such arrangements. What can be done to distinguish potentially pro-competitive settlements from those that are likely to be anticompetitive? The fact that the settlement involves a payment from the patentee to the challenger is not sufficient to determine that the settlement is anticompetitive. The savings in transaction costs and the risk-allocation benefits could outweigh the potential benefits from a finding of invalidity. Furthermore, parties could attempt to hide payments, for concessions on other products. We suggest the following factors as a guide to assess these settlements. However, none of these conditions, standing alone, is sufficient to determine that a settlement is anti competitive.

- Concerns should be greater if the size of the payment from the patentee to the challenger is a large fraction of the monopoly profits from the patented drug. This would suggest that the patentee has a high expectation that the patent is invalid.

- Concerns should be greater if the transactions costs that are saved by a settlement are small.

- Concerns should be greater if the settlement has not been subjected to judicial review (and ideally, inspection and comment by third parties).

- Concerns should be greater if the patentee would not have been likely to obtain a preliminary injunction against the generic challenger.

- Concerns should be greater if the terms of the settlement clearly delay the date at which a judicial finding of invalidity is likely to occur.[32]

10.7 Patent Abuse Rules and Pro-Competitive Rules

Patent abuse rules and rules to encourage competition are independent of each other although often intertwined. Patent abuses, such as fraud in the patent office and sham litigation may be more difficult to prove than any trust allegations.[33]

10.8 Per Se Violations

Some activities are considered so restrictive of competition that they are treated as violations without the requirement to prove actual restraint of trade; these are often referred to as "*per se* violations". "Among the restraints that have been per se unlawful are price-fixing, output restraints, and market division among horizontal competitors, as well as certain group boycotts and resale price maintenance".[34]

10.9 Rule of Reason

"In the vast majority of cases, restraints in intellectual property licensing arrangements are evaluated under the rule of reason. The Agencies' general approach in analyzing a licensing restraint under the rule of reason is to inquire whether the restraint is likely to have anti-competitive effects and, if so, whether the restraint is reasonably necessary to achieve pro-competitive benefits that outweigh those anti-competitive effects".[35] An arrangement deserves "rule of reason" treatment rather than *per se* treatment if the

---

[32] Extracted from pp. 36 to 38.

[33] See Pitofsky, p. 6.

[34] *Ibid.*, Section 3.4. Kathleen R. Terry in "Antitrust and Technology Licensing" in Journal of the Association of University Technology Managers, 1995, Vol. VII, p. 83, at 85, lists the "Nine No-No's" considered by the Agency (but never ratified by a court) to be *per se* antitrust violations: (1) requiring a patent licensee to purchase an unpatented material from the licensor; (2) grant-back of title to the licensor of the licensee's improvements to the patented technology; (3) attempting to impose restrictions after sale of the patented product; (4) tie-in and tie-out: tying of products or services outside the scope of the patent claims, or restricting the licensee's freedom to deal with other suppliers; (5) an agreement outside the licence not to grant other licences (that is, concealing the exclusive nature of the agreement); (6) mandatory package licences; (7) any broadening of the royalty base; (8) restriction on sale of products made with the patented process; and (9) price fixing.

[35] U.S. Antitrust I.P. Guidelines, Section 3.4.

restraint in question can be expected to contribute to an efficiency-enhancing integration of economic activity. In general, licensing arrangements promote such integration because they facilitate the combination of the licensor's intellectual property with complementary factors of production owned by the licensee. A restraint in such a licensing arrangement may further such integration by, for example, aligning the incentives of the licensor and the licensees to promote the development and marketing of the licensed technology, or by substantially reducing transaction costs. If there is no efficiency-enhancing integration of economic activity and if the type of restraint is one that has been accorded *per se* treatment, the Agencies will challenge the restraint under the *per se* rule. Otherwise, the Agencies will apply a rule of reason analysis.[36]

10.10   Hot Spots

Although not *per se* violations, transactions that should give immediate concern for violation of the restraint of trade rules include:

(a) Technology transfers between horizontal competitors;[37]

(b) Resale price maintenance;[38]

(c) A "tying" arrangement — *i.e.*, "an agreement by a party to sell one product . . . on the condition that the buyer also purchases a different or 'tied' product or at least agrees that he will not purchase that [tied] product from any other supplier".[39] Instead of products, the offence could relate to the tying of the acquisition of one intellectual property right (for example, a patent) to the acquisition of other intellectual property rights (for example, a trade secret);

(d) Packaged Licensing — *i.e.*, the licensing of multiple items of intellectual property in a single licence or in a group of related licences;[40]

(e) Exclusive Dealing — *e.g.*, preventing "the licensee from licensing, selling, distributing or using competing technologies";[41]

(f) Cross-licensing and pooling arrangements[42] — *i.e.*, "agreements of two or more owners of different items of intellectual property to license one another or third parties";[43]

(g) Grant-back — *i.e.*, an arrangement under which a licensee agrees to extend to the licensor of intellectual property the right to use the licensee's improvements to the licensed technology:[44] These grant backs

---

[36] See para. 10.5 of this text for a statement of the Canadian Analytical process.

[37] *Ibid.*, Section 5.1.

[38] *Ibid.*, Section 5.2.

[39] *Ibid.*, Section 5.3.

[40] *Ibid.*

[41] *Ibid.*, Section 5.4.

[42] *Ibid.*, Section 5.5.

[43] *Ibid.*

[44] *Ibid.*, Section 5.6.

can be non-exclusive or exclusive; the former is "less likely [than the latter] to have anti-competitive effects";[45]

(h) Acquisitions rather than licenses — These will be reviewed applying the "1992 Horizontal Merger Guidelines" rather than the U.S. Antitrust I.P. Guidelines; and

(i) Enforcement or attempted enforcement of invalid intellectual property rights.[46]

Strategy: Add the Hot Spot Checklist to the Per Se Checklist.

10.11 How to Conduct Business without Fear of Antitrust Violation

As mentioned above, each technology transfer agreement must be reviewed by competent counsel to determine if there is a possible violation, using many of the principles set out in the Canadian and U.S. Guidelines. Unfortunately, it may be costly to obtain even a very restricted opinion. The legal advisors have to anticipate how the markets may develop, using the limited market information available for such analysis. In contrast, the Agencies or the self appointed "private attorneys-general" have the benefit of hindsight. Additionally, the Agencies have material available to them that is not available to the general public.

10.12 Analysis

The analysis to determine the balance between the economic benefits of the arrangement and its anticompetitiveness can be both extensive and expensive. The market must be narrowed, to the extent data is available, "to the smallest group of technologies and goods [and services] over which a hypothetical monopolist of those technologies and goods would exercise market power, for example, by imposing a small but significant and non-transitory price increase".[47] The "markets" consist of "goods markets",[48] "technology markets"[49] and "innovative markets".[50] In the analysis, the Agencies "will not engage in a search for a theoretically least restrictive alternative [to the offending activity] that is not realistic in the practical prospective business solutions faced by the parties".[51] The parties should be able to establish that there are no existing practical and significantly

---

[45] *Ibid.*

[46] *Ibid.*, Section 6.

[47] *Ibid.*, Section 3.2.2.

[48] *Ibid.*, Section 3.2.1.

[49] *Ibid.*, Section 3.2.2.

[50] *Ibid.*, Section 3.2.3.

[51] *Ibid.*, Section 4.2.

less restrictive alternatives to their selected arrangement; their claims to efficiency are not enough.[52]

10.13 Safety Zone

To "provide some degree of certainty" and to reduce the costs associated with antirestraint of trade opinions and defences, "the Agencies will not challenge a restraint in an intellectual property licensing arrangement if (1) the restraint is not facially anti-competitive and (2) the licensor and its licensees, collectively account for no more than 20% of each relevant market significantly affected by the restraint".[53] A challenge to an arrangement in a technology market or innovation market is unlikely (but not precluded) if:

    (a) the restraint is not "facially anti-competitive" — in violation of a *per se* rule or other similar rule "that would always or almost always tend to reduce output or increased prices";[54] or

    (b) in addition to the parties for the technology, there are four or more parties in that technology market or innovation market.[55]

If these safety zones are exceeded, there is not an automatic violation; arrangements outside the safety zone are encouraged and are assessed under the U.S. Antitrust I.P. Guidelines.[56]

Strategy: Take comfort in the safety zone, but remember that it is a moving standard; the qualification is determined at the time of entering into the transaction as well as at the time of "the subsequent implementation of the restraint".[57]

EMPLOYMENT CONTRACTS

10.14 Reasons for Restrictions on Competition

Because an employee, (including, in this context, independent contractors who are similar to employees) gains access to sensitive trade secrets, an employer will wish to impose restrictions on the employee's use of these trade secrets. The employer may wish to restrict the employee from using the information for any purpose other than the specified project and from developing a competing product or service. Without adequate protection the interest of the public, as

---

[52] *Ibid.*
[53] *Ibid.*, Section 4.3.
[54] *Ibid.*
[55] *Ibid.*
[56] *Ibid.*
[57] *Ibid.*

well as the interest of the employer, could be harmed: "businesses would cease to invest sufficiently in these activities and overall levels of economic development would suffer".[58] The employee, on the other hand, does not want his or her professional expertise to be restricted; the employee will wish to preserve employment mobility. Just as the U.S. courts have done in the antitrust cases, the courts can be expected to impose a standard of reasonableness on employee-related restrictive covenants.

10.15   The Test of Reasonableness

The Canadian rules will be examined to develop the basic principles involved, their application in any locality, including a Canadian jurisdiction, must be examined in light of local law as it applies to the particular fact situation. This Chapter is not intended to develop legal principles that may be relied on; it is intended to develop only the basic principles. Any restrictive covenant must be reasonable, not only in regard to the interest of the parties, but also in regard to the interest of the public.[59] The basic Canadian premise is that "all restraints of trade themselves, if there is nothing more, are contrary to public policy, and therefore void".[60] Restraints are justifiable "if the restriction is reasonable — reasonable, that is, in reference to the interests of parties concerned and reasonable in reference to the interests of the public, so framed and so guarded as to afford adequate protection to the party in whose favour it is imposed, while at the same time it is in no way injurious to the public".[61] The public interest is "always upon the side of liberty, including the liberty to exercise one's powers or to earn a livelihood".[62]

10.15.1 Only "Adequate" Protection will be Provided

Adequate levels of protection can be identified by means of five distinct elements:

> (1) only proprietary interest will be protected; (2) such interest will be protected no more extensively than is reasonably necessary; (3) the onus of proving both that a legitimate interest exists and that it is not too wide normally falls upon the promisee; (4) failure to meet this onus in either respect will often result in the unenforceability of the entire restrictive covenant (that is, it will generally not be

---

[58]   Trebilcock, *The Common Law*, p. 52.
[59]   *Nordenfelt v. Maxim Nordenfelt Guns & Ammunition Co.*, [1894] A.C. 535, at 565, [1891-4] All E.R. Rep. 1 (H.L.).
[60]   *Ibid.*, at 565 (A.C.).
[61]   *Ibid.*
[62]   *Mason v. Provident Clothing & Supply Co. Ltd.*, [1913] A.C. 724, at 739–40, [1911-13] All E.R. Rep. 400 (H.L.).

severed); and (5) where a covenant is held to be enforceable, the primary relief for breach is injunctive.[63]

10.15.2 Proprietary Interest

Interests that are deserving of protection include protection of trade secrets, which should not be improperly divulged or used, and relations with customers which should not be subject to improper solicitation by employees or ex-employees.[64]

Strategy: Define clearly what activity is being restricted and establish why the proposed restriction on that activity is reasonable.

10.15.3 Reasonable Scope

Trebilcock writes:

> In practice, a restrictive covenant "will be too wide," and hence unenforceable, if it is found to: (a) endure for a longer time period; (b) apply to a wider range of types of employee activities; or (c) apply across a greater geographical area, than is considered by the courts to be reasonably necessary for the adequate protection of the employer's legitimate interest.[65]

Reasonableness is decided "at the date at which the agreement was entered into",[66] taking into account the parties then-existing expectations of what might possibly happen in the future.[67]

Strategy: Design the restrictive covenant, for the specific facts, to apply only for a reasonable time period and within a reasonable geographical area.

10.15.4 Onus

The party wishing to enforce a restrictive covenant has the responsibility or onus to establish that it is reasonable *in the interest of the parties*. The party wishing to resist enforcement of a restrictive covenant has the onus to establish that it is not reasonable *in the public interest*.[68]

---

[63] Trebilcock, *The Common Law*, p. 67.

[64] See *Herbert Morris Ltd. v. Saxelby*, [1916] 1 A.C. 688, [1916-17] All E.R. Rep. 305 (H.L.) and Trebilcock, *The Common Law*, pp. 67 ff.

[65] Trebilcock, *The Common Law*, p. 70.

[66] *Gledhow Autoparts Ltd. v. Delaney*, [1965] 3 All E.R. 288, [1965] 1 W.L.R. 1366, at 295 (C.A.).

[67] *Tank Lining Corp. v. Dunlop Industrial Ltd.* (1982), 140 D.L.R. (3d) 659, at 665 (Ont. C.A.).

[68] *Ibid.*

10.16 Application of Test of Reasonableness to Employees

The test of reasonableness applies to restrictive covenants imposed on employees (such as secrecy obligations, non-solicitation or non-competition covenants). There must be a reasonable balance between the interests of the parties, and the result must not injure the public interest. The employer has the obligation to establish that the restriction is reasonable for the parties; the employee has to establish that the restriction is not within the public interest. One factor to be considered is the bargaining power of the parties. The court will protect an employee who is not in a strong bargaining position with the employer against any restriction that may prevent the employee from using his or her professional expertise. But if the proprietary interest of the employer is exceptional, a broad restrictive covenant may be appropriate.

> Whether a restriction is reasonably required for the protection of the covenantee can only be decided by considering the nature of the covenantee's business and the nature and character of the employment. Admittedly, an employer could not have a proprietary interest in people who were not actual or potential customers. Nevertheless, in exceptional cases, of which I think this is one, the nature of the employment may justify a covenant prohibiting an employee not only from soliciting customers, but also from establishing his own business or working for others so as to be likely to appropriate the employer's trade connection through his acquaintance with the employer's customers. This may indeed be the only effective covenant to protect the proprietary interest of the employer. A simple non-solicitation clause would not suffice.[69]

10.16.1 Dimensions to Reasonableness

There are three "dimensions" to reasonableness of the scope of employee-restrictive covenants that are designed to prevent unauthorized use of trade secrets, solicitation of customers, or non-competition agreements: "(i) the range of people that the employee will be prevented from serving; (ii) the range of services that he will be prevented from providing; and (iii) the duration of the restraint".[70]

SELLER OF A BUSINESS

10.17 Seller of a Business

A non-competition covenant is a standard part of the sale of a business, including an assignment of all intellectual property rights for specified technology.

---

[69] *Elsley v. J.G. Collins Insurance Agencies Ltd.* (1978), 83 D.L.R. (3d) 1 at 7, [1978] 2 S.C.R. 916, 20 N.R. 1, 3 B.L.R. 183, 36 C.P.R. (2d) 65.

[70] Trebilcock, *The Common Law*, p. 99.

The courts are more likely to find an equality of bargaining power in a case involving a sale of a business than would be found in a case involving an employee.[71] Therefore, although the same dimensions of reasonableness generally apply to restrictive covenants granted on the sale of businesses as apply to employees, the specific determination of what is acceptable is often provided.

SEVERANCE

10.18 Severance

Frequently, at the time of drafting a restrictive covenant, it is difficult to determine what scope, duration and area, is reasonable. The drafter of the restrictive covenant will be concerned that if the clause is too broad it will be held to be unenforceable and no restrictive covenant will be in place. The drafter would like the courts to decide what is appropriate and then reduce the scope of the restrictive covenant accordingly. Unfortunately, the Canadian courts will not do that. "The courts have always resisted rewriting a contract that the parties have made".[72] This may be the opposite result to the position taken by some American courts who "have asserted a jurisdiction to rewrite contracts to provide reasonable restraints where the covenant agreed between the parties has been held to be unreasonable".[73] The Canadian courts will restrict themselves to severing unenforceable covenants from enforceable ones. "[T]he severance can be effected when the part severed can be removed by running a blue pencil through it".[74] This "blue pencil" rule does not authorize a Canadian court to add words or to rewrite the clause.[75] The part that is left after a severance must "be a sensible and reasonable obligation in itself and such that the parties would have unquestionably had agreed to it without varying any other terms of the contract or otherwise changing the bargain".[76]

10.18.1 Telescope Clauses: Uncertainty Versus Severability

Some drafters, counting on severability of void clauses, provide a series of decreasing areas of restriction. The British Columbia Court of Appeal has refused to sever the components of a telescope clause that said that the "employee will not compete in (a) Canada, (b) British Columbia, and (c) Vancouver, for (i) 10

---

[71] *Elsley, supra,* note 69, at 5–6 (D.L.R.).

[72] *Canadian American Financial Corp. (Canada) Ltd. v. King* (1989), 60 D.L.R. (4th) 293 at 305, 36 B.C.L.R. (2d) 257, 25 C.P.R. (3d) 315 (C.A.).

[73] *Ibid.,* at 303 (D.L.R.).

[74] *Attwood v. Lamont,* [1920] 3 K.B. 571, at 578, [1920] All E.R. Rep. 55 (C.A.), quoted favourably in *Canadian American, supra,* note 72, at 299–300.

[75] *Canadian American, supra,* note 72, at 306 (D.L.R.).

[76] *Ibid.*

years, (ii) five years, and (iii) one year". It held that the clause was void for uncertainty and it refused to make it valid by severance.[77]

10.18.2 Draft as Separate Covenants

Some writers will now draft a Canadian restrictive covenant selecting the widest
geographical area that can be bargained, and stating that the covenant will be
construed as a series of separate covenants, one for each province (or smallest
area that is reasonable). The agreement could specifically provide why the protection is necessary. The same principle could be adopted for each of the restricted activities. The intent of the drafter is to provide certainty on the agreed
restrictions but to allow them to be independently severed, leaving the balance
of the agreement a complete and reasonable bargain without change.

---

[77] *Ibid.*

Part V

CONSIDERATION

Chapter 11

PAYMENT

a billion here, a billion there, and pretty soon you're talking about real money[1]

11.1 Introduction

Payments for the technology transfer may be made in a number of ways; what is best may depend on the individual nature of the parties to the transfer as well as on the technology.[2]

11.2 Fixed Payments

As a result of valuation and negotiation, the parties will establish a price for a technology and as a result the "cost to the buyer and the benefit to the seller is fixed, certain, and immediate".[3] In addition to offering administrative simplicity, a fixed payment or instalment licence will be attractive to:

(a) competitors who do not want to reveal their sales/financial records to each other;

(b) a transferor which does not have the staff to collect and audit running royalties;

(c) a transferor who needs the working capital immediately to continue development of either the technology that is the subject-matter of the transfer or the development of other technology that it wishes to commercialize.[4]

Lump-sum technology transfer fees are appropriate when the continuing benefit of the technology that a licensee can be expected to receive can be calculated

---

[1] Everett McKinley Dirksen, quoted in John Bartlett, *Familiar Quotations: A Collection of Passages, Phrases, and Proverbs Traced to Their Sources in Ancient and Modern Literature*, ed. Justin Kaplan (Boston: Little, Brown, 1992), p. 694, No. 4.

[2] The prevailing tax system may influence the choice of payments. See Chapter 12 of this text.

[3] Richard Razgaitis, *Early-Stage Technologies, Valuation and Pricing* (John Wiley & Sons, Inc., 1999), p. 201.

[4] For a discussion on Customization, see Chapter 8 of this text and, for Improvements, see Chapter 9 of this text. The payments will vary according to preserved value; see Chapter 2 of this text.

with reasonable accuracy and then discounted to take into account the time and risk factors. But, as was discussed in Chapter 2, it is very difficult to arrive at an evaluation precise enough to produce a fixed figure that both parties will consider in the long run as fair and equitable. Razgaitis writes:

> It is precisely this certainty of valuation that makes it challenging to use only cash as the basis of a technology license. Sellers must make projections on the potential range of outcomes, high to zero, and settle on one number for which they are willing to part with the technology and live with that decision. Similarly, buyers need to reduce all uncertainties to one number, and that number has to be equal to or higher than the seller's number or no deal is possible.[5]

11.2.1 One-Time Fixed Payments

The simplest licences to administer generally involve a fixed-cash payment made in one instalment at a specified date, with the transferor preferring to receive the payment on the execution of the licence and the licensee preferring to pay on the attainment of a specified result or milestone.

11.2.2 Fixed-Periodic Payments

Instead of the fixed-cash technology transfer fee being payable in one instalment, the payment could be made over a period of time in fixed amounts, perhaps dependent on certain milestones being attained.

Strategies: In the case of fixed periodic payments, consider:
(a)   *acceleration of the remaining payments if an instalment is missed;*
(b)   *interest on delayed payments or overdue payments (but watch for laws relating to usury or laws that prohibit a higher rate after default than the rate that was charged before default); and*
(c)   *the possibility that the delayed payments will still be payable even if the subject patents are declared invalid (in contrast to a running royalty, payment of which might then cease to be enforceable in the United States as a result of U.S. patent misuse rules).*[6]

11.2.3 Fixed Payments Credited Against Future Royalties

In some cases, the fixed payment is an advance against royalties that will subsequently be earned.

---

[5]   Razgaitis, pp. 201-202.
[6]   See §11.9 of this text.

Strategies:

(1) How much of the running royalty payment will be credited against the advance? The licensee may need some of the funds for income taxes and working capital for on-going research and development.

(2) Is the advance non-refundable if the earned royalties do not cover the advance?

(3) What is the effect of bankruptcy of the transferee on the application of the advance? Will the licence continue to have the on-going right to offset the advances against earned royalties?

A variation of this model is the grant of an option for a fixed price that gives the transferee the right to obtain a licence only when certain milestones have been met, such as further development of the technology to a specified state.

11.3 Running Royalties

When it is difficult to determine the potential commercial success of the technology, when the parties cannot agree on the valuation of the technology or the discount rates, or when the licensee cannot afford an appropriate lump-sum payment, running royalties may be appropriate. Running royalties may be combined with a fixed payment, which is either independent of the running royalties or is an advance against them.

11.3.1 Different Royalty Rates for Different Intellectual Property Rights

In the case of a technology transfer consisting of a number of intellectual property rights, such as a number of patents or a combination of patents and trade secrets, it may be appropriate to separate the consideration for each component, or, at least agree on the amount of reduction of the consideration if one or more of the rights is invalid or ineffective (for example, a patent application not resulting in an issued patent, an issued patent being declared invalid, or a trade secret entering the public domain).[7]

11.3.2 Variable Consideration

The running royalty could be based on the following:

(a) A flat sum per unit — this basis is attractive to the transferor because payment is made at an early stage in the manufacturing and distribution cycle. It is a useful standard when the technology that is transferred is

---

[7] See also §11.9 of this text.

included as one of many components of a product marketed by the licensee, or when the licensee does not wish to reveal its sales revenue.

(b) A fixed percentage of revenue — this method allows the royalty to reflect the commercial success of the technology that is transferred and is often the fairest allocation of the risks and benefits of commercialization. What is considered to be "revenue" will require careful consideration.

   (i)   It will be net of sales taxes, but will it be net of the costs of packaging, transportation, return allowances, sales commissions or other appropriate deductions?

   (ii)   Will the revenue that is the subject of the royalty calculation include indirect benefits provided by the transferor to the licensee such as installation services, maintenance or support, and training, or will these items be charged for separately? The manner in which indirect benefits are handled could amount to significant benefits to the licensee and significant costs to the transferor, especially in the case of licensing software which could entail material labour costs.

   (iii)   Are Canadian tax credits for research to be considered as a source of revenue?

   (iv)   If the products that embody the licensed technology will be bundled with other products and there are not separate prices for each component product of the bundle, it may be very difficult for the parties to establish a method of separating the royalty for the licensed product from the value delivered by the rest of the bundle. One such method is to assume that each component product contributes to the overall price of the bundled product in proportion to their respective list prices. For example, if Product A has a list price of $100 and Product B has a list price of $200 and the combined list price is $210, then Product A will be deemed to earn one-third of the revenue of the bundled product or $70. However, where each component does not have a separate list price, the parties can expect vigorous negotiations on what the component technology contributed to the overall value. In this case the parties will want to consider a flat price per unit.

   (v)   A cap on the maximum amount to be paid by way of royalty could be established; after which the licence would become fully paid-up.

(c) Increasing or decreasing rates — in order to encourage a prompt incline in the growth of sales, the royalty rate may decrease as certain milestones are reached — the "wedding cake" model. Conversely, the entry into the marketplace may involve significant one-time costs and, thus, will initially require low royalty rates that can be increased as the licensee's fixed costs are being amortized over a higher level of sales — the "inverse wedding cake model".[8]

(d) Flat periodic sum — the licence could provide that the annual royalty will have minimums or maximums. If the transferor is concerned about its technology not being adequately exploited, it may require a minimum royalty payable for each specified time period. If there is concern that the transferor's revenue could be excessive in comparison to its contribution to the successful commercialization of the resulting product, a maximum aggregate amount could be specified.

11.3.3 Base for Calculation of Royalty

The base for calculating royalties could be:

(a) the number of units manufactured, processed or produced;
(b) the revenue generated;
(c) the quantity of supplies or raw material used; or
(d) the profits generated by the licensee. This is a standard that is conceptually attractive to the acquirer of the technology since a top line calculation based only on revenue does not take directly into account the profitability of the technology. However this standard is probably the most difficult one to use because it is very difficult to decide what deductions from revenue will be permitted.[9] Razgaitis writes: "However, because all the costs between the top line and the net income of the bottom line are largely controlled by the buyer, there are only rare and special cases where the parties agree to basing royalty on any value below the top line and doing so is perilous to the seller".[10] Further he writes, "In general, because of the auditing complexities in computing the royalty base anywhere below the top line, it is still rare that parties agree to such a provision".[11]

11.4 Non-monetary Consideration

In addition to payment by way of cash, the consideration payable to the transferor could include the following:

(a) Equity shares issued by the licensee — the transferor will wish to determine what restrictions will be placed on the marketability of these shares, either as a result of securities regulations, regulations imposed by a stock exchange, or by the number of shares being actively traded in the

---

[8] See Razgaitis, pp. 235-236.
[9] For a further discussion see §2.8 of this text.
[10] Razgaitis, p. 203.
[11] Razgaitis, p. 203.

open market. A thin market may prevent trades in a timely fashion. Consideration should also be given by the parties to the following:

(i) If the transferred technology will be a core asset for the acquirer, equity will be of strong interest to the transferor as a royalty based on sales will not fully reflect the value and goodwill that the technology brings to the acquirer. In addition, with equity the transferor will share more closely in the spin-off results and the convoyed sales.

(ii) A significant factor to the acquirer is a reduction in the amount of cash that has to be expended to acquire the technology. Dot.com start-ups were highly proficient in using equity instead of cash as a method of payment for everything from office space to technology acquisitions to legal fees.

(iii) Pricing will be a significant issue. If the shares trade publicly, the price used to determine the number of shares to be provided to the transferor on one particular day or a particular moment in that day may not be representative of underlying value. A 20-day rolling average may be more fair to use. With a private company, pricing will be even more difficult. Alternatives include using the price established by the most recently preceding private placement or the next one to be placed if the former is no longer relevant. The transferor would favour equity in a private company when it could anticipate significant growth through the step-ups in value as a result of the exploitation of its intellectual property.[12]

(iv) Dilution as a result of subsequent offerings should be considered by the transferor. Legitimate further rounds of financing would normally be considered acceptable when the company has progressed as expected while dilution in favour of the founders by way of excessive stock options or warrants or as a result of the founders' errors or incompetence would be less acceptable.

(v) Equity is a valuable component of an overall compensation scheme that also includes cash and a royalty or other form of earnout.

(b) Goods or Services — The transferor may have a need for products or services that the acquiror can better provide, such as conducting research or clinical tests, obtaining regulatory approval, providing expertise or know-how, or providing products or services that can be used in the course of the transferor's business;[13]

(c) Funding of continued research — as government funding shrinks, the need for university funding of continued research may prevail over the desire for royalties in the longer term.

(d) Appointment to advisory boards — such appointments allow the inventor to maintain continued involvement in the development and

---

[12] For a further discussion on this topic generally, see Razgaitis, chapter 10, p. 201ff.
[13] For further discussion see 3.24.1(g) for a brief discussion of the synergetic business model.

marketing of the product and may give him or her prestige; conversely, the appointment may give prestige to the licensee by the inventor lending his or her name and reputation.

(e) First rights — the transferor may have certain first rights granted by the licensee, such as a first right to all improvements, a right of first refusal to market the technology once it is developed, a first right to research or develop improvements, or to make, use or sell improvements. Some first rights are only for first negotiating marketing rights to obtain a licence of the subject technology after clinical or other tests are performed by the licensee.

(f) Grant-back of improvements — a pooling of improvements through an "improvements club" allows all licensees to share improvements and know-how with each other.[14]

(g) The settlement of outstanding litigation between the parties, including a claim of infringement.

11.5 Release for Past Infringement

One consideration in a technology transfer agreement may be the release of the licensee for past infringements, which might be effective only upon a certain level of royalties or other performance levels being attained. The release may be for specifically stated infringements or may be a general release of all infringements by the licensee for using specific intellectual property.

11.6 Duration of Period for Payment of Royalties

The period during which royalties are earned and, thus, are payable must not only satisfy the applicable antitrust rules but also good business practices — both often conclude that no payment should be required if no benefit is received.[15] Often, royalties are payable during the life of any patent that is a subject-matter of the licence, but this is not necessarily a good correlation between cost and benefit. Royalties should reflect the benefit received by the licensee and should correlate to a patent that is core to the transaction, rather than to all patents that are the subject of the licence. A licensee will also want to contemplate decreasing royalties payable for the licensed rights where they become less valuable as a result of obsolescence.

---

[14] For further discussion see Chapter 9, "Improvements and Joint Ownership".

[15] Unfortunately, antitrust rules are less flexible to compensate for changing economic demands than are good business practices.

11.7 Royalties Payable to Others

When preparing the technology transfer agreement the licensee will want the agreement to contemplate the licensee being required to pay a royalty to a third party for use of the technology, perhaps as a result of underlying patent rights of the third party, a combination of many protected technologies being incorporated into one product that includes the third party's technology, or a claim by the third party for infringement producing a settlement that requires a royalty to be paid to the third party for the continued use of the technology.[16] Usually, it would be fair for the licensee to deduct any third party payments from the royalty payable to the transferor and if so, the transfer agreement should permit such deduction. If the parties decide to take out patent infringement insurance to resolve the foregoing, the issue as to who should pay the premiums should also be addressed.

11.8 Interest on Overdue Payments

There should be a provision levying a pre-agreed reasonable interest rate on delayed payments. Some jurisdictions do not automatically provide for interest on amounts awarded in a court judgment; others allow for a rate that is lower than a commercial rate. A reasonable rate should reflect the fact that payment is in arrears and, thus, the licensee does not deserve or qualify for preferred rates, such as a bank's prime lending rate.

11.8.1 Other Consequences of Failure to Pay

The technology transfer agreement could go on to provide other consequences of a failure to pay, including termination. The local bankruptcy rules will have to be examined for any rules that may prevent termination for failure to pay if the licensee is in bankruptcy.

11.9 Effect of Invalidity/Expiration of Intellectual Property Rights

The effect on payments if the subject intellectual property expires or is held to be invalid must be addressed in a licence.

    In the United States, the *Brulotte* case[17] establishes that it is patent misuse for a licensor to demand payments on account of a licence of a patent when that patent has expired. The same principle applies when a patent has been held invalid. This is not the accepted rule in Canada; there is a significant risk that the

---

[16]   See Chapter 16 of this text.

[17]   See *Brulotte v. Thys Co.*, 379 U.S. 29 (1964); rehearing denied, 379 U.S. 985 (S.C. 1965), and *Lear, Inc. v. Adkins*, 395 U.S. 653 (1969).

contract will govern. In the U.S., there has developed the practice of requiring a royalty as long as any licensed patent has not expired and any claims in that patent remain valid. In respect of this practice and the effects of the *Brulotte* case, there are a number of business issues that must be considered with local legal advisors:

(a) Should the royalty continue if a key patent has expired where a family of patents was licensed, or if no key patent claim remains valid?

(b) Does *Brulotte* apply if the licensee is a U.S. company but the only patent licensed is a Canadian patent? What if there was a U.S. patent as well as a Canadian patent where the former has expired or no patent claim remains valid but the latter continues in effect.

(c) Does *Brulotte* apply if there is a hybrid licence of a patent and a trade secret and there is a blended royalty? A practice has developed to expressly provide in a hybrid licence a lesser royalty rate if the patent has expired, or is invalid.[18] This may not produce fairness if the trade secret contributed the bulk of the value unless substantial competition is encountered that evidences the value of the expired or invalid patent?

(d) Should there be a reduction in, or elimination of, royalties if:
  (i) the subject of the licence is a patent application and the patent does not issue (consider specifying a time period in which it must issue).[19]
  (ii) the subject of the licence is a trade secret and the secret enters the public domain without fault of the license? It should be noted that *Brulotte* does not cover trade secrets.

(e) Does *Brulotte* apply if the patent licence called for a lump-sum payment, which was financed over an extended period of time, and in that time period the patent was declared invalid?

(f) Does a governing law clause that provides for U.S. law produce the application of *Brulotte* when the parties are all non-American?

11.10 Payment When Licensee Challenges the Transferor's Patent

In the event that the licensee challenges the licensor's patent, the licence agreement could consider forcing the licensee to choose to:

(i) repudiate the licence; or
(ii) continue to pay the royalty and not challenge.

---

[18] See Michael D. McCoy, P. Higgins, and Lance A. Lawson, "Trade Secrets and Related Licenses", Technology Transfer Seminar 2001, Licensing Executives Society, p. 22.

[19] *Aronson v. Quick Point Pencil Co.*, 440 U.S. 257 (1979) held a royalty valid where it was reduced pursuant to the agreement as a result of the patent application not producing a patent within five years.

Otherwise the licensee would be able to have the best of both worlds – challenge the licensor's patent but not be subject to infringement if the challenge is lost. Local law will have to be examined in the event that this issue arises.

11.11 Periodic Reports

To satisfy the transferor that the proper royalty is being paid, the licensee will issue periodic reports, based on the same period used for calculating royalties. In addition to providing data to summarize the calculation of the royalty, the report could include details of competition encountered, complaints being made by customers about product quality, suggestions for modifications or additions to the offered products or services, forecasts of future sales (usually non-binding), marketing efforts made by the licensee, methods adopted to satisfy required standards of production and maintenance of confidentiality and compliance with field of use or other restrictions imposed by the technology transfer agreement.

11.11.1 Duty to Maintain Records

The licensee will be required to maintain records that will enable it to prepare these periodic reports. If accounting records are involved, the agreement should specify the generally accepted accounting principles to be adopted. The difference between generally accepted accounting principles of the relevant countries should be taken into account.

11.11.2 Right to Inspect

The transferor will want to inspect some, or all, of these records from time to time. The transfer agreement should contemplate whether it is only accounting records that may be inspected or whether any document or other information that relates to the exploitation (or non-exploitation) of the transferred technology (such as other licences of other technology owned by the licensee that were made at the same time to the same transferee where there is the possibility of sifting compensation between the different technologies). In some cases, the transferor and licensee are competitors and this inspection could reveal confidential information that is not within the scope of the transferor's review. In such a case, the transfer agreement could provide for an inspection by an independent entity, such as a firm of accountants, (chartered accountants in Canada or certified public accountants in the United States). Further, if the scope of the inspection is beyond accounting matters, the transferor may wish to retain a firm that understands the nature of the subject technology transfer agreement. In addressing this issue in a transfer agreement, some agreements specify that the independent auditor cannot act for competitors of the parties as well as not act for either party. It should also be noted that some agreements give the auditors the right to interview directors and officers – which should be avoided.

Practice Point: the licensee should restrict this right to only the CFO or equivalent person who should be required to acquaint himself or herself of the facts. The transfer agreement should also address how far back the auditors can go in performing their review? Perhaps some period less than the statutory limitation period would be appropriate? Finally, the transfer agreement should ensure that the individuals making the inspection are bound by secrecy obligations.

11.11.3 Frequency and Cost of Audit

The licensee does not want to be subject to frequent and vexatious audits and may want to limit the frequency of audits to no more than one every 12-month period. The parties will also wish to allocate the cost of the audit — many agreements allocate cost depending on whether errors are found. Generally, it is the size of the errors in relation to the size of the transaction that should determine the allocation of the cost and this allocation should not be chosen arbitrarily. A $5,000 (5%) error threshold may be appropriate for an agreement producing royalties of $100,000 in the period audited.

11.12 Withholding Taxes

Many countries require a licensee to deduct withholding tax on payments being remitted to foreign transferors. The technology transfer agreement should address whether the licensee must "gross up" the payment so that the transferor receives the full amount owing to it and in such a case, the right of the transferor to obtain a tax credit in its home country in respect of the tax paid should be taken into account. Whether the transferor is earning sufficient taxable income to gain full benefit of such a local credit is also a relevant factor.[20]

11.13 Sales Taxes

In some jurisdictions, sales tax is considered to be included in the price for the goods or services, unless expressly stated to be in addition to such price, as is the case with the Canadian Goods and Services Tax. If so, the agreement should specify that the stated prices are net of all such applicable taxes.

11.14 Currency

In international transactions the currency of payment is relevant. Some countries require licensees to pay in the local currency (all too often those countries have a volatile currency exchange rate). The possibility of currency controls being imposed should also be of concern. If revenue is being earned in a currency

---

[20] See Chapter 12 of this text for further discussion.

other than the currency used for establishing royalties, the method of timing of the conversion will be relevant. Will that time be the time of receipt by the licensee or the time of payment by the licensee or some time arbitrarily selected by the parties, or an average conversion rate applicable throughout the reporting period?

11.15 Method of Payment

The negotiators will wish to take into account the time and place for payment, the method of effecting payment and the "clearing" relationship between the parties' bankers.

11.15.1 Payment Milestones

If the technology that is being transferred is not fully developed or proven, payments may depend on milestones being achieved.[21]

11.15.2 Security for Payment

If the licensee is not a solid financial entity or is located in a country where recovery by court action is not practically or economically available, the transferor may require some form of security for payment, such as a letter of credit drawn on a credible bank. Conversely, the licensee may want the transferor's warranties of performance guarantees to be supported by some method of security. Some technology transfer agreements include a charge on the licensee's assets to secure payment; in such a case, registration under the local personal property security rules may be necessary.

---

[21] See Chapter 8 of this text for a discussion on customization and acceptance tests.

Chapter 12

TAXATION

A technology transfer agreement should not only satisfy the commercial goals of the parties. It should also ensure that the most advantageous tax consequences are achieved. For a cross-border transfer of technology, this means considering the domestic tax laws of two or more countries, as well as the applicable tax treaties. It can be a complicated exercise. However, it is important to at least have an appreciation of the tax consequences of exporting technology before starting to negotiate a technology transfer agreement.[1]

12.1 Moving Complexity

The process of determining the tax consequences of a technology transfer agreement reflects the complexity of the applicable taxation legislation and international tax treaties. Hardly can a person become expert in the tax treatment of a technology transfer agreement before the rules are changed as the taxing authorities perceive another loophole to be closed or another social policy to be implemented. Today's social policy is tomorrow's loophole. This Chapter does not attempt to provide anything other than guides as to what basic principles should be raised by negotiators to a technology transfer agreement when meeting with their tax advisor.

Strategy: Obtain up-to-date tax advice from an expert for each territory involved.

12.2 Characterization of Payment

Payments under a technology transfer agreement will be treated either as a "capital" receipt or an "income" receipt. The manner of treatment required by generally accepted accounting principles does not necessarily determine treatment for tax purposes. The treatment under the domestic tax law in one country may differ from the treatment in another, and there may be a tax treaty that

---

[1]   Shelley J. Kamin, "The Tax System and Technology Transfer Agreements" in M. Goudreau, G. Bisson, N. Lacasse and L. Perret, eds., *Exporting our Technology: International Protection and Transfers of Industrial Innovations* (Montreal: Wilson & Lafleur, 1995), p. 389, at 389.

overrules both. The following sums up the issues for the parties to a technology transfer agreement.

> The income tax consequences arising from a technology transfer often depend on three key factors. The first is the legal classification of the technology, for example, whether it is the subject of a copyright or patent, or whether it is "know-how". The second is the form of the transfer, namely, whether the technology is being sold or assigned outright, or whether it is being licensed. The third factor is the method of payment, which is generally a lump sum or periodic royalties or both. A payment may be regarded as a lump sum payment, even though it is made by a series of instalments. It is important to keep these factors in mind when drafting a technology transfer agreement. Otherwise, the tax treatment of amounts paid under that agreement may not be the same as the parties had intended.[2]

Strategy: For licensing, know the tax treatment for each party to a technology transfer agreement.

12.2.1 Capital Versus Income

For tax purposes, payments characterized as "capital" are often treated more favourably than payments that are characterized as "income".[3] The tax treatment of receipt of the payment by the transferee, however, is not always the same as the tax treatment of the acquisition costs incurred by the other party making the same payment. Also, a payment that normally would be characterized as "capital" can lose that characterization for certain reasons. For example, in Canada, a payment that is based on production or usage will be treated as income, even though the same payment in another country may be treated as capital.[4] Additionally, even though a transaction in Canada would normally be treated as a capital one, it may be treated as giving rise to income for Canadian tax purposes on the basis of being a "venture in the nature of a trade" if it is one of a series of similar transactions.

Strategy: Watch for the other party's sensitivity to its tax treatment.

12.3 Tax Credits

In Canada, some types of expenditures qualify for special treatment. Some qualify as credits against tax paid (in contrast to being deductible against income

---

[2] *Ibid.*

[3] See Catherine A. Brown, "Tax Aspects of a Transfer of Technology: The Asia-Pacific Rim," Canadian Tax Paper No. 87, pp. 388 ff., The Canadian Tax Foundation 1994. Helpful Discussion on Tax Treatment from a Canadian Point of View.

[4] See s. 12(1)(g) of the *Income Tax Act*, R.S.C. 1985, c. 1 (5th Supp.).

only). Some qualify for actual payments from the government to a taxpayer who does not generate enough taxable income to benefit from a tax credit.

Strategy: In any strategic alliance, look for potential tax consequences or favourable tax programs encouraging social policies, such as research and development.

12.4 Applicable Taxing Authority in an International Transaction

Taxing authorities establish complex rules attempting to tax all the income earned within their country by domestic and foreign businesses. These rules will reach strenuously to include a business or its income within its taxing jurisdiction. Thus, "transfer pricing" is a material issue, particularly if the parties are not dealing at arm's length.

Strategy: Each technology transfer relationship must be examined to determine its potential for bringing businesses within the scope of foreign taxation authority.

12.4.1 Withholding Tax and International Treaties

The Canadian and U.S. income tax legislation impose a duty on a domestic transferee of technology to withhold portions of payments made to a foreign transferor of that technology; this withholding can be as much as 25 per cent of the transfer consideration. In attempts to reduce the amount of withholding tax and to avoid double taxation (*i.e.*, taxation by the country requiring the withholding and taxation on the same payment by the country in which the transferor is sited), countries such as Canada and the United States enter into tax treaties. Canada and the United States entered into an Income Tax Convention signed September 26, 1980 which has been periodically amended by Protocols. Some types of payments are subject to withholding, some are exempt.

The Treaty provides for the taxation of 13 general categories of income. These include income from real property, business profits, transportation, dividends, interest, royalties, gains from alienation, personal services, artists and athletes, pensions and annuities, government services, payments to students and other income. In a technology transfer arrangement, the relevant Treaty articles would depend on how the technology is transferred. . . . [A] typical technology transfer agreement might include all or any combination of the following: know-how, trade secrets, patents and related technology, industrial designs, copyrights, trademarks, formulas, processes, models, prototypes, machinery or equipment, as well as a range of technical and professional services. Therefore 7 of these Treaty provisions will normally affect technology transfer arrangements: royalties (Article 12), business profits (Article 7) and, where applicable, the permanent establishment rules (Arti-

cle 5), independent and dependent personal services (Articles 14 and 15), gains from
the alienation of property (Article 13), and other income (Article 21).[5]

Strategies:
  *(1)   The domestic tax law does not necessarily characterize a payment the
          same way the treaty does, so reference to both domestic rules and
          treaty rules will be necessary.*
  *(2)   Each party to an international technology transfer agreement should
          determine the international tax consequences to the other party; do
          not assume that they "mirror" its domestic tax treatment.*

12.4.2 Double Taxation

The Canada/U.S. Tax Treaty, often endeavouring — sometimes successfully,
sometimes not — to avoid double taxation by allocating which country may tax
the proceeds of a transaction under domestic law, requires the home country to
provide a credit for the tax paid to the foreign country. Even with credits for tax
paid in a foreign country, serious problems may be encountered if the transferor
has no income and, therefore, cannot utilize the tax credit. Do not assume the
tax credits will produce a neutral tax result.

12.4.3 Zero to 10 Per Cent in Seconds

The parties to a technology transfer agreement that is within the scope of the
Canada/U.S. Tax Treaty will be anxious to determine if the applicable rate is 10
per cent or 0 per cent.[6] One solution to the problem may be "separate multi-
stage agreements" which will separate out the payments for each type of technology that is within the scope of the technology transfer agreement. Be cautious, however, because there are no guidelines as to when, or how, contracts
will be "linked" to determine which characterization will dominate.[7] Obviously,
the taxing authorities will attempt to characterize an agreement that transfers
different types of technology as substantially one that would trigger the maximum withholding tax.

> It may also prove cumbersome to separate out a portion between technology pay-
> ments which will be subject to withholding and those which will not. This would
> occur, for example, even in the simple case where payment for the use of a patent
> is coupled with rental payments for the use of tangible property. The tax bureau-
> crat will be concerned first, about whether he can unbundle the payment; second,
> about the apportionment between exempt and non-exempt portions of the license
> fee and finally, about any documentation required to support the allocation, cur-

---

[5]   Catherine A. Brown, "The Canada–U.S. Tax Treaty: Its Impact on the Cross-Border Transfer of
       Technology" (unpublished), pp. 10–11.
[6]   *Ibid.*, p. 12.
[7]   *Ibid.*, p. 37.

rently as well as on an annual basis. This may prove to be a substantial burden. As one author has pointed out, "if periodic valuation is necessary to support a taxpayer's allocation of royalties between technology and taxable intangibles such as trademark, it will impose an enormous system cost to both taxpayer and revenue authorities".[8]

Strategy: "Attempts by the licensee to allocate between the exempt and non-exempt royalty portions of the contract may also be met with some resistance by the licensor, whose obligation it is to withhold and remit. This may not be a . . . risk he or she is prepared to assume."[9]

This "substantial burden" may interfere unnecessarily with the global market for technology. Why should competitive technology developers in either Canada or the United States be placed at a disadvantage to competitors by tax rules?

12.4.4 Sales Tax

Payments under any technology transfer may give rise to tax being levied under a sales tax, goods or services tax, or value added tax regime. Some jurisdictions require very little "nexus" to demand payment of a sales tax. Often, the sales tax regime imposes responsibility on the transferor to collect the tax. The Canadian Goods and Services Tax (or the Harmonized Sales Tax in Nova Scotia, New Brunswick and Newfoundland) provides that if the tax is not separately specified in an exigible transaction, the tax is considered to be included in the purchase price.[10]

In Ontario, software programs have been deemed to be tangible personal property in certain circumstances and a supply of software (including installation, maintenance and upgrade services) may therefore be subject to the Ontario retail sales tax.

Strategies:
  (1)   Watch for a sales tax being levied on a technology transfer.
  (2)   Allocate who bears responsibility for the sales tax. Do not assume that silence on the issue places the responsibility with the other side.
  (3)   Decide whether the tax is in addition to, or included in, the consideration paid on account of the transfer.

---

[8]   *Ibid.*, pp. 37 and 38 (footnotes omitted).
[9]   *Ibid.*, p. 38.
[10] See *Excise Tax Act*, R.S.C. 1985, c. E-15.

Part VI

TERM

Chapter 13

TERM AND TERMINATION

13.1 Introduction

The term of the project refers to the length of the agreement between the parties, albeit for a definitive period, or a perpetual period. Generally, the term will regardless of its length terminate on the occurrence of specified material breaches of duty imposed on the defaulting party.

13.2 Specify Term

The commencement of the term of the rights granted does not always coincide with the date of execution of the agreement; in such cases the commencement date should be specifically stated. If the agreement causes the term to commence retroactively, avoid the possibility of an automatic default arising for failure to report or to pay royalties after the commencement date of the term but before the date of execution of the agreement. The agreement could have some specific provisions relating to the "pre-execution" term, the performance of which may be conditions precedent to the grant and continuance of the grant of permitted rights. If the technology is not yet proven or must be customized before the term commences, and the term of the licence will not commence until it is proven or customized, the negotiators should make sure the commencement of the term is finite and not susceptible to a dispute over the possibility that unauthorized activities have occurred outside the term.

13.2.1 Term Calculated on External Matters

Many patent licences provide that the term is for the life of a patent or for the life of the last patent of a group of patents to expire. This method of calculation may be used to avoid violations of an antitrust rule[1] while still providing the maximum term legally available. The licensee should examine the term of each patent, selecting only those patents that are material and calculating an appropriate term based on those patents rather than

---

[1] See Chapter 10.

agreeing to pay royalties even though the remaining patents may be immaterial. The parties could provide a method of re-establishing royalties when material patents have expired.

13.3 Automatic Renewal

Although the parties may be reluctant to agree on a long initial term, they may accept a shorter term that is automatically renewed. For example, they could provide for a five-year term that will be automatically renewed for a further three successive five-year terms unless either party gives at least six months' notice to the other party of its desire for termination at the expiration of the current five-year term. Automatic renewals must be distinguished from "evergreen" contracts where there may be a basic term with an automatic extension for an indefinite term thereafter, terminable only after expiration of the basic term by one party giving the other party an appropriate notice. For example, a five-year project could be renewed indefinitely and be terminable after the fifth year on five months' notice.

13.4 Events Giving Rise to Termination

These events include:

    (a) failure to attain specified performance requirements (this could terminate exclusivity or terminate all rights);

    (b) ceasing to do business;

    (c) breaching any provision of the agreement. Consider whether a particular breach can be remedied, and if so, whether time for a "cure" should be permitted before termination is effective. Some breaches, such as breach of secrecy obligations, cannot be cured; some can be cured promptly, such as payment of money, and some can be cured only with the expenditure of time and effort, such as improving product quality; and

    (d) bankruptcy.

13.4.1 Bankruptcy

If a licensee becomes bankrupt, under Canadian law the transferor cannot terminate the licence for failure to pay royalties that arose prior to the bankruptcy.[2] The effect of the transferor's bankruptcy must also be considered. The U.S. case, *Lubrizol Enterprises Inc. v. Richmond Metal Finishers Inc.*, established that a trustee in bankruptcy of the transferor could renounce licences granted by the bankrupt if they were "executory".[3] This produced unfair results, particularly

---

[2] *Bankruptcy and Insolvency Act*, R.S.C. 1985, c. B-3; 1992 (en. 1992, c. 27, s. 30), s. 65.1.

[3] 756 F.2d 1043 (1985).

when the licensee had made a material investment in the acquisition and exploitation of an exclusive licence. The U.S. *Bankruptcy Act* was amended to overcome some of the perceived unfairness.[4] It is not clear that a *Lubrizol*-type decision could be made in Canada; the two Bankruptcy Acts are very different.[5] The U.S. curative legislation covers only the transferor becoming bankrupt and provides no remedy for an assignor of intellectual property rights that is receiving payment by way of royalties from an assignee in a relationship that, economically, is very similar to a licensee.

13.5 Terminating Agreement Versus Terminating Rights

Rather than terminating the agreement, it is preferable to terminate specific rights and obligations, leaving the balance of the provisions of the agreement in effect. Drafters who terminate the agreement often have to go to great lengths to specify what provisions survive. It is more helpful to the negotiators to a technology transfer agreement to specify what provisions terminate and then set out the consequences of termination.[6]

13.6 Consequences of Termination

The following are some of the consequences of termination that negotiators to a technology transfer could consider including in their agreement.

(a) The licensee ceases to use or exploit the licensed technology, including trademarks and logos.
(b) The licensee returns to the transferor all copies of confidential information and licensed products in its possession.
(c) After termination, if the licensee may sell the inventory on hand in the market-place, the transferor might want to have the right to perform an audit of this inventory to determine what is there to be sold, to avoid continued production, particularly if easily reproduced software is involved. The transferor may wish to have the right to repurchase that inventory rather than permitting the licensee to sell it in the market-

---

[4] Section 356(n) of the U.S. *Bankruptcy Act*, U.S.C. §356(n).

[5] See also *Re Erin Features #1 Ltd.* (1991), 8 C.B.R. (3d) 205 (B.C.S.C.), and see the case comment by Gabor G.S. Takach and Ellen L. Hayes in (1993), 15 C.B.R. (3d) 66. See also John R. Morressey, "Insolvency and Intellectual Property" presented at Learning Executives Society Seminar Meeting 2001; Piero Ianuzzi, "Bankruptcy and the Trustee's Power to Disclaim Intellectual Property and Technology Licensing Agreements: Presents the Challenging Effect of Licensor Bankruptcy in Canada", 18 CIPR 367; Martin Kratz, "Bankruptcy, Insolvency and Receivership: How to Protect Your Interests" Negotiating and Drafting Intellectual Property License Agreements 2001.

[6] See Ronald B. Coolley, "Importance of Termination Clauses" in *les Nouvelles*, the Journal of the Licensing Executives Society, Vol. XXV, No. 4, December 1990, p. 169.

place. The right is especially appropriate if such a right to sell is permitted or required by the local legislation.

(d) The licensee pays all royalties earned pre-termination and (if it has the right to continue distribution) after termination, and

(e) The transferor has the right to audit the licensee's books and premises to satisfy itself that it has been paid in full and that the licensee has ceased to use, or otherwise exploit, the licensed technology.

Part VII

LIABILITY

Chapter 14

WARRANTIES

You wanted it to work?!

14.1 Introduction

It is often very difficult to find a fair allocation of risk of imperfection or in-fringement in technology transfer agreements, making it very difficult to negoti-ate the appropriate warranties. Sometimes it is difficult even to establish your own position as a bargainer: the balance of fairness and the proper allocation of risks is not always apparent. As we move into the information economy, many of the rules we established for a physical goods economy no longer apply. Re-cent studies and model legislation will give us guidance.

14.2 Distinction Between Representations, Warranties and Conditions

The words "representations", "warranties" and "conditions" are not words that should be used interchangeably, nor should they be used without the drafter being aware of any peculiar meaning that may be given by local law. According to Milgrim:[1]

   (a) a representation is a statement as to the existence or non-existence of a fact or state of affairs, or state of mind, for which act is an inducement to contract;

   (b) a warranty is a guarantee, an assurance of the existence or future existence of a fact upon which the other party may rely; and

   (c) covenants are simply contractual promises to do certain acts or refrain from doing certain acts.

Strategy: Rather than think in terms of warranties, representations or condi-tions, which do not produce clear concepts, it might be better to think only in terms of performance obligations.

---

[1]   R.M. Milgrim, *Milgrim on Licensing*, looseleaf (New York: Lexis Nexis, 2001), para. 23.00.

The essence of the distinction may be in the legal remedy that results. The following oversimplified discussion may illustrate the point:

(a) The remedy may be a claim for damages. In the case of a breach of a representation, or of a statement of fact, the circumstances of the remedy may provide only for a right to damages. The breach in this case may require the non-defaulting party to continue to perform "independent" promises in the agreement even though the defaulting party has breached one promise. Thus, agreements usually permit the termination of the agreement or other obligations in the case of material breaches.[2]

(b) The remedy might be the right to reject the goods or rescind the contract. Under the U.S. system, a breach of warranty may give rise to this remedy, but under Canadian common law sale of goods laws, a warranty may only give rise to a claim for damages – only a breach of "conditions" may give rise to such a remedy.[3] In other circumstances in Canadian common law, a breach of warranty may give rise to a right to reject or rescind.

Strategy: Specify the remedy.

14.3 Allocation of Risk

The negotiators of a technology transfer agreement do not have the benefit of hindsight, as does a court; they must endeavour to foresee who should bear the risks some of which are not only unknown in kind but also unknown as to the economic result. Some of the standards the courts use may provide useful guidelines to the negotiators to a technology transfer agreement:

(a) Which party can better insure against the risk[4] or otherwise bear the loss?[5] It should not be assumed that this is the producer of the product; software developers may not be able to obtain product liability insurance at a reasonable cost due to the difficulty of assessing the risk.

---

2   See Chapter 13 of this text. See also *Milgrim on Licensing*, para. 23.01.

3   See *Manual and Technology Transfer Negotiations, United Nation Industrial Development Organization*, Vienna, 1996, General Studies Series ("U.N. Manual") at pp. 273-274. See also Sheldon Burshtein, *Representations on Warranties and License Agreements, Negotiating and Drafting an Intellectual Property License Agreements*, the Canadian Institute, Vancouver, April 10-11, 2000, pp. 2-4. Hereafter in this Chapter, the writer will refer to warranties to cover any promise in the nature of a guarantee and will no longer distinguish between warranties, representations and conditions for the ease of reference.

4   See S.M. Waddams, *Products Liability*, (Scarborough, Ont.: Carswell, 1993) p. 34. Also see Chris Reid, *Limiting Risks in International Transactions: U.K. and EEC* (London: University of London, 1991), p. 15 (hereinafter "Reid, *Limiting Risks*").

5   See Waddams, *ibid.*, p. 11. See also Ontario Law Reform Commission Report, p. 228 and Reid, *Limiting Risks*, p. 15.

(b) Which party can better avoid risks being actually realized? For example, can an intermediate user recognize the defect and stop the use that otherwise would give rise to the risk?[6]

(c) Which party can better determine or, perhaps, even control the scope of the risk? For example, one party may not have the ability even to foresee the type of use, which is often the case with many software licensors.

Particularly with technology that does not have a well proven record, the extent of warranties granted will be the subject of serious negotiation. The licensee will want some assurance, or "warranty", that it will get at least the quality or economic rights and benefits it expected. It often has good reason to be concerned about "untimeliness, inadequate productivity and questionable quality".[7] It will also be concerned about risks of ownership, freedom to use and exploit the intellectual property, with the anticipated exclusivity. This allocation of risk appears in three sections of the technology transfer agreement. First there is the scope of the warranties set out usually in the middle of the agreement. Second, there are the remedy clauses: what remedies are available (e.g. damages, rejection, rescission, termination). Third, there is the indemnification process and exposure to damages. Experienced practitioners prefer to establish the scope of the warranties and related liability exposure before they establish the price. The indemnification and liability clauses often baffle non-legal negotiators due to the legalese (not legal-ease), and they may overlook that the indemnification provisions take away all the protection they expected as a result of the warranty clauses where their attention was focused. The transferor will want to limit its exposure to liability from what it considers to be unreasonable expectations by the licensee.

PART ONE: WARRANTIES OF QUALITY

14.4 Causes of Defects

Product liability can result from a defective design or defective information, defective manufacture or production, defective testing procedures, defective use,

---

[6]   See, for example, C.A. Wright, A.M. Linden and L.N. Klar, *Canadian Tort Law: Cases, Notes & Materials*, 9th ed. (Markham, Ont: Butterworths, 1990), pp. 16-19 – 16-20 (hereinafter "Wright and Linden, *Tort Law*"), quoting *Phillips v. Chrysler Corp. of Canada Ltd.*, [1962] O.R. 375, 32 D.L.R. (2d) 347 (H.C.J.) and *Haseldine v. C.A. Daw & Son Ltd.*, [1941] 2 K.B. 343, [1941] 3 All E.R. 156 (C.A.).

[7]   Douglas E. Phillips, "When Software Fails: Emerging Standards of Vendor Liability Under Uniform Commercial Code" in American Bar Association, Section on Business Law, The Business Lawyer, November 1994, Vol. 50, p. 151, at 153 (hereinafter "Phillips, 'When Software Fails'").

defective repair and defective user instructions or warnings.[8] Each of these possible defects should be considered in designing the warranties in a technology transfer agreement.

14.5 The Nature of Warranty Depends on the Nature of Deliverable

The quality warranty chosen will depend on whether the subject matter of the warranty is:

(a) A physical good (and there the warranty will vary depending whether it is a harmless or potentially dangerous good);
(b) Services, such as the development of custom software, the design of a physical good, the provision of training or software support;
(c) Software (custom or mass marketed); or
(d) Other types of information.

14.6 Two Types of Warranties

Quality warranties may be divided into:

(a) Result based warranties. Here the warranty focuses on the obligations about the quality of the product rather than the process of producing the product. The quality deliverables are compared to some objective quality benchmark and found satisfactory or deficient. For example, the goods could be compared for conformance in all material respects to certain "functional specifications". Result based warranties are often used with fixed price contracts. To be useful, they must co-relate to a realistic and precise standard; and
(b) Efforts based warranties. Here the warranty focuses on the "manner in which a contract is performed, the process rather than the result".[9] The deliverables are expected to be produced in accordance with a certain level of efforts, such as reasonably careful "workmanlike" efforts. Efforts based warranties are often used in time and material contracts. To be useful, the standard of efforts must be well defined – "workmanlike" although often used may not be highly meaningful. These types of warranties often have different remedies, for example:

---

[8] For further discussion see Waddams, *Products Liability*, p. 38 and Woodley/World Intellectual Property Organization *Guide on the Licensing of Biotechnology* (Geneva: WIPO and LES, 1992), pp. 86–87.
[9] *Uniform Computer Deformation Transactions Act*, 1995 draft (UCITA 1995) §2B-403, reporter's note 3.

(i)   In a fixed price contract, a results based warranty may require the transferor to repair or replace the deliverable until its meets the standard, at its own cost;

(ii)   In a time and materials contract, an efforts based warranty may require the transferor to take reasonable measures to remedy the defect, but at the cost of the licensee.

Strategy: Co-relate the type of warranty with the remedy.

14.7 Examples of Quality Warranties

Warranties as to quality include:

(a)   Warranties of merchantability. Here the benchmark is what an objective acquiror of the deliverable would consider to be the minimum acceptable standard – just enough to avoid rejection. Merchantability does not require perfection, but it does require conformance to average standards applicable to that kind of deliverable destined for that type of user.[10]

(b)   Warranty of fitness for the ordinary purpose. Here the deliverable must be fit (on an objective standard) for the ordinary purposes for which deliverables of that description are used. The deliverable does not have to be the best or most fit or indeed fit for all purposes.[11] A Canadian case has stated:

> The implied warranty is that the products would pass without objection in the trade under the contract description and are fit for the *ordinary* purposes to which such goods are used. The product need not be perfect. Breach of warranty turns on separating acceptable flaws from defects that go beyond the ordinary.[12]

(c)   Warranties of conformance to an objective standard which are set out in negotiated functional specifications, or documents such as a user manual. Here the parties adopt their own standard rather than using a merchantable or ordinary fitness standard that may have little application to their facts. Consider:

(i)   Does the word "conform" imply that there must be 100 per cent conformance?

(ii)   Does the phrase "substantially conform" help? If 90 per cent of all the features are there, will this be acceptable to a licensee who wanted the 10 per cent that is missing?

---

[10]   See *Uniform Computer Deformation Transactions Act*, final version (UCITA Final) §4.03 official note 3.a.

[11]   See UCITA Final, §4.03 note 3.a.

[12]   See text 14.9.1.

(iii) Is "conformance in all material respects" better? It may solve the problems of substantial conformance missing the mark, but it may leave open to dispute what is "material".

At least, however, conformance recognizes that there will be imperfections, particularly with software. The UCITA Final reporter writes:

> It is often literally impossible or commercially unreasonable to guarantee that software of any complexity contains no errors that might cause unexpected behaviour or intermittent malfunctions, so-called "bugs". The presence of such minor errors is fully within common expectation. The question for merchantability is not whether errors exist but whether the program still comes within the middle belt of quality in the applicable trade or industry, i.e., whether it is reasonably fit for the ordinary purposes for which such programs are used in accordance with average levels of quality and reasonable standards of program capability. A great deal of theoretical and practical work is currently focused on techniques to reduce the time and cost needed to determine program "correctness". Professional standards also exist for software quality evaluation. Commercial reasonable use of existing testing techniques can be one benchmark of whether a computer program is merchantable in law. As industry standards evolve, what constitutes a merchantable program will evolve along with those standards.[13]

(d) Warranties against viruses in software. The licensee will want an assurance that its system will not be contaminated by the transferor's software or services. It may be unreasonable to require a warranty that no virus will exist; it may be more reasonable to require that the transferor will take reasonable or specified measures to avoid transmitting viruses.

(e) Warranties of accuracy of information. The licensee may require a warranty that all information provided is complete, truthful and accurate. The licensor would prefer a warranty that accuracy will be within specified parameters. If the transferor of information is transferring information compiled by others, it may want to limit its warranty to a provision that: "no inaccuracy in the informational content [will be] caused by [its] failure to perform with reasonable care".[14] The UCITA Reporter writes in official comment 403.2:

> What constitutes reasonable care depends on the commercial circumstances and the contracted for duties. For example, in a contract to transmit computer information, there is no duty to screen or vouch for accuracy, but merely to avoid a lack of reasonable care in the transmission that causes inaccuracies. A data provider in a context where major loss of human life is possible has a higher degree of care than a provider in other settings.

---

[13] UCITA Final §403 Official Comment 3.
[14] UCITA Final §404 (a).

a. *Ordinary Standards as Described.* Informational content is accurate, if, within applicable understandings of permitted errors, it correctly portrays the objective facts to which it relates. Whether or not data are inaccurate is based on expectations gauged by ordinary standards of the relevant trade under the circumstances. In most large commercial databases, ordinary expectations are that some data will be incorrect. Variations or error rates within the range of commercial expectations of the business, trade or industry do not breach the warranty. If greater accuracy is expected, that must be made express in the agreement.

(f) Warranties of "workmanlike" effort. The licensee may require that the transferor exercise the skill and knowledge normally possessed by a person in the licensee's trade or profession, or he or she will possess the skill and will exercise the diligence ordinarily possessed by well informed members of his or her trade or profession.[15]

Instead of these efforts based warranties, the licensee may require a results based warranty such as a warranty that the transferor will select, develop and furnish suitable information, rather than an efforts based warranty that the information will not fail to achieve the licensee's particular purpose as a result of the transferor's lack of effort.[16]

(g) System warranty. If the transferor is providing or designing a series of components to be integrated into a system, whether or not produced by the transferor, the licensee may want a warranty that the components selected or provided will function together as a system. Thus the licensee can rely on one party to remedy defects rather than be caught in a IT WASN'T ME scenario.[17] Note that this warranty does not provide that this will be the best system; that quality warranty must be provided separately.

(h) No warranty. In addition to the usual disclaimers of merchantability and fitness for the purpose, consider:
    (i)   There is no warranty that the information [software], our efforts, or the system will fulfill any of your particular purposes or needs.[18]

A client of mine, a university professor who had a good sense of humour and who was marketing to other university professors who, he hoped, shares his humour, wrote,

> We strongly recommend that you test the program thoroughly before relying on its results. This disclaimer and limitation of liability that is included in this licence is absolutely sincere. Approach the program with skepticism. You should assume that it is a schizophrenic and bug-infested program and

---

[15] See UCITA 95 §403 note 13.
[16] See UCITA Final, §405 and §405(a)(2).
[17] See UCITA Final, §405(c).
[18] UCITA Final, 406 (b)(2).

that it is completely unreliable until you have proven to yourself that the data sampled by your equipment in your environment is valid.

(i)   Except for express warranties stated in this contract, if any, this information or computer program is provided with all faults, and the entire risk as to satisfactory quality, performance, accuracy and effort is with the user.[19]

(ii)   "as is". This may imply more words in some U.S. legislation, but should not be used without adding the implied words where the U.S. legislation does not apply.

IMPLIED WARRANTIES

14.8 Social Policy

In the 1800s the courts of the United Kingdom, Canada and the United States were each developing judicial social policy by establishing standards of quality that products could not fall below. They found it unconscionable for sellers to take money for products that were not merchantable or fit for the intended purpose. The courts were prepared to find liability for defective products based on negligence (a subdivision of the legal "tort" that imposes duties of care) or on contract based on implied warranties. This judicial social policy as it applies to the sale of goods has been enacted into statutory codes in many jurisdictions: in Alberta and many of the other Canadian common-law provinces as the *Sale of Goods Act*, based on the English *Sale of Goods Act* (now replaced by *The Unfair Contract Terms Act*);[20] in many U.S. states as the *Uniform Commercial Code*, Article 2; and, for international contracts, in many countries by the adoption of the United Nations Convention on Contracts for the International Sale of Goods.[21]

14.8.1 *Warranties Implied by Law may Depend on the Nature of the Transaction*

Notwithstanding a position common to Canada and the United States that transactions considered to be unconscionable will not be enforced, the social policies

---

[19] UCITA Final 406(b)(3).

[20] See Report on Sale of Goods, Ontario Law Reform Commission (hereinafter "Ontario Law Reform Commission Report"), Vol. 1 (1979) p. 7. See also Waddams, *Products Liability*, p. 9.

[21] For example, for adoption of the United Nations Convention in Alberta, see the *International Conventions Implementation Act*, S.A. 1990, c. I-6.8, s. 2. See also Peter Winship, "Changing Contract Practices in the Light of the United Nations Sales Convention: A Guide for Practitioners", American Bar Association, Section on International Law and Practice, The International Lawyer, Fall 1995, Vol. 29, No. 3, p. 525 (hereinafter "Winship, 'Changing Contract Practices'").

concerning the remedies resulting from a supply of deficient goods, services and information have been handled differently from jurisdiction to jurisdiction. Most jurisdictions have enacted legislation that covers the sale of goods, but all too often this legislation is not sufficiently flexible to cover the licensing of technology, the supply of custom software or the provision of information. Recognizing the demand produced by changes in technology, courts seemingly may stretch the facts, fitting them into one category or another, to allow the court to impose an appropriate remedy. For example, the task of classifying something as a "good" or a "service" can be very difficult. Software sold in a package at a retail store is likely to be considered as a "good" for the purposes of the sale of goods legislation. If, however, the same software is transmitted electronically, that transaction may no longer be a sale of a good but may now be classified as a provision of a service because there is no tangible component.[22]

These implied warranties are often referred to as the warranties of "merchantability" and "fitness for a particular purpose". For many purposes other than for disclaimers, it is difficult to distinguish between these two warranties.[23]

14.9 Disclaimer of Implied Warranties

In negotiated technology transfer agreements express warranties should be designed to properly allocate risks between the parties and then all implied warranties could be disclaimed.

14.9.1 Disclaiming Implied Warranties on the Sale of Goods

A disclaimer of implied warranties of the product quality of goods should do the following:

(a) expressly disclaim the implied warranties; the express warranties are in addition to the implied warranties unless they are inconsistent[24] *i.e.*, expressly disclaimed;

(b) mention the word "merchantability" to disclaim the implied warranty of the merchantability for U.C.C. purposes;

(c) make it clear that the acquiring party has notice and has agreed to accept the disclaimer;

(d) be conspicuous; the U.C.C. states that the disclaimer must be conspicuous, and if it is in BLOCK CAPITALS it is deemed to be conspicuous for U.C.C. purposes. Consider breaking BLOCKS OF BLOCK CAPITALS into different parts to maintain the actual

---

[22] See Reid, *Limiting Risks*, p. 5.

[23] See in Winship, *"Changing Contract Practices"*, pp. 546–47.

[24] Section 16(7) of the *Sale of Goods Act*, R.S.A. 2000, c. S-2, and see *Fording Coal Ltd. v. Harnischfeger Corp. Of Canada* (1991), 8 B.C.A.C. 25, 17 W.A.C. 250, 6 B.L.R. (2d) 157 (C.A.).

conspicuousness that may be required by other jurisdictions such as the Canadian common law provinces; and

(e) use both the words "conditions" and "warranties" in the disclaimer. The statements that give rise to the right to treat the contract as at an end are sometimes referred to as "conditions"; statements that are not so essential or fundamental are then referred to as "warranties". Many *Sale of Goods Acts* are derived from the English *Sale of Goods Act* and use the word "condition" in reference to minimum product quality. They allow the buyer of deficient goods to choose between treating a contract as at an end (relying on a condition) or continuing the contract but seeking damages (relying on a warranty).[25] Under Article 2 of the U.S. *Uniform Commercial Code* (U.C.C.) "an express warranty is any affirmation, promise or description that becomes part of the basis of the bargain of the parties".[26] Any disclaimer of implied warranties where a party is subject to any *Sale of Goods Act* derived from the English *Sale of Goods Act* should add the word "condition" to the U.C.C.'s standard word "warranty".

14.9.2 Provision of Services

A technology transfer agreement may include a provision of services; these services could include the customization or further development of technology, or training and support.[27] The law may imply a warranty that the "service provider has the skill to complete the task" and that such skill will be applied with "reasonable care and diligence".[28] It is more questionable whether there is an implied warranty that a desired result will be achieved by the provider of services.[29] A disclaimer of these implied warranties requires different words than those used for implied warranties relating to the sale of goods; such a disclaimer may have to specifically disclaim negligence.[30] Consider: There is no warranty that our efforts will fulfill any of your particular purposes or needs and any implied warranty to that effect is specifically disclaimed.[31] Drafting this type of disclaimer requires considerable creativity; such a disclaimer is "fundamentally at odds with the vendor's marketing goals of persuading the user that the [service] will meet all the user's needs. The marketing goal [may mandate] that the contracting goal remain unspoken" and, thus, ineffective.[32] It is questionable whether "gross negligence" can be disclaimed, except, perhaps, in a negotiated

---

[25]   See, for example, the *Sale of Goods Act*, R.S.A. 2000, c. S-2, s. 13(1).

[26]   Nimmer and Krauthaus, *Commercial Law*, p. 22.

[27]   Nimmer and Krauthaus, *Commerical Law*, p. 24.

[28]   *Ibid.* See also UCITA 95 §403, note 13.

[29]   Waddams, *Products Liability*, p. 101.

[30]   Nimmer and Krauthaus, *Commercial Law*, p. 26.

[31]   See UCITA Final §406(b)(2).

[32]   Phillips *"When Software Fails*," p. 160.

contract between parties with equal bargaining power, who are not "consumers" under any legislation designed to protect consumers.[33]

14.9.3 Provision of Information and Implied Warranties

The relationship between an information provider and its customer will be examined by a court to determine if "there is an implied obligation imposed on the information provider to provide an accurate and complete result" or whether the emphasis is "more on the process by which the contract is performed", the former producing a higher duty of care than the latter.[34] An information provider may have a duty to provide accurate and complete information if

(a) the information was provided in the course of "his business, profession or employment, or in any other transaction in which he has a pecuniary interest";

(b) the recipient was justified in relying on that information and did rely on it;

(c) the information provider "failed to exercise reasonable care of competence in obtaining or communicating the information"; and

(d) there was a special relationship that justified a duty of reasonable care.[35]

A disclaimer for information might say there is no assumption of responsibility for the accuracy of the statement.[36] The disclaimer may have to address completeness as well as accuracy[37] and "might refer specifically to either a disclaimer of negligence or a disclaimer of any responsibility for the accuracy of the information provided".[38] Consider: There is no warranty that this information will fulfill any of your particular purposes or needs.[39] Or: This information is provided with all faults, and the entire risk as to satisfactory quality, performance, accuracy and effort is with the user.[40] It is not clear if a properly drafted disclaimer puts an end to liability; reliance in light of the disclaimer may have to be reviewed for reasonableness.[41]

---

[33] See Ontario Law Reform Commission Report, p. 288.

[34] Nimmer and Krauthaus, *Commercial Law*, p. 27.

[35] Adapted from Nimmer, *ibid.*, pp. 29–30, who was quoting from the *Restatement of Torts (Second)* §552. See *Hedley Byrne v. Heller & Partners Ltd.*, [1964] A.C. 465, [1963] 2 All E.R. 575 (H.L.) and *Queen v.* Cognos, [1993] 1 S.C.R. 87 p. 110 and *Hercules Managements Ltd. v. Ernst & Young*, [1997] 2 S.C.R. 105.

[36] Susan A. Griffin, Hedley Byrne Revisited; Torts – 221, Continuing Legal Education Society of B.C., April 11, 2001 found at <http://www.fmc-law.com> at p.7, referring to the Hedley Byrne approach ("Griffin").

[37] See Griffin at p. 10 referring to *Queen v. Cognos*.

[38] Nimmer, *ibid.*, p. 30. See also Griffin, p. 7 and p. 12.

[39] UCITA Final 406(b)(2).

[40] UCITA 406(b)(3).

[41] See Griffin referring to *Micron Construction Ltd. v. Hong Kong Bank of Canada*, 2000 BCCA 141 (Q.L.).

14.9.4 Unconscionability

Implied warranties cannot always be disclaimed. Legal systems "have long recognized the need to balance the freedom to contract with the need to protect the weaker party against over-reaching by the stronger party".[42] Some jurisdictions, therefore, have passed legislation that prevents disclaimers of implied warranties in "consumer transactions" and even in some commercial transactions. Even without enabling legislation, some courts will not enforce disclaimers of implied warranties where the parties do not have equal bargaining power and enforcement would be unconscionable.[43] The quality is measured not only in financial strength but also in technical expertise and market position. In some jurisdictions it may be "unconscionable" to disclaim warranties when the inherent risks are very high, particularly if they could result in death or personal injury.[44] Factors that a court may consider concerning the possibility of unconscionability or imposition of unreasonable terms include an examination of the negotiation process, as to length of time in dealing, length of time for deliberations, the experience or astuteness of the parties, whether counsel reviewed the contract, and whether the buyer was a reluctant purchaser.

14.10 Implied Warranties and Duties as Guidelines

The negotiators to a technology transfer agreement might use the warranties implied by law as guidelines for their negotiated express warranties and then agree that these express warranties are the only ones that will govern their relationship. These negotiators could consider the following:

    (a) a warranty that the technology will perform substantially in accordance with stated specifications — perhaps the transferor's published specifications;[45]

    (b) a warranty that the technology will be fit for the licensee's expressly stated purposes;

    (c) if the contract contemplates customization or further development:

        (i) detailed benchmarking and acceptance tests could be set out. "The acceptance test provision should define a clear and objective procedure for deciding when the supplier has satisfactorily completed performance".[46]

        (ii) a warranty that the transferor's efforts will be representative of the "skill that it represents itself to have";[47] and that the transferor

---

[42]   Ontario Law Reform Commission Report, p. 153.

[43]   See Waddams, *Products Liability*, p. 203. See also Toedt, *Licensing Law Handbook 1987*, p. 6-30.

[44]   See U.C.C. § 2-719(3).

[45]   Reid, *Limiting Risks*, p. 13.

[46]   *Ibid.*

[47]   Nimmer and Krauthaus, *Commercial Law*, p. 25.

"will exercise that skill in a workmanlike and reasonably careful manner";[48] and

    (iii) a warranty that the transferor's efforts will achieve a specified result;

(d) if information, such as databases, are included in the technology transfer:

    (i) a warranty that the information will cause the technology to obtain the intended result; or

    (ii) a warranty that information will be accurate and complete; and

(e) what defects attributable to one party give the other party the right to repudiate the contract rather than only the right to damages, or whether the right of repudiation is the only remedy.

14.11 Outline of Matters to be Considered When Negotiating Express Warranties

The negotiators to a technology transfer agreement could use the requirements of the *Magnuson-Moss Warranty Act*[49] as a checklist for matters to be dealt with in the warranty clause:

(1) the identity of all persons who are entitled to the benefit of the warranty;

(2) a clear description of the covered product or components;

(3) a statement of the remedy if there is a defect;

(4) when the warranty period begins and its duration;

(5) a step-by-step explanation of the procedures to obtain performance of any warranty obligation;

(6) information about the availability of any informal dispute settlement mechanism;

(7) any limitations on the duration of implied warranties; and

(8) any exclusions or limitations on relief, such as incidental or consequential damages.[50]

14.11.1 Conditions to Effectiveness of a Warranty

The effectiveness of an expressed contractual warranty may be subject to certain limitations. The warranty might

(a) become invalid if the product is improperly used, maintained or repaired;

(b) become invalid if it is modified or improperly combined in use with any other product;

---

[48] *Ibid.*

[49] 15 U.S.C. §§2301–2312.

[50] Pegi A. Groundwater, "*General Considerations in Drafting Software Licenses*", a paper presented at the Licensing Executives Society Annual Meeting, October 26, 1992, pp. 3-34 and 3-35 (hereinafter "Groundwater '*General Considerations*'").

(c) become invalid if it is otherwise tampered with or damaged;

(d) be effective only if the transferor is properly notified of the defect; or

(e) be effective only if the defect was not caused by other technology or by an unauthorized combination with other technology.

The warranty might be restricted in time and might be effective only if the transferor is properly notified of the defect. In any event, the particulars of the conditions to effectiveness should be reasonable and relevant to the specific technology.

14.11.2 Duration of Warranty

The negotiators should consider the duration of the warranty. Should it be less than the time period that would exist under the applicable limitation period? Sometimes it is very difficult to determine a limitation period. The technology transfer agreement could thus provide that the period for making a claim under the warranty is one year, commencing on delivery of the technology or some other mutually acceptable milestone being attained.[51] Some legislation that is designed to protect consumers will not allow a disclaimer of the implied warranties but will allow a limitation on the duration of the warranty.[52]

14.11.3 Scope of Warranty

The parties to a technology transfer agreement should agree on who will be protected by the warranty; consider: the licensee, its sublicensees, its customers, and those who have no contractual relationship but who may be affected by the product, service or information. The agreement could also specify under what circumstances the warranty will extend to a particular class of persons.[53]

14.11.4 Duties

The technology transfer agreement could specify

(a) the duties of care imposed on each party. In many cases the manufacturer/producer will be required to prove it used all of the modern methods available to make the product safe;[54]

---

[51] D.C. Toedt III, ed., *Licensing Law Handbook 1987* (New York: Clark Boardman Co., Ltd., 1987), pp. 5-36 and 5-37 (hereinafter Toedt, "*Licensing Law Handbook 1987*").

[52] For example, see the *Magnuson-Moss Warranty Act*, 15 U.S.C. §231, referred to in Toedt, *Licensing Law Handbook 1987*, p. 5-47.

[53] Nimmer and Krauthaus, *Commercial Law*, p. 21.

[54] See Wright and Linden, *Tort Law*, p. 16-61, quoting Professor Plant in (1957), 24 Tenn. L. Rev. 938.

(b) the duties to warn users and, where appropriate "learned intermediaries"[55] of inherent risks and damages. This duty can be described as follows:

> The duty to warn is a continuing duty, requiring manufacturers to warn not only of dangers known at the time of sale, but also of dangers discovered after the product has been sold and delivered: ... All warnings must be reasonably communicated, and must clearly describe any specific dangers that arise from the ordinary use of the product: ...

> The rationale for the manufacturer's duty to warn can be traced to the "neighbour principle", which lies at the heart of the law of negligence, and was set down in its classic form by Lord Atkin in *Donoghue v. Stevenson*.... When manufacturers place products into the flow of commerce, they create a relationship of reliance with consumers, who have far less knowledge than the manufacturers concerning the dangers inherent in the use of the products, and are therefore put at risk if the product is not safe. The duty to warn serves to correct the knowledge imbalance between manufacturers and consumers by alerting consumers to any dangers and allowing them to make informed decisions concerning the safe use of the product.[56]

If the consumer is being advised or assisted in the use of the product by someone who can be described as a "learned intermediary," such as a doctor in the case of breast implants, there is a duty on the manufacturer to warn that intermediary so that the intermediary can behave in a "learned" fashion. Warning the learned intermediary can be in addition, or in substitution,[57] to warning the consumer, depending on the circumstances.

(c) the duties to provide a user manual designed and written to be understandable to the normal user; and

(d) warnings to the users to have the product maintained only in accordance with the user manual and by an authorized service provider.

14.12 Know Where Your Warranties Are

In addition to appearing in a section of the agreement specifically dedicated to warranties, warranties can be found in:

(a) technical specifications or other forms of description of the technology being transferred;

---

[55] For example, see *Hollis v. Dow Corning Corp.* (1996), 14 B.C.L.R. (3d) 1, 129 D.L.R. (4th) 609, [1996] 2 W.W.R. 77, 190 N.R. 241, 67 B.C.A.C. 1, 27 C.C.L.T. (2d) 1, 111 W.A.C. 1 (S.C.C.).

[56] *Ibid.*, p. 618 (D.L.R.).

[57] *Ibid.*, p. 622 (D.L.R.).

(b) the negotiations leading up to execution of the definitive agreement, which could have been lengthy and may have included contradictory descriptions of the technology involved;[58]

(c) promotional material, sales literature or product specification sheets;[59]

(d) personal correspondence; or

(e) oral communication.

14.13 Puffery and Salesmanship Versus Misrepresentation

Not all product descriptions (or representations) have the same legal effect.[60] Some statements are not intended to be relied on: they are merely "salesmanship or puffery".[61] These "statements... are only intended to extol the virtues of the seller's goods and are not usually regarded by the ordinary, reasonable buyer as being of any [significance]".[62] It is a question of fact for each case whether a statement is meant to be binding on the parties.[63] It may depend on how central the feature described is to the transaction.[64] "The closer an alleged representation lies to the central features of the deal, the more likely a court will recognize it as an express warranty".[65] Often practitioners will include an entire agreement clause in the transfer agreement that limits the agreement between the parties, including all representations and warranties, to those that are expressly stated in the agreement.

14.13.1 Innocence Versus Fraudulent Representation

A statement about the features of the technology that misrepresents the true features could be made innocently or fraudulently. A misrepresentation made innocently that is not fundamental to the transaction may give rise to a claim for damages, particularly if the misrepresenting statement was made negligently. If a statement made by one party could be considered as essential or fundamental to the deal between the parties, it might entitle the other party to repudiate or "rescind" the contract and permit that party to ask the courts to place it in the position it would have been in if the contract had not existed.[66] If there is a fraudulent misrepresentation by one party, the other party may have the right to

---

[58]　To the author's consternation, in reviewing an agreement, all previous (and contradictory) descriptions were attached to the agreement as a substitute for expressly drafted warranties. There were great difficulties sorting out which ones would prevail in the event of a conflict.

[59]　Groundwater "General Consultations", p. 3-62.

[60]　Gerald H.L. Fridman, *Sale of Goods in Canada* (Scarborough: Carswell, 1995), p. 149 (hereinafter "Fridman, *Sale of Goods*").

[61]　Nimmer and Krauthaus, *Commercial Law*, p. 22, and see Fridman, *Sale of Goods*, p. 149.

[62]　Fridman, *Sale of Goods*, pp. 149–50.

[63]　*Ibid.*

[64]　Nimmer and Krauthaus, *Commercial Law*, p. 22.

[65]　*Ibid.*

[66]　Fridman, *Sale of Goods*, pp. 157–58.

repudiate the contract or to claim damages.[67] This remedy may not always be as appealing as it initially looks; such a rescission may result in the licensee infringing the intellectual property rights to the technology that is the subject-matter of the licence since the rescission will result in the loss of the licence. Such a rescission may also disentitle the licensee to damages.

PART TWO – OWNERSHIP/EXCLUSIVITY/INFRINGEMENT

14.14 Introduction

The licensee will want assurance that its continued use of the transferred intellectual property will be uninterrupted but rather will provide the full enjoyment of expected benefits and rights. The risks facing the licensee are:

(a) Ownership or title risks:
    (i) Risk of loss through bankruptcy or security;
(b) Exclusivity risks:
    (i) Risks of information being in the public domain;
    (ii) Risk of the intellectual property being invalid or unenforceable;
    (iii) Risks of there being co-ownership with another entity that can exploit the intellectual property independently; and
    (iv) Risk of a prior or subsequent grant or transfer in an exclusive license;
(c) Infringement risks.

14.14.1 Ownership Risk

Often a licensee will request a warranty that the transferor owns the intellectual property, or is the holder of the registered title to the intellectual property. Unfortunately it is not clear what "ownership" means. It often indicates that no one can deprive the owner of the benefit of the asset. With intellectual property, does that mean that the licensee will gain the benefits of the intellectual property to the exclusion of all others, that the value of the intellectual property will not disappear as a result of invalidity or unenforceability, or that its quiet enjoyment of its rights to the intellectual property will not be interrupted or interfered with. If the licensor concedes to a warranty of ownership, at all, it will want to specify that the warranty does not cover validity, enforceability or other provisions that could be inferred and thus will want to define clearly what the word "own" means. Referring to "registered owner" does little to help since there is no guaranteed registry of title for intellectual property such as there is for land under the Alberta Titles system. Milgrim writes:

---

[67] *Ibid.*, p. 152.

In the industrial and intellectual property area, public recordation of ownership may be sketchy, delayed or nonexistent. For example, there is often a gap between the filing of an interest in a patent (such as an assignment or a security interest) or a trademark registration application and its appearance as a matter of public record. If one must determine whether a particular mark is confusingly similar to other marks which predate it, one must take into account that there is a six month to one year delay in the Patent and Trademark Office for the issuance of registrations. Moreover, even a federally registered mark, not yet incontestable, can be inferior to a "common law" mark, which by its nature is *unrecorded*.[68]

Although there is a register for copyright, registration is not required and registration is not a conclusive indicia of ownership. The situation is even worse for trade secrets: by their nature there is no register and ownership is difficult to determine.[69]

14.14.2 Security Interests

The licensee will want assurance that it will not lose its rights in the subject intellectual property as a result of a lender realizing on its security.

14.14.3 Bankruptcy

The licensee will also be concerned about the effect of the bankruptcy of the transferor on its license. In the United States, this has been addressed in part by the amendments to the *United States Bankruptcy Act*, although this appears not to apply to the licensing of a trademark. As a result of this amendment, the licensee is not at the same significant risk it was before the remedial legislation came into effect. In Canada, no amendment to the *Bankruptcy Act* has been passed so licensees from Canadian transferors have a risk of losing their licence as a result of the bankruptcy of the transferor and this risk is difficult to assess; prudent drafters of technology transfer agreements take the position that the licensee is at risk and that some other measures are necessary to protect the licensee, such as a security interest in the intellectual property.[70]

14.14.4 Non Interference Warranty

UCITA Final suggests using a non-interference warranty such as "no person holds a rightful claim to, or interest in, information [for example patent rights, software] which arose from an act or omission of the licensor which would interfere with the licensee's enjoyment of its interest".[71] The drafter may want to

---

[68] *Milgrim on Licensing*, § 23.03.
[69] See *Milgrim on Licensing* § 23.03. See also Burshtein, p. 18.
[70] See also Chapter 13 of this text.
[71] UCITA Final § 401(a).

exclude infringement and misappropriation from this clause if those risks are covered by another clause.

14.15 Exclusivity Risks

The licensee will be concerned that for some reason it will not get the exclusive or exclusionary rights it expected.

14.15.1 Public Domain

There is the risk that the rights purportedly conveyed are in the public domain.[72] This may result from the information not being a trade secret as expected.

> The "public domain" risk deals with the affirmation that the subject matter consists of rights controlled by the transferor and not in the public domain. Most contracts deal with this explicitly. If the transferee relies on the rights in creating a product for third parties, this affirmation is the entire deal. Copyright licenses commonly contain a representation that the subject matter is not entirely in the public domain and failure of this *implied* representation violates a warranty and yields a failure of consideration. M. Nimmer & D. Nimmer, The Law of Copyright §10.13[A]. The analysis is not clear in patent licenses. The validity of the patent is subject to the fact that subsequent court or administrative actions may invalidate the claim. One can infer that there is a warranty or other obligation that the patent documentation shown to a licensee is real, but there is no warranty that the patent is valid and will remain enforceable.[73]

14.15.2 Validity or Unenforceability

The patent may be held to be invalid or unenforceable with the result that the disclosure of the intellectual property makes it free for others to use, and the licensee does not get the expected exclusionary rights.[74] Whether a patent is valid or invalid might be so complex that it can only be determined by a court. The negotiators will focus on which party should better assume the risk of an unfavourable interpretation. However there are matters that are more within the control of the transferor. Thus the validity warranty could be restricted to a knowledge warranty such as "to the knowledge of the transferor" the licensed patent rights are valid.[75] But whose knowledge? Is it the knowledge of anyone in a 6,000 person firm, or is it knowledge restricted to named individuals who should know? The transferor will also want to explicitly state that it is actual

---

[72] See UCITA Final § 401 official note 3.

[73] UCITA 1995 § 401 Reporter's Note 8. This note does not appear in UCITA Final.

[74] See also Chapter 11 "Payment" of this text where the consequences of invalidity and enforceability are discussed.

[75] See UCITA Final § 401 (b)(2)(A).

knowledge without any duty to make inquiry at all or beyond a precisely stated duty to enquire.

14.15.3 Co-ownership Risk

If someone other than the transferor owns a co-interest in the transferred intellectual property rights, then that co-owner may have rights to exploit the intellectual property independently of the other co-owner, with these rights, differing between Canada and the United States.[76] Thus the licensee may not have got the exclusive and exclusionary rights it expected.

14.15.4 Prior Grants

While exclusive rights clauses often prohibit future grants of licences or other interests, the representation that no prior grants have been made is occasionally overlooked. The licensor of a trade secret could warrant that it has not granted rights to another person, but will resist a warranty that no other person has independently developed the licensed information.[77]

14.16 Disclaimer

The transferor might try to disclaim all such warranties by stating that it does not warrant that competing claims do not exist, and that it grants only the rights it has. Consider: "There is no warranty against interference with your enjoyment of the information or against infringement".[78]

14.17 Infringement

The licensee will be concerned that its exploitation of the intellectual property will be prevented as a result of an infringement claim by a third party or that it will be permitted to use the technology only after a payment of compensation to a third party. The transferor will want to provide that the infringement risk applies only to existing intellectual property rights and not to a patent not yet disclosed by being laid open to the public or issued. The allocation of the risk of the unknown, such as the risk of a submarine patent[79] emerging after the date of execution of the agreement, is hard to make fairly. The transferor will wish to restrict its warranty to a warranty that it has no actual knowledge of any fact that

---

[76] See paragraph 9.15ff of this text.

[77] See UCITA Final § 401, official note 3.

[78] UCITA Final § 401(b).

[79] That is a patent application filed on the date of the agreement but not then available for review either as a result of not being laid open or as a result of not being issued.

would give rise to a claim for infringement of a valid patent and has no duty to enquire as to infringement.[80]

14.17.1 Infringement of the Transferred Intellectual Property Rights by Third Party

In order to gain the expected exclusivity, the licensee may request the transferor to take action against any third party that infringes the transferred rights. The transferor might resist this since it would not be able to determine in advance who the infringer will be and the economic merits of launching the infringement suit. The transferor will endeavour to restrict its warranty to a statement that it has no actual knowledge of the third party's infringing the transferred intellectual property rights at the date of the agreement.

14.18 Allegation Versus Successful Claim

The transferor will endeavour to restrict its obligation to indemnify the licensee against successful claims. Infringement suits can be brought for vexatious or competitive reasons and not always on the merit of the challenged intellectual property right. Some indemnity clauses require the transferor to defend all of the claims; the transferor might wish to have the right but not the obligation to defend. If the licensee defends, the transferor will wish to restrict its liability for defence costs to successful claims but will want to be involved in any settlement to the transferor who permits the licensee to defend if it is concerned about a prudent defence where the transferor's long-term interests are kept in mind rather than merely satisfying the short term and specific needs of the licensee.

14.18.1 Withholding Payments

Some agreements provide that the licensee may withhold payment of ongoing royalties until an infringement suit has been resolved, to protect itself against double payment. To avoid leaving the transferor at risk and being unable to collect from the licensee when the suit is successfully defended, some agreements provide for the payment of the ongoing royalties into escrow. Still, this does not address the cash flow problems of a smaller transferor. The licensee will have to assess the risk that ongoing improvements or continued research may not be available if the transferor is cash strapped as a result of the infringement suit.

---

[80] See *Milgrim on Licensing*, § 23.08.

Chapter 15

LEGAL REMEDIES — CONTRACT AND TORT

Men's actions are so diverse and infinite that it is impossible to make any general laws which may aptly meet with every particular and not fail in some circumstances.[1]

NATURE OF REMEDIES

15.1 Introduction

The purpose of this Chapter is to set out the legal remedies that are available in the event of a breach of a contractual or tortious duty. It is important that the negotiators of a technology transfer agreement be aware of these remedies when allocating risks of breaches of duties and deciding on the appropriate remedies.[2] The negotiators must examine how these basic remedial principles have been applied in their jurisdictions. The remedies that are appropriate to any particular case may depend on the nature of the breach. Breach of duties to deliver acceptable technology, to pay royalties when due, or to restrict competitive activities require different remedies.

15.2 Available Remedies

Before the parties negotiate an allocation of risk of liability arising out of a breach of contractual or tortious duty, they should be aware of the various remedies that are available. Some of these are:

    (a) injunctions — an injunction is an order usually prohibiting a party from engaging in specified conduct. Injunctions are granted in the discretion of the court; injunctions can be either granted for an interim period or granted permanently. To obtain a pre-trial injunction, the plaintiff must be able to show that there is a serious issue to be tried, that its claim is not frivolous or vexatious, that at least arguably it has the rights it is claiming to have and that its rights are being infringed in some fashion.

---

[1]   Lord Ellesmere in *Pearl of Oxford's Case* (1615), 1 Ret. Ch. 1, at 6.
[2]   Remedies for infringement of intellectual property rights will be discussed in Chapter 16.

Next, the court will consider whether the defendant's conduct is causing irreparable claim to the plaintiff. Irreparable harm is literally harm for which an award of money can provide no adequate recompense. In deciding whether to grant a pre-trial injunction, a court will consider whether the balance of convenience in general favours the plaintiff or favours the preservation of the *status quo* until the final disposition of the action. The "balance of convenience" takes into account such issues as whether it would cause greater hardship to grant or refuse the injunction. Injunctions are appropriate where damages are not an adequate remedy because the wrong is continuing;

(b) Anton Piller Order — this is a somewhat Draconian order derived from a case of that name that came before the House of Lords. It requires the defendant to open his or her doors to the plaintiff. The plaintiff may then search and seize offending material and pertinent books and records as a result of an order obtained without notice to the defendant. The purpose of such an order is to provide a quick and efficient means of recovering infringing material and of discovering the sources from which the material has been supplied and the persons to whom they are distributed before those concerned have had time to destroy or conceal them. The essence of the success of this remedy is surprise; the defendant does not have time to destroy the incriminating evidence. The grounds for such an order are an extremely strong *prima facie* case and very serious damage, potential or actual, to the applicant; there must be convincing, concrete, factual evidence that the defendants have in their possession such incriminating evidence, and would likely conceal or destroy that evidence if given notice of the plaintiff's claim in the ordinary course. This order is often used in copyright infringement cases in countries, such as the United Kingdom and Canada, where the judicial decisions are influenced by the judicial House of Lords;

(c) damages arising directly out of the breach of duty;

(d) damages that are incidental to the breach;

(e) damages that are consequential to the breach, including economic loss of profits;

(f) punitive or exemplary damages;

(g) aggravated damages;

(h) costs — when authorized by law, the court can award costs against the losing party to compensate the successful party for its litigation costs. Costs awards in Canada are usually a partial indemnity only, but in exceptional circumstances they can be awarded as a full indemnity of the successful party's litigation costs;

(i) interest — under the appropriate circumstances, the court can award interest on the damages that were assessed;

(j) right to reject.

15.3 Direct Damages

The basic purpose of an award of damages "is to put the party complaining, so far as it can be done in money, in the position the party would have occupied if the wrong had not been done".[3] Under Canadian law, the plaintiff must establish that it has suffered a loss and that the loss was caused by the defendant's wrong. The loss must not be too remote; it must be a loss that could reasonably have been contemplated by the parties on entering into the contract or that was reasonably foreseeable at the time of the occurrence of the tortious act. The Canadian courts are very reluctant to award damages for economic losses that are considered too remote. One component of direct or compensatory damages on a failure to deliver acceptable technology is the cost of obtaining acceptable substitute technology, if that is available.[4] If substitute technology is not available then the market value of the non-delivered technology valued as promised will have to be determined, and that value less the unpaid contract price will establish the quantum of damages.

15.4 Incidental Damages

The injured party may be able to recover damages that are incidental to curing the breach. These are out-of-pocket expenses; in the sale of goods context they include expenses incurred in the receipt, inspection and transportation of the goods, and expenses incurred in procuring substitute goods.[5] There may be a right to incidental damages, even if not specifically provided in applicable legislation, as a result of common law.[6]

15.5 Consequential Damages for Economic Loss

The Canadian courts have great difficulty in deciding what damages for economic loss are permitted. They are concerned about the remoteness of the economic losses and the possibility of opening a "floodgate" of lawsuits. In the

---

[3] S.M. Waddams, "The General Principles of the Law of Damages", *Law of Remedies*, Special Lectures of the Law Society of Upper Canada, 1995, p. 15, at 15 (hereinafter "Waddam's 'General Principles'").

[4] See the *Uniform Commercial Code*, §§2-708(1) and 2-706 (hereinafter "U.C.C."), *per* Raymond T. Nimmer and Patricia A. Krauthaus, *Commercial Law of License Contracts*, September 9, 1993 (unpublished), p. 40 (hereinafter "Nimmer and Krauthaus, *Commercial Law*") and the *Sale of Goods Act*, R.S.A. 1980, c. S-2, s. 51.

[5] U.C.C. §2-715 and D.C. Toedt III, ed., *Licensing Law Handbook 1987* (New York: Clark Boardman Co. Ltd.), p. 5-30 (hereinafter "Toedt, *Licensing Law Handbook 1987*").

[6] Nimmer and Krauthaus, *Commercial Law*, p. 44, and see the Report on Sale of Goods, Ontario Law Reform Commission, Vol. 1 (1979), p. 420 (hereinafter "Ontario Law Reform Commission Report"). See also Waddams "General Principles," p. 9.

United States, consequential damages are a matter of course.[7] From the point of view of the transferor of technology,

> incidental and consequential damages pose the greatest single threat that can flow from ineffective warranty disclaimers [and limitations on liability clauses]. One of the problems posed by such damages is that they bear no relationship to the cost of the [technology]. In addition, [the transferor] may have little or no idea of the nature of use and abuse to which customers [and licensees] may subject the [technology]. Under these circumstances, it is frequently difficult to form even a reasonably accurate estimate of potential damages.[8]

Indeed, absent a contractual limitation on liability, the transferor could be liable for damages amounting to many times the amounts paid by the licensee and many times the profit the transferor could hope to derive from the technology transfer transaction;[9] all of this may occur without any "form of moral culpability" or negligence as a result of strict liability arising out of breach of warranty.[10]

15.6 Costs

In the United States, in suits based on contract or tort, costs incurred by the successful party are not normally recoverable from the losing party. In Canada, costs are recoverable, but the award usually covers only a portion of actual costs. A technology transfer agreement could provide that all costs incurred to enforce an agreement must be paid by the losing party; this clause should be designed to award costs where costs would not otherwise be awarded and to increase costs from the level normally awarded by a Canadian court to the full amount of costs incurred.

CONTRACTUAL LIMITATIONS ON LIABILITY

15.7 Pre-agreed Allocations of Risks

The negotiators to the technology transfer agreement should decide in advance what remedies would be available to each other for a breach of contractual or tortious duty owed by one party to the other. These remedies may very well be different than those available for an infringement of intellectual property rights or a breach of duty to maintain secrecy.

---

[7] U.C.C., Article 2.
[8] Toedt, *Licensing Law Handbook 1987*, p. 5-32, referring to software.
[9] Adapted from Ontario Law Reform Commission Report, p. 486.
[10] *Ibid.*, p. 46.

Strategies: The following are some pre-agreed allocations of losses arising from a breach:

(a) the fixing of a dollar amount for the maximum damages. This must be a reasonable pre-estimate of these damages; it should not be too high, as it may constitute a penalty, and not too low, as it may be set aside as unreasonable or unconscionable;[11]

(b) the pre-agreed estimate of damages shall exclude the application of all other remedies. If that is done, the negotiators might want to consider a back-up remedy in case that pre-agreed estimate is held to be invalid; the software licence can provide that the pre-agreed estimate of damages shall equal the aggregate of the amounts paid by the licensee through the date of the breach (assuming that the licensor is the breaching party);

(c) the disclaimer of liability for incidental or consequential damages; and

(d) the disclaimer of punitive or exemplary damages.

15.8 Repair or Replace

Where equipment is provided with the technology transfer, a remedy for defects could be a requirement to repair or replace the defective components of the equipment. For many licensees, the important feature will not be that "there are no problems with the product, but that any problems that do occur will be corrected".[12] The warranty to repair or replace may permit a disclaimer of remedies for the implied warranties or merchantability or fitness for a particular purpose, but, perhaps, only to the extent that such repair or replacement, if made, will cure the defect.[13]

Strategies:

(a) Always have a back-up remedy to cover the possibility that the "repair or replace" remedy fails its essential purpose[14] (or, as is referred to in some other jurisdictions, is "fundamentally breached");

(b) Consider stating in the agreement that the parties agree that equitable relief, such as restraining orders, is appropriate under the circumstances, in order to encourage the courts to exercise their discretion and grant these types of orders; and

(c) Contractually provide for the recovery of full direct costs externally expended by the successful party to a lawsuit.

---

[11] See Toedt, *Licensing Law Handbook 1987*, pp. 6-31 and 6-32 and Pegi A. Groundwater, "General Considerations in Drafting Software Licenses," a paper presented at the Licensing Executives Society Annual Meeting, October 26, 1992.

[12] Toedt, *Licensing Law Handbook 1987*, p. 5-8.

[13] *Ibid.*, p. 6-26.

[14] *Ibid.*, p. 6-27.

SUIT FROM A THIRD PARTY

15.9 Risk of Third-party Law Suit

The allocation of risks between the parties will not affect the rights of third parties who are able to sue in tort (negligence and product liability).[15] The parties could agree which one of them is to assume:

(a) responsibility for third-party claims, perhaps allocated according to nature or quantum; and
(b) responsibility for insuring against third-party claims, perhaps with the insurer having no right to claim over against the other party.

An indemnity may have economic meaning only if it is backed up by insurance or some other form of security.

---

[15] See §14.3 of this text.

Chapter 16

Intellectual Property Remedies

16.1 Introduction

In this Chapter, special remedies available as a result of infringement of intellectual property rights are reviewed. These remedies are specialized variations of the remedies for breach of contractual or tortious duty that were discussed in Chapter 15. These remedies will be of interest to negotiators of a technology transfer agreement as they allocate the risk that the transferred technology infringes rights possessed by others as well as the duty to prosecute infringers of the rights to the technology that is the subject-matter of the technology transfer agreement, together with the right to share in any resulting damages (awarded either in their favour or against them). The remedies vary depending on the type of intellectual property rights involved and the jurisdiction in which the judicial action is conducted. Remedies for infringement of intellectual property rights may be in addition to any contractual or tortious remedy that is concurrently available.

16.2 What Constitutes an Infringement?

For a discussion of the activities that constitute an infringement of intellectual property rights refer to Chapters 3 to 6 of this text.

PATENT INFRINGEMENT

16.3 Damages Provided by the U.S. Patent Act

Section 284 of the U.S. *Patent Act*[1] *allows the following:*

    (i)   damages adequate to compensate for the infringement, *i.e.*, "computed so as to place the patentee in the position that it would have been in had the infringement not occurred",[2]

---

[1]   35 U.S.C.

[2]   Raymond T. Nimmer and Patricia A. Krauthaus, *Commercial Law of License Contracts*, September 9, 1993 (unpublished), p. 34 (hereinafter "Nimmer and Krauthaus, *Commercial Law*").

(ii)   damages shall not be less than a "reasonable royalty for the use made of the invention by the infringer" (note that this establishes a minimum; royalties are not the only standard of measuring damages.);

(iii) the court may increase the damages up to three times the amount found or assessed (*i.e.*, treble damages); and

(iv)   interest and costs as fixed by the court.

16.3.1 Loss of Profits

One method of determining damages is by the amount of lost profits that the patentee suffered. To establish lost profits, the patentee must prove what the profits would have been "but-for" the infringement.[3] The leading U.S. case of *Panduit Corp. v. Stahlin Bros. Fibre Works*[4] sets out "four criteria, all of which the patentee must prove if the remedy is to apply, namely: (1) Demand for the patented product; (2) Absence of acceptable non-infringing substitutes; (3) Manufacturing and marketing capability to exploit the demand; and (4) The amount of profit he would have made".[5]

16.3.2 Royalties

Instead of loss of profits as the measure of damages, a fair royalty rate can be used to establish damages. The leading U.S. case, *Georgia-Pacific Corp. v. United States Plywood-Champion Papers, Inc.*,[6] sets out factors to be used by a court for establishing a fair royalty rate. Goldscheider[7] lists 13 of these factors:

(a)   royalty rates generally available to licensees of the holder of the infringed patent;

(b)   royalty rates paid by the infringer for comparable technology;

(c)   the nature and scope of licences giving rise to royalties used for comparison purposes, *e.g.*, do not compare royalties payable for exclusive licences to royalties payable for non-exclusive licences;

(d)   the practice of the patentee not to grant licences to anyone, instead keeping the technology for its own exclusive use;

(e)   the commercial relationship between the parties, *e.g.*, are they competitors?

---

[3]   Robert Goldscheider, "Litigation Backgrounder for Licensing", *les Nouvelles*, Journal of the Licensing Executives Society, Vol. XXIX, No. 1, March 1994, p. 20, at 21 (hereinafter "Goldscheider, 'Litigation Backgrounder'").

[4]   575 F.2d 1152, at 1156 (6th Cir. 1978).

[5]   Goldscheider, "Litigation Backgrounder," p. 23.

[6]   318 F. Supp. 1116 (1970).

[7]   Goldscheider, "Litigation Backgrounder," p. 23.

(f)   the extent to which the infringer gained by marketing the infringing technology in conjunction with other products or services offered by the infringer, *e.g.*, "derivative or convoyed sales";[8]

(g)   the remaining duration of the patent and the duration of the "licence" to the infringer;

(h)   "the established profitability of the product made under the patent, its commercial success, and its current popularity";[9]

(i)   the nature and benefits derived from the patented inventions;

(j)   "the extent to which the infringer has made use of the [patented] invention and . . . the value of that use";[10]

(k)   the traditional profit margin;

(l)   the portion of the profit attributable to the infringing invention;

(m) the amount that the patentee and the infringer would have agreed on

    (i)   at the time the infringement commenced;

    (ii)   if both at had been reasonably and voluntarily trying to reach an agreement;

    (iii) giving a reasonable profit margin to the infringer;

    (iv)   giving a reasonable reward to the patentee;[11]

    (v)   considering the relative bargaining position of the parties;

    (vi)   the extent to which the infringement prevented the patentee from using or selling the invention; and

    (vii) the market to be tapped.[12]

Goldscheider[13] suggests that three additional factors were added by a judge in his jury address in *Honeywell v. Minolta*:[14]

(n)   the relative bargaining positions of Honeywell and Minolta;

(o)   the extent to which the infringement prevented Honeywell from using or selling the invention; and

(p)   the market to be tapped.

16.4 The Canadian Patent Act and Damages

To be entitled to claim damages for patent infringement, a patent holder (or someone claiming under the patent holder) must show that the infringement

---

[8]   *Ibid.* See also *Prism Hospital Software Inc. v. Hospital Medical Records Institute* (1994), 97 B.C.L.R. (2d) 201, [1994] 10 W.W.R. 305, 18 B.L.R. (2d) 1, 57 C.P.R. (3d) 129 (S.C.).

[9]   Goldscheider, "Litigation Backgrounder," p. 23.

[10] *Ibid.*

[11] The four factors, (a) – (d), are adapted from Goldscheider's list in the discussion of the *Georgia-Pacific* standards (p. 23).

[12] The three factors, (e) – (g), are adapted from Goldscheider's comments on *Honeywell v. Minolta*, Civil Nos. 87-4847, 88-1624 (D.N.J. January 28, 1992) (p. 23).

[13] At p. 23.

[14] *Supra*, note 12, p. 69.

actually caused the loss.[15] Section 55 of the Canadian *Patent Act*[16] outlines the remedies for infringement by stating that:

(1)   A person who infringes a patent is liable to the patentee and to all persons claiming under the patentee for all damages sustained by the patentee or by any such person, after the grant of the patent, by reason of the infringement; and

(2)   A person is liable to pay reasonable compensation to the patentee and to all persons claiming under the patentee for any damage sustained by the patentee or by any of those persons by reason of any act on the part of that person, after the application for the patent became open to public inspection . . . and before the grant of the patent, that would have constituted an infringement of the patent if the patent had been granted on the day the application became open to public inspection. . . .

16.4.1 Loss of Profits

If a Canadian court is having difficulty calculating the amount of the patentee's lost profits, the patent holder may be able to claim an amount equal to the net profits the infringer made from the infringement.[17] To this end, the patent holder may be able to claim for sales to all customers of the infringer, even to a customer who would not have purchased from the patent holder.[18] In addition, the patent holder may be able to claim for some loss of normal business if it is proved that the loss was caused by the infringement.[19]

16.4.2 Royalties

Similar to the United States, royalties will be awarded in Canada where it is difficult to prove the loss of profits to the patent holder. The amount of royalties will be based on either (1) the amount the infringer is liable to pay under a licence agreement, or (2) in the absence of a licence agreement, an amount that is established as an equivalent market value for a licence of the subject-matter.[20]

---

[15]   George Francis Takach, *Patents: A Canadian compendium of law and practice* (Edmonton: Juriliber, 1993), p. 145, Section 10.34 (hereinafter "Takach, *Patents*").

[16]   *Patent Act*, R.S.C. 1985, c. P-4, s. 55 (rep. & sub. R.S.C. 1985, c. 33 (3rd Supp.), s. 21).

[17]   Takach, *Patents*, p. 145, Section 10.34(a), quoting *Collette v. Lasnier* (1886), 13 S.C.R. 563 at 576. This remedy is similar to an accounting of profits, which also may be available where there is a very close relationship between the infringer and the patent holder, such as that of principal and agent. See Takach, *Patents*, p. 147, Section 10.36.

[18]   *Ibid.*, p. 146, Section 10.34(a), quoting *Electric Chain Co. v. Art Metal Works Inc.*, [1933] S.C.R. 581 at 589, [1933] 4 D.L.R. 240.

[19]   *Ibid.*, p. 146, Section 10.34(c).

[20]   *Ibid.*, p. 146, Section 10.34(b), quoting *Colonial Fastener Co. v. Lightning Fastener Co.*, [1937] S.C.R. 36 at 45, [1937] 1 D.L.R. 21.

16.4.3 Other Remedies

Other possible remedies for infringement are an interim injunction,[21] a final injunction, an order to deliver the infringing products and destroy them, interest, legal costs and the potential for punitive damages.[22]

COPYRIGHT

16.5 The U.S. Position

The holder of copyright is entitled to recover the actual damages the holder has suffered as a result of the infringement, together with the profits of the infringer that were not included in those actual damages and, in any event, at the minimum statutory damages. Note that there is a dual award — the actual damages and the profits of the infringer. The recovery of actual damages is the normal standard for a breach of contract; the addition of the amount that the infringer's profits exceed those actual damages is intended to "prevent the infringer from unfairly benefitting from a wrongful act".[23] It is up to the infringer to establish the costs and, thus, make the proper deduction from revenues.[24]

16.5.1 Statutory Damages

The U.S. *Copyright Act* allows a copyright owner to elect, at any time before a final judgment is granted, to receive an amount not less than $750 and not more than $30,000 per action. The actual amount awarded will be at the discretion of the court[25] and may be varied depending on whether the infringer knew of the copyright and who has the burden of proving the infringement.[26]

16.6 The Canadian Position

A Canadian case, *Prism Hospital Software Inc. v. Hospital Medical Records Institute*, sets out the various remedies available on infringement of copyright.[27]

---

[21] An interim injunction is used to stop an infringer from doing an activity before the case can get to court, whereas a final injunction is an order made by the court in the disposition of the case.

[22] See, for example, the discussion in *Prism Hospital Software Inc. v. Hospital Records Institute, supra*, note 8, at 303-306 (C.P.R.).

[23] Nimmer and Krauthaus, *Commercial Law*, p. 33.

[24] *Ibid.*, pp. 33–34.

[25] U.S. *Copyright Act*, 17 U.S.C. §504(c)(1).

[26] If the infringement was wilful (the copyright owner has the burden of proving this), the award may be as high as $150,000. If the infringer meets the burden of proving "such infringer was not aware and had no reason to believe that his or her acts constituted an infringement of copyright," the award may be as low as $200. See the U.S. *Copyright Act*, 17 U.S.C. §504(c)(2).

[27] *Supra*, note 8.

In that case, Prism Hospital, the plaintiff, licensed its software to Hospital Medical Records Institute, the defendant, for distribution to Canadian hospitals, permitting the defendant to modify the software. Not being satisfied with its role as a distributor, the defendant released its own software in place of the plaintiff's software. The "replacement" software copied substantial portions of the plaintiff's software, errors and all. The Court stated that the remedies "given should be tailored to attempt to place Prism back in the position [it] would have been in but for the breaches of contract and copyright".[28] The orders granted by the Court in the *Prism* case included:

(a) a declaration that the defendant's software was an infringing work;
(b) an injunction prohibiting further copying of the plaintiff's work and *of the infringing work*;
(c) withdrawal of the defendant's software from the installed sites;
(d) delivery up to the plaintiff of all infringing copies in the defendant's possession, except as necessary to provide continued maintenance during the transitional period;
(e) delivery up to the plaintiff of all necessary information to permit conversion of all user's data to the plaintiff's software;
(f) costs associated with changing the user sites from the defendant's software to the plaintiff's software; and
(g) immediate cessation of the marketing of the defendant's software.

The injunction permitted the defendant to maintain the software during the transitional period.

16.6.1 *Canadian Compensatory Damages for Infringement of Copyright*

Section 35 of the Canadian *Copyright Act*[29] is very similar to section 504 of the U.S. *Copyright Act*. It provides:

> 35(1) Where a person infringes copyright, the person is liable to pay such damages to the owner of the copyright as the owner has suffered due to the infringement and, in addition to those damages, such part of the profits that the infringer has made from the infringement and that were not taken into account in calculating the damages as the court considers just.

The Court in the *Prism* case notes that the "damages described are cumulative not alternative".[30] The "burden of proof is on the plaintiff to show what its losses are".[31]

---

[28] *Ibid.*, at 154 (B.L.R.).
[29] R.S.C. 1985, c. C-42.
[30] *Prism Hospital Software Inc. v. Hospital Medical Records Institute* (1994), 97 B.C.L.R. (2d) 201, [1994] 10 W.W.R. 305, 18 B.L.R. (2d) 1, 57 C.P.R. (3d) 129 (S.C.), at 158 (B.L.R.).
[31] *Ibid.*, at 157.

The Canadian *Copyright Act* now also gives copyright owners the right to elect statutory damages, "in a sum of not less than $500 or more than $20,000 as the court considers just".[32] The minimum can be reduced to $200 if the defendant did not know, and there were no reasonable grounds to believe, that the defendant had infringed copyright.[33] The minimum can also be reduced below $500 or $200 in the case of infringement of multiple works if the minimum "would result in a total award that, in the court's opinion, is grossly out of proportion to the infringement".[34] For claims by collective societies, the statutory award of damages is "a sum of not less than three and not more than ten times the amount of the applicable royalties, as the court considers just".[35] The factors to be considered by the court in assessing statutory damages include (but are not limited to):[36]

(a) the good faith or bad faith of the defendant;
(b) the conduct of the parties before and during the proceedings; and
(c) the need to deter other infringements of the copyright in question.

Punitive or exemplary damages may be awarded in addition to statutory damages.[37]

TRADEMARKS

16.7 Introduction

As mentioned in Chapter 5, trademarks are within both federal and provincial/state jurisdiction. This section on remedies will be restricted to remedies under the Canadian and U.S. *Trademark Acts.*[38]

16.8 Canadian Remedies

The remedies for infringement of a Canadian trademark are Anton Piller relief, interim and permanent injunctions, damages, accounting for profits, delivery up or disposal of infringement materials and prohibition of importation of products bearing an infringing trademark.[39] In Canada, the plaintiff can have compensa-

---

[32] Section 38.1(1). Education institutions and some other types of parties are exempt from having statutory damages awarded against them: s. 38.1(6).
[33] Section 38.1(2).
[34] Section 38.1(3).
[35] Section 38.1(4).
[36] Section 38.1(5).
[37] Section 38.1(7).
[38] *Trade-marks Act*, R.S.C. 1985, c. T-13, (hereinafter *Trade-marks Act* (Canada)) and U.S. *Trademark Act*, 15 U.S.C.
[39] *Trade-marks Act* (Canada), ss. 53, 53.1 and 53.2 (rep. & sub. S.C. 1993, c. 44, s. 234).

tion only for the loss the plaintiff sustained or an accounting of profits earned by the defendant, but not both.[40] The plaintiff is not to be better off because of the infringement; the plaintiff is only to be restored to the same position it would have been in if the wrong had not occurred.[41]

16.9 U.S. Remedies

The U.S. *Trademark Act* provides that the plaintiff shall be entitled, subject to certain provisions and subject to principles of equity, to recover[42]

(1) defendant's profits,

(2) any damages sustained by the plaintiff, and

(3) the costs of the action. The court shall assess such profits and damages or cause the same to be assessed under its direction. In assessing profits the plaintiff shall be required to prove the defendant's sales only; the defendant must prove all elements of cost or deduction claimed. In assessing damages the court may enter judgment, according to the circumstances of the case, for any sum above the amount found as actual damages, not exceeding three times such amount. If the court shall find that the amount of the recovery based on profits is either inadequate or excessive the court may in its discretion enter judgment for such sum as the court shall find to be just, according to the circumstances of the case. Such sum in either of the above circumstances shall constitute compensation and not a penalty. The court in exceptional cases may award reasonable attorney fees to the prevailing party. In certain provisions the court must, unless there are extenuating circumstances, enter judgment for three times such profit or damages, whichever is greater, together with reasonable attorney fees.

TRADE SECRETS

16.10 No Single Law

In both Canada and the United States, no single piece of legislation covers trade secrecy.[43] In the United States, many states have adopted some version of the *Uniform Trade Secrets Act*, which separately provides remedies appropriate for those states. None of the Canadian common-law provinces has passed any legislation relating to trade secrets. The remedies, therefore, will vary depending on the locality.

---

[40] David J.A. Cairns, *The Remedies For Trademark Infringement* (Toronto: Carswell, 1988), p. 144.

[41] *Ibid.*

[42] 15 U.S.C. §1117.

[43] See Chapter 6 of this text.

16.10.1 Contract Law versus Trade Secrecy Law versus Trust Law

In trade secrecy cases, the courts have drawn on three areas of the law. They will impose remedies arising out of any contract between the parties, they may rely on a separate duty of trade secrecy or they may find a fiduciary duty and apply trust law.[44] In some states, these areas of the law provide mutually exclusive remedies. The remedies available in trade secrecy cases, in principle, mirror those available under contract or tort laws.

(a) injunctions — the injunction could be designed to prevent a continued use or disclosure of the trade secret and even to extend to the production of the resulting product by any process and not just the secret process.[45] The duration of the injunction may be the time "it would have taken defendant to independently develop or reverse engineer the technology";[46]

(b) damages equal to the loss suffered by the plaintiff;[47]

(c) damages equal to the profits unjustly received by the defendant;[48]

(d) a combination of damages lost by the plaintiff and new profits unjustly received by the defendant (which is comparable to the standard of damages allowed for copyright infringement).[49] A Canadian court is unlikely to allow such a double recovery;

(e) a reasonable royalty rate — particularly valuable when the first two approaches will not produce a "logical amount of damages"[50] drawing analogy to patent cases. Litigation Backgrounder favours the reasonable royalty standard and provides the following guideline:

> In calculating what a fair licensing price would have been had the parties agreed, the trier of fact should consider such factors as the resulting and fore-

---

[44] See the difficulty that the Supreme Court of Canada had in the *Lac Minerals* case. The judges disagreed about the appropriate causes of action and remedies. See *International Corona Resources v. LAC Minerals Ltd.*, [1989] 2 S.C.R. 574, 69 O.R. (2d) 287, 36 O.A.C. 57, 61 D.L.R. (4th) 14, 101 N.R. 239, 44 B.L.R. 1, 26 C.P.R. (3d) 97, 35 E.T.R. 1, 6 R.P.R. (2d) 1.

[45] See *General Electric Co. v. Chien Min-Sung*, 843 F. Supp. 776 (D. Mass. 1994); *Apotex Fermentation Inc. v. Novopharm Ltd.* (1998), 162 D.L.R. (4th) 111, 80 C.P.R. (3d) 449, 129 Man. R. (2d) 161, [1998] 10 W.W.R. 455, 42 C.C.L.T. (2d) 133 (C.A.).

[46] See American Bar Association, Section on the Intellectual Property Law, *Annual Report* 1994–95, p. 343 (hereinafter "ABA *Annual Report*, 94/95").

[47] See Goldscheider, "Litigation Backgrounder", p. 28.

[48] *Ibid.*

[49] The *Restatement of Law (Third)*, Unfair Competition, Preliminary drafts 1 to 3 indicated that the plaintiff should be entitled only to the greater of the two numbers and not to both of the two numbers. The *Uniform Trade Secrets Act*, however, provides that "a plaintiff can recover both damages for the actual loss as well as unjust enrichment, so long as the unjust enrichment loss is not taken into account in computing damages for actual loss". See ABA *Annual Report*, 94/95, p. 352.

[50] Goldscheider, "Litigation Backgrounder," p. 28.

seeable changes in the parties' competitive posture; the prices past purchasers or licensees may have paid; the total value of the secret to the plaintiff, including the plaintiff's development costs and the importance of the secret to the plaintiff's business; the nature and extent of the use the defendant intended for the secret; and finally whatever other unique factors in the particular case which might have affected the parties' agreement, such as the ready availability of alternative processes.[51]

TIME LIMITATIONS ON REMEDIES

16.11 Take Action in Time

All remedies available to a patent, copyright, trademark or trade secret holder are subject to limitations relating to the passage of time. These limitations may be a result of statutory provision[52] or a result of common-law principles.[53] For example, the holder may be "estopped," or, in other words, prevented, from using a certain remedy because the holder knew the infringer was committing the activity and did nothing about it, or the holder may possibly be limited by "laches" because the holder waited too long to take the action.

NEGOTIATION ISSUES

16.12 Allocate Risks of Product Failure

When allocating which party bears the risk of infringement of third-party intellectual property rights, consider:

    (a) Implied warranties of title/against infringement — Under both the *Sale of Goods* legislation and the *Uniform Commercial Code (U.C.C.)*, there are implied warranties of title, *i.e.*, the seller of a good implies it has the

---

[51] *Ibid.*, quoting from *University Computing Co. v. Lykes-Youngstown Corp.*, 504 F.2d 519 (5th Cir. 1974).

[52] Most jurisdictions maintain a *Statute of Limitations* that governs the time within which an action can be commenced. See, for example, the analysis of the former Alberta *Limitations of Actions Act*, R.S.A. 1980, c. L-15, in *Lubrizol v. Imperial Oil Ltd.* (1992), 45 C.P.R. (3d) 449 (Fed. C.A.), at 475-477.

[53] See *Cadbury Schweppes Inc. v. FBI Foods Ltd.* (1994), 1 B.C.L.R. (3d) 258, [1995] 4 W.W.R. 104, 59 C.P.R. (3d) 129 (S.C.); additional reasons at (1994), 93 B.C.L.R. (2d) 318, [1994] 8 W.W.R. 727 (S.C.), where the Court held that the owner of a trade secret for "Clamato Juice" was not entitled to an injunction due to the passage of time, but was still in time to claim other remedies. The Supreme Court of Canada upheld this decision, although the Court was somewhat less emphatic on the impact of the owner's delay on the request for injunction: [1999] 1 S.C.R. 142, at 188-190, 167 D.L.R. (4th) 577, [1999] 5 W.W.R. 751, 59 B.C.L.R. (3d) 1, 83 C.P.R. (3d) 289, 42 B.L.R. (2d) 159.

right to pass title of that good to the buyer. Additionally, in the *U.C.C.* but not in the *Sale of Goods* legislation, there is an implied warranty against infringement. Can a warranty against infringement be implied either from the common law or from the use of the word "title"?

Strategies:
(1) Out of prudence, a negotiated technology transfer agreement should provide express warranties of title/against infringement appropriate for the transaction and should expressly disclaim any implied warranties.
(2) In Canada, a prudent negotiator should not assume that a warranty of "title" does not include a warranty against "infringement".

(b) Express warranties of title/against infringement — It may be beyond the knowledge of many parties whether there has been an infringement on their part. In the case of copyright, was the creator truly employed? Was the relationship within any statutory work-for-hire rules? Is there any possibility of joint ownership? Did the creator include only original work or include something copied from another source? Instead of providing an express warranty that there is no infringement, the parties might provide a warranty that the party has no knowledge of an infringement and include a separate covenant imposing full responsibility on one party for defence of infringement and any damage suffered. Thus, the party is not providing a warranty that it cannot verify, and is avoiding a suggestion that such a warranty was fundamental to the transaction and was fraudulently given.[54]

(c) Scope of Warranty and Defence/Indemnity Obligation — Some of the factors that negotiators to a technology transfer agreement might consider when allocating risk of infringement are:
   (i) territorial restrictions on the indemnity; even if the licence is world-wide, should the indemnity be effective only for the jurisdictions where the bulk of the commerce is expected?
   (ii) which party receives the greatest benefit from the exclusivity granted or retained by the technology transfer agreement. If the technology transfer is exclusive, that party may be the licensee; if the technology transfer is non-exclusive, that party may be the transferor;

(d) The allocation of risk of infringement if the licensee has been granted a licence only in one of many fields of use, and other fields of use have been reserved to the transferor or its licensees;

(e) Which party should bear the risk of a patent issuing after the agreement has been signed, the details of the patent application not having been

---

[54] See, for example, American Bar Association, Section on Patent, Trademark and Copyright, Committee on Computer Programs, *Draft Model Software License Provisions*, Committee Chair: D.C. Toedt III of Arnold, White & Durke, Houston, Texas, Article 7.

previously disclosed (either as a result of issuance or as a result of disclosure under the 18-month rule);[55]

(f) Will the transferor have the right to modify or replace the allegedly infringing technology with non-infringing material? What criteria will be used for the functional and performance specifications of the substituted technology to make sure that the qualities of the transferred technology are maintained?

(g) Will either party have the right to enter into a licence to obtain continued use of the infringing material; can that licence be obtained only when infringement has been established, or when the claim is first made or somewhere in between, perhaps based on an infringement opinion from qualified legal counsel?

(h) Who will have the right to conduct the defence and who will have the right to settle? Consider the following:
  (i)   who will decide the merits and costs of a settlement?
  (ii)   the economics of replacing or modifying the allegedly infringing technology so that it becomes non-infringing but has substantially similar capabilities to the allegedly infringing technology;
  (iii) the economics and uncertainties of litigation;
  (iv)   potential non-litigious methods of settlement of any such claim;
  (v)   the seriousness of the alleged infringement;
  (vi)   the strength of the patent infringed;
  (vii) the importance of the patent infringed to the business of each of the parties;
  (viii) the expected costs of the proceedings;
  (ix)   the difficulty of obtaining the necessary evidence to support the proceedings; and
  (x)   the risk of any third-party infringer making a serious challenge to the validity of a patent or patent claim;[56]

(i) Do the royalties continue after infringement is alleged, but before infringement is proven?

(j) Which party will maintain documents in anticipation of litigation, in accordance with pre-agreed specifications of quality and type?[57]

(k) What conditions, if any, apply to protection offered against infringement?
  (i)   prompt notification[58] (is there really an essential correlation between prompt notification and right to an indemnity?);
  (ii)   the indemnitor has the right to have conduct of the action;
  (iii) the indemnitor has the sole right to settle; and
  (iv)   infringement did not result from misuse or a combination of uses that separately were non-infringing;

(l) What limitations on exposure to liability will be pre-agreed?

---

[55] See §3.18.1 of this text.
[56] See also ABA *Annual Report*, 94/95, p. 389, for patent litigation strategies.
[57] See ABA *Annual Report*, 94/95, p. 389.
[58] American Intellectual Property Law Association, 1994, 1995, "A Guide to Patent Law Harmonization: Towards a More Inventor-friendly Worldwide Patent System", p. 122 E.

Chapter 17

DISPUTE RESOLUTION

Currently, much creative experimentation is taking place with the aim of improving dispute resolution processes. The experimentation embraces innovative dispute resolution methods, new models of dispute resolution, and variations and combinations of these methods and models.[1]

17.1 Introduction

Most parties to a technology transfer agreement are familiar with the traditional methods of dispute resolution: court proceedings and arbitration. As a result of concern over the cost and effectiveness of these traditional procedures, there is a movement to find alternative methods. These methods range from some form of negotiation, to the use of a mediator/facilitator, to some form of adjudicator.[2] The distinction between the separate methods is becoming blurred as parties try to combine the processes for their particular purposes, but always with the intent of producing a better result than could come from a normal court proceeding. Article 2022 of the North American Free Trade Agreement ("NAFTA") provides that Canada, Mexico and the United States "shall, to the maximum extent possible, encourage and facilitate the use of arbitration and other means of alternative dispute resolution for the settlement of international and commercial disputes between private parties of the free trade area".

17.2 The Court Process

Court proceedings are attractive because they involve well-tested evidentiary rules and principles intended to produce just results. Since the cost of the courtrooms, reporters and judges is paid by the government, this method of dispute resolution can be the least costly of the alternatives (but occasionally excluding

---

[1]   Alberta Law Reform Institute, "Civil Litigation: The Judicial Mini-Trial," Dispute Resolution Special Series, Discussion Paper No. 1, August 1993, p. 1 (hereinafter "Judicial Mini-Trial").

[2]   Tom Arnold, *A Vocabulary of ADR Procedures, Introduction to Patenting & Licensing*, Licensing Executive Society (U.S.A. and Canada), Inc., 1995 Manual (hereinafter "Arnold *Vocabulary*"), pp. 1–2. This material also appears in the manual *Technology Transfer 1996*, Licensing Executives Society (U.S.A. and Canada).

the cost of the result), especially if the circumstances are not appropriate for mediation.[3] But court proceedings often produce surprises including:

(a) the expense of lawyers and expert witnesses in protracted court motions, discoveries, trial and appeals;

(b) the allocation of business resources from revenue-producing efforts to the court proceedings;

(c) the stress the court process puts on key witnesses who are also trying to carry on normal family/business activities;

(d) the failure to establish at trial facts that previously were thought to be obvious;

(e) the decisions of some juries; and

(f) the fallibility of some judges, which may or may not result from inability to comprehend the factual/legal issues.[4]

17.3 Insert an Arbitration Clause only with Discernment

Instead of automatically inserting an arbitration clause, the negotiators to a technology transfer agreement might consider the broad spectrum of alternatives available to them. Alternative dispute resolution has produced not only a multitude of dispute resolution centres but also libraries of material on the topic. This Chapter will merely try to acquaint the reader with some of the alternatives.

17.4 Progressive Management Involvement

If the parties have a similar management structure, it is often appropriate to require progressive management involvement before a dispute is referred to arbitration or court proceedings. The American Bar Association Draft Model Software Agreement[5] designates the three levels of management required to deal with a dispute and provides a time period for each level of management to deal with the dispute before the dispute moves on to the next level.[6] The levels of management and the time period could vary depending on the subject-matter of the dispute involved.

The proposed clause reads:

This Section will govern any dispute between the Parties arising from or related to the subject mater of this Agreement that is not resolved by agreement

---

[3] See §17.8, below.

[4] Adapted from Judicial Mini-Trial, p. 13.

[5] American Bar Association, Section on Patent, Trademark and Copyright Law, Committee on Computer Programs, *Draft Model Software License Provisions*, Committee Chair: D.C. Toedt III of Arnold, White & Durke, Houston, Texas (hereinafter "ABA Draft Model Software Agreement").

[6] ABA Draft Model Software Agreement, Section 1021.

between the respective Personnel of the Parties responsible for day to day administration and performance of this Agreement.

Prior to the filing of any suit with respect to such a dispute (other than a suit seeking injunctive relief with respect to Intellectual Property Rights), the Party believing itself aggrieved (the "Invoking Party") will call for progressive management involvement in the dispute negotiation by notice to the other Party. Such a notice will be without prejudice to the Invoking Party's right to any other remedy permitted by this Agreement.

The Parties will use their best efforts to arrange personal meetings and/or telephone conferences as needed, at mutually convenient times and places, between negotiators for the Parties at the following successive management levels, each of which will have a period of allotted time as specified below in which to attempt to resolve the dispute:

	LICENSOR	**LICENSEE**	**ALLOTTED TIME**
First Level	___ Manager _____	___ Manager _____	10 business days
Second Level	___ VP _____	___ VP _____	10 business days
Third Level	___ CEO _____	___ CEO _____	30 days

The allotted time for the first-level negotiators will begin on the effective date of the Invoking Party's notice.

If a resolution is not achieved by negotiators at any given management level at the end of their allotted time, then the allotted time for the negotiators at the next management level, if any, will begin immediately.

If a resolution is not achieved by negotiators at the final management level within their allotted time, then either Party may bring suit to resolve the dispute in a court of competent jurisdiction and venue.

17.5 Negotiations in Good Faith

If progressive management involvement is not appropriate, the agreement could provide for an obligation to negotiate in good faith before the parties move to adjudication. Since what is "good faith" is often debatable, the agreement could either provide a short time period or permit any party to refer the matter to adjudication if it feels that "the good faith" negotiations are not proceeding to its satisfaction.

17.6 Injunctive Relief

If immediate action to stop an activity that could have highly injurious results is necessary, the agreement could provide that the requirement to negotiate does not preclude the right to apply for an injunction or similar relief. If the arbitrators have the ability to grant injunctive relief that will be enforceable under the local law, the agreement could give the arbitrators the power to grant that relief. Interim injunctions as well as permanent injunctions must be contemplated. The availability of interim relief can be particularly valuable in many intellectual property contexts in order to stop irreparable harm to the interests of the owner of an intellectual property right.

It is not uncommon, for example, to seek interim injunctive relief to prevent the marketing of a product that allegedly infringes a patent or a trademark, to prevent disclosure of trade secrets or to prevent destruction of evidence establishing that an intellectual property right is being infringed or assisting in quantifying damage done by infringing actions. In these cases, the lack of interim relief can cause damage that cannot be rectified or adequately compensated by subsequent determination on the merits of the dispute.[7]

17.7 Wise Counsel[8]

As an adjunct to good faith negotiations, some agreements contemplate referring specified issues to a panel consisting of "wise" individuals employed by the parties. The facts and arguments are placed informally before this panel. If the panel agrees, their decision will be binding on all parties. If the panel does not agree, the dispute can be referred to mediation or some form of adjudication. Instead of using a panel of individuals drawn from the parties, there could be a neutral and, perhaps, expert fact-finder, or someone who assumes the role of an ombudsman.

17.8 Mediation

Mediation works best when it is voluntarily selected by parties who want to resolve the dispute and to continue to do business together.[9] Mediation is a non-adjudicative process that facilitates settlement negotiations. The mediator acts as a facilitator and takes a very pro-active role in trying to facilitate communications between the parties, often shuttling back and forth between the parties who are occupying separate rooms.[10] Mediation allows the parties to maintain control over the proceedings by using a mediator of their choice with appropriate privacy in a process that encourages enhanced negotiations carried on in an informal atmosphere.[11] "Justice is not the mediator's primary goal";[12] facilitating

---

[7] "Consultation document prepared by the International Bureau, Proposed WIPO Supplementary Emergency Interim Relief Rules," World Intellectual Property Organization, April 19, 1996.

[8] See Arnold, *Vocabulary*, pp. 4 – 8.

[9] *Ibid.*, p. 12.

[10] *Ibid.*, pp. 10 –14.

[11] Joanne Goss, "An Introduction to Alternative Dispute Resolution", Alberta Law Review, Vol. XXXIV, No. 1, October 1995, p. 1, at 9.

[12] Arnold, *Vocabulary*, p. 11.

communication between the parties with the intent of producing a mutually acceptable resolution is the common goal.[13] Mediation is a "safe procedure"[14] that often produces timely and cost-effective results. Mediation is not effective

(a) if there is a severe power imbalance between the parties;

(b) where a party is in need of a legal precedent;

(c) where an individual in charge of the dispute resolution for one party wants to avoid ultimate responsibility and, thus, personally needs a decision from a mutual third party;

(d) where the parties distrust each other or there is no need for a continued relationship.[15]

17.9 Mediation and Arbitration ("MED-ARB")

MED-ARB stands for some combination of mediation and arbitration.[16] If mediation fails, the technology transfer agreement could provide for an automatic transfer of the issue to arbitration, either before the individual(s) who served as mediator(s) or before new arbitrators who have not been exposed to the frank and full discussions that mediation is intended to encourage.

17.10 Private Mini-trials

There are two types of mini-trials — private and judicial. Private mini-trials involve presentation of facts and argument to the individuals who represent the parties and have the authority to settle. This procedure may be useful when the proceedings have progressed far enough to expose the majority of legal and factual issues, usually as a result of the discovery process in an adjudicative proceeding. The parties must be "committed to resolving the dispute with a minimum of expense, delay and disruption".[17] The neutral advisor in a private mini-trial usually does not take a pro-active role, as a mediator does, but can take on any role requested by the parties.[18]

> For settlement to occur, the persons present must have the authority to settle. In a private mini-trial, the case is presented to the parties themselves (the "principals") who receive "a crash course on the subject of the dispute". The principals "are responsible for hearing the presentations and making decisions for each party". The persons selected must have "positions of organizational authority sufficient to al-

---

[13] *Ibid.*

[14] *Ibid.*

[15] *Ibid.*, p. 14.

[16] *Ibid.*, p. 17.

[17] Judicial Mini-Trial, p. 16, quoting Edelman and Carr, "The 'Mini-Trial:' An Alternative Dispute Resolution Procedure" (1987), 42 The Arbitration Journal 7, at 11.

[18] See Judicial Mini-Trial, pp. 2–3, for a list of possible roles that can be taken.

low them to make unilateral decisions regarding the disputes". Furthermore, they must not have been "personally or closely involved" in any part of the dispute. They must also "be prepared for some amount of second-guessing upon successful conclusion of a mini-trial" and "be of sufficient stature to withstand" pressures from within the organization. In addition to the qualities already identified, they "must possess the temperament and skills to negotiate a settlement fair and reasonable to both parties based on both the facts presented and on their background knowledge".[19]

17.11 Judicial Mini-trials

Instead of presenting the case to the parties, as is done in a private mini-trial, in a judicial mini-trial the case is presented to a judge or to someone acting like a judge, who is a neutral, "characteristically expert in the subject area . . . who initially presides over the proceedings and hears evidence partially in a passive role like a judge though also cross-examining points and commenting on evidence and arguments here and there to put them in perspective, and who presents a conclusion without prior private conversation with any party or party representative (on this point different from mediation)".[20] Like the private mini-trial, the intent is to produce a negotiated settlement. One of the greatest strengths of the mini-trial, in contrast to traditional court proceedings, is the flexibility it offers to the parties.[21] Like mediation and the private mini-trial, the judicial mini-trial is not appropriate where there is no relationship to be preserved[22] or where the case involves "unsettled or novel questions of law — especially if the unresolved legal issue involves the establishment of important legal precedent — 'the credibility of witnesses, multiple parties', unusually 'factually complex,' 'lengthy, or factually contested cases', multiple party disputes, and cases that are 'potentially tainted by fraud'".[23]

> The judicial mini-trial can be conceptualized, philosophically, either as an "advanced negotiation technique" or as an "expedited litigation". The resolution of the litigation will have been expedited if settlement is achieved. Short of settlement, the mini-trial process may help counsel to clarify and narrow the issues, eliminate some, and thus shorten the length of the trial that does take place. Participating in the mini-trial process will give the lawyers a headstart on their preparation to present and argue the case at trial, thereby promoting "more efficient use of legal time than may occur during the drawn-out preparation that takes place over many years in the typical big case".[24]

---

[19] Judicial Mini-Trial, pp. 27–28 (footnotes omitted).
[20] Arnold, *Vocabulary*, p. 38. See also Judicial Mini-Trial, p. 6.
[21] Judicial Mini-Trial, p. 17.
[22] *Ibid.*, p. 18.
[23] *Ibid.*, p. 19 (footnotes omitted).
[24] *Ibid.*, p. 5 (footnotes omitted).

If the judicial mini-trial does not produce a settlement, the trial will come before a different judge than the one who participated in the judicial mini-trial,[25] though the neutral expert could become a mediator if that is appropriate.[26]

17.12 Arbitration

Arbitration is a form of adjudication that produces a binding win-lose result. Some arbitration is referred to as non-binding, but that type of arbitration is merely a variety of mediation. Arbitration has much of the formality and inflexibility of a court proceeding (both are virtues under the right circumstances). There are, however, many varieties of arbitration and the negotiators to a technology transfer agreement should not casually accept any arbitration clause or treat it as irrelevant legal boilerplate. Some arbitration rules specify three arbitrators if the parties do not designate a specific number; some specify a single arbitrator. Some rules of arbitration permit arbitrators who are not independent. Some rules require detailed decisions, others require no decision unless otherwise specified.[27] Some rules specify a foreign location for arbitration, which can be extremely inconvenient and expensive when disputes arise. A negotiator should be aware of the rules that will apply to arbitration arising out of their agreement. Tom Arnold provides an annotated set of principles that the drafters of technology transfer agreements should consider. Some of these principles are:

(a) the number of arbitrators to be involved, the experience required of each, and how they are selected;
(b) all disputes will be referred to arbitration;
(c) contrast a dispute arising out of the due payment of royalties with a dispute over the rejection of technology based on functional defects;
(d) should the different topics be referred to different types of arbitration with different adjudicators being preferred?
(e) time and place of arbitration; language to be used and availability of experienced interpreters;
(f) the necessity for reasons, taking into account the delay and increased costs that result from reasons being required;
(g) the procedural rules to be followed;
(h) payment of costs; and
(i) the enforceability of the arbitrator's award through the court system in the local country (which is particularly important in less developed countries).[28]

---

[25] *Ibid.*, p. 33.
[26] Arnold, *Vocabulary*, p. 39.
[27] Tom Arnold, "Arbitration? Here Are Real Recommendations" in *les Nouvelles*, Journal of the Licensing Executive Society, Vol. XXVII, No. 1, March 1993, p. 24, at 24.
[28] For an excellent checklist of matters to be considered see Tom Arnold's 32-point checklist in *Vocabulary*, p. 29.

17.13 Baseball Arbitration

Derived from arbitration used to settle pay disputes with baseball players, baseball arbitration requires the parties to write out their proposed settlement and to present it to the arbitrator before proceeding to arbitration. At the completion of the arbitration, the arbitrators will be required to open the sealed proposals for the first time and to select one of the proposals.[29]

17.14 Mediation And Last Offer Arbitration ("MEDALOA")

This is a combination of Mediation And Last Offer Arbitration (a variety of baseball arbitration). In essence, the parties proceed through mediation and, if the mediation fails, they proceed to arbitration. In simple cases the mediator moves immediately to "baseball arbitration" and selects only one of the proposed settlement offers. In more complex cases, the dispute goes through the more traditional arbitration procedure but the arbitrator is still restricted to one of the proposed offers.[30]

17.15 Availability

Before selecting any one of many variations of dispute resolution, the negotiators to the technology transfer agreement must consider the availability and enforceability of the dispute resolution mechanisms under the local law.

---

[29] Arnold, *Vocabulary*, p. 25.
[30] *Ibid.*, p. 26.

Part VIII

LEGALESE

Chapter 18

PRELIMINARY MATTERS
AND DRAFTING STYLE[*]

*The agreement should be precise and concise, using business language without
ambiguity.*
Say it once and say it well.

18.1 Licences are Contracts

Technology transfer agreements are contracts and the general principles for the
drafting and interpretation of contracts apply. Unlike many contracts, however, the
relationship also must contemplate a flexible, vibrant and changing business relationship. The certainty that lawyers prefer is often not available in these agreements. In
the end, it must be recognized that "agreements to agree" are not enforceable, so the
need for business flexibility must be balanced with the legal need for enforceability.

18.2 Parties

The parties to the technology transfer agreement must be clearly and correctly
identified. Because different companies may be incorporated in different jurisdictions with the same names, it is recommended to state each company's name
as well as its place of incorporation, perhaps including the location of its head
office. Upon identifying any party that has any material relationship with the
United States, examine the nature of the party, the transaction and the subject
technology to see where they fit in the U.S. Anti-Trust I.P. Guidelines.

18.2.1 Divisions

A division of a company is not a legal entity; the company itself should be party to
the agreement with the use of the technology restricted to the appropriate division.
The agreement could contemplate the division disappearing in a corporate reorgani-
zation and might use a functional description for the division (for example, if the

---

[*] This material is derived from the author's work, "Dreadful Drafting, The Do's and Don'ts of
Licensing Agreements". Robert Goldschieder, "Licensing Best Practices" to be published in
2002 by Wiley.

technology is an innovative herbicide, describe the part of the company's business that manufactures and sells fertilizer for use on agricultural lands). The agreement could also contemplate the company itself being acquired or merged with another company.[1]

18.2.2 Partnerships

If one party is a partnership, the agreement could state the names of the current partners, and the party signing the agreement should provide a warranty of authority to bind the partnership. In some jurisdictions partnerships must be registered and their registration details could be inserted in the agreement.

18.2.3 Determining the Nature of Business Entities Involved

In some countries it is more difficult to determine the nature of business entity and who has what corporate authority. This has been a significant problem in the countries formerly comprising the U.S.S.R. Local advice may be necessary.

18.3 Effective Date

Because several agreements relating to the same subject-matter could be entered into as the relationship of the parties develops, the first page of the agreement could contain a reference date or refer to an effective date. If the word processor that is used permits "footers" for later determining the location of the document on the computer, a date for each draft can be inserted in the footer for ease of reference.

18.4 Place of Signing

Frequently, agreements will specify where they are signed. This may influence the choice of law, and, thus, the application of local laws, as well as imposition of sales and other taxes.

18.5 Recitals

Recitals are useful for setting out the background to the agreement and for establishing some initial definitions. Recitals can be used to assist a reader in understanding the intention of the parties, their prior relationship, if any, and what each party expects to contribute to, and receive out of, the relationship established by the agreement. No substantive part of the agreement (*i.e.*, a commitment by either party) should appear in the Recitals if they are placed physically

---

[1]   See Chapter 7 of this text.

(as is often the case in Canada) before the statement "IT IS AGREED" (or however worded). Recitals are particularly powerful assists to the business reader, especially if the agreement moves immediately from the Recitals to the essential terms (*e.g.*, the grant clause), with definitions and the usual boilerplate clauses located at the end of the agreement. The definitions can be placed in an appendix for ease of access.

18.6 Benefits Derived from Definitions

Those who negotiate a technology transfer agreement will not necessarily be the same as those persons who will be responsible for its execution and management, since, among other reasons, personnel in enterprises change over a period of time. It is essential, therefore, that the technology transfer agreement reflect definitely and accurately the intention of the parties, and avoid, to the greatest extent possible, ambiguity and misunderstandings. Language is a rich source of possible misunderstandings, particularly in the context of international agreements, since different nuances in the meaning of words in the same language used in different regions of the world are common, and the meaning of concepts differs between languages. For these reasons, a technology transfer agreement commonly contains definitions of key terms in relation to which misunderstandings must be avoided at all costs.[2]

18.6.1 Use Definitions to Isolate Issues

Definitions allow the drafter of the technology transfer agreement to isolate issues for the reader. Definitions reduce the verbiage and the accompanying complexity and, thus, help the drafter to "achieve clarity and consistency without burdensome repetition".[3]

Strategy: Use definitions to achieve clarity.

18.6.2 Expansive Definitions

Some definitions do not truly define the meaning (*i.e.*, confine the meaning of the defined word to certain specifics).[4] Instead, some definitions of the word

---

[2] General Considerations Concerning Licensing, *Guide on the Licensing of Buy-Out Technology*, World Intellectual Property Organization, Chapter 4, p. 39, at 41–42. Some might suggest that lawyers speak a different language than most businesspeople and this has the same cultural impact as travelling from one country to another.

[3] See Robert C. Dick, *Legal Drafting in Plain English*, 3rd ed., (Scarborough: Carswell, 1995), p. 77 (hereinafter "Dick, *Legal Drafting*"), quoting from R. Dickerson, *The Fundamentals of Legal Drafting* (Boston and Toronto: Little, Brown & Co., 1965), p. 98. Dick provides a helpful discussion of the various types of definitions.

[4] David Mellinkoff, *Legal Writing: Sense & Nonsense* (St. Paul, Minn.: West Publishing Co., 1982), p. 26 (hereinafter "Mellinkoff, *Legal Writing*").

expand the normal meaning, for example, "*Software* means the computer program and user manual". Sometimes the definition does not define the word at all but only adds a specific meaning to its ordinary meaning, for example, "*Software* includes the user manual". "Software" is not a term that is defined at all by this definition (does it mean executable code, source code, annotations, flow charts?); this definition, instead of adding certainty, has added an unexpected component (*i.e.*, the "user manual"). Sometimes an expansive "definition" is appropriate; more often it gives rise to confusion.

Strategy: Whenever possible, design definitions to limit and not to expand the meaning.

18.6.3 Forced Definitions

Some definitions are more than expansions of meanings; they give meanings that have no correlation to the normal meaning of the word that is being used, for example, "Software means a user manual". Anyone reading the technology transfer agreement and encountering the word "software" might be misled or, at a minimum, very frustrated each time that he or she has to translate the common meaning to the forced meaning. Forced definitions are found even in patent applications.

Strategies:
  (1)   A reader of any document should check the definition section carefully to arrive at the intended meaning and should watch for forced meanings that disguise the business intent.
  (2)   Better yet, do not use nor permit others to use forced definitions in negotiated technology transfer agreements.

18.6.4 Sources of Definitions

The use of definitions that have been used previously and, perhaps, even discussed in judicial decisions can assist in acheiving clarity and precision. Definitions can be found:

  (a)   in legal dictionaries;
  (b)   in specialized manuals;[5] and
  (c)   in published precedents.[6]

---

[5]   For example, Robert P. Bigelow, *Computer Terminology: Judicial and Administrative Definitions*, Computer Law Association, 1993; the *1993-94 Licensing Law Handbook*; and "Samples of Selected Definitions of Biotechnology Terms Occurring in License Agreements", Chapter 6 of the *Guide on the Licensing of Biotechnology*, Woodley/World Intellectual Property Organization (Geneva: WIPO and LES, 1992), p. 97.

[6]   For example, The ABA Draft Model Software Licenses and the AIPLA Software Licensing Compendium.

Strategy: Use previously interpreted definitions.

18.6.5 Unless the Context Otherwise Requires

Drafters often write "in this Article 2, the following words shall have the following meanings, *unless the context otherwise requires*". The last five words negatively influence the definition section. Each time a defined word appears, the reader will be required to decide whether the definition applies or whether the "context" of the agreement here, or in any other place, requires another meaning. The goal of the use of definitions is to increase precision and ease of reading and analysis.

Strategies:
    (1)   The words "unless the context otherwise requires" reduce precision and make the agreement more difficult to read.
    (2)   Drafting laziness should not detract from precision.

18.7 Coupled (Tripled?) Synonyms

The traditional drafting style suffers from the long-standing use of strings of synonyms.[7] We often see the use of well-worn phrases such as "releases, relinquishes, quits and forever discharges". Some strings of synonyms always seem to appear together; some writers seem to feel incomplete without all the words being there.[8] Sometimes strings of synonyms are used by drafters who are insecure about the meaning of the individual word, and, as a result of their insecurity, they include them all.[9] Some strings of synonyms can be reduced to one or two words without changing the legal meaning. Long-established precedents should be rewritten to keep the meat and throw out the filler.

Strategy: Eliminate redundant words — less is more.

18.7.1 Long, Long Sentences

Some writers seem to like long sentences — in some cases, 500 words or more without a period. These long, long sentences significantly increase the risk of errors in typing and in proofreading. Errors are lost in the mass of words.

---

[7]   See Dick, *Legal Drafting*, p. 126.

[8]   Mellinkoff, *Legal Writing*, p. 126, states: "The explanations for wordiness in legal writing do not justify keeping it that way".

[9]   Dick, *Legal Drafting*, suggests, at p. 127, that this insecurity may result from inadequate training. This is true to some extent, but many adequately trained and skilled drafters still suffer from this insecurity.

Strategies:
   (1)   Avoid verbose, sloppy writing that may produce surprising results.
   (2)   Carefully proofread long, long sentences.

18.8 Plain Language

Increasingly, clients are demanding "simple" documents.[10] Too often this results in legal principles being discarded with the legal language. As Mellinkoff notes in "Rule 5" of his superb book on drafting:

> Rule 5: WRITE LAW SIMPLY. DO NOT PUFF, MANGLE OR HIDE.

> The only thing about legal writing that is both unique and necessary is law. To simplify legal writing, first get the law right. You can't simplify by omitting what the law requires or including what the law forbids. The better you know the law, the easier to decide what law ought to go in, and what is overkill or window dressing.[11]

18.8.1 Inclusive Language

As a result of the plain language movement, document drafters increasingly are endeavouring to use inclusive language.[12] With modern word processors, documents can be customized. For example, if all parties are female, the feminine gender could be used throughout, instead of using the masculine gender and relying on a phrase saying that the masculine gender includes the feminine gender. Unfortunately, writing in genderless English is very difficult[13] and sometimes obscures plain language rather than creating it. The use of "you" and "we" in documents may help.

---

[10] So are many legislators. See, for example, the EC Directive on Unfair Terms in Consumer Contracts (Directive 93/13) which imposes an obligation that all contract terms must be drafted in plain intelligible language which, amongst other things, may require suppliers of goods distributed throughout Europe to draft contracts in the national languages of each state or, perhaps, to prepare separate contracts for use in each state. Investment in translations of contractual terms may be a simple step in the direction of compliance with the Directive.

[11] Mellinkoff, *Legal Writing*, p. 101.

[12] Beware of the mischievous typographical error; one document provided "words importing the masculine gender shall include the feminine and *neutered* gender". The word "neutered" might apply to my "Garfield" sized ex-tomcat, but it would seem to have little other application.

[13] See Dick, *Legal Drafting*, p. 165.

18.9 Visual Appeal

With improved laser printers and libraries of available fonts, documents can be made visually attractive as well as comprehensible. Visual appeal may overcome a reader's initial negative reaction to a complex document.

18.9.1 Block Capitals

Many agreements use block capitals for every defined word. For example, "TRANSFEROR" and "TRANSFEREE". These capitalized words frequently BLOCK communication flow; a feature that should be retained for emphasis has been squandered on a defined word.[14] The use of initial upper-case letters serves the purpose of distinguishing defined words.

Strategy: Do not use BLOCK letters for defined words; they BLOCK the communication flow.

18.10 Marketing

The marketing process does not stop once the drafter of the technology transfer agreement puts pen to paper (or fingers to keyboard). The document should continue to market the technology being offered, not serve as a hindrance to the marketing and negotiating process.

Strategy: Market! Market! Market!

---

[14] The use of BLOCK CAPITALS is a breach of Netiquette — it is equivalent to shouting or "flaming".

Chapter 19

LEGAL RULES AND PROCEDURES

19.1 Introduction

The legal boiler-plate in a technology transfer agreement often seems tedious and endless. There is a tendency to overlook the importance of the rules that innocently sit at the back of the agreement because they do not directly deal with business issues. The boiler-plate, however, may materially alter the position of the parties. The governing law clause may introduce unexpected social policy; the entire agreement clause may exclude promises that one party had expected. This boiler-plate may also provide standard warranties and some legal rules.

19.2 Governing Law and Forum

The branch of law known as "conflict of laws" applies if there is any element of a contract that involves a foreign party. In this context, "foreign party" often refers to a party from another province, another state or another country.[1] A "conflict" may arise if the parties are from different jurisdictions, or the contract is made or is to be performed in a foreign jurisdiction. The conflict of law rules resolve three questions: (1) Which jurisdiction's courts will be entitled to adjudicate on the issue? (2) Which jurisdiction's laws will apply? and (3) Will a foreign award be recognized in each party's home jurisdiction?[2] For example, in an electronic transaction, the transferor could be in Calgary, the licensee in Houston and the technology in London. Will the contract law of Alberta or Texas apply? Will the intellectual property rules of Canada, the United States, or the United Kingdom govern? These conflict of law questions are the subject of statute and common law, and each must be examined to determine how the law applies to the particular facts. Usually, the parties are able to select which jurisdiction will provide the governing laws. A party should not necessarily assume that its own law or judicial system is best. An effective restraining order may be

---

[1] See Dicey and Morris, *The Conflict of Laws*, 12th ed. (London: Sweet & Maxwell, 1993), Vol. 1, p. 3.

[2] *Ibid.*, p. 4.

available only from the defaulting party's home jurisdiction.[3] When choosing the jurisdiction whose laws will govern consider the following:

(a) the selected jurisdiction should have "ample precedents" on the matters in question;[4]

(b) the agreement should exclude the governing law's "conflict" rules; parties adopting a governing law usually intend to adopt a law that applies to parties domiciled in the same jurisdiction, carrying on activities only in that jurisdiction;

(c) the parties should review the selected law to determine whether it favours the transferor or the licensee;

(d) "important idiosyncrasies" in the law of the chosen jurisdiction must be examined, such as the required method of disclaiming implied warranties. For example, not all jurisdictions require "CAPITALS" as required by the *Uniform Commercial Code*. Some jurisdictions have unusual rules relating to penalties or to "consumer" rights;[5] and

(e) the effect on a world-wide marketing plan if the law of different jurisdictions are applied to the same standard form contract.[6]

When deciding on the appropriate jurisdiction that will provide the judicial forum for determining the legal issues, consider the following:

(a) the availability of experts who can testify about rules if the forum is not in the same jurisdiction that provides the governing law rules;

(b) the relationship of each party to the selected jurisdiction;

(c) the ability of the aggrieved party to effectively enforce the award in the defaulting party's home jurisdiction;

(d) whether, in the selected jurisdiction, there is a choice of courts (*e.g.*, federal versus state), and, if so, the benefits offered by each court system as contrasted with the disadvantages.

19.3 Standard Warranties

In addition to warranties about product quality, title and against infringement,[7] warranties of authority and against material adverse facts are appropriate, including:

(a) a warranty of valid corporate subsistence;

---

[3] Pegi A. Groundwater, "General Considerations in Drafting Software Licenses," a paper presented at the Licensing Executives Society Annual Meeting, October 26, 1992.

[4] *Software Licensing Compendium* (Boston: American Intellectual Property Law Association, 1992), Vol. 1, p. 129.

[5] *Ibid.*

[6] *Ibid.*

[7] See Chapters 14, 15 and 16 of this text.

(b) a warranty of power and authority to enter into the agreement;

(c) a warranty that the execution and performance of the agreement will not contravene any other subsisting agreement;

(d) a warranty that there is no "kick back" payable as a result of the execution of the agreement; and

(e) a warranty that there is no existing fact (including bankruptcy) that would prevent the party from fulfilling its obligations under the agreement.[8]

19.4 Survival

If the agreement terminates (rather than the project), some clauses should survive the termination.[9] These include confidentiality obligations and restrictive covenants as well as the obligation to pay amounts then due. Promises made before execution of the agreement should also "survive".

19.5 Assignability

If an agreement is characterized as a "personal services" contract, it is usually not assignable. Otherwise, the agreement usually is assignable. Rather than having assignability determined by often conflicting rules of the common law, the agreement should establish the assignability rules. Some agreements prohibit assignment under any circumstances; some permit assignment with the consent of the other parties; some merely request notice to be given to the other party once the assignment has occurred. If assignment requires consent, the agreement should provide the guidelines for approval or rejection of a proposed assignment. Some agreements require the assignor to provide details of the financial, production and marketing capabilities of the assignee, and whether the assignee is a competitor of the non-assigning party.

19.6 Entire Agreement

The transferor and the licensee may have had lengthy negotiations; the transferor may have promoted its technology by using all sorts of superlatives. The agreement could exclude all that puffery by combining an "entire agreement" clause with a limited and narrow warranty. This clause states that the only promises that will be binding will be those actually written in the agreement and that all others are excluded. The transferor wants this clause to provide certainty to its obligations. The licensee will want to make sure all representations and

---

[8] American Bar Association, Section on Patent, Trademark and Copyright Law, Committee on Computer Programs, *Model Software License Provisions*, Committee Chair: D.C. Toedt III of Arnold, White & Durke, Houston, Texas, para. 1051.2.

[9] See Chapter 13 of this text.

warranties are included in the agreement and should not rely on any "gentlemen's" or side agreements.

CONCLUSION

A successful licensing arrangement is virtually assured (assuming the technology has merit) if the negotiations leading up to the licence are full and frank, if the licence agreement is well drafted for the particular purpose and if the developer works at maintaining a continuing relationship of support for its customer.

Index

(References to section numbers)